FEB   2011

I Walked with Giants

JIMMY HEATH

and JOSEPH McLAREN

■

Foreword by Bill Cosby

Introduction by Wynton Marsalis

I Walked with Giants

The Autobiography of
JIMMY HEATH

TEMPLE UNIVERSITY PRESS  PHILADELPHIA

Temple University Press
1601 North Broad Street
Philadelphia, Pennsylvania 19122
www.temple.edu/tempress

TEXT DESIGN BY KATE NICHOLS

All attempts were made to locate the owners of and the people in the photographs published in this book. If you believe you may be one of them, please contact Temple University Press, and the publisher will include appropriate acknowledgment in subsequent editions of the book.

Library of Congress Cataloging-in-Publication Data

Heath, Jimmy.
  I walked with giants : the autobiography of Jimmy Heath / Jimmy Heath and Joseph McLaren.
    p. cm.
  Includes discography (p.), list of compositions (p.), and index.
  ISBN 978-1-4399-0198-4 (cloth : alk. paper)
  1. Heath, Jimmy. 2. Jazz musicians—United States—Biography. I. McLaren, Joseph. II. Title.
  ML419.H357A3 2010
  788.7′165092—dc22
  [B]

                                                                              2009020108

♾ The paper used in this publication meets the requirements of the American
National Standard for Information Sciences—Permanence of Paper for Printed Library
Materials, ANSI Z39.48–1992

Printed in the United States of America

2 4 6 8 9 7 5 3 1

■

To the **Creator**;

my mother and father, **Arlethia** *and* **Percy**;

my wife, **Mona**;

my sister and brothers, **Elizabeth, Percy, Jr.,** *and* **Albert**;

my children, **Mtume, Roslyn,** *and* **Jeffrey**;

my nieces and nephews;

and all of my grand and great grandchildren

■

You say you walked with giants
well I say that you are one

To compare your spirit
with their greatness
well I can say it can't be done

From the time I can remember
you were special
yet not quite strong

You were heading toward your greatness
it just hadn't come along

You were searching
you were seeking
though you had not found your way

Peace finally settled within you
and ever since that day
you've focused on that quest
nothing could stop you from moving on

And today that
same great spirit
comes soulfully through
your horn

We are blessed to know
your goodness
what a privilege to know that smile

Yet the music
you have lent us
is only ours for
just a while

We can't keep it
nor can we own it
for it's yours,
it's part of you

But you share it
oh so freely
this precious gift
that's you

So to say you walked with giants
is an understatement—true
for the giants that you walked with
were not half as big as you

—BETH JACKSON, "Jimmy's Song"

Contents

■

Part Three ▪ Third Chorus (1969–1986)

Part Four ▪ Fourth Chorus (1986–)

Appendixes

Illustrations follow pages 24, 104, and 216

Foreword

■

In the Basement

We have to start with family, with the grandparents and the parents, all of the people who offered support. Jimmy's father, Pop, played clarinet in the Elks Quaker City Marching Band in Philadelphia, and Mom sang in the choir after leaving Wilmington, North Carolina. Mom and Pop didn't do this for a living, and it wasn't a hobby.

European people came to the United States with their traditions of classical music. When people say, "Well, do you listen to classical music?" we assume that it's Wagner or Beethoven, but each culture has its own classical music: People from China have their own, people from India have their own, people from Bosnia have their own, and people from Africa have their own.

In all of their neighborhoods, people who migrated to this country worked at various jobs—a watch repairman, a dockworker hauling vegetables off trucks, a fruit-stand vendor, or an auto mechanic. When workers came home at the end of the day, they turned on the radio or Victrola, and after dinner, and maybe a cigar and a half a glass of wine, they shook off the dust from a violin. They weren't planning to go to Carnegie Hall, hadn't studied for that. They played the music that they loved.

In the house in Philadelphia Pop pulls out his clarinet, and Mom sings in the church. There's music in the house, which they bought, and in the house there's a basement. In Philadelphia, in Baltimore, and in Wilmington, Delaware, houses like this were famous for what went on in the cellar, where there was also the coal furnace and the coal bin. The coal vendor would say, "How much you want?" and the answer might be, "Give me fifty cents' worth of that cut." Then the vendor would slide that long shovel down through the hole, past the screen and the window. He would mark off fifty cents' worth of coal. You could hear the coal slide down into the coal bin like a long drum roll, a press roll, a Max Roach roll, and the coal dust rose up in the air. Then the coal man would pull that long slide out and close up the window, and the coal was ready for the furnace, ready to heat the house.

Blocked off in the basement was a section for getting together, and Jimmy would say to his friends, "Come on. We're going to play some music." They would go down into the cellar to practice, to talk about their classical music—African American music, Negro music, the devil's music, the music of Duke Ellington, Don Redman, Louis Armstrong, Jimmie Lunceford, Erskine Hawkins, Benny Carter, Dizzy Gillespie, and Charlie Parker.

There was young James, and nobody told him what he should be playing. He made his own choices. He played with his friends, but Pop was always there in spirit or in person with the clarinet, their strength and their stronghold.

On Thanksgiving Day in Philadelphia, down Broad Street marched the Elks Marching Band. I saw them, and I probably saw Pop, but I didn't know who he was. I stood there at Broad and Parrish when the Elks Marching Band went by. I was waiting for Santa Claus, but I was also very proud when the all-Negro marching band passed by, because everything was segregated back then. There wasn't any integration in those bands, and very few black school bands marched by to fill us with pride. Then came the Elks Lodge all-black marching band. They were resting before they struck up again. The cadence that the drummer struck on the snare and the bass drum, the way they walked, their rhythm, made me feel connected and proud. They hit it, bam, but the drumming was different from those other bands—the kick, the emphasis, the crescendo from the cymbal player. They still played 1, 2, 3, 4, just like everybody else, and they marched straight and stood tall, but I'll be damned if there wasn't a little attitude that came through. They just couldn't help it. There was something mythical, something real, something mysterious. The Elks band continued on down the street, and I could still hear those black men, who were marchin' on and taking their attitude, taking their happiness, taking their education, taking their "I work for a living to support my family" attitude along with them. It ain't a hobby. It's a love.

Somewhere back there in South Philly there was house with a cellar called a basement, and there were chairs waiting for musicians whom Jimmy had chosen for his band. One of them would say, "Let's go over this or go over that. Let's practice this scale or this chord." They were saying, "Let's study; let's learn, yeah." It's in the cellar; it's in the basement. It's in the mother, it's in the father, and it's in the children. When these young men became professional musicians and were playing in a nightclub, it was weird when a patron would say, "Play something where you go crazy," because nobody was crazy. That's what people were taught to think, that this music was being played by musicians who were just going crazy. I don't think so, because it's in the basement, it's in the cellar, it's in the mother and father, passed on to the children to learn and to study.

Bill Cosby
September 2007

Acknowledgments

∎

Acknowledgments from the Authors

The authors thank the following people—some of whom have gone on to the big bandstand in the sky—for their assistance or contributions: Monty Alexander, Dave Bailey, David Baker, Ed Berger (Institute of Jazz Studies, Rutgers University), Howard Brofsky, Dave Brubeck, Ray Bryant, Benny Carter, Ron Carter, Joe Chambers, Johnny Coles, Stanley Cowell, the Reverend Herbert Daughtry, Marcia Diggs, Paquito D'Rivera, Jon Faddis, Art Farmer, James Forman, Frank Foster, Curtis Fuller, Johnnie Garry, Dizzy Gillespie, Don Glanden, Benny Golson, April Grier (Institute of Jazz Studies, Rutgers University), Billy Griffin, Slide Hampton, Winard Harper, Barry Harris, Antonio Hart, Roy Haynes, Albert "Tootie" Heath, Mona Heath, Percy Heath, Roslyn Heath, Beth Jackson, Frank Jackson, Milt Jackson, Hank Jones, Orrin Keepnews, Felix Leach, Bill Leonard, Ed Levine, Hy Lockhart, Andy McGhee, Billy Mitchell, James Moody, Mtume, Jimmy Owens, Maurice Peress, Amrita Persaud, Gerald Porter, Lewis Porter, Benny Powell, Larry Ridley, Sonny Rollins, Michael Rothbard (Inter-Media Arts Center), Phil Schaap, Dr. Lee Shelton, Akira Tana, Billy Taylor, Dr. Phil Terman, Clark Terry, Cedar Walton, Frank Wess, Phil Woods, and Ike Wright. We also thank the copy editor, David Updike, and the staff of Temple University Press, including Editor-in-Chief Janet Francendese, Ann-Marie Anderson, Gary Kramer, Matthew Kull, Emily Taber, and Joan Vidal.

Special Acknowledgments from Jimmy Heath

I am grateful to Dave Bailey, for endless friendship and respect; Dr. Howard Brofsky and Maurice Peress, for believing in me; Camille and Bill Cosby, for their ongoing love, support, and friendship; Colleen Forester, for her interest in starting this project; Dizzy Gillespie, for his musical direction; Orrin Keepnews, for giving me the chance to record my music; Wynton Marsalis, for his respect, dedication, and perseverance; Joe McLaren, for his tireless research; Steve Rodgers, for his discographical work; Danny Scher, for producing the *Brotherly Jazz* DVD; Rudolf Schramm, for broadening my musical world; Dr. Billy Taylor, for offering me many opportunities; and Clark Terry, for giving me much career support and affection.

Introduction

∎

I guess the old bard summed it up years ago: "To be or not to be." And then Dizzy went on to qualify it: "To BE, or not . . . to BOP." What we choose determines what we will be. Choosing is serious business. The most provocative memoirs inspire us to make informed choices in our own lives. That's why we love to check out other people's lives. From the pen of a master storyteller, Jimmy Heath's memoirs instruct and entertain.

Jimmy's has been a life rich in experience, full of the bittersweet ironies and extremities that make you want to laugh, to cry, and to sing the blues. He tells stories with the homespun humor of a true American original. Through him, we get an accurate take on those fabulous musicians who swung across the globe throughout the twentieth century. Possessed of originality, resilience, pride, and a deep understanding of our common humanity, their lives burned brightly and quickly against a backdrop of segregation and injustice. Still, their music projected the joys and sorrows of real life with unsentimental optimism. It was romantic and wise, virtuosic and earthy—the perfect antidote to the difficulties of modern life.

These musicians believed that times would always be improving and that the syncopated rhythms and on-the-fly improvisations of their brand of jazz would help. They played with a swagger forged in the Great Depression, tested by the war, and proven in the cultural neglect of postwar prosperity.

In the early twenty-first century, Jimmy Heath is one of the last of these jazzmen. Past the civil rights movement, the rock 'n' roll revolution, and the computer age; through generations X, Y, and Z; and up to the hip-hop nation, his presence speaks to the ageless vitality of this music. He stays very much on the scene, composing, arranging, teaching, and playing with wit and vigor. Jimmy brings the generosity of spirit and downright soul that makes jazz worth the dues paid to play it.

At a rehearsal of James Moody's music with the Jazz at Lincoln Center Orchestra, Jimmy Heath walks in and lights up the room. Men, some of whom are close to sixty years younger than he is, stop playing to salute him. All are happier than they were the moment before. He hugs Moody and calls him "Section." Man, they played at different times in Dizzy Gillespie's saxophone sections in the 1940s, and here they are talking 'bout "Section" as if it were yesterday. One thing is clear—they love each other and this music. The passage of time has only strengthened those bonds.

While there may be some confusion about the identity of jazz in present-day critical circles, in educational institutions, and even among musicians misinformed by both, Jimmy Heath is unquestionably the embodiment of the spirit and practice of this music. He is always showing us how to live in jazz, how to be . . . jazz. Coming into the twenty-first century, there could be no more perfect figure to call us home. He walks that walk, and what he talks is exactly what we need to be reminded of in this moment. Enjoy the words of a master.

Wynton Marsalis
October 2007

PART ONE

∎

First Chorus

(1926–1949)

1

Finding a Rhythm

■

Philadelphia and Wilmington, North Carolina

My parents were Carolinians but from different states. My father, Percy, was born in Wilmington, North Carolina, on March 19, 1898, and my mother, Arlethia, in Sumter, South Carolina, on June 4, 1903. They moved to Philadelphia in 1923. My grandmother on my mother's side was Ella Wall, and her husband was Sandy. My mother and father had very little but gave us so much. They taught us respect and love, how to share, and they gave us music. My brothers, Percy and Albert, my sister, Elizabeth, and I were aware of the sacrifices they made for us. We were extremely lucky and blessed to have parents like them. They were honorable, lovable, hard-working people. The world would be a much better place if there were more folks like them. Not a day goes by when I don't thank them for their example of how to live.

I was born on October 25, 1926, in my parents' house at 5710 Ludlow Street in Philadelphia. I was in a hurry to get here, so I couldn't wait for my mother to get to a hospital. My first chorus began when I entered this world at home thanks to my grandma, who acted as the midwife. I had an older brother, Billy, who died of pneumonia at nine months old. My sister, Elizabeth, was born in 1921; my older brother, Percy, who later played bass in the Modern Jazz Quartet for over forty years, was born in Wilmington, North Carolina, in 1923. My younger brother, Albert ("Tootie"), who took up the drums, was born in Philly in 1935. I don't think my parents could have predicted that their three sons would all become professional musicians known as "The Heath Brothers." Elizabeth had her own names for us: "Lord Percy," "King James," and "Prince Albert." I guess that was her sarcastic way of "feeling a draft" because she wasn't in the music business.

As a family, we moved around Philly quite a bit. We lived in West Philly and South Philly. Philadelphia had one of the oldest black communities in the United States, dating back to just after the American Revolution, when they called it the "free black community." I went to elementary school at the Smith School in South Philadelphia until 1939. It was a ghetto school, so everybody was black. My father and mother were on welfare during the war. My father had been an automobile mechanic, but at that time he was on welfare and worked on bridge building with the WPA. He wasn't doing that well financially. When I left Smith School, for financial reasons, I attended high school in Wilmington, North Carolina, but I returned to Philly in the summers. Percy had gone to school down there too, and we both eventually graduated from Williston Industrial High School in Wilmington.

In Wilmington, Percy and I lived at 412 McRae Street near Eighth and Redcross, a major crossroads in the city. My great-grandmother on my father's side, Carmella, was born during slavery, and I remember seeing my great-grandfather driving a dray on the dirt roads. Carmella's daughter, my grandmother, Mattie, had white blood.

Mattie and her second husband, Oliver Fisher, had a grocery store in Wilmington, and they were doing better than my father and mother. It was an independent business, and they sold groceries and supplies to the black schools in Wilmington. I sold newspapers and shined shoes until I was fifteen, and then I went to work at the store, clerking and delivering groceries on a bicycle. Although he ran the store, my step-grandfather couldn't read or write. He had a mind like a computer, but the best he could do was to write down figures. If I wasn't in the store, or my uncle or my grandmother was out, and somebody called in for an order of food, my step-grandfather would write down all the numbers and could tell you exactly which order belonged to a customer, although he couldn't write down the name.

In 1941, my father sent me a saxophone for Christmas. It was a silver Conn, an alto. Percy, Jr., had already been playing violin in junior high school, and my sister Elizabeth had had piano lessons. My father had said that I would be the next one to be given a musical chance. When my older brother was studying violin, his teacher, Professor Pugsley, would crack Percy's fingers with a pencil if he missed a note. The violin was covered with tears and dust, so when Pop asked me what I wanted to play, I said, "Not that violin." I had heard Benny Carter and Johnny Hodges, so I wanted a saxophone. When he sent me the saxophone, the first thing I did was to take it completely apart, as any curious youngster would do. That was the last time I ever took a saxophone apart! I got it back together successfully that time. I wouldn't dare try it again. Now I don't have the same kind of inquisitive mind that I had at that time.

I started playing sax at football games in the Williston High School Marching Band. My father was a clarinet player in the Elks Marching Band, and my mother sang in the church choir of the 19th Street Baptist Church, and they were interested in seeing that all of us had an opportunity to play. My father's clarinet stayed in the pawnshop a lot because of his financial troubles, but he practiced whenever he could. He would get the clarinet out of the pawnshop and have rehearsals with the band on Sundays before they'd go on a marching band trip in Philly or Atlantic City for conventions of the Quaker City Elks Lodge No. 720. My mother was in the marching club at the lodge.

I'd been interested in music since I was six years old, when my mother took me to see Duke Ellington at the Pearl Theatre on Ridge Avenue in Philadelphia. I'll never forget when Duke Ellington patted me on the head and said, "Hello, sonny." They used to have shows of mainly "race music," as it was called then, which featured a lot of the well-known bands of the time. People would spend the whole day enjoying the big bands. When Lionel Hampton's band would play, I would take my lunch there. They had four shows a day during the summer. I saw other groups such as Shep Fields and his all-saxophone band. The other orchestras were Benny Carter's, Georgie Auld's (which included Howard McGhee and Shadow Wilson), Cab Calloway's with Chu Berry, Erskine Hawkins's, and Jimmie Lunceford's. They also had stage shows—vaudeville shows with singers, bands, and musical reviews. My parents were also friends with Eddie and Grace Hart, who owned a record shop on South Street and were big jazz fans. We were notified of all the new releases and bought lots of them, the so-called "race records." I also saw a lot of white bands such as the Mitchell Ayres Band, the Glenn Miller Orchestra, and Tommy Dorsey and Jimmy Dorsey's orchestra. I also saw Gene Krupa and his band with Roy Eldridge and Anita O'Day.

As I grew older, I became a lover of the music, an autograph-seeker. I was fascinated with Lionel Hampton's band with Earl Bostic and Arnett Cobb. Arnett played tenor like a Baptist preacher delivering a sermon. He was part of the Illinois Jacquet era of the Texas tenor players, who had a strong spiritual playing style. The bands would play for the various acts, jugglers and dancers. Most of the bands had their own singers, who were incidental parts of the band. Bands as background for singers came later. At that time, the bands would play three or four choruses before the singers would come in. It was the instrumental music that was most important to the people. The bands always had improvisation, and they also had good saxophone and trumpet soloists.

PERCY HEATH

We have a family picture of Jimmy up on a pony. Jimmy had a couple of teeth showing. I remember that date pretty well. A photographer would come through the neighborhood with a little horse, and he used to take pictures of children. We were renting a place in West Philadelphia, in the house of a West Indian lady, 5710 Ludlow Street. . . . Jimmy must have been about a year old. . . . I must have been about four. At that time, my mother was a housewife. She later became a hairdresser. Much later, after we had moved several times, she had her own business as a hairdresser. That was when we moved to South Philadelphia. That move took place before I was six years old because when I went to kindergarten, it was right across the street from where we were living. We lived right across the street from an all-black grade school. The principal, the teachers, everyone was black.

We moved around two or three times in South Philadelphia while we were growing up. Although we moved, I was still going to the same grade school. We probably stayed in that location until I was in the sixth grade. Although Philadelphia was a segregated place from the beginning, we lived next door to an Italian family and there were other Italian families on our block. They had to walk several blocks to a segregated grade school. We played in the streets together and were in and out of each other's homes: Carmen, Dominick, Butch, Rita, and Johnny Verone. Jimmy used to follow behind me. My parents would say, "Take your brother with you." One day we went to play by some railroad cars over on Washington Avenue, and we played over there for a couple of hours. Jimmy and I got very dirty from playing in a coal car. My grandmother and mother were looking for us. I got a terrible whipping for taking Jimmy, who followed me over there.

I started playing violin at the age of eight. My father was a clarinetist in the Elks Band. We had music in the house all along; blues, gospel, and even comedy records were played on the old Victrola. At that time, I couldn't hardly turn the handle of the Victrola. I had to reach up to it to play the records. My mother sang in the choir, and her mother too. They sang at the Nineteenth Street Baptist Church. We went every Sunday to Sunday school morning service and again in the evening. I used to sing with my mother, grandmother, and cousin Gertrude. We had a gospel quartet called the Family Four. Jimmy was too young to be involved with that. I was only about ten or eleven then. I also played violin at church teas, fundraisers, and other occasions.

When we were grown, back in 1975, Jimmy mentioned something about sibling rivalry. He said he always felt that he was trying to catch up to me. I never even realized it. I was the big brother, so I didn't expect him to compete with me about anything. We had a close relationship as brothers.

In Wilmington, I studied with Mr. Wall during the winter, and we practiced marches for the marching band. It was an extracurricular activity that we didn't have every day. I spent the summer months in Philadelphia and studied music there. I took lessons from Mr. Terry, a man who had a beautiful tone like Johnny Hodges. The one thing I regret is that he really didn't teach me about breathing. But what he taught me was something similar to the "easy" methods that you find in certain books that helped you to play little songs very quickly, which I was able to do. I could play "Intermezzo," "Frenese," and "Maria Elena" and many of the songs that were popular during those days. I joined with a friend of mine called James "Sax" Young, who later changed his name to Rashid. In the summer of 1942, I studied with Paul Amati, who taught at the Theodore Presser School of Music and was connected with the Philadelphia Orchestra. I studied with him for one summer and that was the extent of my formal training on the saxophone.

In Wilmington, I got my diploma when I graduated from the eleventh grade, because the school was really separate but not equal. The courses were mainly for black males; it was a vocational school where we had courses in bricklaying and carpentry. We didn't have algebra or higher forms of math, geometry and trigonometry, like they had in white New Hanover High, although we did study black history, people like Frederick Douglass. I was being trained to be a cabinetmaker, which is why I've always done things around the house.

In 1942 we started a jazz band in Wilmington and played stock arrangements. Mr. Wall, one of our music teachers, wrote certain things out for us,
as did Mr. Page, another teacher who had played bass with Count Basie for
a while. Andy McGhee, who was a couple of years younger than I was, also
played in the band. Andy would later play with Woody Herman and other
bands and would become a teacher at the Berklee College of Music in
Boston. Walter Best was the finest trumpet player down there, but of all the
players from Wilmington at that time, Andy McGhee and I were the only
ones who made music a career.

ANDY McGHEE

*I think Jimmy and I got our horns the same Christmas. When we got back to
the school after the holidays, Jimmy was picking stuff off the records. Before
Jimmy and I started playing the horn in the band and rehearsing together,
we just hung out socially. We were chasing the same girl, Dorothy McNeal.
After we joined the high school band, Jimmy and I became friends because we
sat next to each other in the sax section. I never visited the store his relatives
owned because I didn't live in that location, but I knew his cousin Jookie. I
lived further up, on North Fourth Street. Every time Jimmy and I got together,
it was always mellow. We talked about music or chasing the ladies.*

*The band director, Mr. Melvin Wall, was the first band teacher who really
gave us some inspiration. He was a saxophone player, and just like most music
teachers at that time, he knew a little bit about everything. He showed us the
saxophone fingering and told us to play whole notes. When he found out that
we could play, he put us in the band. Both of us could read only a little bit,
but we were good enough to function in the band. Jimmy and I were so short
that we could hardly carry the horn. We called Jimmy "Jeep," like the car, because he was so little. . . . The marching band played for all the football games
and we played concerts and traveled. We competed in Greensboro in the state
competitions at A&T in the early forties when Mr. Wall had the band. I think
Jimmy was there when we won first place. Jimmy was as mellow then as he
is now. He stayed sharp all the time, and he would always come back from
Philadelphia looking good. I was young but I liked to hang out with older
cats, and so the group that I hung out with was Jimmy's group. Mansfield
Ready was in the same class as Jimmy. I could tell when Jimmy came back
from Philly that he had improved because I was a competitive type. We were
very friendly but still everybody wanted to play first chair. The next teacher,*

Mr. Robert Page, came from Tuskegee. He was a good musician, and it was a blessing when he took over after Mr. Wall went into the navy.

Mr. Page could write and organized a small jazz band, which he called the Melody Barons, named after the Tuskegee Melody Barons. The group included some of the members of the marching band. There were three saxophones and two trumpets, and Mr. Page played bass. Billy Richards, who was a very good reader, and Jimmy were the two alto players. The tenor player, Grover, used to play at the carnival. Lee Shelton played trumpet, and there was a professional trombone player, Freddy Bennett, a Wilmington guy, who was a hell of a player. He liked to play with carnivals like Silas Green's. The piano player was an experienced performer from New York. The Melody Barons played around Wilmington for five dollars a night. The band played every Wednesday and Friday night, Wednesday night at the white U.S.O. Club and Friday night at the black U.S.O. Club.

I wasn't in the band at that time. Jimmy, who was two years ahead of me, got picked. I was waiting for one of the guys to drop out, stumble over a stone or something, but that didn't happen. Jimmy stayed there about a year or more, maybe between 1942 and 1943 because he graduated in 1943. When Jimmy graduated, I took his place.

The black people who owned the Barn were personal friends of mine, Mrs. Carrie Whitty and her husband, a businessman. It was located on the outskirts of Wilmington, out in the boondocks a little bit. Mr. Whitty wanted to bring in big bands, and so he remodeled this big old house, put a floor in it, and started bringing in bands. It looked almost like a tobacco warehouse, long and big enough to hold two hundred people, enough for Mr. Whitty to make some money. There was a stage and benches on the side. That's where all the white folks would sit. The Barn was integrated. When something was really happening, a few whites would sit on the side.

Mr. Whitty was shrewd, because he saw that there was a market for bringing in big bands. He booked mostly black bands. Once I played with a white band from Baltimore that came through. He booked Ella Johnson, Red Prysock—the best drawing band—Lucky Millender, and Duke Ellington. Some people didn't dig the very sophisticated Duke that much, but Jimmy and I did because Johnny Hodges was there. People in the South were a little funny. Duke's band was the most undisciplined band you ever saw. That was a little strange for us, but the band was smoking. Down South, where blues was very strong, they liked people like Eddie "Cleanhead" Vinson, Cootie

Williams, and blues singers like Etta Johnson. The Melody Barons didn't play in the Barn, but later I played there in 1946 with a band I organized for one of those sorority things. The Melody Barons band was kaput by that time. When Jimmy came down with Calvin Todd, Mr. Whitty booked the group at the Barn.

Jimmy's growth was faster than mine. When he was with Howard McGhee, I was studying at the New England Conservatory. There are two ways to learn how to play the horn, in school or on the street, and that's what Jimmy was doing. Both ways work. They were calling him "Little Bird" and he was killing everybody. Even "Trane" [John Coltrane] couldn't surpass "Little Bird." When Howard McGhee broke his band down, he was at the Apollo Theater, and he had to make a choice between the two. He thought Jimmy was the stronger, so he took Jimmy.

I went by to see Jimmy when he was in Boston. They were at the Ballroom on Huntington Avenue. Diz's band was there and Jimmy was playing lead and Coltrane was playing second. They had Matthew Gee, and it was a hell of a band. I think Paul Gonsalves was on tenor too. Jimmy took John Brown's place in Diz's band. When I saw him that night, Jimmy was wearing John Brown's uniform, but John Brown weighed about four hundred pounds, so Jimmy had the uniform wrapped all around him about fifteen times.

Jimmy's demonstrated that there are two ways to skin a cat. You don't have to go to a conservatory to be a hell of a player. His music and his talent speak for themselves. Jimmy's one of the finest arrangers. He's right at the top. I played a lot of his compositions in my workshops at Berklee, such as "Big P," "Heads Up! Feet Down!" "Sound for Sore Ears," which is one of my favorites, and "Gingerbread Boy," which Dexter recorded.

LEE SHELTON

Williston started the first high school band around 1940. It was a marching and concert band. That's how we got started playing horns. The band played for football games and other events. The bandmaster, Melvin Wall, taught us how to play our first instruments. A man named Mr. Blue gave me some private lessons. My formal training was limited, but I had a pretty good ear and good tone and could read the music. I could improvise. The Williston High School band won a state band competition in Laurinburg.

I started playing in a dance band, the Melody Barons, while in high school. We played in nightclubs where patrons smoked, drank liquor, and flirted with *the band members. The older members of the band protected me and encouraged me not to adopt any dangerous habits such as smoking weed, drinking liquor, and chasing skirts. We played what was popular at the time, like "After Hours," which featured the piano player. We played blues and tunes like "One O'Clock Jump" and traveled to other cities. When Fletcher Henderson came to town, I sat in with his band and was offered a job. I declined then and later at Howard University when he came through D.C. I had always wanted to be a physician.*

Jimmy was interested in being a musician and was serious about his horn. He played more expertly than we did (my two brothers and I). He left us in high school and we were not in touch for several years. Meanwhile, Percy, his brother, became famous with the Modern Jazz Quartet. Later, we became aware of Jimmy as a rising star in jazz and were proud to be acquainted with him.

Wilmington had hardcore segregation. We sat in the back of the bus and up in the balcony of the theater. I stopped going to the movies because I didn't like sitting in the balcony. At that time there were no racial incidents. Wilmington was the kind of town where black folks didn't "make waves" due to the history of violence during Reconstruction, when white folks rioted, drove the black mayor and other politicians out of town, and destroyed businesses such as the black newspaper. I walked three miles to high school past the white high school three blocks away.

During the civil rights movement, Wilmington was not in the forefront, and "The Wilmington 10" had the distinction of being sentenced to prison for their activities. Black folks and white folks didn't back them up like they did civil rights fighters in other cities.

In 1943, after finishing high school in Wilmington at age sixteen, I started playing with Arthur Woodson. Sax Young was also in the band, and we worked with him at a carnival show, where we learned to play popular songs such as "Jersey Bounce" and "Let Me off Uptown," the way Gene Krupa and Roy Eldridge performed it. We learned songs by ear, "Tuxedo Junction" and "One O'Clock Jump," which had been played by Basie and a lot of other groups. We copied a lot of popular tunes of that time and played carnivals. On one occasion, we played a carnival in New Jersey, where we were called the "Dixie Red Hots." The sign advertising the band had images of the darkest black people they could find, with exaggerated lips, stereotypes of African Americans. We had to "bally" before we performed to draw people into the show by going outside and playing so that the crowd would come into the tent and see the performance. I remember when someone first told me to go out and "bally." I didn't know what he was talking about. All of us went outside and "ballied"; even the piano player had to come out and play a piano they had outside. This was the start of our group. We made other gigs and amateur hours. In fact, we won an amateur contest. I knew at this time that music would be my life's work. It was like finding a rhythm, something I felt.

Later that year, I joined Calvin Todd's band in Philadelphia and stayed around Philly for a while. Sax Young was in that band too. Calvin Todd had played with Arthur Woodson, Sax Young, and me for some of the carnival gigs. Sax Young, who was later a member of my big band, which I started in 1946 and which included John Coltrane and other musicians from Philly, was one of my first musical associates. He used to play a C melody saxophone. When I was just getting started, we used to get together in the summer at the same time I was taking lessons from Mr. Terry. In fact, Sax Young was the best tenor in my big band. At that time, he could play better than Benny Golson and Trane, and he could improvise better than most of us, although he never got recognized. He later drove a cab in Los Angeles and was just as good as some of the musicians out there.

The Calvin Todd Band, which was soon enlarged to about ten pieces, was my first real band because we had more arrangements than the group led by Arthur Woodson. Calvin enlarged the group to about ten pieces. Calvin liked Louis Armstrong and Roy Eldridge and played in that style. Calvin wasn't playing like Dizzy Gillespie. In fact, at that time Dizzy was playing like Roy Eldridge, who was his idol. But Calvin was a very good player and I often wondered why he never took off. I guess he got married too early and got bogged down in Philly with a large family. He started working for the Post Office and didn't follow through musically. It wasn't his fault; things just didn't happen for him.

If we weren't playing stock arrangements like "Tuxedo Junction" and "9:20 Special," we would do head arrangements. One person would say, "You play this" or "You try that." We would get the tunes together that way; that was the way we arranged "One O'Clock Jump," for example. One guy who entered the band, Johnny Acea, who also played in my big band, wrote music for the band at one point. Johnny, who had gone to the Mastbaum

School of Music in Philly, played piano and trumpet and also knew how to write. Eventually he started giving arrangements to Calvin, and we ended up getting a booking to tour down South.

BILL GRIFFIN

In 1943, I met Calvin Todd at a carnival along with Sax Young and a piano player named Arthur Woodson, who played gospel but never really got into serious jazz. Woodson recruited us and we traveled with the band to Maryland. Arthur, who was gay, lived around Twenty-first and Kater Street. One of the tunes we played was "Sweet Sue," when the bally would come up. We played only about eight or sixteen bars to get the crowd interested, and after the crowd got there, we went inside the tent and played. We didn't play that much because we mostly played for the comedian. I don't think there was a singer. Arthur Woodson played boogie woogie with his left hand so we didn't need a bass. He had good rhythm. I understand that Jimmy had played with Arthur earlier at a carnival in New Jersey.

Calvin Todd started a band that Jimmy was in. I was playing tenor and Jimmy was playing alto. The band started out playing stock arrangements and eventually progressed to original arrangements. Some of the top arrangers in Philadelphia, like Johnny Acea, Gabe Bowman, and Leroy Lovett, were involved. The personnel of this band was five reeds, three trumpets, and three rhythm, which was augmented on special occasions with the addition of two trombones. We had the gig down at Rosedale Beach, Delaware, for one summer with Calvin Todd. [Billy] Braithwaite, lead alto, couldn't make the gig because his parents wouldn't let him go. I was playing tenor along with Alonzo Hagins, but I was also doing a lot of the business matters, so we needed another tenor. Zack Wright joined the band and that really stabilized things, put us on a different track, because he was a professional, a real pro. He gave us a lot of direction because he had so much experience. He held his tenor on an angle like Lester a little bit. We bought some of those royal blue coats when we had a couple of gigs at Town Hall. Jimmy McIntyre played piano in Calvin Todd's band. Chick Jones was on drums but Lenwood Ewell played with the band sometimes. He was a little bit more advanced than we were, so we would use him when we really needed some professionalism, but Chick Jones was the main drummer. In 1944, Calvin Todd's group was becoming the most popular dance band in the Philadelphia area. Jimmy started out playing third alto, but because of the war and personnel changes, Jimmy moved up to first alto. With the move to first alto, Jimmy progressed and matured. He led the reed section by putting his individual style in place. Hearing him lead the reed section with the tone that he had developed, I knew that the alto was his predestined instrument, not the tenor. In 1945, Calvin Todd's band went on the road to tour the South, and I went to the West Coast, so I didn't see Jimmy until after the war. After I returned to Philadelphia in '45, Charles Parker (Bird) and Diz had hit the scene and the music was changing. Big bands were not as prominent as they were, and the style of playing was changing rapidly. Around 1946, small groups were now popular. During this period, Jimmy organized his big band. This band was really a workshop heading in new directions with arrangements and soloists. Jimmy used to come over to my house, and we practiced the new chords, experimenting with flatted fifths, augmented thirteenths, substitute chords, different voicings and progressions. This is also when John Coltrane was beginning to get noticed.

With Jimmy's orchestra, we played the Strand on Tuesday, and we floated around on Friday and Saturday because those were the dance nights.

GERALD PORTER

I met Jimmy Heath in 1943. Bill Griffin had heard me play and wanted me to join him in the Calvin Todd Band. I tried to convince him that I was not up to the level of those guys, but he said, "Come on out." I think we went to the Strand Ballroom, where Calvin Todd and the group were rehearsing. Bill Griffin introduced me, and Leroy Lovett asked me to play "Jumping at the Woodside," which was in the book. I must have done all right. Lovett said, "You're with the band." I told them I was studying at the Granoff School of Music, and Jimmy very astutely looked at my horn and said, "What kind of horn is that?" I wasn't sure myself, and he said, "It's a Brun." Jimmy said, "I have never in my sixteen or seventeen years of life heard of a Brun. From now on you are Brother Brun." That was my initiation with Jimmy Heath and Calvin Todd's band.

I thought Calvin Todd was an extremely talented guy. He just had a musical gift. He could play saxophone, trumpet, guitar, and bass. He helped to engender the kind of camaraderie that we had. We weren't making any money, but we had a good time and we had some focus.

When we were on the road, we stopped at Jimmy's grandfather's store in Wilmington. During the war, you couldn't buy cigarettes. Jimmy's grandfather sold me a carton for about a buck and a half. He could have sold them *for almost three or four times that amount. We rode down South in banjo Bernie's bus. With Todd we went back down there to perform at the Barn on Tenth and Mears. We also worked in Philadelphia on Tuesday nights at the Wharton Settlement. That was a regular gig. We also worked regularly at the Richard Allen Homes.*

One time on the road with Calvin Todd, we had a car accident. I was asleep when we got hit and the back of the bus caught on fire. The first thing I did was grab my saxophone and the cigarettes and got out of there. That was the first time I ever saw anybody die. A big Delaware state trooper arrested our bus driver, and we played the gig that night with these big state troopers watching us.

Another time in 1945 in Kinston, North Carolina, we were sleeping in the colored waiting room of the bus depot because our bus had broken down. This trooper came in and started beating us on the feet. I said, "What have I done? I'm sleeping in the colored waiting room." I guess I had no business sleeping.

With Todd, we encountered either overt or covert racism all along the path. We played the gig for the white folks the first night and the black folks the second night. One time we played at Seymour Johnson Army Base right outside of Goldsboro, North Carolina; we played for the officers. We had a couple of waltzes, so we pulled out what we called the white book. We played what the white folks wanted to hear. When we played for the black audiences, we would pull out "Jumping at the Woodside" and "One O'Clock Jump." Calvin Todd played the twelve-bar blues. We used to wear out a set of riffs behind the twelve-bar blues.

Jimmy's mother and father would have thirteen guys practicing in the living room or the basement because we didn't have anyplace else. Jimmy's mom and dad would say, "It's all right." That kind of support helped to make Jimmy the kind of musician he became.

The jazz scene in Philadelphia in the forties was very kinetic because the war was over and there were always musicians coming from various parts of the country. Some of them had been in the army, and they wanted to find out where the music was being played. There were clubs like the Woodbine Club on Eleventh and Master and a club at Thirteenth and Poplar where Bass Ashford used to play. One of the saxophonists was Vance Wilson. Specs Wright was a very good personal friend of mine. He was an extremely competent drummer and a very unassuming one. His lady at that time was a girl named Dorothy Tucker, who lived up in North Philly. She went to West Philadelphia

High School with me. One day she said, "If you like jazz, come on past my house." She was very knowledgeable, and she had the largest collection of 78s that I had ever seen. We used to go home from school at 2:15 P.M., and I would stay at her house until eight o'clock at night listening to her albums.

Trumpeter Red Rodney [Rodney Chudnick] and Al Steel used to play at the Down Beat. The Blue Note was at Fifteenth and Ridge, and I saw Jimmy, Diz, and Coltrane at the 421 in 1948 or '49 or later than that. It was located at Fifty-sixth and Wyalusing. Another club was the Zanzibar. Some of the other musicians were Richie Kamuca, tenor; Marty Gold, trumpet; and Buddy Savitt. Ziggy Vines could cook.

Jimmy was on the road a lot, and he wrote me a letter when I was in the army in 1945 or '46 when he was playing with Nat Towles. Jimmy lived at 2626 North Twenty-fourth Street in Omaha, Nebraska, when I was stationed in Kansas. I made a couple of gigs at the Orchid Room.

In 1945, the Calvin Todd Band booked a southern tour, a real starvation tour, where we ate potted ham and crackers just to survive the gig. We bought a bus and began playing gigs that paid two or four dollars. We even played gigs for ninety cents, or we would get a percentage. (Later, when we got in the Musicians' Union, we made two dollars and then eight dollars scale. Eventually we made ten and twelve dollars. We got together then and bought an old school bus.) We didn't go into the Deep South; mainly we played North and South Carolina. On the tour, a guy named Leroy Lovett started writing for us, and so did Johnny Acea. We played the book of original arrangements. Of course, we still played the standards such as "Flying Home," "Tuxedo Junction," and "One O'Clock Jump" and used quite a bit of Johnny Acea's and Leroy Lovett's arrangements.

We were in Wilmington, North Carolina, in 1945 and played a place called the Barn. I stayed with my grandmother while the other guys in the band stayed in the bus. At that time, the Ernie Fields Band from Tulsa, Oklahoma, was passing through Wilmington. We knew that this was a very good band; it wasn't quite a big band, but they had excellent arrangements. I met Bill Evans, who is now known as Yusef Lateef; he played with the Ernie Fields band and had a big tone on tenor saxophone. The all-black Ernie Fields group was a hell of a band as far as we were concerned. They were much better than we were and a little older. They had also been on the road a lot longer than we had been. I was completely carried away by the arrangements written by Charles Sherrill. One other thing about that band is that they had a very good singer, Melvin Moore.

In the Ernie Fields band, Yusef was playing all right, and the whole reed section sounded pretty good. We went to a lot of their rehearsals and heard a lot of Sherrill's music. They had lead choruses and other arrangements that we didn't have that made their sound more intricate. At that time, I didn't notice any overwhelming ability in Yusef's playing. He just had a good sound. We didn't really become friends until he was with Dizzy. When I saw Yusef much later, I was able to recall and sing some of the arrangements of that 1944 band because the backgrounds were so advanced.

On one occasion with the Calvin Todd band, we had a gig in Rosedale Beach, Delaware. It was quite a long ride. We rode all night in the old yellow school bus we had bought for a thousand dollars, and it kept stalling out. Eventually we had to get out and push it because it conked out a few miles from where we were going to play. We stalled right in the middle of the highway, and we all got out except the bus driver. All of our baggage and instruments were in there. It was pitch dark. Realizing that we were supposed to play an hour or two later, we started to push the bus. There were four or five of us in the back pushing and another four on the side. Suddenly, when we looked around, there was a car coming, a black Ford doing about eighty or ninety miles an hour and heading straight for the back of the bus. When I saw the car coming, I hollered, "Look out! Look out!" Everybody jumped to the side just in time. We came so close to getting killed, but nobody in the band got hurt. Some of us jumped into the ditch on the side.

The white soldier who had been driving the Ford must have been drunk; he didn't see the bus and rammed right into the back of it. The bus caught on fire. After it was all over, I stopped trembling. There was glass in my pocket from the accident. The Delaware state troopers came with their big Boy Scout hats on. We were all scared because they were talking about charging our bus driver, Al Stevenson, with manslaughter because of the bus stalling in the middle of the highway. Also, we didn't have the proper lights. We ended up getting to the gig that night, and the band sounded like Guy Lombardo's band, saxophones with a lot of vibrato; we were all so shook by the soldier killing himself by running into the back of the bus. The next day, our bus driver had to go down for the hearing and the inquest. That was one of my first experiences on the road. Another time later on, when I was with the Nat Towles Orchestra, the bus almost ran off a cliff near Omaha, Nebraska.

In Philly, I still worked with local bands like Mel Melvin's or Calvin Todd's until 1945. At that time, Felix Leach, who played trombone in Melvin's band, joined the Nat Towles Orchestra from Omaha, Nebraska, and I soon followed him. I was about eighteen years old and already had about two or three years' experience playing in bands. Joining Towles's band meant that I would have to leave home to play on the road. My mother didn't want me to go; she was afraid because I was so young. My brother Percy had already left home to join the Army Air Corp, and I was the first professional musician in the family. On July 3, 1945, I played what was probably my first gig with Nat Towles in Wayne, Nebraska.

Leaving home and being on the road from age eighteen, I saw a lot of America. We were a "territory" dance band and traveled through the Midwest, South, and Southeast. Besides playing the known cities, we played small towns. I kept a diary of the dates. We were in such places as Wayne and Chadron, Nebraska; Ortonville and Austin, Minnesota; Boscobel, Wisconsin; Woodward, Iowa; Quincy, Illinois; Bird City and Concordia, Kansas; Moberly, Missouri; Beresford and Waubay, South Dakota; Leland and McComb, Mississippi; Tallulah and Monroe, Louisiana; El Dorado and Camden, Arkansas; Paris and Texarkana, Texas; and Julesburg, Colorado.

The Nat Towles Orchestra made headlines in the Midwest, like when we played the Prom Ballroom in St. Paul, Minnesota, in the fall of 1945. As the October 13, 1945, *Pittsburgh Courier* article "Nat Towles Ork Smashes St. Paul Ballroom Mark" reported, "[The] significance of the entire event is the fact that Nat is the first sepia leader to play the noted ballroom. That shows, without a doubt, that Nat's unique way of presenting his music has caused the critics everywhere to take notice, and therefore enable him to step further ahead in his field by accomplishing bookings of this type" (p. 11). That October we were also in St. Cloud, but we went east in January 1946 for an engagement at the Royal Theatre in Baltimore. I got paid eighty-four dollars for the week of January 11–17. One of the final entries in my diary was May 11, 1946, in Ames, Iowa.

In the Nat Towles Orchestra, Billy Mitchell, a tenor player from Detroit, was the "straw boss." Buddy Pearson from Boston played lead alto. All of the guys in the band were good sight readers, but I couldn't really read that well then. Leach got them to send for me because they needed an alto player. Mitchell was instrumental in my staying with the band. He told Nat Towles, "Keep the little guy." When I auditioned for the Nat Towles Orchestra, I was chosen over the other applicant although I couldn't read as well as he could. Billy, having the power of persuasion, also told me that there was a small room at the rooming house where he lived that would be perfect for me. You might say that Billy was responsible for my professional career. He always referred to me as the "little guy." Billy could read "fly shit," and he went on to a brilliant career playing with Basie, Thad Jones, Dizzy, and others.

2

Big Band Connections

■

Whe I was with the Nat Towles Orchestra, in the band was a saxophonist from Kansas City, Missouri, named Clifford Jedkins. He was an ultra-modernist who claimed he had a tenor saxophone that was once Charlie Parker's. Clifford was one of the most unique musicians in the way he played and in his lifestyle. I had never met anyone quite like him. When he joined Nat Towles, he had few clothes, but he did have a large suitcase filled with marijuana. He also could identify the plants that we would pass on the road in places like Council Bluffs and around Omaha. He would ask us to stop the bus, pretending that he had to relieve himself, and he would pick plants by the roadside. At that time, I wasn't into any of that. I did notice the way he played so-called flatted fifths on a lot of his solos. He had learned that from Charlie Parker and Dizzy, but he would exaggerate this particular harmonic sequence. Nat Towles was a very conservative, square type of leader. Each time Cliff would play a solo, he would play things that sounded strange to Nat, who frowned as if he were thinking, "What the hell is he playing." The guys in the section knew that Cliff was trying to play in the modern bebop style. Cliff didn't last in the band very long. I don't know if I left before he did, but Nat got rid of him. Another tenor player in the band, who we called Buddha, was more soulful. In Nat Towles's book were some great arrangements by Frank Greer. The guys in the band told me that Neal Hefti, who became a well-known composer-arranger with the Woody Herman band, traveled with them gratis just to check out Frank's music.

As band members, we had to wear white shirts each night we played, and Clifford had only two white shirts. He was the one who first told me that I could turn a shirt inside-out and wear it on the other side. When we did one-nighters, it was necessary to do that. He would turn his shirt over on the opposite side and button it up backwards, and his tie would cover the name tag on the back of the shirt.

When we first went up to the "Land of Ten Thousand Lakes—Minnesota—where most of the inhabitants were of Scandinavian origin, race relations in the lower states were not that good. In Minnesota the racism was not as obvious because there weren't many black people in the state. One day, Billy Mitchell and I went in the five-and-ten-cent store in Mankato, Minnesota, and a couple of clerks, young girls, asked us, "Are you guys in the band?" We said, "Yeah. We're playing here tonight for a dance." Most people in town knew about the dance, and the clerks wanted to attend. I was about nineteen, and the clerks were about our age. Billy and I were not out of line with them as far as age was concerned, so we invited them to the dance. They came that night, and during intermission, they jumped up on the stage, sat down, and started to talk to us.

One of the girls said, "I really loved the music. It was so beautiful. How many are in the band?"

Billy said, "It's a sixteen- or seventeen-piece band."

One of the girls replied, "And all niggers!"

We said, "We're not niggers. We're Negroes." She turned red because it was so embarrassing, and she apologized for the next five minutes. She didn't mean it viciously, but it was the way she had heard black people identified. To her, that's what we were.

I also hung out with Billy around the time when the bass player with the band gave notice that he was leaving. On a day off, Billy and I went from Omaha to Lincoln, Nebraska, to see a band led by Snookum Russell, which was playing in a local theater. When the band finished the set, we went backstage to talk to the bassist, who was killin'. His name was Ray Brown. Billy and I told him who we were and who we worked for and that Towles needed a bass player. Ray said he would consider the offer. We never heard any more from Ray, but when we picked up a *Down Beat* magazine a little later, we read that he had joined Dizzy's band.

Another time with Nat Towles, we went on the road to Dallas, Texas. One day, Billy and I were walking across the street in Dallas, and we jay-walked. We heard a loud police siren and the police ran up on us. One said in a Texas drawl, "Where you boys from?"

I said, "I'm from North Carolina."

He said, "I know you weren't from around here because if you cross the street like that around here, some of these Dallas niggers will run over you down here."

BILLY MITCHELL

In 1945, I was working with the Nat Towles Orchestra when I first met Jimmy. He was wearing a little blue beret that was the hit in those days and a tan trench coat. We needed an alto player. Evidently Felix Leach must have recommended Jimmy, and somebody else had recommended another guy from Chicago. Leach, a trombone player from Philadelphia, joined the Nat Towles band before me and Jimmy. I got the job with Towles when he was at the Paradise Theater in Detroit. Jimmy was about a year and half in the band. I was the straw boss, which equates to foreman, with the same activities as if you were a foreman in a foundry, a musical foreman. Instead of running to the leader of the band, you would go to the straw boss. As straw boss, I told people what to do in regards to the music.

It was a good band. We had arrangements. Nat Towles didn't write. He was a bass player in earlier years, but he never played with us. He just handled the business. Our book was a nice size, a good book with 100 or 150 arrangements. We played the standards and the hits of the day like "Nine-Twenty Special" and "One O'Clock Jump"; everybody had those and they had their own things too. You could buy them as stock arrangements. If a band had a hit, you could get a stock on it. Most every band got them because people naturally wanted to hear the latest hit. "Tuxedo Junction," played by Erskine Hawkins's band, was real hot for years. Some of our arrangements were written by Wild Bill Davis, Charles Thompson, and a fellow in the band named Burple. Everything was dance then. A lot of the people who were in the big bands of Lionel, Duke, and Basie came through the Towles band. Lionel, Duke, Basie, Fletcher Henderson, and Lunceford were the top of the heap. They got the most recognition. The other bands weren't the top bands, but they were the breeding grounds for all of the musicians who got to be in top ones.

Territory bands cover a certain area, from this town to the next town. The Nat Towles Orchestra was based in Omaha and it played the South, the Southwest, and the Midwest—Iowa, Nebraska, Kansas. Occasionally we might come east. Maybe Towles was in the Apollo Theater one time during the whole time he had the band, never when I played with him. Omaha was the base for the Towles Orchestra. We always left out of Omaha and came back when we weren't working. Omaha was like any other town, black people on one side and white people on the other. There used to be a couple of clubs around in Omaha that we would go to. Downtown there was a white place we used to play at once in a while. I remember jamming down there one night with alto saxophonist Eddie Vinson, who came in with the Cootie Williams band— George Treadwell (trumpet), James Glover (bass), and Leonard Gaskin (bass). Williams had two basses.

All the engagements we had with the Nat Towles Orchestra were for mostly black audiences. Even the big-name bands were playing all-black audiences, except maybe some places like New York or Detroit, where they would play for white people too. At the local theater, black people could go, but generally speaking most black bands of that day played to all-black audiences. Most of the big bands didn't play that much in the East and the West. They all went south.

Jimmy and another sax player joined us on the road and played for a couple of nights while Nat was trying to decide which one he wanted to keep. The other fellow could read a little better than Jimmy. Jimmy could spell but he couldn't really read music then. We used to play dances, and instead of playing arrangements, somebody would stand up for a solo on one of the ballads. Towles had already made up his mind that he was going to keep the other cat, but just before he let Jimmy go—Jimmy was supposed to leave the next day—he pointed to Jimmy to play a solo and Jimmy stood up and played "I Should Care." That knocked me out. Buddy Pearson, who was also in the band and played saxophone too, looked at me and we listened to what Jimmy was doing. It was just so pretty. The other cat was all right. We didn't have anything against him, but Jimmy was our age too. We had that in common. Plus, I also had a room that had two beds in it and one of the beds was a little bitty bed. It was made to order for him. That was half of my room rent, so we, the two saxophone players, told Towles, "No, man, we want to keep Jimmy." Jimmy sat between me and Buddy on the bandstand. Towles said, "He can't read." But we said, "That ain't nothing." After all, reading is memorization too. I can remember when I was the one who taught Jimmy to read and now he can write reams.

If you ever saw Duke's band or Basie's band, you didn't see them reading the music. They knew it by that time and that's what all reading is. You run it down two or three times and you've memorized it really. You've memorized what's coming; even if you have to read it, you know what's coming next. If it's a really difficult part, the trick is to memorize it and know when it's coming. If it's something difficult and you know it's coming, you might experience a little anxiety. "Here comes this tricky part." If you memorize it, it ain't no problem. Jimmy learned with everybody's assistance. We all learned everything we knew by imitation. You see somebody else do something and then you learn to do it. We all assisted each other at that time. Remember, didn't none of us really know shit. Just some of us knew a little more than the others about certain things. As the saying goes, "We're all ignorant, just on different subjects."

Jimmy has the same attitude and personality now as he had back then, just a little nice cat. There was a club in Omaha called the Blue Room, Twenty-fourth and Lake, where all the cats jammed, and I could go in there and jam every night because I was big and looked older. Jimmy would have to sit outside waiting for me. On intermission I would bring him one beer and by the time I'd get back, that one beer would make him high as he could be. So he had to sit outside in front and listen while I could go inside and jam. Drinking age was twenty-one. He was eighteen or nineteen and looked sixteen.

Towles relied on Buddy and me about Little Bird, as he was later called, when we said we would rather have him. After all, we were the two best saxophone players in the section. We would rather have Jimmy because we had more in common. The old man was smart enough to see that too. Jimmy just sat there and absorbed from us, imitation. Buddy and I were both good readers. Sitting between the two of us, Jimmy knew if he made a mistake or if he felt he would make a mistake, he could lean on any one of us. When he saw how we did it, he would look at how it sounded and how it looked on paper. The next time he saw that, he knew what it was. It wasn't a matter of teaching. There is no such thing as teaching. It's all learning, and learning is imitation. Imitation develops and evolves into styles or uniqueness. He learned by experience. The parts he was weak on, we were strong on. The things he was doing naturally stimulated us. If he was teaching us, we were teaching him. Now, anything he plays is going to be special at any time. That's just a rule of thumb.

When you're living together in a bus twelve months out of the year, everybody knows everybody's personality. We had a couple of nuts in the band. Joe Timmons, the singer in the band, was after Little Bird one night. He was a big cat, weighed about as much as I did. He got mad at Jimmy about something and was talking about hitting him. That was out of the question. Nothing big ever came of it. I doubt if anybody has ever raised his hand at Jimmy

■ Jimmy in a baby carriage, Philadelphia, 1927. (Jimmy Heath Collection, photographer unknown)

■ Jimmy and pony, Philadelphia, 1927. (Jimmy Heath Collection, photographer unknown)

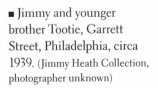

■ Jimmy and younger brother Tootie, Garrett Street, Philadelphia, circa 1939. (Jimmy Heath Collection, photographer unknown)

■ Jimmy wearing Big Apple hat, Philadelphia, circa 1940. (Jimmy Heath Collection, photographer unknown)

■ Percy, Sr., and Arlethia (Jimmy's father and mother) in their Elks uniforms, Philadelphia, circa 1940. (Jimmy Heath Collection, photographer unknown)

■ Williston High School, Wilmington, North Carolina, class of 1943. Jimmy is in the bottom row (standing), twelfth from the left. (Jimmy Heath Collection, photographer unknown)

■ Calvin Todd Orchestra, Town Hall, Philadelphia, circa 1944. *Top row, left to right*: Lenwood Ewell (drums), Quenzell McCall (vocalist), and unknown (vocalist). *Middle row, left to right*: unknown (blocked; trumpet), Ethel Wilson (trumpet), Monroe Pitts (trumpet), unknown (trumpet), James McIntyre (piano), and unknown (bass). *Bottom row, left to right*: Sax Young (tenor sax), Billy Braithwaite (alto sax), unknown (leaning over; baritone sax), Jimmy Heath (alto sax), Bill Griffin (tenor sax), Gerald Porter (tenor sax), and Harry Crafton (guitar). *Out front*: Calvin Todd (trumpet; leader). (Jimmy Heath Collection, photographer unknown)

■ Nat Towles Orchestra on tour in the Midwest, 1945. *Left to right:* Kingfish (trombone), Baptiste (baritone sax), unknown (trombone), Milton "Burple" Thomas (trumpet), unknown (tenor sax), Felix Leach (trombone), Russell Emory (trumpet), Buddy Pearson (alto sax), Nat Towles (leader), Jimmy Heath (alto sax), Nat Williams (drums), Billy Mitchell (tenor sax), Joe Timmons (vocalist), and Roosevelt (piano). (Jimmy Heath Collection, photographer unknown)

■ Jimmy Heath with alto sax, Philadelphia, 1946. (Jimmy Heath Collection, photographer unknown)

■ *Facing page:* Howard McGhee Sextet, Les Ambassadeurs, Paris, May 1948. *Left to right:* Jesse Powell (tenor sax), Jimmy Heath (alto sax), Howard McGhee (trumpet; leader), Percy Heath (bass), Specs Wright (drums), and Vernon Biddle (unseen; piano). (Jimmy Heath Collection, photographer unknown)

■ Jimmy Heath Orchestra, Club Elate, Broad and Fitzwater Streets, Philadelphia, 1947. *Seated on bandstand, left to right:* Bill Leonard (trombone), Howard Scroggins (trombone), Sax Young (hidden; tenor sax), John Coltrane (alto sax), Bill Massey (unseen; trumpet), and John Joyner (alto sax). *Standing:* Charlie Parker (alto sax) and Jimmy Heath (leader). (Jimmy Heath Collection, photographer unknown)

or if Jimmy has ever raised his hand at anyone. At five-foot-three and one hundred and twenty-five pounds, you don't go around intimidating people. I saved Jimmy.

I didn't receive any worse discrimination in 1945 with Nat Towles in Nebraska that I didn't experience with Woody Herman in 1949. In Iowa you could be treated like a king and then go a hundred miles in any direction and still be in Iowa and it would be shitty, a whole different scene. It was based on the attitude of people in the area. Wherever there aren't many of us, we don't frighten them. For example, Minnesota was like heaven in those days. There was no discrimination. People would bring their children up to you on the street so they could see what a colored person looked like. There weren't many colored people up there, very, very few up in Minnesota then. You don't experience as much discrimination as an artist when you're known. For example, in the South, when we came to town, there were places where they closed the restaurant.

We played in Marysville, Kansas, once a month, and the dance hall was a small building outside of town. The first thing about that dance hall that tickled me was the sign on it. "Men in overalls not admitted." That was for the farmers. When we got in town in the afternoon, they closed the restaurant to just feed us and nobody else. I got through eating early and I went out on the porch. While they were feeding us, the sheriff was standing on the porch. About that time two colored cats came along, and they saw me standing on the porch and the sheriff standing on the porch so they started up the steps into the restaurant. The sheriff says, "Where you going, boy?" They said, "Well we're going in the restaurant. We saw them other colored fellows in there." The sheriff said, "That's a different kind of nigger than you."

Another time, one night we were on the road somewhere in the South. Our driver, named Kingfish, would scratch his head if he were talking to a white person. He'd give the white folks just what they wanted, "No, sir" and "Yes, sir." He knew how to talk to them. He could put the Uncle Tom routine on quick, but it wasn't no act. It was natural. There's such a thing as Tomming in a situation and there's such a thing as Tomming so much that it was a part of your life. He just shifted roles. At that time, during the war, there was a speed limit of thirty or thirty-five miles an hour. You couldn't drive any faster, highway or anywhere. That night we heard a siren and the highway patrol pulls up. We must have had a light out or something. Kingfish straightened things out, "Sir, the bulb went out about five miles back and soon as I get a bulb at *a gas station, I'll fix it." The highway patrol was satisfied. They got what they wanted and they went on. Just at that moment, Towles woke up.*

"What's going on out there?"

The highway patrol said, "Who are you?"

Nat Towles said, "Well, I'm Nat Towles. I own this band."

The patrolman said, "Oh yeah. You own this band?"

"Yes," said Towles. It was quiet.

Towles said, "Yes."

The patrolman said, "Nigger, I'll give you one more chance." He said, "Do you own this band?"

Towles said, "Yes, sir."

If Towles had kept his mouth shut, we would have been gone. It was humorous then after he let us go. It wasn't funny as long as we were stopped.

One time we had a valet with the band. He stole some clothes, my suit and someone else's, and sneaked off in Hattiesburg, Mississippi. We were going to go to the police station to report it. Little Nat, the drummer, told us, "Man, don't do that." I was from Detroit, and so with my Detroit shit, I went to the police station. When we got down to the police station, the first thing that happened is that they wanted to know what we were doing down there and they gave us a grilling. They asked Russell Emory, who I think was the other person, "Where you from, boy?" and took his draft card. He's from Kansas. They took my draft card, looked at it and said, "Detroit." There had been a big race riot in Detroit in 1942.

The policeman said, "You one of them race riot niggers, ain't you?"

I said to myself, "Oh, shit."

Then I said, "No, sir. I'm from Missouri, sir. I just turned eighteen traveling with this band, and while we were in Detroit, that's where I had to register."

So he said, "Okay," and gave me the card back. Then he told the guy sitting in the room with him about the suit. "If we see the black bastard, we'll know what to do about it. Lock these two up until the morning."

They didn't want us walking around downtown at night. The cop who gave the order walked out. After about five minutes the one sitting behind the desk, who had his shoes off, said, "Y'all get out of here." And we did.

I left Jimmy in the band in 1946.

FELIX LEACH

I joined the Nat Towles Orchestra through one of the guys in the band, Abe Meeks, when they were playing down at the Strand Ballroom in Philadelphia.

Jimmy and I were the only two Philadelphians with Nat Towles. A guy from Chicago named René Hall was writing arrangements that were setting our ears back. He even wrote numbers for shows, when we played the Rhumboogie Club in Chicago. Jimmy wrote a couple of very good arrangements too.

We always looked at Jimmy as quite unusual because when Charlie Parker came out, Jimmy jumped on that right away. He knew exactly what those guys were doing because he was the one that first pointed out what Charlie Parker was doing, how he would end up at an unusual note in an unusual place in a tune. You were looking for him to end the phrase at a certain point. Jimmy Heath was doing the same thing at that time. Jimmy latched right onto it, and he was playing it. He was playing bebop way before a whole bunch of guys were doing it. Most of us were looking for the same groove we always got and we called it swing, but Jimmy was jumping into the next generation of music right then. . . .

Nat Towles was a stepping stone. Burple, Milton Thomas, received a telegram from Cootie Williams because Cootie Williams had a big band at that time too. We ran into him up in New York at a benefit, I think at the Loews State Theater. Cootie Williams played before we did, and Billie Holiday was singing on that same show. When Cootie started off that first number, those guys sounded like thunder.

Omaha was a small town, and it had one main stem where all the blacks hung out. Right on the corner was a place called McGill's Bar, where a little band played every night and you could go in there and jam. I don't know if Jimmy was there one night after we had been out playing all these white gigs. That night the whole band showed up at McGill's Bar and we played Nat's book. Everybody knew the music by heart. When we left town, Nat bore down on us. He said, "You guys are out there giving a free concert." He was upset because he didn't get a gig out of it.

Once on the bus after we played a gig in North Dakota, we were driving down out of the Black Hills and ahead of us was this great big herd of buffalo coming right across the road. We thought the bus driver was going to stop, but he didn't. He pulled that big air horn and the buffalo parted and we passed through, but when we got on the other side of the herd and he slowed to a stop, the driver said, "I ain't got no brakes." That's why he didn't stop for the buffalo.

HY LOCKHART

In 1946, the week before I got discharged from the navy, I stopped in Chicago to buy a new trumpet. I was on the train headed back to my hometown,

Troy, Alabama, when I met Chester Thomas, a tenor player with the Nat Towles Orchestra. He took my name, address, and phone number, but I never expected to hear from him again. After about a week at home, I received a surprise telegram from Nat Towles asking me to join the band when they came through Troy. When I got on the band bus, I had the feeling that all the guys were thinking, "Who's this country boy coming aboard. I wonder if he can play." One of the first people I met was Jimmy Heath. We kind of hit it off because we were the same age, nineteen. We were the two youngest in the band, and both of us liked bebop. While traveling, we'd hum tunes and scat sing all the hits that Diz and Bird used to play. I roomed mostly with Jimmy, who was more established in the band because Nat gave him a lot of solos. Jimmy attracted people when he stood up and soloed in the bop style. I was in the band for about a year and a half.

The trumpet section was nice. The first trumpet was Russell Emory from Wichita, Kansas; another trumpet player was "the Whistler," Leo Sheppard, out of Charleston, South Carolina, who later went with Lionel Hampton. The other trumpet was Joe Bentley, an impressive talent from New Orleans but kind of erratic. He used to get into a lot of trouble in his free time because he would drink heavily and end up in jail or beaten up and in the hospital.

Nat Towles was a very likable guy. Musically speaking, he was no Jimmie Lunceford or Duke Ellington. He didn't have that kind of musical respect. Towles didn't do his own writing. Some of the charts were by the piano player, Sir Charles Thompson, and Neal Hefti, a white arranger who wrote for Woody Herman's band, did a lot of the charts too.

With us in the Nat Towles Orchestra was a blues guitarist and singer named Lonnie Johnson, and Lonnie used to do the same tunes every night. Sometimes Jimmy would make fun of that. We were in our room one day when we were in New Orleans, probably at the Patterson Hotel, and Jimmy was practicing and holding his saxophone like a guitar. He was singing like Lonnie, "I cover the waterfront," and then he said, "Wrong chord." Jimmy didn't know that Lonnie was standing in the doorway. Lonnie got so mad that he went to his room to get his gun, which he kept in his guitar case. I followed him to his room and told him that it was all in fun, that nobody meant any harm. I really calmed him down, and I may have saved Jimmy's life. Lonnie did play a lot of wrong chords.

Jimmy was always striving to learn more about chords. We had a record player on the road, and we used to play recordings by Billy Eckstine's big band. Jimmy would play right along with the lead alto, picking up on his phrasing.

The most exciting musician in Towles's band was Chester Thomas. He could stand next to Coleman Hawkins and play "Body and Soul." He amazed Jimmy, who used to say that Chester Thomas was a tough man. Jimmy learned something from Chester. We all learned from each other. Jimmy was first alto, and back then he sounded a lot like Bird. I've heard from others that the reason he switched from alto to tenor is that he didn't want that label, being called "Little Bird." Jimmy also used to impress me with how he saved his money. On the nights that we got paid, the next day Jimmy would go to the post office and send his mother the money. We were making eighteen or nineteen dollars a night; the first-string guys were probably making more.

Our bus driver, Brother Wes, was a handsome black guy. He was well liked by all the guys in the band. One evening in Iowa or Kansas, we were starving and Nat said, "I'll be right back. I'm going to see if we can get some food." When he came back, he said, "We got to wait about half an hour, and then we're going to be served at this restaurant." When we walked into this place, it was empty. The guy had pulled the shade down and hung the closed sign on the door. He had told Nat that he would serve our band, but he wouldn't be able to let his white customers in while he was serving us. When people tried to get in, the owner said, "I'll be opening in about an hour and a half. I have a colored band that I'm serving here." They served us some of the best food I've ever had on the road. The steaks were gigantic and delicious. Whites used to attend some of the dances we played, but they would have to sit in the balcony. It was the reverse of segregation in the South for blacks.

The band was very popular in most cities through the South and the Midwest. We were like a family; we protected each other. We stayed in a lot of black hotels, and in Chicago I stayed at the Hotel Evans, Sixth-third Street. We played at the Rhumboogie Club at Fifty-fifth and Garfield Boulevard in Chicago, and it was unforgettable. It was owned by Joe Louis, and the night that he fought Billy Conn for the second time, they wouldn't let the show hit until after the fight. Louis won that fight, and what a night of celebration it was. Everything was on the house. We're talking about really balling. They had a hell of a floor show, with eighteen chorus girls, and they put on a fabulous show every night. On Sunday mornings we got off at 4:00 A.M. and after breakfast played a breakfast dance from 6:00 to 8:00 A.M., and the place was packed.

I left the band for Boston to go to the New England Conservatory of

Music, but Jimmy and I kept in contact. My father lived in Philadelphia, and it turned out that my father's second wife and Jimmy's mother were very good friends. When I traveled to Philly in the early fifties, I'd go over to Jimmy's house. I was very impressed with his family. It was just the kind of family that I often wished I had because I was an only child. The family feeling was great.

We need more people like Jimmy out there. He has always been a gentleman, someone who's never too busy to talk to the young musicians, encourage them, and pass along some knowledge. If we had more people like that, the world would be a hell of a better place, especially in the music end of it.

I left Nat Towles and came back to Philadelphia in May 1946 on Percy's insistence that he knew Dizzy Gillespie. By the time I got back to Philly, Dizzy no longer had the small band that I had heard on records, with him and Charlie Parker playing compositions like "Shaw 'Nuff" and "Hot House." Dizzy had started his bebop big band—which I really liked—in '45, but I hadn't met him yet. I had heard him on records and had seen him live at a concert on June 5, 1945, at the Academy of Music in Philadelphia. Benny Golson and Trane were there too.

The general concert scene in Philly hadn't really taken off until 1945. Elliot Lawrence's band, a small group playing in a concert format, didn't really begin until about 1945. It was still the era of the big band, and there were a lot of them. The small groups didn't take hold until Dizzy, Bird, and Charlie Shavers formed their groups. Charlie Shavers was playing with John Kirby at the time, and the Savoy Sultans were also on the scene. But the big bands were still in vogue because there were a lot of theaters around the country where they could perform: the Howard in Washington, the Regal in Chicago, the Apollo in New York, the Riverside in Milwaukee, the Earle and the Fays in Philadelphia.

I wanted to write big band music, but I had no formal training. When I was with Nat Towles, I tried to learn how to write for the band by asking questions of the guys. If I liked the sound of a chord, I asked somebody, "What note did you play?" It might have been the trombonist. He would give me a note, and I would write down the notes that were played and then figure out the chords I liked. I learned some voicing by that crude method.

I started my own big band in late 1946 into '47. The original members were Wilbur Campbell and James "Sax" Young, tenor sax; John Joyner and John Coltrane, alto sax; Joe Adams, baritone sax; Willie Dennis, Bill Leonard, Howard Scroggins, and Joe Steinberg, trombone; Johnny Coles, John Drew, Johnny Lynch, and Bill Massey, trumpet; James Forman, piano; Nelson Boyd, bass; Harry Tucker, drums. It would have been my brother Percy on bass, but he couldn't read well enough at that time; he had just come out of the service and was studying at the Granoff School of Music. I had worked with Sax Young in a small group when I first started playing saxophone, with me on alto and Sax Young on C melody. We had both gotten our saxophones around the same time.

When I started the big band, there were a couple of arrangers in Philadelphia—Leroy Lovett, who had a commercial group that included Danny Turner and Dottie Smith, and Johnny Acea, who had played with Dizzy's band and could play all the instruments: piano, trumpet, and saxophone. He's from Philly, and I think he had met up with Dizzy when Dizzy was with Frankie Fairfax. Acea wrote a couple of arrangements for Dizzy's band and was transcribing some of the music for my band. Lovett was also writing some of the music for my band, and I was transcribing whatever I could understand and whatever I could hear. Those transcriptions were the source of some of our music. I did write an arrangement on "Mean to Me" that was later recorded by Gil Fuller on his album *Bebop Boys*. We didn't transcribe everything that Dizzy had done, just some things.

John Coltrane also joined my band. He decided to write one arrangement for the band, for "Lover Man," and it was a wonderful orchestration. If Coltrane had wanted to take the time to be an orchestrator, he would have been one of the greats. There was a particular line that was so pretty that I still play it when I do "Lover Man." When Lee Morgan and I played together in the sixties, I played the counter-line that Trane wrote. Lee said, "Shorts, where you get that from?" I said, "Oh man, this is something that Trane wrote on the arrangement for the band." He said, "I like that." Everybody who heard that line associated it with one of Trane's lines because of its beauty. I tried to get Trane to write more arrangements, but he said, "Jim, I ain't got no time to write no arrangements. I got to practice." He was more interested in performing and playing than writing. Years later, Trane wrote about working in my band, in the September 29, 1960, *Down Beat* article "Coltrane on Coltrane," with Don DeMicheal:

> I had met Jimmy Heath, who, besides being a wonderful saxophonist, understood a lot about musical construction. I joined the group

in Philadelphia in 1948 [actually 1947]. We were very much alike in our feeling, phrasing, and a whole lot of ways. Our musical appetites were the same. We used to practice together, and he would write out some of the things we were interested in. We would take things from records and digest them. In this way, we learned about the techniques being used by writers and arrangers. (p. 26)

The band existed for a year and a half to two years, with occasional changes in personnel. At some point, Benny Golson replaced Wilbur Campbell, Calvin Massey substituted for John Drew, and John Burris for Johnny Lynch. We were known around Philly, and we had some gigs elsewhere in Pennsylvania, and in New Jersey and Wilmington, Delaware. We made a demo recording but it got lost. Also, one time Lionel Hampton came to Philly and we auditioned for him at the Earle Theatre for his record company, and he promised to record us, but that never came about.

BILL LEONARD

There were a lot of jazz clubs in Philly in the mid-forties. Broad Street was busy and things were jumping. The Club Zanzibar was a beautiful, brand-new place where Billie Holiday, Jug (Gene Ammons), Sonny Stitt, and all the groups performed. Philly Joe Jones, who was driving a trolley car during those years, would pass by and stop the trolley car so he could play a few sets at the Zanzibar. Café Society on Columbia Avenue was a very active music scene. There was also Essie Marie's Ballroom and the Strand. Catherine's on South Street, Fifteenth and Sixteenth, was very ultra–high society. Sugar Ray Robinson used to go there when he had a fight somewhere near Philadelphia. He used to bring his entourage, and I'll never forget that pink Cadillac of his.

I met Jimmy at a bar called Budweisers at Sixteenth and South, where during those war years big-time musicians used to jam. That's where I first saw Roy Eldridge. I started jamming with Jimmy Tisdale and another fellow, a great guy named Kid Haffy who used to sing ballads and blues. When I met Jimmy, he told me he was trying to get his band together and he wanted me to play first trombone. Many trombone players can play an awful lot of jazz, but some aren't very good on melodic lines. I had a straight tone and I loved beautiful melodies. We had a trombone trio that played some of the melody lines.

Our first concert was at Reynolds Hall in 1946, a great big place up on Broad and Montgomery Avenue, where the Elks used to meet. The audience that first night at the Reynolds Hall was very appreciative. It was the first time that they had heard modern jazz of that time. It was basically modified bebop, especially in the melody lines. The Jimmy Heath Orchestra was very advanced as far as big bands were concerned. A lot of the musicians in town came to hear us, and many of them wanted to be in the band.

I had about five to six performances with the Jimmy Heath Orchestra, mostly dances and mostly in Jersey. We played Atlantic City for the Elks Ball at the convention hall.

At that same time, little old Tootie Heath [Jimmy's younger brother] was nothing but a young boy. He had a set of little toy drums and he'd be sitting up there grinning and looking at us while we were practicing. It was a wonderful family, wonderful rapport we all had together. We used to rehearse sometimes in Jimmy's basement on Federal Street. His sister, Elizabeth, was a wonderful person too.

We used to listen to Dizzy an awful lot. He was our mentor. We all had tams and we tried to grow goatees to emulate Dizzy. Jimmy was crazy about Charlie Parker, but I was in love with Johnny Hodges, Lawrence Brown, and the Ellington band. Then J. J. Johnson came up there and blew my cool. He revolutionized the way music was played, but Johnny Hodges to me had the most beautiful tone and sound.

In Jimmy's orchestra, I had a number of solos on ballads like "I Don't Stand a Ghost of a Chance with You." Leroy Lovett arranged "Mam'selle" and Johnny Acea arranged "Night and Day." Jimmy wasn't writing a lot of the arrangements at that time. He was learning. With most of our arrangements, like "Red Top," we would just get the melody together, and each person would put his own harmony to it. We did mostly head arrangements.

Eventually people started writing arrangements for us. I don't know whether they ever got paid. We started getting some ballads together and numbers to play for dances. We developed a nice size book. My brother Jim Leonard was an artist, and he designed the music stands. The band never made any money because there wasn't any money around for the bands. The big bands were breaking down into combos. We tried to get money just to rent a hall, just to hear the music, to see what it sounded like, and we enjoyed ourselves.

The night at Club Elate when Bird sat in was one of the happiest times I've had in the music business, just seeing Bird and hearing him play. Ike Wright, who was with Club Emanon, was well-connected with modern music.

He was a debonaire man, a handsome dresser. He always had an umbrella, gloves, and a derby, a big fedora hat. He was a complete gentleman.

Coltrane came to my apartment when I lived at Sixteenth and Bainbridge Street. He used to go to a place off Bainbridge Street, Broad and Bainbridge, where there was a dance hall. Whenever we had enough money, we would rent the place to rehearse. We were struggling along, trying to get into the big time.

Jimmy's orchestra performed for mostly white audiences, and they couldn't dig our modern sound. They were used to Sammy Kaye, Benny Goodman, and Artie Shaw. We came with this new sound, with flatted fifths and scat singing. They didn't take to it too well in Jersey. There was a lot of prejudice during those years.

I was like the father of the band because I was the oldest member. I used to keep those boys straight. I was doing bad things too, because I was drinking wine, but they were doing those other things, which I was scared to do. I wasn't an old fogey but I was going on thirty. They looked up to me and looked after me, and I would bawl them all out. I used to try to tell Specs [Wright] to get himself straightened out. They used to duck me to a certain extent, but I wasn't going to degrade them. I had a problem too, with alcohol, one of the demons. I was just as bad as they were, but I didn't shoot that stuff.

One time Dizzy Gillespie had a big band affair at the Reynolds Hall, and Jimmy and I went to the hotel where Diz was staying. Dizzy pulled out some of them great big fat reefers and I puffed on one of them suckers and didn't do it right because I never got high. The Lord was protecting me some kind of way because I didn't get high off of it. Maybe I didn't know what to do with it, but I'm glad.

Diz was very instrumental and very helpful to the band because he thought a lot of Jimmy and Jimmy thought a lot of him and all the members of the band. We were very close during that two-year span when the orchestra was together. Howard McGhee, a fine gentleman, took the band over, but I didn't go with him because I was married and my wife was in the family way.

On trumpet was Johnny Lynch from Dizzy Gillespie's band. Lynch had already recorded with Dizzy on "Things to Come" and was also in Dizzy's big band film, *Jivin' in Be-Bop* (1947). Johnny Coles and John Drew were also in the band. Drew's father was one of the wealthiest black men in Pennsylvania; he owned bus lines and had sold a franchise to Red Arrow and made a lot of money. Drew's brother was with the Katherine Dunham Dance Company. Drew didn't play that well, but because his father had money, he bought the outfits for the band. We wore brown cardigan jackets, white shirts, and maroon ties. Drew also helped to publicize the band. He was the straw boss and manager and a very nice man. Six members of my band and I eventually played with Dizzy's big band: James Forman ("Hen Gates"), piano; Nelson Boyd, bass; Specs Wright, drums; John Coltrane, alto and tenor sax; and Benny Golson, tenor sax.

BENNY GOLSON

At only eighteen or nineteen years of age, it was quite evident that Jimmy had a solid grip on the pulse of jazz with all its indigenous peculiarities. And this was at a time when jazz was undergoing radical and dramatic changes in concept. New and developing things were being rapidly added to the distinctive repertoire of creativity. It was totally incomprehensible how he could be so erudite. How could someone so young be so far ahead in his perception of things? Time, though, taught us that he had a natural proclivity for this thing called jazz—degradingly called be-bop at that time—which was tearing at his young mind and heart in an attempt to supplant the older and more traditional forms of jazz we had known and tried to perform before. Yes, before ever really getting a strong grasp on the already deeply entrenched music that occurred before our time—the more traditional approach—we all "had" to suddenly recast our thinking in order to gain the forward motion that was so necessary in our moving ahead to yet newer things. What an adventure all of this was.

Jimmy, a forerunner among us in his acute, perceptive thinking, was a good, analytic listener. He was able to listen to the jazz recordings of all our idols and not only derive great joy from what he heard, as we did, but . . . reproduce those things in graphic detail through music notation—no small feat for our young ages. Not only melodies and solo transcriptions but duplication of actual parts for larger works, which required additional musicianship in order to realize their performance.

It was a time of enlightenment, and Jimmy was certainly one of our illuminators. We were fortunate enough to have him right there in Philadelphia with us, thank goodness. Even though he was not aware of it, he was . . . a (natural) teacher, which resulted in our learning a great abundance from him.

He played an important part in all our lives, a fact I'm sure he's not aware of. But Jimmy had great organizational skills too.

At about age twenty or twenty-one, he formed a big band that was unlike any big band Philadelphia had ever heard before. It was made up of young musicians, of course, but Jimmy brought such organization and professionalism to it that age was never a factor unless one paused to marvel at what they heard and saw. He taught us how to play together: how to think as one; how to phrase as one; how to play with dynamics so as to color what we played; how to articulate and personalize what we played, giving it shape, character, and identity. There was only room for fifteen of us in that remarkable band, so that each chair was highly coveted. We who occupied those chairs knew we were in a highly privileged position. I was one of them; John Coltrane was another. After all the intervening years, I still lovingly call him Jimmy "boss."

Enough cannot be said about Mr. and Mrs. Heath, his mother and father, who continuously put up with all of us who used to come to their home in South Philadelphia, remove all of the furniture in the living and dining room, then begin our rehearsal. No matter what we did, how much noise (music) we made or how late we did it, they were always our champions. It was their support that, in part, enabled us to grow. And grow we did.

Those memorable rehearsals always turned out to be concerts for the entire neighborhood—the neighbors seemed to love it, which psychologically gave us added impetus. There was so much controversy over this band that news of it soon reached New York City. And in doing so, it prompted some well-known arrangers to write for us, including the late Tadd Dameron and Johnny Acea. But, I must say, Jimmy's reputation as a gifted alto saxophonist went ahead of him, even before the reputation of his newly formed big band. As a result, giants like Charlie Parker, Dizzy Gillespie, Coleman Hawkins, Max Roach, and J. J. Johnson were often seen at his house. How proud—and, yes, envious—we were of him. We had the recordings in our homes to listen to, but Jimmy had the recordings and the heroes as well.

Whatever he learned he would always pass on to the rest of us, who were waiting like hungry little pups at feeding time. It wasn't long after this that he left for New York City. But this was inevitable; Philadelphia could no longer accommodate his quantum growth. His potential—that which existed in possibility—was becoming awesome. He had no choice but to get closer to the source.

3

Organizing and Melodizing

■

Bill Massey was a trumpet player who lived in Darby, Pennsylvania, where John Drew lived. I met Massey through Drew, and Massey introduced me to Coltrane. They had been in the navy band together at Great Lakes. Trane was playing alto when he came out of the navy. One day I was having a rehearsal and in walked Bill Massey and his cousin, Calvin Massey, from Pittsburgh. Calvin and I became good friends. He played in my band along with Coltrane, and he and Coltrane became real good friends too. Calvin and I ended up writing a piece together called "Fiesta" for Machito's band. Calvin wrote a number of compositions that Trane and others recorded.

When I had the band, my mother would let us rehearse in the living room in her home. I could fit a sixteen-piece band in there to rehearse — that's how much my mother and father were into the music. It took some organizing, and they really supported us. At our home in Philly, we had a piano in a little extra extended kitchen, an enclosed back porch. It was cold out there because the room wasn't heated.

A group of young working-class black guys in Philadelphia started a social club called Club Emanon, named after Dizzy's composition "Emanon" ("no name" spelled backwards) from *Dizzy Gillespie and His Orchestra*, a 1946 recording. Those club members were in love with bebop. One of the guys in the club was Ike Wright, Specs's older brother. The club presented concerts around the city of Philadelphia and would feature my big band.

We performed at the Elks Home and at the O. V. Catto Lodge at Sixteenth and Fitzwater. The lodge was named for Octavius Valentine Catto, who was a black activist for voting rights in Pennsylvania back in the 1860s. On Election Day, October 1871, he was shot through the heart during attacks against blacks in Philadelphia.

At that time, I was having trouble getting people to dance to the music the band performed because it was bebop. I continued to melodize, writing melodies to the beat of life. Ike said, "When my brother Specs gets out of the service, he's the drummer for your band." Sure enough, when Specs came out, he was the guy.

IKE WRIGHT

I always liked the big bands. When I got out of the army and returned to Philadelphia, I heard people talking about how Jimmy Heath had been away with Nat Towles so I wanted to meet Jimmy. I went down to Federal Street, below the tracks near Washington Avenue, which separated the turf. Broad Street was a turf boundary. I stopped at Jimmy Heath's house because I already knew Percy, who told me, "You know what. I think I'm going to play bass." We laughed at him, but the next thing you knew he was thumping back. Between my house up above the tracks at Sixteenth and Catharine and Jimmy's on Federal Street, I'll bet money that most of the bop era musicians had been in one of those two houses.

Around the time Jimmy was rehearsing his big band, Johnny Lynch, my buddy over in Camden, said, "Man, why don't you come to a rehearsal?" I said, "Okay. I'd love that." The drummer didn't show and although they just made it through the day, Jimmy was kind of warm under the collar. I had been telling Jimmy that my brother could play drums and that he should give him a chance. He said, "Yeah, okay. I'll get to that." So one of the next times I went to the rehearsal, I took my brother and Jimmy let him play. Jimmy said, "Wow." From then on my brother, Specs, was in. They started making gigs together, Jimmy and my brother and the band.

My brother and the guys were rehearsing one day at my house. One of the guys introduced my mother to a saxophone player from North Carolina, and he told her that the guy could play good. I said, "Well, you know my mother can't read music, but she's got an ear. If he can play, Mom will pick it up, and if he can't, she'll know that too." I said, "Jimmy, who's that guy?" He said, "His name is John Coltrane." So I nicknamed him "John Col-

Truck." Trane, who was a little shy guy then, started playing with Jimmy's group after that.

Jimmy can write, just like other guys from Philly like Benny Golson. They could have written music for Duke. Jimmy is a perfectionist just like Diz, who was a musician and a showman.

JOHNNY COLES

Jimmy and I came up in the same boat. I started begging my parents for a horn, and it took me four years of begging to get a trumpet. I got my horn before Jimmy got his. I played with Jimmy's father, Percy, Sr., in the Elks Quaker City Band in 1940, and later on I met Percy, Jr., who told me, "You're the guy that my daddy used to always talk about. Pop used to say, 'I think we got a little young trumpet player who's going to be all right.'"

I don't know exactly when I met Mel Melvin before I met Jimmy in '44. I went out on the road with Melvin and got stranded before Jimmy joined the band. Bill Barron and I played in the Mel Melvin band, and we both went to Mastbaum High School. Ray Bryant, who played piano for Jimmy, used to come up to my house when I had sessions from 12:00 P.M. to 12:00 A.M.

I played in the band that Jimmy organized around '46. Jimmy was a big force for progress as far as I was concerned. He would seek out the latest musical ideas and tell us about them at rehearsals. He liked the sound of the Dizzy band, and when Jimmy stood up in front of his own band, he emulated some of Dizzy's movements. Harry Tucker was playing the drums when I played in Jimmy's band. Flame, Ronald Tucker, a South Philly drummer, was an excellent player too. The orchestra played at the O. V. Catto, which was a basement club, where you had to have a cabaret card to perform.

When I started actively making gigs in the early forties, I worked at a place up on Ridge Avenue past the Blue Note, near Fifteenth Street. I worked with a saxophone player named Byron Garrison, who played old-time sounds. We left that gig and played at a club called Simms' Paradise. We were playing shows and a little bit of dance music, but we were mainly a show band.

In the forties there were many jazz clubs but they weren't always called that. Budweiser's at Sixteenth and South was a favorite place. It was famous through all of Philadelphia and places outside. That's where I saw Benny Carter play with Jimmy Tisdale, a trumpet player, a little short red dude like me. The Zanzibar was at Nineteenth and Columbia. It may have been open then. The Watts brothers, black entrepreneurs, owned it. There was also a place called Billy

Hughes' up at Seventeenth and Dauphin. The Blue Note was open too, and we were jamming there. Jimmy Oliver used to work at Irene's up on Twenty-second and Ridge on the third floor, over the top of the pawnshop. The Woodbine was on Twelfth Street in between Thompson and Master, not far from Trane's house, just about a minute. I think the Showboat was open at that time but not Peps. When I was living in Trenton and just learning a little bit about the trumpet, I was on this kiddy hour program that used to be at the Nixon Grand in Philly. The Nixon Grand Theater was at Broad and Columbia Avenue on the second floor. I played "New Organ Grinder Swing" in E natural. I also went to the Earle Theatre and I got my butt beat for going there. I used to go there all the time to hear the Ellington band, which was the only band I would hooky school for. I hung out with Ray Nance. I also went to the Fays Theatre at Fortieth and Market. State Theater was on Fifty-second Street and Chestnut.

RAY BRYANT

I first started playing around Philadelphia at age twelve or thirteen. Later we used to have little jam sessions at the home of Johnny Coles, the trumpeter, who lived right around the corner from me. Jimmy Heath would come to those sessions. Jimmy had one of the first bebop big bands around Philadelphia. I probably played in the band once or twice as a sub. He had James Forman, "Hen Gates," on piano, but I would go to rehearsals. I was somewhat younger and looked up to them, but they considered me one of them. At the jam sessions, I would get a chance to play. The jam session would start by word of mouth. Anybody who wanted to participate was welcome. At the sessions, a tune would be called and if a guy didn't know it, we would teach it to him so he could learn and experiment. There was no competition at all. This is what we all loved and everybody helped everybody else. It was just a sense of complete and beautiful camaraderie. It was a place to learn, and then the next level was an actual gig.

Johnny Coles's house was one of the key meeting places for musicians. The guys in New York heard about it after a while. That's where I first met Charlie Rouse. At Johnny Coles's house, we played the bebop tunes from the day, including "Billy's Bounce," "Now's the Time," and "Confirmation." When Charlie Parker had a new release, every bebop player and fan in the country would latch onto it.

There were different areas of Philadelphia: North, South, West, and Northeast. The black sections of town were mostly in North and South Philadelphia, but there were some out in the West too. The immediate area that Jimmy lived in was mostly black just like the area where Johnny Coles and I lived. There were still some white people there at that time, but they were thinking about leaving.

Philadelphia had a pretty thriving musical scene around that time, but if you really wanted to get into the circles, you had to go to New York. That was the Mecca. This is where it all was coming from as far as we were concerned down in Philadelphia. Pittsburgh, Detroit, and Chicago all had their musical communities, but the guys in those other cities still looked to New York as being the headquarters. At that time, New York seemed much farther away. It's tremendous that so many guys came out of Philadelphia who have really made huge contributions: Coltrane, Benny Golson, Lee Morgan, McCoy Tyner, and Bobby Timmons. There's something about Philadelphia that made it unique. They used to say it was the water. The atmosphere was fertile at the time and there was a rash of musicians who were actually making a livelihood. It was one of the places to be if you wanted to really develop. There were so many guys to listen to and to learn from.

Jimmy was my connection to Charlie Parker because I hadn't met Bird at that time, or any of the guys like Dexter Gordon or Dizzy Gillespie. They all knew about Jimmy's big band. When I heard it, I was very much impressed. It was a bebop big band as opposed to a swing big band. We had some other big bands around town, like those of Jimmy Gorham, Jimmy Tisdale, and Charlie Gaines, but they were playing more or less in the swing tradition, which is great because that's where bebop came from. But Jimmy's band was playing the new music. Jimmy was carrying the swing tradition further, moving it forward into the bebop era.

It's ironic that Jimmy and I started out in Philadelphia and ended up living about a half a mile from each other in Corona, Queens. When I first moved to New York, quite a few musicians were living in Queens, guys who just didn't want to live right in Manhattan any longer. They wanted to get out where there were a few more trees. Charlie Shavers helped me get a place in Queens not too far from where he lived. Dizzy lived right around the corner from where Jimmy lives right now.

In 1946, when I started reorganizing my musical life and direction, my social life was also going through a change. I had met a beautiful young lady, Bertha Preston, who lived in the next block from my house. Our relationship began to get more serious as time went by, and soon Bert and I were in love. Within a year's time, she became pregnant, and that was a proud and happy time for us. We started to discuss marriage, and I gave her a cheap engagement ring. In January 1947 our beautiful son James was born, and we seemed very happy as he began to grow.

Meanwhile I had met Dizzy in '46 as well and one of his arrangers, Gil Fuller. Birks, as we sometimes called him (Dizzy's full name was John Birks Gillespie), was changing personnel about a year later and was interested in my piano player, James Forman. "Hen Gates" was his nickname, given to him by the guys in Philly because of the way he comped, played chords for a soloist, which was like Dizzy, who had used that name as an alias on one of his recordings. I later got Hen Gates a job with Dizzy through Gil Fuller when Dizzy needed a piano player.

JAMES FORMAN

I lived in South Philadelphia, not too far from Jimmy. My neighborhood was primarily Italian but black people lived there too. There were more blacks where Jimmy lived. I went to two high schools but ended up graduating from South Philadelphia High. I used to play in the high school band. I played boogie woogie primarily, and it was my first introduction to jazz piano. I was interested in jazz but not to the degree that Jimmy was. My biggest chunk of knowledge came from a piano player named Luchi De Jesus. I got my first gig of any note through Sax Young during the summer. It was at the High Steppers Café in Wildwood, New Jersey, and that's where I met Luchi De Jesus, who was playing in a trio. When I came home in September of 1946 and met Jimmy, I had really grown a lot musically. That's when I heard about Jimmy wanting to form a band. Jimmy had already been on the road with Nat Towles when I met him, around 1946 or 1947, through John Joyner and Sax Young. When Jimmy formed his orchestra, I was able to take the piano chair. I could read, so that's one of the reasons I was picked. When we started rehearsing, I was the first piano player. That was my real baptism into jazz. At Jimmy's house in the daytime, we would just have sessions, where we exchanged ideas about chords. I was learning from Jimmy and whoever else was around. Later on in my career, "Hen Gates" became my nickname. Dizzy made a record under that name, and when Max Roach found out, he started calling me Hen Gates and then everybody started calling me that. It stuck.

There were a lot of clubs in Philadelphia in the mid-forties. The Showboat and the Zanzibar club that the Watts brothers had up on Columbia Avenue were two of them. People like Dexter Gordon would come there. There were clubs all up and down Columbia Avenue, which was the strip. Now they call it Cecil B. Moore Avenue after the lawyer who was very prominent in civil rights and who lived in the North Philadelphia area. I knew about the Down Beat Club on Eleventh Street even though I couldn't go in there. Philadelphia had a blue law, where everything had to close up on Saturday at 12:00 midnight, but there were some after-hour places like the Elate Club. I hung out more in the northern part of the city.

Jimmy's orchestra played in and around North and South Philadelphia and Delaware. We played in the Metropolitan and the Mercantile Hall up North Broad Street. We played the O. V. Catto and the Elks Lodge. We were playing there on weekends mostly.

Back in '46 and '47, when we heard those tunes like "Blue and Boogie," "Billy's Bounce," and "Now's the Time," we were like the kids who like rap music today. We were interested in what was going on that was "new." We would sprinkle dance music in so the audience wouldn't get mad. We would play three or four tunes, and then we would play some of what they would refer to at that time as bebop. We also played "Flying Home," naturally, and "Disorder at the Border," which was semi-modern but a good dance tune. In the band, first Bobby Ross and then Jimmy Thomas were the vocalists.

We were playing primarily for blacks but there were some white people who were interested in what we were doing. They would come and listen. Most of the time the white people would come to the Elate Club in South Philadelphia. At that time North Philadelphia didn't have such a good reputation but the more adventuresome white people would still come.

Jimmy still had his band when I went out of town. He was going on other gigs because the band didn't work every week. We'd work maybe two gigs in a month and then sometimes we were lucky and we would get three or four. But we were still trying to do other things, playing with other musicians in order to have some money to spend. In fact, Jimmy was working with Howard McGhee. Jimmy and Percy got me the gig with Howard McGhee in late '47 or early '48. The Jimmy Heath Orchestra lasted until '48 because Jimmy joined Dizzy's band and so did Trane. When I left Jimmy's orchestra, they were all happy for me. I was afraid to leave, and they gave me the encouragement that I needed because I kept saying, "I can't do this." Dizzy was an icon. I never even dreamed that I would play with him.

In 1946, name bands continued to come through Philly, like the Luis Russell Orchestra, which included at that time another giant-to-be, Bostonian Roy Haynes, whose folks were from Barbados. A master drummer, Roy has performed with energy and virtuosity. He's played with small groups and vocalists too—from Charlie Parker to Sarah Vaughan to John Coltrane, to name a few.

ROY HAYNES

I met Jimmy around 1946 when I was with Luis Russell and we played the Earle Theatre in Philadelphia. A lot of the big bands would come through the Earle. We stayed at the Douglas Hotel, which was in South Philly. That was the hotel where a lot of the big black bands stayed. I met Jimmy before I met his brothers. They used to say that Jimmy and I looked alike. We were both short and had big eyes, the whole thing. Back then, his nickname was "Little Bird."

Another time, when I was with Charlie Parker in 1949, Jimmy invited us over to his house when we played the Showboat, which was in the Douglas Hotel. There was a matinee on Saturday, and between the matinee and the evening show we went over to his house. I met his mother and his father. We were kind of close then. I saw Jimmy with his son Mtume (James), who was just starting to walk. His son must have been less than two years old at the time. We played together a lot back then. Then Jimmy got involved with you-know-what and disappeared for a while. He came back to New York years later. Also, when the Heath Brothers played Jazzmobile concerts, I played with them once or twice in Queens. We also played Gerald's, located on Linden Boulevard. Now that we're both in our eighties, we've become closer. We call each other periodically and sometimes on our birthdays; the beat goes on.

When Dizzy's big band came to Philly in July 1946, before I went to New York, I went to see them at the Elate Club at 711 South Broad Street (at Fitzwater Street). That was the same place where I had a picture taken with Bird playing with my big band. Percy and I invited the whole band to our house—John Lewis, James Moody, and the others—and Mom fixed food.

On December 7, 1947, when I had the big band with Trane and Cal Massey, many of the cats played a benefit at the same club for a six-year-old girl from the neighborhood, Mary Etta (or Marietta) Jordan, who had gotten her legs cut off by a streetcar. her. The house was packed, and we were able to raise $1,500. Earl Bostic, Leroy "Slam" Stewart, Jimmy Oliver, Beulah Frazier, and Charlie Parker were on the bill. Bostic was a great alto saxophonist who had recorded popular records such as "Temptation," and the general public was probably wowed by him because he had so many records. But the musicians were in awe of Charlie Parker.

That night at Club Elate was the highlight of my having the band. It was the same week that Bird came to Philly with his quintet and played at the Down Beat Club on Eleventh and Market streets. He had Miles Davis, Tommy Potter, Duke Jordan, and Max Roach in his band. Bird came to town without his horn, so he called me about using my horn that week, and I was thrilled. I took my horn to Charlie Parker at the Down Beat, handed it to him, and he played his gig, two sets. After he finished, I took the horn back and he split. He was commuting back to New York every night. The next night I'd bring the horn and hand it to Bird and he'd play, and Bird would leave his mouthpiece on the horn. Since I was a young Charlie Parker fanatic, I would just grab my horn the next day and say, "Wow! Charlie Parker played this horn, man!" I had the feeling that he would leave some of his music in the horn. When I played it, it was just the same old stuff, sad as ever to me.

When the weekend for the benefit arrived, I asked Bird if he would come down and play and he said, "Yeah!" Max Roach came, and Specs Wright got off the drums and let him play. Bird sat in with my big band. I was directing the band, and Bird was playing my horn. Trane was watching Bird with his mouth open in amazement, concentrating so hard on what Bird was playing that he almost burned his hand because he forgot about the cigarette he was holding. I was amazed too. Everybody in the band was in awe of Parker. Any musician who'd ever seen him had that reaction of disbelief. Even Dizzy Gillespie said he was in awe of Parker and that Bird had the bebop style perfected.

Another great musician who came to Philly was Coleman Hawkins, "Bean" or "Hawk." He came to town one night in 1947 with Freddie Webster and Theodore "Fats" Navarro. They were working at the Zanzibar, and Freddie came down to hear my rehearsal with the big band. He said, "Man, you come when they call you Little Bird, don't you?" He was suggesting my reaction was some kind of orgasm. I said, "Yeah, I sure do!" Freddie was one of the finest trumpet players that ever lived. Dizzy, Miles, and Fats loved his big sound.

The night that Bean played the Zanzibar with Fats Navarro, Fats was late coming back after the break, and Bean started without him, playing "Dynamo A and B" or "Dizzy Atmosphere." The tune is in A flat, but Bean was playing it in A natural. So when Fats finally arrived and started in on the song, he thought he was out of tune. Bean just looked at him with a sly expression. Fats then realized that Bean was playing a joke on him. However, Fats soon caught on and proceeded to play it in A natural, including the hard-to-play "out-chorus." Eddie Locke, the drummer who played with Hawk, later said that Coleman had mentioned that incident to him. Hawk spoke of his admiration for Fats and his ability to play in all keys.

My big band continued to get some gigs in 1947, not just in Philly but in the surrounding area. On May 16, we featured Calvin Todd, vocalist Jimmy Thomas, and vibraphonist Walt Dickerson, when we played Rosedale Beach, Millsboro, Delaware. In Philly, we were at the Met Ballroom at Broad and Poplar on June 27 along with Johnny Moore's Three Blazers. You could get in for just a buck fifty and dance from nine o'clock "until." I was also part of events like the Jazz Guild's swing concert on November 22 at the Elate Ballroom, where I played baritone sax. There were more than one hundred people at that one.

While I still had the big band, I also worked some gigs in a small group with Howard McGhee in Chicago. That was also the first time I met Wilbur Ware, in 1947. We played a place called the Argyle Show Lounge on the North Side, which was very white. We stayed on the South Side with the black people; we were living at 4140 Drexel and would get off the train at the end of the line. At the end of the week, the guy who owned the Argyle gave Howard a check. When Howard went to the bank and tried to cash it, they said, "No funds available." The check was rubber. We went back to the guy and Howard said, "Man, the check is no good. I tried to cash it." Then this white man opened up his coat and showed us the gun he had on his belt. He said, "I said the check is good." Howard said, "Man, I tried to cash the check; the check is . . ." The owner repeated, "I said, the check is good!" We split and went on back to 4140 and hung around there for a while eating canned biscuits and whatever we could get hold of while Howard tried to get the musicians' union to get us some funds. We were stranded in Chicago until he finally got the money from the union.

At some point that year, Howard, a jazz star, took my band under his name for a couple of gigs and we went on the road. We played one gig in Kansas City in back of Billie Holiday. Howard was from Oklahoma, but he had lived in California. He was also in an interracial marriage. The police didn't like that out there, so they wanted Howard out of town. Howard told me that the narcotics squad came into his apartment, and one cop reached underneath his bed with his hand closed and came out with a package. The cop said, "This is what we're looking for." They had set him up, floated him out of Los Angeles. That's when Howard left the West Coast and came to New York. We also went to Chicago. It was there in the Englewood train station that the whole music book for my big band was lost. I never got the music back.

Back in Philly, my big band started getting good "headliner" notices in the papers. At that time, writers were calling me an "up-and-coming" musician. Ramon Bruce, a former football player who hosted a WHAT radio show from the Club 421 Monday to Wednesday nights from 11:00 to 11:30 P.M., highlighted our gigs. In the February 28, 1948, *Philadelphia Afro-American*, he wrote, "Jimmy Heath and his 16-piece band are really going places. They are at the Elate Club every Tuesday night with Jimmy Thomas as vocalist" (p. 9). That same month we were also at the Embassy Ballroom in Camden, New Jersey, for some Sunday shows. Since we weren't exactly local, we were identified in the papers as a Philly group. For example, the February 10, 1948, *Philadelphia Tribune* article "Thru the 'Spy' Glass," by Squire Bryant, stated, "The 'Heath Mob' is naturally a group of young Philadelphians who can play anything . . . from a wild Hampton Ride to a smooth Ellington riff" (p. 5).

Howard was taking me, Percy, and Specs Wright with him on the road. He also started using a piano player named Vernon Biddle from Chicago and a tenor player named Jesse Powell, who had a smoke shop on Broadway in the Bronx and, later, was in Dizzy's band when I joined. We recorded with Howard on one of his albums, *Howard McGhee Boptet*, on May 15, 1948. We joined McGhee because of the gigs he could secure. The loss of the music was kind of a turning point for the big band. Otherwise, I might have stayed with it longer.

We went to Paris for one or two weeks with McGhee in May 1948, my first trip to Europe. It was the year of the First International Jazz Festival. It was also my first time on an airplane. Percy, a Tuskegee Airman pilot, had come out of the Army Air Corp, and so he knew about flying. He tried to ease my mind during the flight. We were on a four-engine plane called the Constellation, and the flight took seventeen hours to get to Paris. When I looked out the plane window, I could see fire coming out of the back of the engine. This was before the jet age. I said, "Percy, looks like the thing's on fire." He said, "It's cool. Everything's cool." We stopped in Gander, Newfoundland, and then we took off again for Shannon, Ireland. When we got to Orly in Paris, there was a big reception of beautiful young women. I don't know if they were members of a jazz club in France, but they met us and gave us flowers. Photographers were there and our pictures appeared in the local newspaper. Before we even got into town, the women were asking us to take them jitterbugging. It was 1948, right after the war, and we were welcomed like heroes. We played at a place called the Théâtre Marigny on the Champs-Élysées and stayed at the Hotel Du Bois on Avenue Victor Hugo and Rue De Dom. Maybe those places are still there. Parisians don't change their architecture as readily as we do here.

Kenny Clarke was living in Paris at that time. He had been in the service, and so had John Lewis. They played with Coleman Hawkins on the same tour package I was on with Howard McGhee. I was just twenty years old and really nervous. The headliner was Le Grand Coleman Hawkins, as they say in French, and the bill also included "The Slam Stewart Trio" with Slam Stewart on bass, John Collins on guitar and, an unknown to the French, a pianist by the name of Erroll Garner. It was a sensational tour. I was part of "The Howard McGhee Sextet de Bebop."

In Paris, we were playing tunes like "Donna Lee," things from the bebop era, some of Howard's music, "Sweet and Lovely," "Out of Nowhere," and "I Surrender Dear." I wrote one blues composition, which Howard called "Maggie's Draw," but it was really "Maggie's Drawers." He was cleaning it up for the recording. Certain things couldn't be said then.

While we were in Paris, I went to a record date to hear Erroll Garner. That was the first time in my life that I had been to a recording session involving any of the giants. It was also the only time I've been on a recording with any of the giants of music that went down that smoothly. I have been on sessions with J. J. Johnson, Miles Davis, Art Farmer, Clark Terry, Milt Jackson, and many others. Almost everyone makes at least a couple of takes, but Erroll Garner would play a song straight through. Then he would play the next song and play that one straight through. The only time they had to stop Erroll Garner was when the tape ran out. He was such a natural, although he couldn't read any music. But he was a gifted person from God, and he could just sit down and play. He was incredible, as was all that happened while we were in Paris. Howard and I played "I Surrender Dear" with Erroll Garner at a live concert.

Before returning to the States, Percy and I bought some hats in Paris. When we got off the plane in New York at Idlewild Airport, now JFK, a white baggage handler made some negative remarks about the hats we were wearing. I said to Percy, "We're back in America." We had just got through playing for upper-class people in Paris, who had accepted us royally, but when we got back to the States, we heard negative remarks from a baggage handler. We thought we were hip with those big wide brims that were in style at that time.

Back in the States, we worked Fifty-second Street in New York with Howard. We also played the Paradise Theater in Detroit, possibly November 5–11, 1948. The headliner of that show was Illinois Jacquet, who had a hot record with "Robin's Nest," a composition written by Sir Charles Thompson. Sarah Vaughan was next, and then came Howard McGhee. I met a lot of the Detroit musicians at that time and later when I played with Dizzy there. Some of them became well-known, such as Barry Harris, Tommy Flanagan, and Kenny Burrell.

In New York, Howard got me a gig at the Three Deuces on Fifty-second Street. This was probably my first trip to New York as a performer. I was in awe of everybody on Fifty-second Street because you could go from one club to another and people were playing on both sides of the street. All the clubs were there, the Onyx Club, the Downbeat, and the Spotlite, where Dizzy's big band played. Fifty-second Street was a fertile area for the music.

To see all those clubs, to be in New York with all the giants of music, I was as nervous as you could be. I met the pianist Hank Jones at that time. He had an apartment in New York, and one night he took me to his place after his gig. He had put some blankets in his piano over the hammers so he could play at night and not get any static from the neighbors. That night Hank played "Cherokee" through the keys, all twelve keys. It blew my mind. I said, "Oh, this is what I have to do to play like these guys. I have to learn how to play all the tunes in different keys." You might know a tune in one key, but someone might start playing it in another key. That experience really made me aware of my inadequacies.

I stayed with Howard in New York. He had an apartment at 121 East 115th Street, and Fats Navarro and his wife were staying up there with Howard. When Fats moved out, Bill Massey, the trumpeter who was in my band from Philly and who had been in the navy with Coltrane, came to town. We roomed together in New York. I had met Milt Jackson, "Bags"; Bags and Howard McGhee were the people who first started calling me "Little Bird" because I was trying to play like Charlie Parker, playing all of Parker's licks. Massey and I hung around on 115th Street because we didn't have any money. It was great when Howard announced that after his tour with Norman Granz's Jazz at the Philharmonic (JATP), he was going to open in December 1948 at the Apollo Bar on 125th Street. The group would include Milt Jackson, Percy, Specs Wright, Vernon Biddle on piano, and me on alto and baritone.

Percy and I also went back to Philly in February 1949 for a gig with Howard at the Club 421, where singer Wynonie Harris was also on the set. In a February 5, 1949, *Philadelphia Tribune* article, Ramon Bruce had some good things to say about all of us: "Howard McGhee and Wynonie (Mr. Blues) Harris are most madly keeping the joint jumping. . . . It's really great to see Philly boys Percy and Jimmy Heath with Howard McGhee along with Mr. Blues. . . . One has only to dig the swaying heads and feel the rhythmic foot-beats to know that the cats . . . are digging these two great acts at the Club 421" (p. 12).

MILT JACKSON

The first time I met Jimmy was 1946, when I went to Philadelphia with Dizzy Gillespie's band and he and Percy came to the concert. That's when I first got to know him, and we got to be good friends from there. I didn't hear him then. The first time I met him I didn't meet him on the job where he was playing. I met him when he came to the dance at the Elate Ballroom on Broad Street in South Philadelphia, and Jimmy, Percy, and Tootie, of course, lived in South Philly. At that time, dancing was still very popular with all kinds of music. The dance was in a packed ballroom. Most of the black people lived in the center of the city, I guess you would say, between South Philly and North Philly, and a lot of them lived in West Philly.

I got to meet Jimmy probably at intermission, or something like that, and we talked. From there, we just got to be good friends. He invited us to his house and we met his mother and his father. I remember something about Jimmy's father that pertains to Charlie Parker. One of the first times I went to their house for dinner, Jimmy's father put Charlie Parker records on and told everybody that we had to be quiet till dinner because he had Bird on. I was really astounded because it was the first time I knew that any older people were involved with Charlie Parker and had that kind of interest in him. It was one of those moments you always remember. I thought of Jimmy's father along with another era, Louis Armstrong or back in that day, the Jimmie Lunceford days. Jimmy's father played a little clarinet in the Elks Band. He had a little musical knowledge, but it was just really very amazing that here I am at dinner and Mom and Pop are insisting, "You can't be making no noise now. We got Bird on." I'm saying, "What! I don't believe this." That's really what drew me into the whole family, including all three of the brothers and sister, and we became so close as friends.

Philadelphia was such a prominent town for musicians that often I went over there just to hang out with the musicians who were working in different clubs. . . . I would take the train from New York to Philly and just hang out two or three days, before I got married. I was free. I didn't have anything to do. That also enhanced my close association with Jimmy because when I did go to Philly, I'd always go to their house and hang out no matter wherever else I was going.

In 1948 Jimmy and I played together with Howard McGhee's band with Percy and Specs Wright on drums. We played several theater gigs; plus we played in Chicago. Jimmy and I doubled playing piano because we didn't have a regular piano player. When "Maggie" [McGhee] soloed, I played piano. When Jimmy soloed, I played for him and Jimmy would play for me. Sometimes Maggie would sit down and play piano. Howard McGhee was one of the innovators for his style of playing, so everybody accepted that. The guys who were up front and who served as innovators and leaders were all to be respected because that's how we all got our jobs and came into our own prominence.

Howard McGhee's band was off and on for about a year. We played the Paradise Theater in Detroit. This was all in '48. We played the Apollo Theater in New York, and we played a Chicago engagement. We must have stayed there three or four weeks because in those days, you went into a nightclub and stayed three or four weeks at a time, which is one of the things that is missing today, nightclub appearances. Now it's just one week at a time or just a weekend. It's been broken down to that and that's a matter of economics.

I don't really remember how the band broke up. When it was formed, it wasn't to be permanent anyway. We all had our own destinies and directions.

Jimmy always did have a positive attitude. Plus he had the talent. You find some guys that are well-rounded. I preach that, from my father's philosophy, you can't really be a jack of all trades. Pursue one thing and be good at it. Of course, in music it's fortunate that you can be good at some things and be well-rounded. For example, Quincy Jones was a trumpet player yet he chose to pursue composing. He felt that he was probably better at that. He turned out to be a genius at it. Some guys have a forte one way or the other. I've always contended that you really can't be successful in doing two or three things. But then I think that's questionable. It depends on who's doing the judging. If you were to look at somebody who can do a number of things, Jimmy would be one of the prime examples. Not only is he a composer and arranger; he can still play a lot of those reed instruments and play them very well.

PART TWO

■

Second Chorus

(1949–1969)

4

High Note–Low Note

■

Dizzy and Miles

While I was living at Howard McGhee's in New York in 1949, I became close to Gil Fuller, the orchestrator for Dizzy Gillespie's band. Bill Massey and I used to do handyman jobs for Gil. He was a landlord and had several apartments, and we helped paint some of them. He was also some kind of policeman, and I think he had a degree in engineering and one in music, and he was a real estate entrepreneur. He was a heavy. Gil showed us things about orchestration because he had studied the Joseph Schillinger system, maybe from the same teacher I eventually went to, Rudolf Schramm.

I started working with Gil's band in 1948. He had fallen out with Dizzy over money involving his music or arrangements. Gil's band had a lot of the guys who had played with Dizzy. It might have been an interim period for Dizzy, who had gone to California with Chano Pozo that year and made a big splash. Gil was a super orchestrator. The band was rehearsing somewhere near the Savoy, or maybe in the Savoy. It was a song by Leonard Feather, "Signing Off"—it's a ballad that Sarah Vaughan recorded—and while we were rehearsing the arrangement, he wrote an introduction for it and passed it out to the guys. It was sensational. I had never seen anybody write music as if writing a letter. He wrote all the parts, handed them out, and it was terrific.

Things were going well for me musically, but personally I received a serious shock. On occasion, Bert did house work for some rich families in Philly. One day in 1948, she told me she was going on one of those jobs for a couple days and that her mother would take care of our son, so I thought nothing of it. However, she had fallen in love with Hen Gates and was actually going to New York to hang with him. They soon got married. I was completely wiped out. My piano player had taken my old lady. Even so, Hen Gates and I eventually ended up restoring our friendship. He was a nice man, a great stepfather to Mtume.

In the summer of 1949, somebody hooked up a battle of the bands with Gil Fuller's band and Dizzy's band at the Audubon Ballroom. Dizzy, of course, had written "Things to Come." Gil wrote another fast minor tune called "The Scene Changes," which was a kind of answer to Dizzy's composition. I took a solo on it, a fast D minor piece. Gil was trying to get back at Dizzy since Gil had orchestrated "Things to Come" for Dizzy's band. In a way, Gil was saying, "I've got some new stuff; the scene changes." Gil had a competitive spark, and there was always competition, but in this particular case, it was Gil against Dizzy. He was trying to pay Dizzy back for whatever happened to them personally. We played that night at the Audubon Ballroom and we played well; Dizzy's band, with Teddy Stewart on drums, played well too. I don't know what the opinion of the general public was or which one outblew the other. Dizzy had the rep. We couldn't outblow Dizzy regardless of what Gil Fuller had.

Back then, what happened with Bert hurt me so bad that I was vulnerable and open. The night that we played the battle of music with Dizzy's band, Teddy Stewart said, "Man, Bert was over here with Hen Gates." He said, "Look, man, I know how you feel. Try some of this. Snort some of this; you'll feel better." That was my first introduction to snorting heroin. From the first time you do it, it's like an addiction because you get to like it and you start doing it more and more.

In the beginning it didn't affect my music, and I continued to pursue my life's work. July 11, 1949, was the date of my first recorded big band arrangement, the Gil Fuller Orchestra's *Bebop Boys*. The lineup was Dave Burns, trumpet, who had played with Dizzy and left; Bill Massey, trumpet; Abdul Salaam, trumpet; Mustapha Dalee, trumpet; Clarence Ross, Ripp Tarrent, Charles Johnson, and Haleen Rasheed, trombones; Sahib Shihab and me, alto saxophones; Billy Mitchell, Pritchard Cheeseman, tenor saxophones; Cecil Payne, who had also been with Dizzy, baritone; Milt Jackson, piano and vibes; Percy Heath, bass; Art Blakey, drums; and Gil Fuller, conductor and vocals. I arranged "Mean to Me" and used some reharmonizations. The vocal leaves a little bit to be desired, but the orchestration is mine. That's the only big band arrangement I had ever recorded until *Little Man Big Band* in 1992. I had written for a lot of ten-piece units, but Fuller's band was full-sized.

Dizzy Gillespie hired me in September 1949. Playing with a master like Dizzy was my highest achievement to date, like being on a musical mountaintop or hitting a high note. Percy and I had always followed Dizzy's big band. We used to wear berets and artist ties. When they played in Wilmington, Delaware, we were there. If they played in New York, we'd come there. If they played in Philly, we'd stand in front of the band dressed like the band and Dizzy would say, "There's the Heath Brothers in the front!" Ray Brown and Bags were in the band at the time, and Kenny Hagood was the singer. Trane and I joined about a month apart. Trane was playing alto then; he had just started to play tenor around Philly when he gigged with Philly Joe Jones. Percy was on one of those gigs as well, at the Ridge Point.

I was living in New York when I joined Dizzy's band. Trane and I replaced Howard Johnson and John Brown, the two alto players. We shared the lead book, the first alto chair. I played some of the first alto chair, and Trane would play some of those parts also. In his autobiography, *To Be, or Not . . . to Bop,* Dizzy talks about that reed section being the best he ever had. In the band briefly with Trane and me was alto saxophonist Rudy Williams, who could also play tenor and who had come from Al Cooper's Savoy Sultans. When Rudy left, Paul Gonsalves, who later played with Duke, joined on tenor. Trane had played a little tenor before he got in the band, but Dizzy wanted an alto player.

One of the first cities we played was Columbus, Ohio, and later we went to Little Rock, Arkansas. This was before school integration, before the notoriety of Bull Connor and the Freedom Riders in Alabama, and before Orval Faubus, the Governor of Arkansas, defied the Supreme Court and tried to prevent black students from going to Little Rock High School. Bebop wasn't the favorite music of people in the South. It was too sophisticated for most of them. They were more interested in strictly dance music. At the gig we played in Little Rock, the audience was so small that the band actually outnumbered them. We could just about have taken them in a fight. Some people called out, "Man, we don't want to hear no bebop now. Go get Buddy Johnson!" Buddy Johnson had a popular dance band at that time. Dizzy was pretty upset, so he picked that night to play "Things to

Come." "Things to Come" had very fast and difficult saxophone passages. What Dizzy didn't realize is that I had been trying to transcribe his music before I joined the band. As it turned out, we made it through pretty well for a first sight reading. I had memorized a lot of it, but it was still quite a feat to get through it. Dizzy had just wanted to try that piece on us anyway.

We traveled by bus to places in the Midwest, such as Peoria, Illinois. The bus would pick us up at 2040 Seventh Avenue in New York, where Dizzy was living. All the musicians really had fun on the bus. Jesse Powell, who I'd played with in Howard McGhee's band, was on tenor, and Al Gibson was the baritone player. I heard about a saxophone giant-to-be when we played Wilberforce University in Xenia, Ohio, on October 4, 1949; there might have been around twelve hundred people there for that event. When Trane, Teddy Stewart, and I were walking on the campus of Wilberforce, we heard about this saxophonist named Frank Foster.

A few days later, on October 7, we had a week-long gig opening at the Earle Theatre in Philadelphia, back in my hometown. At that time, Teddy Stewart started going with Dinah Washington, and he quit in the middle of the week to be her road manager. Dizzy and Teddy had some sort of disagreement, and Teddy said, "Well, shit, I'm splitting." When he left, Dizzy was kind of uptight because he didn't have a drummer, so I told him, "Man, I got a drummer who was with my band. I can call him up now and get him to come up here and run the show down. He can read and everything and fill in." Dizzy said, "Okay, call him up." That's how I got Specs Wright the gig with Dizzy, and that worked out fine. Dizzy liked Specs.

Unbeknownst to Dizzy, who didn't like his musicians using narcotics, there were six or seven guys in the band who were snorting heroin. Charlie Parker had torn his ass and made it real obvious, and Sonny Stitt, who had played with Dizzy, had been a real addict. Dizzy was through with both of them. Some of the other guys in the band when we toured were Matthew Gee, Sam Hurt, Charles Greenlee, trombone; Al McKibbon, bass; Don Slaughter, Willie Cook, Elmon Wright, and Gerald Wilson, trumpet. In the sax section, we had Jesse Powell and Paul Gonsalves on tenor, Trane and me on altos, and Al Gibson, baritone. Melba Liston also joined the band on trombone. Gonsalves, Wright, Trane, Cook, Gee, Greenlee, and I were all snorting heroin at the time.

One time, when we got to Dayton, Ohio, the price of heroin was three times what it was in New York, and it was in very small capsules. If you had a snorting habit, you were going to become addicted very quickly. It was four dollars for these little teeny-weeny capsules, and you could get a whole lot in New York for that price. So what we got didn't make us high because it was cut and was so weak. It wasn't the same quality, and the stuff didn't keep me from getting sick.

Specs had met a woman named Dee Dee at the theater. We were playing on the bill with Sugar Child Robinson, a boogie-woogie piano player. I didn't feel like playing, and I said, "Look, I'm scared." She said, "I'll do it, I'll hit you." Dee Dee came up with the works, with the needle, but I was always scared of needles. They convinced everybody except Paul Gonsalves—he kept snorting, but everybody else went for the needle. I turned my head and let Dee Dee do it to me. I said, "Okay, go ahead." That was the first time I had shot heroin, and it was downfall number two, first putting it in my nose, and then going through the works. After that, I was a full-fledged junkie.

Heroin would keep you high longer, and you kind of said, "Oh yeah, this is cool; this is good!" But we were always concerned about the illegality of it. We were always ducking around the police, but not as much as when we were on the road with Dizzy's band, traveling to places like Des Moines, Iowa; El Paso, Texas; and Albuquerque, New Mexico. In a lot of places, they had separate dances for blacks and whites. When we toured in Albuquerque, where John Lewis was living, I visited his house. When we got to El Paso, I realized it was segregated too: Spanish, black, and white. We took a trip over to Juarez, Mexico. You could walk across the bridge from El Paso to Juarez. Specs and I were trying to find some stuff.

We played Christmas 1949 at the Apollo, starting on December 23. We were on the bill with The Orioles, a very popular R&B singing group. They had recorded "What Are You Doing New Year's Eve?" The heroin was around, and guys would come backstage with it. It was accessible and available. We came off the stage one night and went out the backstage entrance. There was a mob of young women back there. Specs, Trane, and I, the Philadelphia cats, came out the back door like slick beboppers, but these women were waiting to see Sonny Til, the lead singer for The Orioles. It was kind of drizzling rain a bit, and the chicks had umbrellas. We had these orange-looking coats with bebop ties, and one of the chicks said, "Oh, that's those beboppers. Where's Sonny Til?" When they said that, Specs said, "I sent him to get my laundry!" One girl hit Specs in the head with her umbrella. I said, "Specs, you can't mess with people's heroes, man!" It was so funny. This was the time when R&B was really becoming popular, and the big bands were on their way out. People came to the Apollo to hear "What Are You Doing New Year's Eve?" We were just on the show for some of the people in the audience.

Bebop bands weren't the people's favorite, but there was a certain audience that was completely dedicated to bebop. It wasn't just a black audience—it was mixed. Beboppers had their audiences in New York and other urban areas. Dizzy and Bird had been playing bebop for a number of years by 1949. Dizzy had a successful record with "Manteca" in 1947, so he was established, and there were people who liked us. People were also dancing to bebop. When I toured with Dizzy, they were dancing to the music.

I had a number of memorable moments on the road with Dizzy's big band. On one engagement was the Will Mastin Trio with Sammy Davis, Jr. That was the first time I met Sammy. We both were very young; Sammy was almost a year older than I was. (I saw him again one time on Broad Street in Philadelphia.) The band was in for one week at the Howard Theatre in Washington, D.C., starting on March 17, 1950, and Dizzy didn't like something about the music. He was P.O.'d about something, and one night he kept us in the theater quite late going over a lot of music. Gerald Wilson had written a composition, "Couldn't Love, Couldn't Cry," for a singer from Pittsburgh called Tiny Irving, who was in the band at the time. We went over and over this piece. We kept looking at each other because we thought we were playing it okay, but every time we played it, Dizzy would say, "Let's do it again."

We went to Milwaukee in January 1950, where we played at the Riverside Theater. We got into town on the closing night of the Jimmy Dorsey Orchestra. Coltrane and I went to the theater because Dorsey was quite a famous alto saxophone player, and they let us backstage because we were opening the next day with Dizzy. Jimmy was so drunk. When you admire a person as a hero, you don't always realize that they are human. I was a young man and thought Dorsey was larger than life. I had seen both Jimmy and Tommy Dorsey at the Earle Theatre when I used to go to hear the bands. At that point in Milwaukee, I realized that Jimmy Dorsey was an alcoholic, and it was a surprise to me.

When we opened the next day and played for a week, Paul Gonsalves was on tenor, with Trane and me playing altos. Dizzy had arrangements that featured the tenor, and Trane and I didn't get many solos during theater performances. If we played a dance, we would have a couple of solos each;

for the most part, though, the tenor was featured at theater performances, which were more condensed. This was when I realized that the tenor sound was more important to the audience, more appealing. All the young ladies who came backstage didn't care about me or Coltrane. They wanted Gonsalves: "Where's Paul? Where's Paul?" Paul was the guy. It could have been based on his appearance; he was part Portuguese. It could also have been just the way he sounded—he had this breathy tenor sound that was very beautiful—or simply because he was featured and we weren't.

Trane and I eventually switched to tenor because that was the instrument of choice, especially following the war. After the rhythm section, the audience wanted to hear the tenor. All of this reinforced the importance of the tenor saxophone in my life and Coltrane's life. Also, from hearing the records that were popular, such as *Flying Home* or *Body and Soul*, we realized that the tenor seemed to be more appealing to a mass audience than the alto—except in the case of Johnny Hodges, who had the kind of sound that was beyond the instrument. It sang. It was so personal and so beautiful that people just liked his sound and its special quality. The mass audience wouldn't appreciate Charlie Parker like they did Hodges. He could have gone to any country town in the South and played the saxophone and people would have liked it better than what Parker was doing, which was very fast and modern. Hodges's sound is the sound of music. It was a beautiful, pleasant sound, no unnecessary tricks, no sophisticated chord sequences. Paul Gonsalves also had a sound that was captivating.

These were my formative years with Dizzy, and I was beginning to think of the kind of sound that I wanted to have. In the early years I'd wanted to be like Charlie Parker, but before I had heard Parker, I wanted to play like Johnny Hodges and Benny Carter, who was one of my first idols. I admired both players' sounds on the alto, which were unique. I was searching for a more communicative sound. With Bird, technique was overwhelming, but with Hodges it was the sound that was captivating. They represented two sources from which to draw, two roads I was walking down.

I didn't make many recordings with Dizzy at that time. Trane and I were disappointed in the one recording we did because Dizzy was doing the commercial stuff. It was *Dizzy Gillespie and His Orchestra*, recorded for Capitol Records on November 21, 1949, in New York. Dizzy did this thing called "You Stole My Wife, You Horse Thief," as well as "Say When" and "Tally Ho." Nobody soloed except Dizzy on a couple of things, and Dizzy sang too.

Dizzy ended up cutting loose the big band in June 1950, paring it down to a small group without piano. He had me on alto, Coltrane on tenor, Milt Jackson on vibraphone, Percy on bass, and Specs Wright on drums. We continued to tour as the Dizzy Gillespie Sextet, and on September 16 of that year, with a somewhat different lineup, we made a recording in New York. Coltrane had gotten sick, so Jimmy Oliver played tenor on the date, and Milt Jackson and Percy had also joined us by that time.

Once we were playing in Detroit with the sextet, and in walks Frank Foster, who was very popular around the city. He had a group of people around him like an entourage. This was my first meeting with Frank. You should have seen the expressions on their faces when Coltrane started to play. Nobody knew about Trane—he hadn't been recorded on tenor in his own name at this time—and he was playing so much shit on that instrument. All of Foster's friends, and probably Foster too, had their mouths wide open in amazement. Foster and Trane had a lot in common. They were born on the same day, and Foster was like Coltrane in being such a thorough musician. Trane was seriously on his way in terms of his development.

Percy and Milt Jackson ("Bags") came in at about this time, and Trane was gone. We went to the West Coast, where we did a television show at the Hollywood Palladium, an integrated show. This was my first television appearance, and it was a live show. The headliners were Ray Anthony's Orchestra, a very popular white band, with vocalist Helen Forrest. Art Tatum played solo piano. I had never before been on the scene with Tatum or heard him play in person, and I was overwhelmed by him. I wasn't too impressed by Ray Anthony and Helen Forrest, though they were good. With Dizzy, we played only one or two numbers, possibly "Manteca."

Starting at the end of September 1950, we played a two-week engagement at Ciro's in San Francisco. After the gig one night, I realized that when we were playing onstage, we weren't aware of being sick because our minds were on the music, but as soon as we stopped playing, the withdrawal thing would hit and we would be in serious trouble. Trane was worse, though; he was going through withdrawal on stage. After the gig, Specs and I went back to the hotel; we had purchased some drugs and were going to get high. We were going up the stairs to our room, and when we were almost to our floor, we saw narcotics detectives searching someone's room, not ours. I had the drugs in my hand, and I threw them down on the steps as we were going up. Dizzy was in the lobby. The detectives brought us down to the lobby and said, "Where are the caps?" Dizzy said, "We don't wear no caps. We wear hats." After the police split, Specs and I went back up and found the stuff on the stairs. Then we went into the room and took care of our stupid business.

Another night after the gig in San Francisco, Dizzy came to the room and woke everybody up by banging on the door. "Get up! Get up! I saw a guy at a session playing with his hands backwards on the piano." We all went to see Carl Perkins, a terrific West Coast piano player who worked with Shorty Rogers, Chet Baker, and Art Pepper. André Previn stole a lot of Perkins's stuff. When we heard Perkins, we were amazed by the way he played the piano with his left hand, his thumb facing his chest, and his right hand in the traditional fashion. That was why Dizzy got us up to see him.

We were in Los Angeles in October 1950 when an incident occurred that nearly altered the course of jazz history. We were playing a gig at the Club Oasis on Western Boulevard; the emcee was Benjamin "Scatman" Crothers, a comedian and dancer who later became quite well-known on television. We were staying in a hotel, and Specs and I were still looking to cop. I pawned a watch, and we met this very tall man in a restaurant. We would use the password, so to speak, "What's happening?" and the reply would be, "What you want to happen?" When that was said, you knew you were on your way to copping. You might say, "I want something to get high with." We said that we didn't want any smoke; we wanted some stuff, or "doogie." Coltrane was staying with us. He was trying to make up his mind to quit heroin, and he had already gone through a few days of withdrawal. Specs and I copped from the tall guy, and when we got back to the room to get high, Coltrane changed his mind and wanted some.

Coltrane took off first. He cooked up his stuff, drew it up, and shot it into his arm. He immediately fell out on the floor. The guy who had sold it to us was still hanging in the restaurant, so we asked him to come up and bring some milk so that we could try to revive Coltrane. The milk was supposed to be an antidote, we thought. We were slapping him, throwing water in his face, trying to get him to come to. When the guy brought the milk, we poured that down his throat and eventually Coltrane got up. He said that the last thing he remembered when he fainted was my saying, "Come on, man. Come on, man. Give me the works." If we hadn't revived him, he certainly would have OD'd, and the Coltrane that people know now would never have existed. This was before *My Favorite Things* or *A Love Supreme*.

His monstrous and legendary career came later. Of course, we revived him because he was our friend, not because he was going to make history.

One night in November 1950, toward the end of our West Coast stay, an amazing array of musicians ended up at an all-night jam session at Bop City, a San Francisco club owned by a black guy called Big Jimbo. Dizzy was there, playing piano, as were Kenny Dorham and Miles Davis. Miles just happened to be in San Francisco; he had gotten into some trouble over drugs in Los Angeles. Others who were at that jam session were Roy Porter, Milt Jackson, Percy, the alto player Sonny Criss, and Herb Jeffries's brother, Howard. A woman also sat in on drums during one of the jam sessions, and Carl Perkins was there for one too. Pianist Hampton Hawes was another musician I met out there.

Another thing happened when we were in San Francisco. On our day off, Dizzy took Specs Wright and went back to Los Angeles to make this record with the Johnny Richards String Orchestra, a record that included "Alone Together." Trane and I weren't on that date.

From California we headed to Chicago to play the Silhouette, November 17 to December 7, 1950. During our break one night, Specs and I were down in the basement of the club, and Dizzy caught Specs shooting up. That was the first time he caught us. Dizzy was seriously upset. I had progressed from snorting heroin, when I first joined the band, to shooting up, which started in Ohio. He said, "You junky motherfuckers. You're fired." But he had to give us two weeks notice according to the musicians' union. Dizzy might have been suspicious of us, but until he actually saw us using the stuff, it wasn't something definite. If he had known, he would have gotten rid of us earlier because of the problems he had with Charlie Parker. Dizzy was definitely against heroin. Back when he went to California with Bird, he hired an extra guy, Lucky Thompson, in case Parker didn't show up. In March 1951, we had a gig in Montreal, Canada, at the Seville Theatre. We played on a show with Guy Mitchell, who had a big record on the radio, "You've Changed." I was still on drugs when we got to Toronto, so I would take the train to Detroit to cop and then go back up to Toronto. Coltrane had stopped using drugs at this time.

Being addicted was something I had to hide from everyone, my family and others. Heroin doesn't affect your musical ability as long as you can get it. I felt that mental concentration was better with heroin than with any other stimulant. Alcohol throws your talent out; your technique gets sloppy.

Marijuana makes you get plenty of ideas, but then your mind moves too fast. You move off one idea to another. Heroin was a concentration drug. You only have to look at the numerous users during the bebop era who were outstanding musicians, people like Max Roach, Bud Powell, Charlie Parker, Dexter Gordon, Miles Davis, John Coltrane, Stan Getz, Sonny Rollins, Jackie McLean, and J. J. Johnson. They were labeled drug addicts, dope fiends, or junkies, but in some circles, they were called innovators and geniuses. At the same time, other innovators like Hank Jones, Dizzy, Percy, and Milt Jackson weren't addicts.

In Lexington, Kentucky, where a lot of convicted addicts were sent, research had been conducted on addiction. Some of these addicts had the mentality to be generals, scientists, or anything because of their degree of concentration. With heroin, you could zoom in on something and block everything else out. Nevertheless, I think I would have developed to the same degree if I hadn't been addicted. It's also a myth about playing better on heroin. Some people were drug addicts and still couldn't play. It's a curious thing, and I can't fully explain why so many of the addicts were so great. If you can concentrate better, you can work on things very meticulously. Coltrane used to get high and practice all day. When I would go to see him, he would have nothing on but a pair of pants. Sometimes it was so hot in his house that he would be drenched in sweat, and he would practice endlessly. Heroin enhanced your practice. I don't know if I would have practiced as intensely if I hadn't been on heroin. That's a question mark. I'm not endorsing heroin by any stretch of the imagination, because it has too many things that are bad about it. That's the only thing that was good about it, its effect on your concentration level. Everything else was a drag—your social life, your health, your reputation, all of that was a drag. The side-effects and after-effects are devastating, and the social effects are worse! The physical effects are another thing. It messed me up for seven years.

I can concentrate very well now drug-free, but at that point in my life that was the reason I used heroin. Billie Holiday and Charlie Parker were exhibit A. Parker's depth of thought and concentration, his musical skill, was phenomenal. Dizzy even said that Parker had all the musical stuff together that he himself was looking for. Parker had all of this at an early age. When he was just a kid of seventeen, he was already playing at a level of maturity beyond anyone in the history of our music.

All of the so-called illegal drugs were at one time legal medicines. The negative physical, social, and legal problems that are brought on by the habitual use of drugs of any kind, including alcohol, outweigh the positives. Today, due to semantic-antics, they call the use of drugs "substance abuse," especially if you are famous or upper class.

DIZZY GILLESPIE

Jimmy's a master bopper, a grandmaster bopper, a great-grandmaster bopper. He's well respected among his peers; all the guys who came up under that umbrella of Charlie Parker respect him to the highest. We call him little professor. He's one of the most gifted musicians. This young man is truly one of the outstanding musicians from the forties up, Little Bird, Jimmy Heath. (Inter-Media Arts Center, 1991)

After I was fired by Dizzy, I went back to Philadelphia and borrowed a tenor saxophone from a barber who lived across the street from me, Edgar Holmes, who was also a minister. Around 1951, I had some gigs on tenor, and that's when I really started playing it. I never went back to alto. I was living with my parents, getting my tenor chops together, and hanging around Philadelphia. Many of the jazz names would pass through town, but I didn't get any gigs with them at that time. It wasn't an eventful or spectacular year. My personal life was in the same bag. I continued doing drugs and getting into trouble, playing all those wrong low notes.

I hooked up with Connie around that time, Connie Theresa Ang, for whom I wrote the song "C.T.A." On the record, they said it stood for Chicago Transit Authority, but they were wrong—it was for Connie. I had been writing all along since my days with Nat Towles, but "C.T.A." was one of the first compositions I wrote in 1951 or 1952, and we recorded it in 1953. This was a period when I was just biding my time in preparation for getting to something else. I was deciding whether I was going to move to New York. In Philly, I was on a down from the break with Dizzy. I wasn't on the road anymore, just playing locally, although the gigs I did get were a result of having been on the road. I played with Butch Ballard, who was later Ellington's drummer, in Philly at a club called Spider Kelly's in September 1951. After that gig, in the September 11, 1951, *Philadelphia Tribune*, Francis Cauthorn called me a "boppist" and an "alto dissonance dispenser." All in all, though, he thought that with me in the group "the transformation still leaves a smooth, well-knit outfit with a peculiarly pleasant flavor" (p. 12). Cauthorn wasn't thinking of the kind of personal "dissonance" that was taking place in my life. Even though I wasn't with Dizzy any longer, I was recognized for having been in his group, like when I played in an "All Star Jazz Revue" at Reynolds Hall on North Broad Street on November 17, 1951, and they billed me as "formerly with Dizzy Gillespie." Tommy Monroe's fourteen-piece orchestra also performed at that event. I was able to use my association with Dizzy in other ways.

In 1951 and '52, I played gigs in and around Philadelphia. To capitalize on having been in his band, and having one other person, Specs Wright, who had been with him on occasions, I called the group the Dizzy Gillespie All Stars. My first time playing in Wilmington, Delaware, with a small group was early 1951 at a place called The Spot. My trumpet player was Bill Massey, who had played with my big band. Bill was a fine player and writer. During our first break, a young, shy guy asked if he could sit in and I said, "Yeah, on the next set." He did, and that was an experience Bill and I have never forgotten. It was Clifford Brown. Wow!

During that same period Philly Joe Jones, the drummer, got a week-long engagement at Spider Kelly's in Philadelphia. He hired Sugie Rhodes on bass and Dolo Coker on piano. His front line was Clifford and me on tenor. During the Friday night performance, I noticed a lady down front making a nuisance of herself. When we came off the bandstand, she approached Clifford and me, and we noticed she was sloppy drunk. She pointed her finger in Clifford's face and said, "I don't know what y'all were playing but you were playing the hell out of it." Clifford, in his usual way, blushed and dropped his head as if he had committed a crime. I think this says it all about Clifford Brown. Later, in 1986, while I was teaching at City College in New York, I was offered a gig in Lima, Peru. After missing my plane connection and spending a night in the Cayman Islands, I finally made it. The club was called the Satchmo. The problem was that on the marquee they had a picture of Clifford Brown. I guess we all look alike.

During this period, my group was getting brief notices like the one that appeared in *Down Beat* on November 2, 1951, "Heath Leads Own Unit":

Philadelphia—Former Dizzy Gillespie altoist Jimmy Heath is now leading his own combo at the Pep Music bar here. With him are Cliff Brown, trumpet; Charlie Coker, piano; Bob Berton, bass, and Joe Jones (not THE), drums. (p. 9)

Eventually my father told me that I couldn't stay at the house any longer because of my addiction. That might have been what prompted me to go to New York. The move came in 1951. I wanted to get away from my mother and father and get out on my own. In New York, they required a union membership in Local 802, but there was a rule that you had to establish residence in New York for six months. I had belonged to the black musicians' union in Philly, Local 274, since I had finished high school. It was a separate-but-not-equal union, the same as the high school. However, in New York, I couldn't work steady gigs until I had established residency. I lived with Philly Joe Jones at 446 Central Park West, a sort of hotel rooming place. My addiction continued, and that's why I was in with Philly Joe. I started working odd jobs. I worked at Bloomingdale's during the Christmas season of 1951. Then I got a job at Macy's, working in the men's shoe department. The only thing I liked about it was that I could steal shoes while I worked part-time. All the musicians knew I was working in the shoe department, so I would get shoes for them. I'd take a pair and hide them under my belt underneath the cotton coat I wore as an employee. I would put that pair in a locker at Penn Station when I went for lunch, and I would try to get another pair when I returned from lunch. So I was into stealing shoes. Philly Joe wore size 10½, so he had all kinds of shoes. I would say, "Philly, what you want today, brown suede, black wing tips?" Since he was dealing drugs, I would bring home the shoes and get my stuff. I had a deal with Milt Jackson, who wore size 9B, so I stole this pair of 9B's and brought them uptown to Milt, and Milt said, "Shit, I can't wear these. They too tight." I said, "You told me 9B, so what am I going to do with them? I'm sick. I need my money so I can go cop." I went through this big scene with Milt.

So the next day I got him a pair of 9C's, and that was the last pair of shoes I stole. I had gotten greedy. I was pushing a cart of shoes to the seventeenth floor, where the storeroom was located. I would grab other things, a cashmere sweater, a long shoehorn, and all this stuff. That day, when I got ready to check out, the store detective grabbed me from behind and said, "How long you been working here?" He had seen me picking up things on the different floors. The shoes were worth about thirty dollars, the sweater twenty-five. It was petty larceny. I was taken to the precinct, my first arrest, with five hundred dollars' bail. I had my paycheck in my pocket, about forty-six or fifty dollars. I called Percy and told him I was busted in the tombs, and I was also sick. Percy said, "I ain't going to get you out. Stay there until you get yourself together." I stayed there for about two weeks, and the habit was beginning to wane a little bit.

When I went to court, I had a contract in my pocket for a gig back in Philly. I was still going back home if I had a gig there. The judge said, "I understand you have a job in Philadelphia. You have never been arrested before. Go to your job. Your sentence is suspended." I went back to Philly and made the gig at one of those cabaret parties where there was dancing. It was that gig that helped to spring me.

Miles, Rollins, and all the others who had been messing around would come up to Philly Joe's. We were all in a clique together. At the time, Miles was with the Symphony Sid All-Stars, which also included J. J. Johnson, Percy, Kenny Clarke, Milt Jackson, and Zoot Sims. Miles didn't like Zoot Sims that much, so he maneuvered to get Zoot out and me in. Symphony Sid (Sid Torin), who was white, was the emcee. All he did was announce the band. He was the leader in name because he had gotten all of the gigs. In one place, somebody asked me, "Well, what the hell does Symphony Sid play?" I said, "He plays the microphone. He don't play shit." He had the gigs. Miles was not that big at that time. Miles and J.J. were about at the same level as Bags, all up-and-coming jazz performers. Miles, J.J., and I were all writing tunes. Miles and J.J. were basically in charge of the music. I probably contributed one composition around that time. With the Symphony Sid All-Star Band, in 1952 we had dates at Weekes' in Atlantic City; the Apollo in New York; the Graystone Ballroom in Detroit; the Ebony Show Lounge in Cleveland, July 1; and the Downbeat in New York, July 24.

When we played the Ebony Club in Cleveland, we were staying at the Majestic Hotel, which was two blocks from the club and through an alley. Miles and I were the only two in that band who were using. A famous bass player nicknamed Chocolate was living in the Majestic, and he had the connections. Between sets, we would go through the alley to the hotel, get our fix, and then return to the gig. We would get back late on the set, so my brother Percy would say, "You junky motherfuckers." He would cut me up. Percy was always mean-spirited to me about drugs. He would say, "You motherfuckers are messing the job up." He would mainly jump on me, not much on Miles. I said, "Look, Percy. I'm a grown man. I do what the hell I want. You can't tell me what to do." Years later, when I was in the joint, I wanted to eat those words.

The Downbeat gig, July through August 1952 in New York, was one of the last gigs we had as the Symphony Sid All-Stars. At the Downbeat, J.J., who was the straw boss because he could take care of business a little better than Miles and I could, told us that something was happening with the musicians' union and the money we were supposed to be getting. Symphony Sid was responsible for the problem because he hadn't been paying the union dues. The union people came and jumped on J.J. because Symphony Sid wasn't in the union. He was the contractor. J.J. and Symphony Sid got into this heated discussion, and J.J. ended up punching Symphony Sid in the mouth. Then Symphony Sid brought some Al Capone types with these big hats on, gangsters. They came in the club and were going to kick J.J.'s ass. That was the end of the Symphony Sid All-Stars because gangsters came in and told J.J. that if he touched Symphony Sid again, they were going to fuck him up. We were lucky they didn't beat him up then. It was just a threat and we had a break. The final week of the gig, Miles's father, Dr. Davis, came into town. He had found out that Miles was using drugs. He took Miles off the stage and back to St. Louis. Miles left his horn on the stage, and that was literally the end of the Symphony Sid All-Stars.

In early 1953, I was still in New York and continued drugging around. Percy and Bags had gone with John Lewis, and that was the beginning of the process of forming the Modern Jazz Quartet. When Miles came back to New York, he was still using drugs. I tried to practice every day for at least an hour, scales and so forth. After I got a fix, I would practice all day, but I wasn't doing much composing because I didn't have a piano. Occasionally I would have a chance to use the piano at Miles's place. In April 1953, we made the recording with Miles Davis on which my composition "C.T.A." was included, my second recorded composition. Miles had asked me if I had any tunes to contribute. When I showed him "C.T.A.," he liked it.

I had another recording session with J. J. Johnson on June 22, 1953, along with Clifford Brown, John Lewis, Kenny Clarke, and Percy. This date, which is also a collector's item, was significant because it was one of Brownie's first appearances on a record. J.J. had written a piece for this date titled "Turnpike," which was one of those compositions on rhythm changes that had the cycle of fourths or fifths in the first "A" section. J.J. was meticulous and particular about his recordings. He had worked out some difficult passages on this particular chord pattern. During the course of the recording, chop problems occurred with J.J. missing notes here and there on some of the patterns, and he would stop the recording because he wanted to make sure that his part was right. He would say, "Stop. Stop." We made another take, and as side men, Clifford and I had to go for whatever we could do on each take. We didn't have any lines worked out. The situation was such that we didn't know that particular pattern was going to be called for until we made the rehearsal for the date. However, Clifford was so startling on each take that Frank Wolf, the photographer, said in his German accent, "That Brownie. That Brownie." He was completely taken aback by the creativity of Clifford. As the date progressed, we noticed that Al Lion and Frank Wolf had cornered Clifford in the booth to sign with Blue Note Records. (Don Sickler has said that Clifford had recorded earlier, but that wasn't under his own contract.)

This record date is also significant because I played baritone sax on one track, a piece John Lewis had written called "Sketch I." He wanted me to play baritone and had rented the instrument for me. It wasn't the first time; I had played baritone on one of Howard McGhee's tracks. On the album cover for *Miles Davis Volume 2*, released April 20, 1953, only pictures of Miles and J.J. appear. One of the photos from the session is also included in a jazz encyclopedia from the fifties. The credits for the picture indicate J.J. and Clifford Brown, but there's no mention of the baritone saxophone player. This seems to have been a recurring theme in my career, "little guy passed by." Another example is how certain Miles Davis footage was documented in versions of a 1967 concert in Stockholm, Sweden. When he played "Footprints," Wayne Shorter's title was indicated, but when "Gingerbread Boy" was being played, the title was left out. When I went to Paris for a Charlie Parker celebration in 1989, I was playing with Jay McShann. Percy, Stan Getz, Jackie McLean, Milt Jackson, Hank Jones, Max Roach, and Dizzy were all there too, being awarded the French Medal of Honor. Dizzy said, "Hey, man, you should be over with us." I was left out again.

After the J.J. recording in June 1953, I had some gigs around New York with Art Blakey and his Jazz Messengers big band, which at that time was a big band with Kenny Dorham. We played a couple of gigs at the Rockland Palace in Harlem. Fifty-second Street was going strong around then, but I wasn't a big part of that scene. I had played with Howard McGhee at the Three Deuces in 1947, and also at Bop City and the Royal Roost with Dizzy. Birdland on Broadway opened up in 1949, and I would occasionally get a Monday night gig there. Birdland wasn't technically on Fifty-second Street, but it was still part of the scene.

5

Sharp Dissonance to
Smooth Harmony with Mona

■

This part of my life was entangled with drugs, so it wasn't the most productive musical time for me. That would come later, after 1959. Despite my drug use, I did develop musically because the environment was always conducive to learning. I was around future giants like Miles, who was devoutly working on his music, but he was also sidetracked by drugs and was in a holding pattern. He didn't really arrive until the Coltrane era, 1955–1956. That's when he really started to take off as "Miles Davis," although before that he had a number of recordings. Many of us didn't have much notoriety at that time, since we had a limited number of recording sessions, and I didn't have a recording in my own name. I was recording with the good guys, but I wasn't a leader. This is what using drugs did to my career. Trane was like me at that time because he didn't have a recording session in his own name.

In New York in 1953, my musical relationship with trumpeter Kenny Dorham began to develop with a recording on December 15. I played tenor and baritone saxophone for Debut Records, which Charles Mingus and Max Roach owned. They were trying to go on their own without having to deal with distributors, who were usually considered to be gangsters and unfair to jazz musicians. On this recording, Walter Bishop, Jr., was on piano, Percy on bass, and Kenny Clarke on drums. I had made three record dates in 1953, with Miles, J.J., and Kenny Dorham—April, June, and December, respectively. I wasn't on Miles's 1953 Prestige date, where my tune

"The Serpent's Tooth," named by Ira Gitler, was recorded. It was later part of a recording called *Miles Davis Collectors' Items* and included a 1956 session as well. That 1953 recording was historic because they say it was the second and final occasion when Bird, under the name Charlie Chan, was recorded playing tenor sax. Also, Sonny Rollins and Bird were together on that session, which we're told never happened again.

The Debut Records date was fascinating because of Kenny's playing and his musical ability and quest. We were very close in our search for new harmonies and new ways of playing, as was Miles. We would regularly discuss the music, and our conversations would deal with reharmonization and modernization of songs, especially standards. These sessions would start at the piano, which reminded me of how I learned from Dizzy when he came to my house in Philadelphia. I learned that I needed the piano to create. Kenny could play piano. He would say, "Hey, Shorty. Dig this change here. You can play this here instead of playing that. You can play a half-step up on this instead of the usual change." These were innovations he thought of or had learned from being around Charlie Parker or Dizzy. We would transfer information, and the information in musical terms would usually be about altered chords, what scales could be played on those chords, and how to enhance a composition by selecting certain notes to play the melody. These concepts were part of reharmonizing melodies. We compared original compositions and got suggestions and opinions from each other.

Reharmonization involves working with melody notes. If a composition has a melody note on the third, that might be changed. One of the songs Kenny was working on was "Be My Love," a popular tune made famous by Mario Lanza. Kenny changed the chords. Instead of playing G minor to C7 at a certain point, he would put in a passing chord of C-sharp minor 7 to F-sharp 7, a tritone away. Reharmonization also involved working with the melody. If the melody was on one function of the chord, the 3rd or the root, it might be changed to the 5th or the flatted 5th, 9th, or some other note to give it another quality. For example, you could change a song such as "The Girl from Ipanema." If the melody is on the root, the song sounds "churchy," but if you put the melody on the 5th of the chord, it sounds a little better. When you put it on the 7th of the chord, it has a different sound. Jobim put the melody on the 9th. It's the same melody but on a different function of the chord. You could also put the melody on the 11th, and it would sound even more sophisticated—or on the 13th. It's a matter of changing the function of the chord that the melody is on, usually moving it to a higher function to get a more modern sound. Reharmonization is a technique of jazz artists. It can be done not only with standards but also with original compositions, in order to improve them or develop them. Ellington used to do this, and Art Tatum too. On one chorus, Tatum would play certain chords and melody, and then on the next chorus he might play a different set of chords with that same melody. Bill Evans became famous for doing this, although Tatum had done it way before him. Hank Jones also does this on a lot of pieces, such as what he does with chords to create tension on Ellington's "In a Sentimental Mood." It's in the same key but it involves changing the function that the melody is on.

Back in the 1950s, putting in extra chords was the type of thing we all talked about as musicians. This was part of the musical language: What can you do to get more out of a song, more than what was originally there? How do you use substitute chords? How can substitute chords be placed in arrangements to enhance what is originally there and make it sound hipper, more modern? Some of these discussions would take place at the rehearsal before the record date in a rented studio. Sometimes we would record in New Jersey at Rudy Van Gelder's.

During this period, I was composing songs all the time. My compositions included "Resonant Emotions," "For Miles and Miles," "For Minors Only," "A Picture of Heath," and "C.T.A." With the composing process, you get a germ of an idea until you make a complete composition. You play your horn or sit at the piano until you find a melodic idea and develop it into a song. Sometimes the whole thing is revealed to you, you get a complete idea—but that's very rare. I usually had to work on songs. Sometimes fragments of ideas would come while I was working on one particular song, and I would go back to those germs. At that time, I was mainly thinking about performing on my instrument. Composing would really come later, in 1959. I also got composing lessons from Gil Fuller when Bill Massey and I stayed with him, before I joined Diz. He would show us things, but what he showed us was more about orchestration and arranging.

At the beginning of 1954, I was still living with Philly Joe, and I was continuing to get in trouble with drugs. In the spring of that year, I got arrested for sale of narcotics. A guy with Woody Herman's band was the informer. Philly had gone out of town with Tadd Dameron, who had gone to Atlantic City in 1954. I stayed in Philly's pad, and since he had been a drug dealer, people would call there. This white guy who played saxophone with Woody Herman, Buddy Arnold, called me up to get some drugs. Buddy Arnold was his stage name. His real name was Arnold Grishaver. Even though Philly had suspicions that Arnold was a federal informer, I didn't really worry about the significance of that because I hadn't been involved in anything of that sort. I thought that I was halfway slick. Arnold ordered a couple of glassine bags of heroin. I said, "Okay, man. Meet me in the Ninety-sixth Street subway stop on the A Train line." Before I got there, I put the bags in a matchbook. First, he gave me the money, but I wasn't going to hand it to him directly because that would be a direct sale. So I threw it down in a corner on the subway platform, and he picked it up. Meanwhile, an agent was standing on the other side of the platform observing what was going down. It was an observation sale, not a direct sale. The agent may have given Arnold the money to give to me. I don't know. It was a kind of entrapment. Some time later, the feds picked me up and said I was arrested for the sale of heroin.

When the agents came to bust me, I was at 446 Central Park West. The telephone was in the hallway, and you had to leave your apartment to use it. The phone rang and a woman in the next apartment said, "Hey, Heath. You're wanted on the phone." When I came out in the hall, the agents moved in on me. They said, "We have been watching you down at Birdland." I would hang out and sell drugs down at Birdland to A.T. and other musician friends. The feds took me down to West Street and the federal detention center, where I stayed for some days. Connie, my girlfriend, had arranged a lawyer for me, Eugene K. Jones. I was convicted for the sale of heroin, and he got me a sentence involving a cure in Lexington and two years' probation. Connie overdosed and died a month before my release from Lexington.

Lexington was the place Walter Winchell had called a million-dollar flophouse because they allowed addicts to commit themselves and stay for a cure. The addicts had the key. They could go down to Lexington and stay two weeks and sign themselves out—that is, if you signed yourself in. But if you were convicted and sent there, you couldn't check out. You would have to stay for your cure, which is what I had to do. There were a lot of musicians there, such as Earl Swope from the Woody Herman Band, and Jimmy Forrest, who played with Duke and composed "Night Train." A lot of jazz musicians from Chicago were there. They had a section where all of the women addicts stayed called the Jenny Barn. Guys would court women after they saw them through the windows and would pass notes to them through the kitchen staff. The actor Peter Lorre was at Lexington, and so was Judy Garland, who was supposed to have kicked the habit there.

Before I went to Lexington, I had been offered a gig with Tadd Dameron, but I couldn't go because I was on bail. Sonny Rollins had stopped by Philly Joe's and told me that he had to make a recording the following day and wanted to borrow my horn. He played a song for me called "Stopper," which he ended up recording. Since then, he's joked about that occasion, recalling that after the record date, he pawned my sax. He wrote me a letter calling himself a bunch of dirty motherfuckers because he couldn't help himself. The pawn ticket was in the letter, which my mother eventually received. She got my saxophone out of the pawnshop and sent it to Lexington. I was there for four months.

Lexington had a band, which I became a part of, but I still had to work a job there. I was put in the kitchen, where I had to clean the food carts. They were doing research on anyone who had at least a two-year sentence, which I didn't have. You could have been a bank robber or a drug addict and might have had five years. These guys were eligible for the research program, which meant that they were given some type of a drug. There was one drug called 10A-20. One of my buddies in the kitchen was involved in the research lab. He would say, "Heath, I went down this morning and had my 10A-20, and I'm high off that stuff." When you were on research, you would get time off for good behavior. They were like guinea pigs. They would try anything. These tests would be done with inmates and animals. The story was that dogs and monkeys were being given heroin habits. When a dog went through withdrawal and had come around again after being given the needle, he would put his butt right up there and let them shoot him again. The story was that the men were as stupid as the dogs. There was one case where a monkey was hooked on heroin, and when the monkey went through withdrawal and got sick and all that shit, when they came back with the needles, the monkey went nuts and banged his head against the wall and killed himself before he would take the drug again. The monkeys were smarter than the men. The drug-addict dogs would wander the yard. All of this research was the beginning of methadone development.

In Lexington, there were musicians from all over the country. While those research programs were going on, we were involved with music. Although we would get sleeping pills to help us through, we weren't given any medicine. It was cold turkey withdrawal. I discovered that nutmeg or mace would make you as high as if you had smoked reefer. If you swallowed nutmeg and drank hot cocoa, you would get high for twenty-four hours.

In 1954, after I got out of Lexington, I went back to New York. I played some gigs with Max Roach at a place called Tony's, at Grand Avenue and Dean Street in Brooklyn. Kenny Dorham was also on those gigs. This was when Max was about to start his band, and it was another case where I missed out. Max wanted me to go on the road with his band, but I was on a two-year probation, so I couldn't go, so I missed out on the beginning of the Max Roach–Clifford Brown thing. They told me when I got out of Lexington that if I didn't have any people in New York, I had to go back to Philadelphia. When I went back to Philadelphia, I got into trouble again.

On January 9, 1955, I got arrested, and it was like playing a chorus of sharp dissonance. It started a couple months after I returned to Philly. I was dealing again and fell for the same stupid shit. There was a black guy named Jim Thomas, alias Carbarn Billy. He had a whole bunch of aliases, which I found out when I was taken to court. There was a big drug sweep going on, and I did the same thing, throwing the stuff down in the street so it wouldn't be a direct sale. A black agent, David Wilson, was with Carbarn Billy. When I saw Wilson, I said to myself, "Who is this cat?" An addict peddler is a different kind of hustler. I wasn't peddling drugs to make money. I was just an addict who was going to turn the drugs over to get some stuff to keep my habit straight. If I had a hundred dollars' worth of stuff, I would turn it over and make three hundred and then get more for myself. It was a hand-to-mouth thing. You weren't really doing anything financially. The drug was the pimp and I was a simp. I was a sick man. When this guy Wilson came up to me not looking raggedy like a drug addict, I said, "Who is that dude?" Carbarn Billy said, "That's my cousin. He just started getting high." I said, "I don't like the way this cat looks." But I was still in need of drugs, so I did the same thing again. That's how they got me again for the same thing, but this time in Philly. They put me in the same bag. The agents said that they'd been watching me since I got out of Lexington and they'd been active for five or six months in my neighborhood before they made the sweep on January 9. They probably busted forty or fifty people from my neighborhood, all my boys.

They charged me as a second-time drug offender for drug sale. My brother Tootie was working with organist Shirley Scott, with Bill Carney on congas and Coltrane, who was back in town, playing tenor. He had come back after working with Earl Bostic but hadn't yet gone with Miles. Coltrane and Tootie were working at a place called the Glen Hotel. Tootie wasn't making that much money, but he secured a lawyer for me, Charles Royceman. When I went before Judge Lord, I was told that each sale had two counts, selling, facilitating, and resale, so I had six counts. When the judge started reading the counts, he said, "I sentence you to six years on the first count, six years on the second count, and six years on the third count, six years on the fourth count, and six years on the fifth count. On the sixth count, I impose a $100 fine." When he said that, I said, "Oh, Lord," to myself. I thought it was thirty years, but then he said the first five counts ran concurrently, and I realized I had a six-year sentence.

I was sent to Holmesburg Prison in Philadelphia en route to Lewisburg, which is in central Pennsylvania. Holmesburg is where Willie Sutton, the famous escape artist, escaped from. Designed by a woman, Holmesburg was like a wheel. At the end of each block was solid concrete. The guy in the control center would spin around and look down each block. Most people figured Willie Sutton must have paid some guards when he went over the wall. There was no way you could go into the carpenter shop and come out at the center. It was really escape-proof.

At Holmesburg, they gave me sleeping pills but that was it. It was a horrible experience because I was in a cell with cement floors, two people in the cell, a toilet without a cover, no privacy. That's where I had to kick the habit, and I didn't get any medicine. The main problem kicking was not being able to sleep, and that's why people continue to use—and also because when you're using heroin, you become constipated. When you kick, everything breaks loose. You would get diarrhea, your eyes would run, you would slobber from your mouth, your veins in your arms would quiver. By the time I got to Lewisburg, I was practically cured, but I still couldn't sleep.

In January 1955, I arrived at Lewisburg, a minimum-security prison that wasn't at all like Lexington. When I got there, I saw a wall, not a fence as in Lexington. I was given an IQ test and scored a 120. I was then taken before a classification committee to be given a job. There was an associate warden named Cox, who was definitely gay. He had bags under his eyes as big as you can imagine, a red face, and a potbelly. He had the audacity to carry a Chihuahua around the prison. When I came before the committee, Cox said, "You have an IQ of 120 and they tell me you are a musician. Boy, there ain't no music in here. We going to put you on the main corridor mop gang. We going to keep you on the mop gang for six months, and we going to see if you can learn to type." My heart dropped. This was the same old shit, the prejudice and the racism. I was put on the main corridor mop gang. There was a long hall in the prison, and the mops had to be swung left and right, so that both sides of the floor would be cleaned.

After six months on the mop gang and learning how to type, I was given a job as a clerk for a parole officer by the name of Hitchcock. I worked the rest of my stay there with him. They gave me a few lessons on a machine called the SoundScriber, where you listened to tapes and typed what you heard. My total stay at Lewisburg was four years and five months. I was released on May 21, 1959.

During my first year at Lewisburg, I wrote a lot of songs. When Tootie and my mother visited me on one occasion, I gave Tootie a number of these songs, along with some I'd written in 1953 and '54. Tootie was connected with a Philly bass player named Jimmy Bond, who was playing with trumpeter Chet Baker. Tootie was able to smuggle out a number of compositions, and Chet included them on his 1956 album *Playboys* with tenor player Phil Urso. My compositions were "Resonant Emotions," "For Miles and Miles," "For Minors Only," "Picture of Heath," and "C.T.A." (When Chet died, I received a big royalty check for those songs because his records began to sell again.) That 1956 *Playboys* recording, renamed *Picture of Heath* because so many of my compositions were included, featured Carl Perkins, piano; Art Pepper, sax; Lawrence Marable, drums; and Curtis Counce, bass. Of course, "C.T.A." had been recorded by Miles in 1953 with J. J. Johnson and me. I had composed those tunes back in 1952 to '54 but wrote them out again to give to Tootie so he could get them to Jimmy Bond. At that time, Art Blakey also ended up recording two tunes of mine, "For Miles and Miles," on *Hard Drive*, and "For Minors Only."

At Lewisburg, I was the only professional musician who had a reputation, so I was in charge of the inmate big band. Before I arrived, the band had been floundering. This twelve- to fourteen-piece band of felons was composed of guys who had formerly played music but who had gotten in trouble with drugs or something else. A few of them were bank robbers. Some of our charts were written on funny pink music paper. One officer, Fregley, would open the doors to the auditorium, and another guard, Red

Ramsey, was the DJ in the institution. He had all the jazz records. (When I got out of Lewisburg and played at a jazz festival at the Academy of Music in Philly, Red came to the concert.) The other inmates and I could hear live broadcasts. I heard Specs Wright with Cannonball Adderley in Chicago. I said, "That's my man, Specs Wright. He's got a gig." Also, we heard on the radio one day that Clifford Brown and Richie Powell had been killed in a car accident. Wardell Gray and Charlie Parker died while I was in prison. That was very hard for me to take.

During my stay, I wrote a whole lot of music, some of which I've never recorded. One composition was called "Bruh Slim," for a friend of mine; I did end up recording that one for Riverside. One that was never recorded was "Great Dane," for a guy from New York named Dane. I had access to the piano, which was in the auditorium, and I also had my saxophone. I started playing flute in Lewisburg.

As the long, hard years passed, I waited for every visit. You were fortunate if you received letters and had family. There were guys in there who didn't have anybody and might never get a letter during mail call. You would wonder how those guys could get through it. I was lucky. During everything that I went through, I couldn't imagine not having a mother and a father out there. When I got busted the last time, my father came to the jail and cried. That messed me up because he was a hard guy. If you had a family and people who loved you, you could survive. I don't know how anybody could be successful in the world without having a mother and father who cared. It's hard for me to conceive, but I know there are people who make it without that kind of support. Letters, visits from the family, messages from Miles, all of this helped me.

Lewisburg was near Bucknell University. On one occasion, Bruce Lund-vall, who became president of Columbia Records and was then going to Bucknell, attended one of the band concerts I conducted. Ironically, I would later sign with Columbia Records. On another occasion, Louis Armstrong played for the inmates, with a band that included Barrett Deems, Arvell Shaw, Edmond Hall, and Billy Kyle. That was a treat. Another time, ballet dancers were brought in, and all of the inmates were laughing and admiring the women. They also brought in a white band, headed by Mal Arter, that worked in the western Pennsylvania area. After I got out, I would often see him when I traveled to Harrisburg. When his band came in, they asked me to play because I was a professional, and it was taped.

While I was in Lewisburg, an order came from Washington to integrate the prison. Before that time, white and black inmates were separated in certain dormitories, though I did have in the band an Italian singer, Joe Ritter from New York, who favored Frank Sinatra. The mess halls were segregated. When the black inmates went into the mess hall, we decided that two or three of us would sit at each table. We spread ourselves all over because prior to that we had only a few tables for ourselves and the white guys had the rest. When the white guys saw us sitting all over, they went back to their dormitories. They bought food from the commissary, Oreo cookies, Kool-Aid, Ritz Crackers, and some other junk, for a couple of days. The northern white guys would show up, but they would get their asses kicked by the rednecks. Eventually, after two or three days, those suckers started getting hungry, and that's how the place became integrated in 1955 or '56.

We had a lot of band activities. We rehearsed at the recreation period, when most everyone would show up, but some would hit the yard and wouldn't practice. However, if we had a concert coming up, we would definitely get together. I would write the arrangements for the shows, such as the one I wrote for Joe Ritter on "A World on a String." The band also played on the Fourth of July. I had one roommate, a guy from Pittsburgh, who didn't dig music and objected to my practicing the flute. He was probably the one who destroyed my flute, which I had gotten from the instruments distributed inside. I also roomed with Herbert Daughtry, who became an influential reverend in Brooklyn.

On the whole, the deaths of my friends in the outside world were the low points; the high points were the family visits and the Louis Armstrong performance. At the end of my sentence, they sent me to a place called Allenwood Camp, where they wean you down and give you a little bit of freedom.

THE REVEREND HERBERT DAUGHTRY

At Lewisburg, in that vortex of madness, Jimmy and I were caught. In 1946, I started with marijuana; from there it was the full range of dope: hashish, morphine, cocaine, speed, landing into the clutches of the white lady, or heroin, straight to the mainline.

Jimmy and I became model prisoners. As a result of that, we were accorded certain privileges, one of which was to share a rather spacious room, by jailhouse standards, with soft beds and a TV. We really meshed well. We both have a jovial, friendly, easygoing personality. We sincerely like people and people like us. We love to laugh, always looking for the lighter and funnier side of life. This is not to suggest that we do not take life seriously and that we do not weigh or analyze things carefully. But after saying all of that, we know that life indeed is a mixture of agony and ecstasy, and whoever has found the balance has found serenity and happiness, so long as the balance includes having found something to which they can give themselves, that's bigger than them and that will outlive them.

ALBERT "TOOTIE" HEATH

By ten, eleven, or twelve, I started the drums. I saw Kenny Clarke and Max Roach whenever they came to Philadelphia. Specs Wright, who was from Philly, was one of my main teachers.

From 1947 to 1953, I played locally in Philly with such people as Coltrane, and I was in the house band at the Blue Note, where I played with Thelonious Monk, Slam Stewart, and Beryl Booker, and at the Showboat, where I played with Lester Young, Oscar Pettiford, and Stan Getz. Being Jimmy's brother was to my advantage. Jimmy had more of a reputation than Percy at that time, and a lot of musicians knew Jimmy around Philadelphia and in New York.

When Jimmy was in prison during the fifties, it was a relief from the tension of knowing he was addicted. For my mother, father, and the family, his addiction was a trauma. My parents began to know what was happening after a while, and it got really difficult. It was a relief when Jimmy wasn't in the streets, those people he associated with weren't ringing our doorbell, and he wasn't sick and looking for drugs. Jimmy associated with some people because the only thing they had in common was a drug habit. A lot of the others were musicians. His drug trial was very traumatic, very heavy. He was sentenced to more time than I'd ever heard anybody get. He had six years, concurrent sentences, because he had sold some drugs to a government agent. The police would harass people in the neighborhood. They put him in jail, and while he was in jail, they had this big raid. They didn't kick down our door because he was already in jail.

You're not really yourself when you're addicted to something, but prison stopped all of that. When he was in Lewisburg, we used to go to see him and he had become fat and healthy. The visits to the prison were kind of difficult at first, but then after a while we got used to it. Sometimes my mother, father, sister, and I would all go to visit him. It was about a six-hour drive round trip between Philly and Lewisburg. We went about once every two months, and we also stayed in touch, wrote letters, and sent packages. Percy was in New York at the time, working on his career, and he had his family, so he wasn't really involved in visiting. When Jimmy got out, Percy and I picked him up and Jimmy never looked back.

While Jimmy was in prison, with the help of Cannonball Adderley and Jimmy Bond, a Philadelphia bass player, Jimmy was able to arrange tunes for a whole album of Chet Baker's Playboys. Also, Cannonball told Orrin Keepnews, who started Riverside Records, "This guy in prison, you got to see him, and you got to record him." When Jimmy got out, he started recording for Riverside.

Thursday, May 21, 1959, the day I got out, was a rebirth. I had already made up my mind that I wouldn't use drugs again in my life. From that day, I never touched heroin. I had hurt my mother, my father, and myself and had damaged my career. I wasn't going to do that anymore. It was a clean slate. After degradation, humiliation, and incarceration came regeneration in my life.

I got home the day I was released, after being away four years and five months. There was a coming-home party for me at my parents' house the next day, and that's where I met my wife-to-be, Mona Brown, who had been invited by Tootie. It was like the return of the prodigal son, the one who stumbled and got in trouble. All the family and a few friends filled up the house. I was very shy and quiet. I had been an introverted kind of person anyway, not really gregarious. I found Mona to be a bit standoffish and quiet herself in light of what was happening, but I soon discovered that she was an artist, a sculptor and a painter, who had attended the Rhode Island School of Design and the University of Pennsylvania. I was completely taken by her looks. She lived in proximity of the Showboat and Pep's, which were two important jazz clubs in the city. Mona liked the music and frequently attended club performances in town.

After the day of the party, I asked her if I could stop by and see her sometime. From that point, I started visiting her at her loft on Waverly Street. When she invited me to the loft the first time, it was a strange event. I was shy and so was she. Immediately after that, we started calling each other daily. I realized Mona was a strong-minded, artistic, creative, beautiful person. Who could ask for anything more? We had so much in common; it was the beginning of a sweet song. Mona would also visit me at my mother's house, where the basement was fixed up as a hangout room. Sometimes she would leave our house very late at night, and I would have to call a taxi for her, since we were in a part of town where a white woman wouldn't be seen walking alone around that time of night. My father was curious as to why Mona was interested in me in the first place after learning my history, but my mom, who was very religious, had faith that God would take care of us. The intervals between our meetings got closer and closer, and before we knew it, we were deeply in love. The first song I wrote for her was titled "Waverly Street," which is where she lived. I recorded it with Blue Mitchell in September 1959 for his Riverside album *Blue Soul*. (Blue recorded many of my compositions.) Later I wrote "Mona's Mood" for my own 1960 Riverside release, *Really Big!* Meeting Mona created a feeling of smooth harmony in my life.

In the basement of my parents' house, there were pictures of jazz musicians on the walls, and in the closet were records my mother and father had owned as well as ones I had collected. Mona and I would play albums such as Miles Davis's *Porgy and Bess*, which Tootie had bought. There were a lot of albums that I hadn't heard because I had been away. Often friends and jazz musicians who played at the Showboat would drop by the house for dinner, and Mom would fix the food upstairs. The visitors would go down to the basement, where we would talk, laugh, and tell stories. In later years, people like Horace Silver, Cannonball, Sonny, and Trane stopped by the house when they were in town. In the liner notes I wrote for the Coltrane compilation *The Heavyweight Champion* (1995), I recalled one time when Trane came by the house:

> Much later, when John became famous after "My Favorite Things," he came to the Showboat in Philly. At the matinee he played two-and-a-half hours without stopping. Since he didn't have time to go home to West Philly between sets, I invited him to my mother's house for dinner. When we got there, the food wasn't ready yet. After he spoke to the family, he asked if he could go upstairs and practice until dinner. And he did, knowing he had to play two or more sets that evening!

When I got back home, Tootie had really begun to play well. He had been working and socializing while I was away. Eventually, Tootie moved out and settled in New York, and Mona and I ended up taking his room. Although I had served my time, I was on conditional release, which meant I had to report to the probation officer. A good word had been put in for me at two record companies before I had come home, and I was getting correspondences from Orrin Keepnews of Riverside and Alfred Lion of Blue Note. I had an opportunity to go with either company. Kenny Dorham, Philly Joe Jones, and Cannonball Adderley had given me full endorsements at Riverside. The story I heard was that "Blue Note got Coltrane, so Riverside should get Jimmy." That's what Kenny told Orrin. The money that Blue Note and Riverside were offering was about the same, eight hundred dollars an album as a leader. In 1959, that amount of money was okay. I chose to go with Riverside and made my first recording for the label in 1959.

Orrin Keepnews became almost like a member of the family. He would come to the house in Philly, and my mother and father got to know him. The Riverside record label was like family too. Orrin put up with my restrictions. When I had to record, he would write for permission for me to stay in New York for twenty-four hours. I wrote a song called "24-Hour Leave," recorded by Julian Priester on *Keep Swingin'* (1960).

Orrin was instrumental in my getting a cabaret license. It was very difficult to get a license after you had been arrested; this problem has been publicized in relation to Billie Holiday and Thelonious Monk. A friend of Orrin's father's worked on the State Liquor Authority of New York, and through his help, I was able to get the license. Riverside was a rival of Blue Note, but Blue Note lasted and Riverside didn't. Blue Note recordings are still in existence, and the label is considered one of the important jazz companies. Riverside was important for a period but then went out of business, and Fantasy took over the Riverside catalogue. Riverside didn't have the thrust that the Blue Note organization had. I got in with Riverside right after they had begun, and I was with the company until they folded not long after December 1963. Sometime later I played on a tribute to Orrin at the Monterey Jazz Festival.

After signing with Riverside, I began to work gigs again. When I was offered jobs that took me out of town, I got permission from Mr. Marro, my probation officer. One of my first gigs with someone of international reputation was with Kenny Dorham. We played in a short-lived club called the Diamond Horseshoe Bar way up in North Philly, at Sixth and Germantown Avenue, beginning on June 15, 1959. We were billed in the *Philadelphia Tribune* as "The New, Exciting Kenny Dorham, Jimmy Heath Quintet." I had performed and recorded with Kenny before I had gone to prison, and we had been good friends from that time. That gig with Kenny was the first time that Mona had heard me play with a group, which in this case included on piano McCoy Tyner, who wasn't famous at that time and hadn't yet gone on the road with Trane. Also in the group were drummer Eddie Campbell and bassist Arthur Harper. I played with another group that included Kenny, at the Crystal Caverns in Washington, D.C., which was run by a black man, Tony Taylor. Kenny and I showed up for that gig, but Philly Joe didn't make it. We used a drummer from Washington named Stump Saunders, who ended up playing with Sonny Rollins after Tootie. I really didn't think that much of Stump Saunders's playing.

In June 1959, I got a gig with Gil Evans's big band at the Apollo in New York. Gil needed extra horns to play the show because his usual band had only twelve pieces. The headliner for the show was Dinah Washington, but the bill also included a singing group called The Accidentals and the Thelonious Monk Quintet, a big-name ensemble at that time. The Gil Evans band had Elvin Jones on drums, Ray Crawford on guitar, Bud Johnson on tenor, Lee Konitz on alto, Curtis Fuller on trombone, Eddie Kane on alto and flute, and Tommy Potter, who had played with Charlie Parker, on bass. With Dinah Washington was a Philadelphia woman piano player, Beryl Booker.

CURTIS FULLER

I had the pleasure of meeting Jimmy Heath in Philadelphia in 1959, when I was playing there with Lee Morgan and Tootie Heath. I had asked to meet the family. I was especially interested in meeting Jimmy's father, since my mother was a Heath from Atlanta. I wanted to know if there was any family connection. Jimmy and Mona were soon to be married. I was warmly received by all the Heaths. Later, when Jimmy came back to New York, we worked together and became good friends. We began to rehearse with the Gil Evans Orchestra and played and recorded together. Jimmy helped me with arrangements for recording dates with Freddie Hubbard and Jimmy Cobb. Later we traveled to Europe with the group Jimmy put together: Sam Jones, Stanley Cowell, and Billy Higgins. The band was really out of sight!

We continued working together, traveling together, and recording. I asked Jimmy to be best man at my wedding in July 1981. We are close friends, and I will always admire Jimmy Heath as one of the best saxophonists in the world.

Working with Gil Evans threw me right into the sound I had been hearing when Mona and I were courting, that sound from the *Porgy and Bess* recording. Curtis Fuller soloed on "Summertime" on that beautiful recording that Gil made with Miles. Curtis had an apartment in Manhattan, and he let Mona and me stay there when we played that week at the Apollo.

Shortly after the Apollo engagement, Miles called me from Hollywood, where he was working at the Jazz Seville. He told me that Coltrane was leaving the group. I had known that Coltrane was going to split because he had sent me a postcard dated June 25 from San Francisco telling me that he was going to leave when the group got to L.A. The postcard advertised the club there known as Cousin Jimbo's Bop City. It had a photo of Cousin Jimbo on the reverse side. Trane said, "Hey Jimmy! Remember the fellow on the left? Things haven't changed much out here. Give my regards to the family and I know you all are happy together again—See you soon—Love, Coltrane." Trane knew I had just recently come home, and it was his way of welcoming me back.

Miles wanted me to fly out to L.A. to join him. I consulted with Marro, my probation officer, and everything was cool. Mona and I had been getting closer and closer, and I told her that I would have to go on the road. I flew to California in July to join Miles at the Jazz Seville in Los Angeles. In Miles's band at that time were Cannonball Adderley, Wynton Kelly, Paul Chambers, and Jimmy Cobb. Since coming home from prison, I had become aware of the changes that occurred in the music. Miles had come up with a modal style, but I wasn't that familiar with it. I had no problem with the tunes that had traditional chord changes, such as "On Green Dolphin Street," "Bye Bye Blackbird," or "If I Were a Bell," but I was having a problem with Miles's "So What" because it was a modal tune and my first introduction to the style. I wasn't around when the concept was first being developed.

In modal tunes, there aren't any final endings as in a regular song, where you go through a lot of chord changes and when it gets to the end, it has a definite sound that is familiar to audiences and musicians alike—what we call a dominant seventh, a five chord to the one chord. Modal tunes don't have that pattern. They just stay with the mode. I found it difficult to make a complete musical statement and "get out of it." I wasn't the only one who had this problem. Coltrane, who was also playing modal compositions, had to decide on a good musical ending when he played in that style. One of the reasons Trane kept playing chorus after chorus was that, as he himself said, he "could not find anything good to stop on." I had the same problem because of the modes. Eventually Trane solved that problem through continuous practice, and the rest is history. Of course, I eventually became more comfortable with the modal concept, but at that time it was very confusing. I asked Miles, "How do you play on that Dorian mode in 'So What' and make some sense out of it?" He would say, "That ain't nothing. All you do is play all the white keys on the outside and all the black keys on the bridge." This sounds very simplistic, but it's a fact. When Sonny Stitt was in the band, he would play a D minor seventh all the time on "So What," and Miles didn't like that. Sonny tried to play it like any other tune, where you would play on all the white keys, but in those situations, you wouldn't play in D minor all the time, although the bass was playing a D minor type of bass line. The other chords on the top could be anything on the white keys: a D minor chord, an F Lydian, a G dominant seventh, an A minor seventh, or a B half-diminished seventh, all in the key of C. Consequently, when Miles and Trane played "So What," they found different lines, a different sound. They had a different concept, and it didn't sound like other tunes. Miles got the credit for initially playing the modal-type songs because of "So What." He is credited in most of the books dealing with post-bop. Somebody might have started doing it before him — it could have been an Ahmad Jamal influence — but I don't know of a song that came before "So What" written in the modal style.

Miles was the type of musician who wanted to take the music in a different direction. From the time I first met him, he was always a true Gemini, a person who is very changeable. His musical concept kept changing up until he passed away. Other musicians stuck with proven ways of playing and became famous for playing a certain way, such as Illinois Jacquet, who was a wonderful musician and great player, but he never made any real changes in his music, unlike Miles.

Trane got deep into the modal style and later wrote "Impressions," built on the same pattern. The challenge was there for him, and that was his thing. If he had a challenge, he would jump on it. For me, I tried to meet the challenge when I was with Miles, but I've written only a couple of songs in the modal style since then, "A Sound for Sore Ears" and "Far Away Lands." Modal playing was a unique movement in music, but it's not my favorite. I'm still a chordal person who likes to play a lot of different changes. There's an ongoing question about modal playing: If you play in the modes, can you get as many variations out of it as you can off the changes? That's still an "open sky," as Ornette Coleman would say. The music is still open to that as far as which is more challenging. I was impressed by the modal sound, but I didn't want to go in that direction because I was uncomfortable with it. I didn't stay with Miles long enough to get comfortable with it.

While we were at the Jazz Seville, Paul Chambers, Wynton Kelly, Jimmy Cobb, and I were staying at the Vine Lodge. Miles stayed somewhere else. I kept in close touch with Mona and would call her all the time. Cannonball Adderley was at the Vine Lodge for a while, but he moved up to Doris Duke's house with the pianist Joe Castro, who was a friend of hers. Doris, who has since passed away, was the heiress to a big tobacco fortune in North Carolina and was the richest woman in America for a long period. One day I went to her place with Cannonball and Castro. I'd never been to such an exclusive area before, and I was really impressed by it.

Several things happened at the Vine Lodge that showed me that racism was alive. On one occasion, Paul Chambers, a very handsome person to whom women gravitated, was in the swimming pool with some white women he had gotten involved with. A group of marines who were also staying at the hotel started making remarks about Paul and the women. There was a lot of arguing and hollering, but it never reached the point of a brawl because Jimmy Cobb, a strong guy and a karate expert, came to Paul's defense. The marines had made some racial remarks about Paul, referring to the women and the "nigger" in the swimming pool. In response, Wynton and I went out and bought some lye. We were getting ready for the marines in case they wanted to start a fight. We put the lye and some water in an aluminum pot and hid it in the shower stall. The fight never materialized because the marines eventually left. Jimmy and Paul were pretty hefty guys, and they were ready to go to war if necessary. Wynton and I went to see what had happened with the lye. When we picked up the pot, the bottom just fell out. We wouldn't have been much help in a fight.

I worked with Miles in California for two or three weeks. Then Miles flew to Chicago, where his next gig was and where he had relatives. Cannonball had a 1959 Cadillac Fleetwood, so we drove back from L.A. to Chicago. Jimmy did most of the driving. After we had driven about twelve hours, we stopped to eat near Chicago. Then Cannonball took over the driving into Chicago. It was raining and Cannonball, who was a diabetic, went into a nod behind the wheel. The Cadillac spun on the highway and woke up Jimmy and me.

Jimmy said, "Cannon! What you doing?"

With a dazed look, Cannon said, "I was meditating."

Jimmy said, "Well, meditate in the back!" Jimmy took over and drove the rest of the way. Cannonball almost got us all killed that day. If it had been a two-lane highway instead of four, we probably would have been history.

When we got to Chicago, we played at the Regal Theater. Cannonball, Wynton Kelly, and I were roommates in Chicago. Wynton was a fiery performer and an alcoholic, but even though he drank, he could still play. You could wake Wynton up in the middle of the night and he would be able to play with that same intensity and fire. He was an incredible person who had a real sense of humor, and we got on very well. I was still in the process of catching up with music, the complex arrangements, and the up-tempo speeds, so we discussed the songs in the repertoire. Reharmonization of the changes—superimposition of chords on top of chords—had been introduced in earlier years and was now in full blossom. Although I had the foundation to all of that, I hadn't been able to follow through because I had been off the scene. As a close friend and confidant, Wynton was someone with whom I could discuss the new harmonies and other aspects of the music. Miles was very astute about harmony and had been showing Wynton a number of things. Miles knew what he wanted to hear and what he wanted left out. He would tell Wynton what he really wanted.

We did a week at the Regal starting on July 24, 1959, playing two or three shows a day. We were staying at the South Central Hotel, which was around the corner from the Regal, and we could walk to the show. When Paul Chambers took a solo, the audience related to him a lot. People would holler, "I hear you, Paul." Paul was a very fine bass soloist, but he, too, was a heavy drinker. Sometimes when Paul was drunk, Miles would look at him and call the tune "So What" just to make Paul, who had the bass line, stumble. Sometimes Miles would even call the tune much faster to challenge Paul. Then Miles would say, "Okay, Paul. When we finish, I'm going to take you to get something to eat." Miles would get the food and say, "Eat that food. Eat it." Paul would eat just like a little baby.

At the hotel, Paul was like a kid in a candy store; he would go to the bar and say, "Give me some of that and some of that." I haven't seen anyone do that before or since. As an artist, Paul was a great musician, but as a person, he had weaknesses like anyone else. Wynton could control his drinking but Paul couldn't. Jimmy Cobb was a clean-cut guy. Miles was the "star," so he didn't hang with the guys until we were on stage. Miles wasn't drinking or on drugs at this time. I never liked the effects of alcohol because it made me dense. I couldn't function technically under its influence, so I didn't bother with it. I would drink a little bit when I wasn't working. I was in touch with Mona the whole time, and I missed her.

After Chicago, on August 2, 1959, we played a concert in French Lick, Indiana, the French Lick Jazz Festival, and there Miles stayed in the same hotel as we did. When we were walking together on the grounds of the festival, someone came up and said, "Mr. Davis, can we take a picture?" Miles said, "Yeah. If you catch me walking." Miles's stature had increased since I first met him in 1952. His response to people had changed too—not that I blamed him for his attitude, because people will heckle musicians at times. They often don't give you the freedom to be a regular person. You always have to be on stage as far as they are concerned, giving autographs or posing for photographs. Miles didn't like that, so he would wisecrack. People thought he was a nasty guy but he really wasn't. He was just on the defensive. I was ready to have my picture taken, but it wasn't important to Miles. Miles went through a change when he became a celebrity.

After French Lick, I was supposed to play the Playboy Festival in Chicago with Miles. I called my probation officer, Mr. Marro, and told him that we had a gig in Chicago on the weekend. He told me casually that when I got back to Philly, I should drop by the office before going back out on the road. Since I had time off, I went back to Philly and saw Mona. When I went to see Mr. Marro, he told me that the people in Washington, D.C.—he blamed it on higher-ups—said I had to remain within a fifty- or sixty-mile radius of Philadelphia.

I said, "I got the best job I ever had in my life. I'm making a lot of money, five or six hundred dollars a week. You're cutting me off from making my livelihood." Miles paid better than the average band.

He said, "I can't do anything about it." He had just given me permission before without checking, and now he found out that he shouldn't have—at least that's what he said. I had been arrested twice for drugs, but I had been clean since then.

Miles was very disappointed, but he had friends in Philly; one was a magistrate, another was a police sergeant. They tried to go to bat for me because I couldn't go back to Chicago and join Miles for the next gig of the tour. This was like double jeopardy to me. I had served all of my time—four years, five months. Now I had a job, an opportunity to be with one of the best bands in the land and in the world, and I couldn't go. I was being penalized for my past. Miles tried everybody he knew with authority in Philadelphia, but no luck. That's how I lost the gig with Miles at that time, but I was back with him again on October 21, 1960, for a gig at the Regal Theater in Chicago, where I replaced Sonny Stitt. The Miles Davis Sextet was the headliner, but also on the bill were the Ike Isaacs Trio, the Modern Jazz Quartet (MJQ), and Lambert, Hendricks, and Ross. We were billed as "The Greatest Assemblage of Award Winning Jazz Stars! On Stage! Year's Biggest Jazz Spectacular!" It was good to see my brother Percy, who was with the MJQ. The emcee was Dick Gregory, an up-and-coming comedian in Chicago at that time. He wasn't an activist then, just a comedian. Percy and I hung out one night at a club where Dick was working.

Wynton Kelly and I also did a record date for Vee-Jay in Chicago in 1960 with Vernice "Bunky" Green, an alto player from the city who later taught at the University of North Florida and was president of the International Association for Jazz Education. Donald Byrd was in Chicago at that time, and Bunky put a group together with Donald, Jimmy Cobb, Wynton, Larry Ridley, and me. The record was re-released under Donald's name because he became more famous than Bunky. My own first record, *The Thumper*, had been recorded the previous year with Wynton, Paul, Tootie, Nat Adderley, and Curtis.

6

On the Riverside

■

Since I had signed with Riverside Records earlier in 1959, I was allowed to go to New York that fall to record my first album, *The Thumper.* I took a letter from my probation officer to Orrin Keepnews at Riverside, and he signed it to show that I had been in New York. Since I had played with Wynton Kelly and Paul Chambers and they were available for doing sideman dates around the city, I asked them to be on it. I wanted to feature a sextet so that I could show some of my arranging skills. I had Nat Adderley on cornet, Curtis Fuller on trombone, Wynton on piano, Paul on bass, and my brother Tootie on drums. Nat and his brother Cannonball had been connected with Riverside Records, so Nat was a natural choice. Curtis was a known talent who had also become a good friend of mine since our gig at the Apollo with Gil Evans in June of that year. I had written quite a few originals for the session, including "For Minors Only, "Two Tees" (dedicated to Tootie), "The Thumper," and "Newkeep" (dedicated to Orrin Keepnews). The title "The Thumper" refers to swinging hard with the rhythm section, thumping.

ORRIN KEEPNEWS

Kenny Dorham and a couple of other musicians gave me the impression that Jimmy was a very remarkable player and somebody who clearly had managed to overcome his earlier substance problems. During the course of our first conversation, I became very impressed with this cool, together, levelheaded young man. One of the most interesting things about my first conversation with Jimmy was that he placed a lot of emphasis on having an outlet for his arranging. I decided I was going to sign a contract with him and commit myself to two albums. I could put together dates for him with some of the top young players on the scene at that time. My rhythm sections were already on a Wynton Kelly/Philly Joe Jones–type level. Jimmy's first date for Riverside was The Thumper, recorded November 27, 1959, in New York.

I had recorded the newly formed Cannonball Adderley Quintet, the live date at the Jazz Workshop, which turned out to be a flaming jazz hit record and which was really what put the label on the map. Jimmy joined us at what turned out to be the beginning of a very hot period for Riverside. Our activity accelerated a great deal at that point. Jimmy had this extremely close relationship with the Adderleys; among other things, they lived in the same co-op in Queens.

Jimmy definitely did have a meeting with Alfred Lion at Blue Note, which had a heavier reputation than we did. The conversation Jimmy had with Alfred must have been similar to the one he had with me, except that Alfred apparently was not willing to give him assurances of being able to write.

Jimmy was an impressively pulled-together guy and what he wrote was well constructed. You could almost hear the thoughts that were involved. His arranging skills were there. He very clearly had that freshness, that daring that was characteristic of the music at that time. I thought of Jimmy immediately as an outstanding example of what was going on in that period.

While on probation, Jimmy needed to get written permission to travel more than fifty miles from Philadelphia. The problem was that Jimmy had to get to New York for recording purposes. I was informed that I was supposed to write a letter every time he needed to be up there. I just got aggravated. The concept bothered the hell out of me. I knew it was necessary for him to be granted that permission in order to fulfill the conditions of a legally binding contract, but I didn't at all like the idea of having to ask for permission. I was told that I was supposed to say that "his presence is requested," and what I insisted on writing was "his presence is required" in New York for the recording. It may have been a small point, but it was important to me. Jimmy was an American citizen with a business obligation, not just a guy on probation who could be kicked around.

Jimmy Heath sessions were always easy ones because the music was prepared, and the leader took care of business in the studio. The biggest problem children that I had were bass players and drummers, but with Jimmy there wasn't any problem because whenever possible, it was Tootie and/or Percy on Jimmy's dates. Jimmy Heath sessions were about professionalism.

You have to be knowledgeable to appreciate Jimmy's kind of jazz talent. He's the opposite of flamboyant and colorful. His professionalism sometimes makes you forget that he is an extremely talented, imaginative, and creative jazz musician. Jimmy Heath sessions seemed kind of effortless because of the tremendous amount of effort he put into preparing for them.

Jimmy had an impact on a lot of the musicians he worked with, and his students became more important in later years. He brought a sense of professionalism and stability to his associations with colleagues and friends that is so much at variance with the general cliché picture of the wild, colorful jazz musician. Jimmy was looked on by his contemporaries as a mentor, as a guide, and as a rock, a source of stability. Cannonball had a great appreciation for Jimmy, and he had a lot of success with his sextet performing Jimmy's tune "Gemini." One of the things Cannonball loved about "Gemini" was that it was a very dramatic performance tune. A great ensemble section was played between solos and that really whipped up the audiences. On the record, you can hear that reaction to the song. Cannonball was fascinated by the fact that Jimmy was a damn good, clever, exciting jazz writer and at the same time took care of business. Without being anything other than a contemporary, he was in a certain aesthetic way a father figure to a lot of the people he worked with.

Jimmy was involved in Milt Jackson's sextet recording Invitation [1963] with Kenny Dorham, Tommy Flanagan, and Ron Carter. It's also a wonderful example of Jimmy writing for other people because K.D. and Jimmy did all the writing on that album. There's such a wonderful spirit to it, and the performance level is so high. It was part of the Riverside scene. There was a feeling of relationship between the musicians. On Jimmy's Really Big! [1960], some of the musicians took part not because I called them for it but because they told me that they insisted on being on the date. Cannonball had become a big star by that point, and he's on that album because he said he wouldn't think of letting me use anybody else. The two trumpets, Clark Terry and Nat Adderley, were not necessarily your usual sidemen. That's a wonderful example of the Riverside community, people putting themselves out for other people. It wasn't about making money. It was an exceptionally good thing, and the Adderleys and Jimmy were at the center of that Riverside family.

This period was when I first started doing "dedications"—meaning I would dedicate songs to people I liked and thought worthy, whether family members or professional people that I dug—and it's something I continued throughout my career. "Nice People," one of the originals on the album, was dedicated to all the people in the world who treat you nicely. Sometimes it seems as if there are fewer "nice people" and more of the others. They both know who they are. "Nice People" was a kind of humanistic title. "For Minors Only" had been smuggled out of Lewisburg and recorded by Chet Baker. The title was a pun on young people and the minor key, a dual connection. "Who Needs It?" was based on a lick that Wynton used to play all the time. It was also an expression that Wynton and I used in response to things. It was a humorous inside line that Wynton and I would often say to each other. "Who Needs It?" was written at the record date, but "The Thumper," "Newkeep," "Two Tees," and "Nice People" were written earlier that year. "For Minors Only" was written prior to the rest. Also on the recording were a number of standards, such as the Ellington composition "Don't You Know I Care?" Throughout my recording career, I have tried to record an Ellington or a Billy Strayhorn composition on just about every release under my name. Also on the album was "For All We Know," which I chose because of Gloria Lynne's having made a popular recording of it. My father was a big Gloria Lynne fan. "I Can Make You Love Me" was a song sung by Sarah Vaughan on an early recording. I was very satisfied with my first record, and so was Keepnews. "The Thumper" was released separately as a 45 and was played on jukeboxes.

Starting my recording career was like sailing on a dreamboat down a beautiful river. I felt good about having signed a recording contract, but not so good about the restrictions that were put on me by my probation. I had to wait nine months before I was released from those, around early 1960. By this time Mona and I had become very close, and we were talking about getting married. After my first record, Orrin assigned me as one of the staff arrangers for Riverside. I was writing songs and arrangements for a lot of different bands and playing on different dates. I wrote "24-Hour Leave," which was on a Julian Priester album, *Keep Swingin'*, released January 11, 1960, with Elvin Jones on drums, Sam Jones on bass, Tommy Flanagan on piano, and me on tenor. Musicians would ask Orrin to get me for a date, whether it was Nat Adderley, Sam Jones, Blue Mitchell, or other cats who had signed with Riverside, which was in competition with Blue Note.

This was around the time when rock 'n' roll was really taking off, and in February 1960 I played a show in Philly with Thomas "Beans" Bowles that combined rock with jazz. The February 20, 1960, *Philadelphia Tribune* headline read, "Jimmy Heath, 'Beans' Bowles Jazz-Up Rock 'n Roll Show." Donald Porter, who reviewed the event, said "Heath, a localite, playing lead tenor with the Bill Massey orchestra, treated most of his 16-bar solos with the style most endeared to him while keeping in range of the rock 'n roll trend." I could hear where Beans Bowles was going with his sound, and the reviewer picked up on it too: "Bowles, a native Detroiter, who once fronted his own jazz combo, was almost all rock 'n roll on baritone sax but became daring on flute and went well into the jazz vein" (p. 5). Beans Bowles became a Motown section player and a legend in his own right. He composed for Stevie Wonder and was later chairperson of the Graystone International Jazz Museum.

Eventually Mona and I decided to get married. When I told Marro that I had met someone and we wanted to get married, he said, "That's a wonderful idea. I'm so glad to hear that. She'll be a stabilizing influence." He said that he'd like to see her. When Marro heard the name Mona Brown, he assumed that she was black. When Mona went in to meet him, Marro tried to discourage her from marrying me because of my criminal background and for racial reasons, but it was to no avail. We got married on February 4, 1960, in my parents' living room in Philadelphia. My mother's minister married us, Reverend Banner of the Nineteenth Street Baptist Church. My friends and those of my mother, father, and Mona were there; one of my childhood neighbors, Perry Gordon, took the pictures. Perry lived across the street from my mother's beauty parlor at Twenty-first and Garrett.

My brother Percy had already married interracially when I was with Dizzy in 1950. My interracial marriage was and wasn't a problem. My parents were nervous because they figured that since I had been in prison, Mona couldn't be serious about marrying me. They thought it would only lead to another problem for me to overcome. My father wondered why Mona wanted to marry me. He wasn't sure if she was serious. Mona stopped working at the University Museum after we got married.

MONA HEATH

Jimmy and I are an odd couple. Albert introduced us the day Jimmy came home, Thursday, May 21, 1959. Before that, I never knew there was a Jimmy Heath.

As a child, my best friend next door, Mary Ann Locke, was a cello player. Her mother was our school music teacher, and I loved to listen to Mary Ann practice. We both took piano lessons, but my piano playing was never "music." We sang in choirs in church and in high school. Our choir director, Benjamin Censullo, was the best teacher I ever had.

A year after graduating from high school in 1951 and working in an art-layout design shop, I convinced my father that I should go to art school. The Rhode Island School of Design was my choice, and being the only girl in the architecture department was very interesting. Many of the art teachers were musicians, and they would play traditional jazz on weekends at a club downtown. All their students would show up. My friend Nancy was from Boston, and we would go to the museums and clubs there. We saw Sarah Vaughan and Oscar Peterson with Ray Brown and Ed Thigpen more than once! On my train rides home for the holidays, I would get off in New York City or Philly and go to the museums, the ballet, and Birdland because there was so much going on in the art world and the music world in the fifties. I was doing very well in school and I loved Providence. Then my father said, "You're going to transfer to the University of Pennsylvania." "What?" I said! "They'll never accept me." But they did. I was so angry and heartbroken about leaving Rhode Island.

After two and a half years of struggle with the School of Architecture and the Fine Arts Department at Penn, I realized my father had done me a favor, and I hadn't even met Jimmy yet. It was a miracle that my friend Pat and I graduated in January 1957.

My sculpture teacher, Jim House, recommended me to a team of archeologists working on the ruins of Tikal. My job was to draw the stelae and glyphs that they photographed in the jungles of Guatemala so that they could study them further and publish them. I loved working in the museum in Philadelphia and living with the fantastic collections of art in every room.

Philadelphia had three clubs that we could go to: Peps, the Showboat, and the Blue Note on Ridge Avenue. We were in music heaven. We saw Miles, Max, Clifford, Sonny, Bud Powell, Duke, Dizzy, and our favorite, Count Basie. My best friend from Penn, Alan Mitosky, was a very talented sculptor. We shared a carriage house on Waverly Street. The top-floor space had been a hayloft. It was totally empty, with skylights and room for both of us to have our own private studios. I could walk to work at the Museum, and the Showboat and Peps were two or three blocks away. Perfect!

■ Dizzy Gillespie Orchestra (collage), Apollo Theater, December 1949. *Top row, left to right:* Tiny Irvin (vocalist), Jesse Powell (tenor sax), John Coltrane (alto sax), Jimmy Heath (alto sax), Specs Wright (drums), Paul Gonsalves (tenor sax), Al Gibson (baritone sax), Joe "Bebop" Carroll (vocalist), and Dizzy Gillespie (trumpet; leader). *Center, left to right:* Jesse Powell, John Coltrane, Jimmy Heath, Specs Wright, Paul Gonsalves, Al Gibson, and Don Slaughter (hidden; trumpet). *Lower right, left to right:* unknown (hidden; trumpet), Charles Greenlee (trombone), Elmon Wright (trumpet), and Sam Hurt (trombone). (Photo by Gordon Anderson, Jimmy Heath Collection)

■ Jimmy and his son James (Mtume), Federal Street, Philadelphia, circa 1950. (Jimmy Heath Collection, photographer unknown)

■ Dizzy Gillespie Sextet, Club Oasis, Western Boulevard, Los Angeles, California, summer 1950. *Left to right:* Milt Jackson (vibes; piano), Jimmy Heath (alto sax), Percy Heath (hidden; bass), Specs Wright (hidden; drums), Dizzy Gillespie (trumpet), John Coltrane (tenor sax), and unknown (conga). (Jimmy Heath Collection, photographer unknown)

■ Symphony Sid All-Stars (collage), Apollo Theater, New York, summer 1952. *Clockwise, upper left to right:* Kenny Clarke (drums), Percy Heath (bass), J. J. Johnson (trombone), Symphony Sid, Jimmy Heath (tenor sax), J. J. Johnson, Milt Jackson (vibes), and Miles Davis (trumpet). *Center, left to right:* Percy Heath and Jimmy Heath. (Photo by Gordon Anderson, Jimmy Heath Collection)

■ *Facing page:* Jam session, Bop City, San Francisco, California, 1950. *Top, left to right:* Roy Porter, Specs Wright, Bernie Peters, Jimbo Edwards (club manager), Betty Bennett (vocalist), unknown (hidden; bass), Kenny Dorham, Miles Davis, and Howard Jeffries. *Middle, left to right:* Ernie Lewis, Sonny Criss, Pat (drums), Dizzy Gillespie (piano), and Percy Heath. *Bottom, left to right:* Milt Jackson, Carl Perkins, Jimmy Heath, Henry "Cowboy" Noyd, and Oyama Johnson. (Frank Driggs Collection)

■ Symphony Sid All-Stars, Graystone Ballroom, Detroit, summer 1952. *Left to right*: J. J. Johnson (trombone), Miles Davis (trumpet), and Jimmy Heath (tenor sax). (Jimmy Heath Collection, photographer unknown)

■ Miles Davis All-Stars session, WOR Studios, New York, April 20, 1953. *Left to right*: Miles Davis, Kenny Drew, Art Blakey, and Jimmy Heath. (Courtesy of Michael Cuscuna)

■ Lewisburg Prison Inmates Ensemble, Lewisburg Penitentiary, Lewisburg, Pennsylvania, circa 1958. *Left to right*: Supples (baritone sax), Joe Ritter (vocalist), unknown (alto sax), Jimmy Heath (flute; leader), unknown (drums), Joe Kingston (guitar), unknown (bass), and unknown (piano). (Jimmy Heath Collection, photographer unknown)

■ Gil Evans Band (collage), Apollo Theater, New York, June 1959. *Clockwise from upper left:* Dinah Washington (vocalist), Symphony Sid, Jimmy Heath (tenor sax), Thelonious Monk (piano), The Accidentals (vocalists), Gil Evans (leader), unknown tap dancer, accompanying tap dancer (one of Dinah Washington's sons, either George or Bobby), Beryl Booker (piano), and Gil Evans Band. *Center:* Jimmy Heath (tenor sax). (Photo by Gordon Anderson, Jimmy Heath Collection)

■ Jimmy and Mona's wedding day, 1927 Federal Street, Philadelphia, February 4, 1960. *Left to right*: Jimmy Heath, Mona Heath, Arlethia Heath, and Percy Heath, Sr.

(Photo by Perry Gordon, Jimmy Heath Collection)

■ Mona and Roslyn on Federal Street, Philadelphia, 1962

(Jimmy Heath Collection, photographer unknown)

■ Family photo, Dorie Miller Co-op, Corona, Queens, New York, 1964. *Left to right*: Mona, Jimmy, Jeffrey, and (in front) Roslyn.

(Photo by George W. Martin III)

When Albert brought Jimmy to my studio on his first day home, he invited me to the welcome-home party for Jimmy the next night. I think Jimmy was in shock; he didn't say a word. We began to see each other often and speak on the phone daily at lunchtime. I brought my records to play in his parents' basement. The one Jimmy fell in love with was Miles's Porgy and Bess album with Gil Evans's arrangements. We were getting closer all the time.

Jimmy got a call from Gil Evans to play in New York at the Apollo Theater, and I went to visit him. He was staying with Curtis Fuller. Jimmy's friends had gotten word he was home, and a few weeks later Miles called. He wanted Jimmy to come to California because Coltrane was leaving. When he left to go with Miles, I knew that I wouldn't see him again soon. But the probation officer ordered him to come back, and Jimmy was very angry and hurt. That's when we got really close. He knew he would have to avoid situations that could get him in trouble again, and he had decided that he wanted to get married. I knew that Jimmy was an artist and that I could help him; besides we were madly in love.

By the end of the year, we had decided to get married. We told our families. Mine said, "Goodbye, don't come back." Jimmy's mother said, "Fine," and called her preacher. We were married February 4, 1960, in the living room with Jimmy's family and Mama's friends helping us celebrate. We moved into Tootie's room with the black ceiling and stars painted above. Federal Street was a community that cared for everybody on the block. I learned everything I needed to know in the kitchen with Mama while washing dishes and listening to the family stories.

In 1964, when we moved to the Dorie Miller Co-op in Queens on Fourth of July weekend, Cannonball and Clark Terry welcomed us. They introduced us to all their friends. Our two children instantly made friends, and it was a very good move on our part. The co-op was built by Adam Clayton Powell, Jr., and it was managed by very proud veterans who were determined to live well—and we all did. There were artists, socialists, teachers, musicians, lawyers, corporate executives and business owners, mostly black, and a few white and interracial couples. We started with very little but were able to pay our rent, raise our children, and travel together. Dorie Miller is still home.

When Mona and I sat on the front steps of my parents' house on Federal Street, sometimes the police would slow up and stare. One time they approached her and said, "You all right, Miss?" Things like that would happen.

Our marriage was the start of my life as a family man. When I was away in prison, one of the things I decided to do when I got out was to settle down, get married and start a family. Getting married was a way of protecting myself from that other life. There were a couple of other interracial couples in Philadelphia that I knew; Joe Bay, who wasn't a musician, and Shrimpy Anderson, who was a musician, were married to white women. There weren't a lot of interracial marriages, but people were doing it. In the sixties, interracial relationships involving jazz musicians were becoming more prevalent. The bebop or progressive era had been one of mixing; the music was really intellectual and whites and blacks gravitated to it. The environment was such that white women and musicians could get together. Miles, Charlie Parker, Fats Navarro, Howard McGhee, Benny Harris, Tadd Dameron, Coleman Hawkins, and Charles Mingus were all involved in interracial relationships. Although I was in Philly, I was still into the same kind of musical environment that lent itself to social mixing. There were interracial relationships in the other direction too. Gil Evans, George Wein, and other white musicians were involved with black women. It was socially acceptable in the bebop community, and it was also part of the internationalism of the music.

White women of various backgrounds got interested in jazz. One of the most famous of these was the "Baroness," Nica de Koenigswarter, daughter of the British financier Charles Rothschild, who came to the States around 1951; she was interested in the beboppers and assisted many of them financially. Even in Philly, white women such as Percy's wife, June, were interested in the music. Often it was the Jewish women who hung with the bebop musicians in Philly. June, who wasn't Jewish, was from Tifton, Georgia, where there were lots of crackers. Jewish guys also liked the music. Ziggy Vines, a very good saxophone player, tried to make it with my sister.

During my conditional release period, in early 1960, I was asked to play in a Ray Charles concert in Philly as part of an opening group. The gig was presented by two progressive brothers, Marcus Brown and Charlie Blackwell, an amateur drummer. The venue was the Academy of Music. Jimmy Oliver, one of Philly's favorite saxophonists, and I had been busted before, and so had Ray. A couple of crooked detectives on the narc squad jammed the promoters before the gig, saying they could take Ray, Jimmy, and me downtown for an investigation and stop the concert even if we were clean. So the promoters had to give them some money. After the concert, which was huge, they told Ray about the bribe. Of course, Ray demanded his full salary and Marcus and Charlie had to swallow the bribe. This was my first meeting with Ray, to whom I was introduced just before he went on.

After moving to New York in 1964, another alumni from my big band, Johnny Coles, along with Blue Mitchell, for whose Riverside dates I had composed and arranged, joined Ray's band. They knew Ray was looking for some big band arrangements so they recommended me. Ray commissioned me to do a couple charts for him. I did "A Time and a Place" (also titled "The Time and the Place") and "Togetherness," two original instrumentals that he would use before he began to sing his hits. He paid me five hundred dollars each, and I delivered them to him at Butler Aviation in Queens, where he kept his plane. Ray recorded the two tunes on his label, but I never received any royalties. Many years later, around 1992, while on tour with the "Diz with Love" group in Germany, we opened for Ray. Since Dizzy had been ill, Ray said he wanted to do a tribute to him. He asked Slide Hampton and me if we would do some arrangements. After returning home, we got a three-way call from Ray, still offering us five hundred dollars. Slide told me to talk to him, and he got off the phone. I ended up telling him I was busy too. He was stuck on five hundred dollars. The last time I saw Ray was when the Heath Brothers opened for him in Italy at an outdoor festival in a place called Lago Maggiore, possibly in the summer of 2002. My grandniece Brette, who married David Mayernik, an architect and professor at Notre Dame, was there at the concert.

My writing for Riverside picked up in 1960 after I got married. I would go to New York by train for the day and stay in a hotel overnight because I couldn't be gone for longer than twenty-four hours. When I was in New York for those sessions, I stayed away from the guys I'd been hanging out with before, such as Philly Joe and others who I knew were heroin users. In March 1960, I recorded with a number of the Riverside artists under the name *The Soul Society*, with Sam Jones as the headliner, with Nat Adderley, Blue Mitchell, and Bobby Timmons. Also on that recording were Charles Davis, Keter Betts, and Louis Hayes. Part of the record was recorded on March 8, 1960, and another part on March 10. I contributed one original composition, "All Members," and an arrangement of the standard "Just Friends." "All Members" was inspired by our all being members of the "Soul Society." This was the real beginning of my arranging and composing for others on the Riverside label. My Riverside days were recognized by jazz critic Ira Gitler, who, in a December 1971 *BMI* article, commented on that time:

Most central to establishing Heath's importance as a composer-arranger and player were a series of Riverside recordings, taped under his leadership almost a decade ago. Since then he has continued to grow by not abandoning the past and remaining ever open to contemporary development. (p. 8)

After *The Soul Society,* my second album, *Really Big!* was scheduled for the studio on June 24 and 28 of 1960, but before that my daughter, Roslyn, came into the world on June 17. She was born under the sign of Gemini, so this sparked me to write a song for her titled "Gemini," which Cannonball recorded. The song became a pretty big hit, selling around eighty thousand albums. Roslyn was my second child, since I had a son with Bert Preston, James, who later changed his name to Mtume. Roslyn was born at the University of Pennsylvania Hospital, where Mona had been part of a new program involving induced labor through injection—but Mona never needed that. I think she got so scared that she said, "I'm going to have this baby before I get the needle."

MONA

I went into the hospital on Thursday night at seven o'clock, and my doctor was supposed to induce labor. He had told me earlier in my pregnancy that when I was completely ready and convinced the baby was going to come, he would try to schedule it so that I would not have to rush to the hospital. Jimmy's mother had said, "Who does this doctor think he is, God? Does he think he can tell you when the baby is supposed to come?" I had an appointment to go in on Thursday, June 16, and Roslyn was born at 8:00 A.M. on Friday morning before the doctor got there. Another physician did the delivery because the timing was so perfect that there was no need to induce labor. She arrived right on schedule and was completely normal. It was not a long or difficult labor, but I was terrified. They did give me anesthesia. I was part of a program being designed for wealthy pregnant women who wanted to know the precise time of their deliveries. These clients did not like any brinkmanship. They wanted to be able to plan. I had X-rays and my doctor knew almost exactly when the birth was supposed to occur naturally. This program was for the convenience of the patient and the doctor.

They called Jimmy at home in the morning and said, "Your baby is here." Jimmy and his mother came to see me after I woke up. Later that year, in the fall, Jimmy's father, Pop, had a heart attack, but he was still able to walk and do for himself. Pop was very independent, and for him to stay in the house without driving everybody crazy was a big deal. He used to stand on the corner, hanging out with his friends. When Roslyn was just an infant, we put her in the bed with Pop, and he had to watch her. Pop felt she was his baby. This kept him occupied and at home after his heart attack. It worked well in that way. When she got older, he taught her numbers and ABCs. The baby came along just at the time when he needed a diversion.

Jimmy's mother was wonderful too. Pop and Mama both fell in love with Roslyn, so that made it easier for them to tolerate Jimmy and me. Jimmy's mother had a habit of adopting people. When I moved into the house, there were always other people there, such as Tootie's girlfriend, Marlene. She would come down and see Mama even though Tootie had moved to New York. Marlene was in the house all the time, and she became one of my best friends. She liked to be in the kitchen helping Mama with whatever she was doing. The nieces, Gwen and Beth, were there a lot too. It was a house where you never felt self-conscious because there were always other people in and out. I would also help Mama do this and that. Jimmy and I were trying to contribute to the household. It was like a co-op thing. Our son, Jeffrey, was born September 1963. By the time he was nine months old and crawling up the steps, Pop could not deal with it. He said, "Boy. We can't have it. We can't have him going up those steps by himself. He's going to fall down from the top of the steps and kill himself." We realized it was time to move. We couldn't afford it, but before that we lived as a family in Jimmy's parents' house.

When I saw Roslyn, I just thought, "What a beautiful baby." I was very proud. This was my first experience of being a father where I had to live the experience. There were three bedrooms in my parents' house, and Roslyn made our living together more pleasant for Mom and Pop because they could spend a lot of time with Roz. Pop treated her like a queen when she was growing up. When Roslyn fell down the front steps one time, Pop said, "Why in the hell did you let that child hurt herself?"

I had to take that kind of stuff from Pop. I said, "Pop, I couldn't catch her." Pop went off because nothing was supposed to happen to Roslyn. I was around when she first talked and walked. Christmas of 1961, I bought an eight-millimeter movie camera and took a lot of films of her with her toy kitchen set. Pop would say, "Roslyn, get me some coffee," and Roslyn would get her little tiny coffee cups, open her toy refrigerator, and bring Pop what he asked for. Mom and Pop really had fun with Roslyn, and so did Mona and I. I hadn't been around Mtume when he was growing up, so this was my first real close relationship with one of my children. At that time, Bert was living with her mother and I was living with mine. While Mtume was an infant, I had been on the road with Dizzy, and that was another reason why I didn't have a close relationship with my first son when he was a baby. But Roslyn was close to all our hearts; when we lived with Mom and Pop, it was a co-op thing. I would pay half of this and that because I was earning money gigging around Philly and recording. We stayed at my parents' house until July 1964. Nine months after my second son, Jeffrey, was born, we could afford to move.

MTUME

I was raised by James Forman, the keyboard player from out of Philly, who I called Dad or Pops, but my biological father is Jimmy Heath, who I later named Tayari. Tayari means "ready," and it gives strength like a father has. I'm a pretty strong dude so you know I came from him. His great-grandchildren call him Pop-Pop Tayari. Tayari and I hung out a little bit when I was a kid, but Tayari was incarcerated when I was about six. During those years, I was close to my grandparents and Tootie, who I named Kuumba and who watched over me when he'd come into town. Kuumba was not as much an uncle as he was a big brother, and it was Kuumba who gave me my first conga when I was about thirteen. I was always going over to my grandparents' house when Tayari was gone. My mentoring had come from my dad, James Forman, and my mother, Bert. When Tayari got out, we started to get to know each other, but I was more familiar with Kuumba and my grandparents. I was also close with my aunt and everybody else in the family. Tayari got married pretty much right after he got out, and shortly after that, he moved up to New York. At that time, around '64, I was going into the teenage thing while he was up in New York. I would visit every now and then, but usually I would stay at Kuumba's because Tayari was out in Corona. We maintained and we were cool, but it really got cool when the music thing happened. We began to open up and talk about more stuff, but it was more as men. We got cool on the man shit—father and son as men. My being in the music business just gave us more opportunities to share not just music but a relationship.

I remember that photo of Tayari holding my hand back in Philly when I was just five or six, before he went away. He had on a porkpie hat and I had on a little cap. That's a classic piece. I'm wearing a little beanie that I think my grandmother bought. She bought me all my hip hats. At that time, kids and teenagers were wearing the "Jeff cap." It's almost like an "apple," but the Jeff caps were made out of leather. They cost a lot back then, and nobody had a lot of bread. My grandmother said, "What you want?" and, of course, I said, "I want that Jeff cap."

After Roslyn was born, I went back into the studio on June 24 and 28, 1960, to record *Really Big!* which had more of my arrangements in a larger context. I used a tentet: Clark Terry and Nat Adderley, trumpet and cornet, respectively; Tom McIntosh, trombone; Dick Berg, French horn (Julius Watkins wasn't available); Cannonball Adderley, alto sax; Pat Patrick, baritone sax; Tommy Flanagan, piano, on some of the tracks and on others, Cedar Walton; Percy, bass; and Tootie, drums. It was the first time the Heath brothers had all been on an album together. At that time, Percy was a charter member of the Modern Jazz Quartet and Tootie was freelancing with different people such as Bobby Timmons and J. J. Johnson. *Really Big!* was one of my most successful albums in that the opening tune, "Big P" (dedicated to Percy), was used as a theme song for a California jazz program. On the recording was another original composition, "Old Fashioned Fun," in a Jimmie Lunceford two-four kind of bag; "Mona's Mood," written for my wife; and a Bobby Timmons composition, "Dat Dere." Tom McIntosh wrote the arrangement for that one and "A Picture of Heath." Also on the album were "Nails," another of my originals; "On Green Dolphin Street," which I had played with Miles and which was one of my favorites for improvisation; and "My Ideal," a ballad I knew from way back.

"Mona's Mood" is a ballad that has a kind of melancholy, moody sort of melody. My wife was a quiet intellectual, and I loved her mood. She wasn't moody in a negative sense. "A Picture of Heath" is a kind of bebop tune, and it was titled after a film I liked, *The Picture of Dorian Gray* (1945), which reminded me that a person could look youthful and underneath be an old man. I thought "A Picture of Heath" would represent me as a musician from the bebop school. "A Picture of Heath," a tune with rhythm changes, has a different sequence in the bridge. The title of the album derived from my being small in stature and from a comment by Orrin Keepnews, who said that with my talent I was "really big."

CLARK TERRY

Jimmy is one of my favorite people in the world and definitely one of my favorite musicians of all time. I like everything about him—his playing, his personality. He's a human being who loves the human race. I love both him and his wife, Mona.

Jimmy's saxophone playing is like the sound of joy. He's one of the top composers around and one of my favorite arrangers. It was beautiful back in the early sixties. We had a lot of talented people on the scene. Some people never got the recognition and didn't get to be as big as they should have. Jimmy was one of those who were trying to get their feet on the ground. Once he got his feet on the ground, he never looked back.

I played on his Riverside recording Really Big! which included "Big P," dedicated to his brother Percy. I had been around St. Louis before coming to New York. I played mostly lead trumpet, but I didn't want to get branded as a lead player in New York. I took the chance. Jimmy asked me to play lead on "Big P." He said, "You're going to play this like 'Clark work,'" meaning clockwork. In the studio, he was the most beautiful person to work with, absolutely fantastic, great leader, great improviser. He's just great period.

We played together at Flushing Town Hall on November 30, 2007. That was the second year we did that, and the group was called the Jazz Masters. In the group were his brother Tootie, Benny Powell, the left-handed bass player Earl May, and Barry Harris on piano. There was also a player from St. Louis, me. It was a good concert. There were a lot of people from the Dorie Miller Co-op in attendance. Dorie Miller was my old haunt, and I got Jimmy and Mona in there back in the sixties along with Cannonball and Nat Adderley and a whole bunch of other people. Billy Strayhorn made it possible for me to get in there because he knew the person who was in charge. There were mostly black people living there at that time. We were only paying eighty-nine dollars a month rent back then, and you could rent a parking space for five dollars. You'll never see that again.

Jimmy's funny and has a great sense of humor. He called those thongs chicks wear on the beach "betweenies" instead of bikinis. When the Village Vanguard owner Max Gordon died, Jimmy said, "He was diagnosed with AGE."

After *Really Big!* I recorded with Nat Adderley in August and September 1960 on his album *That's Right! Nat Adderley and the Big Sax Section,* with Nat, cornet; Canonball, alto; Charlie Rouse and me, tenor sax; Tate Houston, baritone sax; Wynton Kelly, piano; Jim Hall and Les Spann, guitar; Sam Jones, bass; Jimmy Cobb, drums; and Yusef Lateef, tenor sax, flute, and oboe. Yusef titled his autobiography *The Gentle Giant* (2006). We musicians call him that because he's one of the nicest people you could ever meet. I later wrote a couple of songs for him, "Angel Man" and "Mt. Hebron." Brother Yusef is a strict Muslim. He abides by the Muslim religion, treats everybody with respect. There's no malice in his heart, nothing evil crosses his mind. My brother Tootie played with him for years. Yusef commissioned me to write some of his big band arrangements from time to time, like the ones I did for his songs "Construct" and "Is-Is." I've written things that he's recorded when Tootie, bassist Bob Cunningham, and pianist Kenny Barron were with him.

I wrote all of the arrangements for *That's Right!* except "Night after Night," which was arranged by Jimmy Jones, and "That's Right!" by Norman Simmons. I arranged "The Old Country"; "The Folks Who Live on the Hill"; "Tadd," written for Tadd Dameron and composed by Barry Harris; "You Leave Me Breathless"; and "E.S.P." My original on that recording was "Chordnation," named as such because there were a lot of chords in the composition.

BARRY HARRIS

In the late forties into the fifties—when Jimmy was with Dizzy, probably—Jimmy, who is just a few years older than I am, came to Detroit with Milt Jackson to play the Paradise Theater, where all of the younger musicians would go. We called him Little Bird, and he was a good musician all the way, but he reminded you of Bird maybe slightly. Standing in front of the band, we listened to the music because we were all trying to play, and they were the people to listen to. Later, in '52, he came to Detroit with the Symphony Sid All-Stars with Milton Jackson, Miles, J.J., Kenny Clarke, and Percy.

I didn't work with Jimmy that much over the years until I started giving big concerts at the end of the eighties and into the nineties. I always wanted to feature the best of our musicians, like Slam Stewart, Slide Hampton, Jimmy, and others. We also worked together along with Clark Terry on the Flushing Town Hall gigs.

A lot of cats are the best because they're on the scene at the right time. That stuff rubs off on you if you were on the scene with Charlie Parker, Pres [Lester Young], and Coltrane. When you think about it, in walk all those cats. Jimmy is in with that bunch, so he has the kind of knowledge that a lot of people don't have. Plus he was in New York. I wasn't mainly there until the 1960s when I joined Cannonball. In 1960, Jimmy arranged two of my compositions, "Tadd" and "E.S.P.," on That's Right! Nat Adderley and the Big Sax Section, *and in 1975 I recorded with him on his album* Picture of Heath *for Xanadu. When you talk about Jimmy, you're talking about quality. He was from what I call the golden age of the music.*

I went to his big band recording session for Little Man Big Band *or* Turn Up the Heath *in Jersey. I don't know how I got wind of it, but I ended up at that studio. It might have been Tony Bennett's son who told me about it. It was a very good big band recording. Jimmy's one of our best arrangers. When you think of arrangers, you have to say Jimmy, Slide, Gerald Wilson, and Frank Foster. Jimmy is in his eighties and he's still going strong for a cat who had a heart attack. There's one thing about him; he's followed all the rules when it comes to eating, when it comes to taking care of his health and himself, and it shows because he's still young and that's the beauty of it. In that young man there's a whole other knowledge of the music.*

He's got his own individual sound, which is a blessing, because most tenor players today don't know anything about that. It's hard to even define them. It's hard to even tell one from the other. You can't mistake Jimmy for them. You can't mistake them for him. The old cats had sounds. You could tell the difference between Pres, Coleman Hawkins, Yusef, Eddie Lockjaw [Davis], and Gene Ammons, all of them. It was a certain way they did things and a certain sound, a vibrato. Jimmy has a sound that's his sound.

He's kept his standards high, and he tried to elevate the music when he used to teach. That's our way of really trying to elevate this music, even though our music wasn't given much of a chance. When was the last time a jazz musician has been on television in prime time? It would have to be when Bill Cosby had a lot of musicians on his show or when Johnny Carson—Here's Johnny—had a big band on his show. It upsets me that [Dave] Letterman doesn't have a big band. They don't have that beautiful jazz sound. The only way we can get that is to have people like Jimmy or Frank Foster writing the music. It's got to be one of those cats. They are the ones who can do it. Thad Jones could do it too. Jimmy is one of the ones.

I met Hank Mobley in 1961 in New York, before he joined Miles. He and the "Bebop Santa Claus," Walter Davis, were part of the New Jersey contingent. When Mobley joined Miles, I saw him at a Carnegie Hall concert that I attended with Orrin Keepnews. The show was a benefit for the Africa Relief Foundation, and we were sitting in the Riverside Records box when Max Roach came on stage in the middle of the set with a sign and protested against the foundation, which, according to Miles's autobiography, Roach thought was a CIA front. When Max sat down on the stage, Miles stopped and walked off. Then the stage personnel picked Max up and escorted him off the stage and Miles continued the set.

My third LP for Riverside, *The Quota*, recorded April 14 and 20, 1961, used a sextet: Julius Watkins, French horn; Freddie Hubbard, trumpet; Percy, bass; Tootie, drums; Cedar Walton, piano; and me on tenor. The title came from my liking basketball and going to games. Mom, Mona, and I would go to the games when Wilt Chamberlain was with the Philadelphia Warriors. When someone fouled out of a game, the famous announcer Dave Zinkoff would say, "That's the quota for" Hal Greer or Wilt Chamberlain or whoever it might have been. I titled the album and one of the compositions after that expression. On the recording, I included my instrumental arrangement I did of "Lowland Lullaby," a traditional song from the Old South that my mother used to sing when we were children:

> Go to sleep, go to sleep, go to sleep, momma's baby.
> When you wake, you get a piece of cake.
> Ride the pretty white horsey, horsey.
> Ride the pretty white horsey, horsey.
> Sheep, sheep, where are the lambs?
> Way down yonder in the valley.
> When you wake you get a piece of cake.
> Ride the pretty white horsey, horsey.
> Ride the pretty white horsey.

Clark Terry was on *Really Big!* and after we did the date he said he would make any of my records for scale because he liked my music so much. Clark was also on the Blue Mitchell record *A Sure Thing*, which featured my arrangements. Others on the date were Pepper Adams and Pat Patrick, baritone sax; Jerome Richardson, alto sax and flute; Julius Watkins, French horn; and Sam Jones, Wynton Kelly, Tootie, and I. The only original I had on that one was "Blue on Blue," dedicated to Blue Mitchell. The other compositions were standards, a Blue Mitchell tune, and a Wes Montgomery tune, "West Coast Blues."

On June 19 and 20 and July 5 of 1962, I went back into the studio for another recording session, which I was very fortunate to be on because it is one of the best big band records of all time: Milt Jackson's *Big Bags*. The arrangements were by two of my heroes and mentors, Tadd Dameron and Ernie Wilkins. Wilkins wrote the arrangements for one side of the album, and Tadd for the other. Willie Ruff played French horn on this album.

Tadd was one of the first writers who really attracted my attention when he composed for Dizzy's big band before I joined. One of my favorite arrangements of Tadd's is of his own tune "Cool Breeze." I also really love his extended works, such as "Nearness," which I recorded on May 4, 1982, with a group called Continuum, with Ron Carter, Art Taylor, Slide Hampton, and Kenny Barron, on the release *Mad about Tadd*. When Tadd was writing for Dizzy's band, he wrote another extended piece, "Soulphony in Three Hearts," which they performed at Carnegie Hall. Most jazz musicians know Tadd's compositions "If You Could See Me Now," "Our Delight," "Sid's Delight," and "Tadd's Delight."

RON CARTER

When I arrived in New York City in August 1959, one of the names I kept hearing was "Little Bird." Hearing how hip New York was with very descriptive names for musicians, I began looking around, trying to find and hear this person. Given the nickname, I was expecting to hear someone that sounded like that, a little bird! Some time later I got a call from Orrin Keepnews, the producer for Riverside Records, to make a recording session, and I was very excited! This was my first recording session with a big band, and I hoped to finally meet "Little Bird"! The date was in June 1962 with the Milt Jackson Orchestra (Big Bags), with arrangements by Tadd Dameron and Ernie Wilkins. When I arrived at the session, and as the music was passed around, there was a guy in the corner tuning and warming up loudly. So, I asked who that was, and . . . I was told that it was Jimmy Heath.

Well, I knew Albert Heath, the drummer, and, of course, Percy Heath, the bassist for the MJQ, but didn't know of Jimmy and I said so. The response was, "Well, you may know him by the name 'Little Bird.'"

I probably started calling him James because, being friends with Albert and Percy, plus playing with Miles, they all called him James. Over the years, we have made six or seven recordings together, mostly with Milt Jackson. However, we did a date on my birthday in 1982, playing the music of Tadd Dameron (Mad about Tadd). It was a beautiful session, with Slide Hampton, Kenny Barron, Art Taylor, and James. Slide and Heath did the arrangements. We walked right through the date because I had to get to my party.

In 1988, we did a recording titled Four Symphonic Works by Duke Elling-ton, *with Maurice Peress conducting the American Composers Orchestra. To come full circle, in 1993 we recorded together with the Riverside Reunion Band. We make gigs occasionally and always enjoy the music and the humor.*

Although he was of the bebop era, Tadd had a romantic quality and a melodic sense that was more lyrical. His compositions lent themselves to words. The melodies weren't quite as complicated as certain bop lines, but they were still interesting in content. Gil Fuller and Tadd were the main writers for Dizzy's band. Gil Fuller did most of the exciting fast-tempo ar-rangements and wild brass figures for songs like "Things to Come," "Algo Bueno," and "One Bass Hit." Of course, Dizzy was often the one who cre-ated the lines. Tadd had a soulful way of writing that I really admired, such as in "Dameronia," the composition he wrote for Clifford Brown. Tadd had an octet with Dexter and Fats Navarro, five horns. I strived to emulate Tadd's concept; he, Kenny Dorham, and I are romantics.

Another arranger I found interesting was Ernie Wilkins, who wrote great swing arrangements; the testament to that is his writing for Basie. I loved Ernie's way of harmonizing standard jazz licks to make them into some-thing classical. He could take any jazz lick, one you probably heard a lot of musicians play, and orchestrate it into something beautiful. Recording with Tadd and Ernie on *Big Bags* was like being in a dream band that included Clark Terry, Jerome Richardson, and James Moody. Moody played the lead on "'Round Midnight" and it was heavenly.

In 1962, I recorded another album in my name, *Triple Threat*. It was a follow-up to *The Quota*, with the same personnel. Around this time, I was getting recognition in my hometown, and it was like the prodigal son had not only returned but was making good. When a long article by Nels Nelson came out in the July 25, 1962, *Philadelphia Daily News*, I was proud that what I was doing musically wasn't being overlooked:

The middle brother of Philadelphia's first family of jazz (the others are Percy, of the Modern Jazz Quartet, and Albert "Tootie" Heath, currently with the Ray Bryant Trio) craves to get his personal Heath-kit warmed up. But it is typical of his musical integrity that Jimmy intends to sweat out the precise conditions he desires. . . . As the Heath luck would have it, Jimmy's hottest tune in years—a haunting air with a Mideastern flavor he calls "Gemini"—is getting most of its spins under somebody else's colors. Cannonball Adderley liked the tune and worked it into a flagwaver for his sextet. The Adderley version came out a short time before Jimmy's own arrangement did (on "Triple Threat," Riverside 400) and slurped up all the attention. Though the author's edition is less spirited, it is better organized and musically more appealing.

So Jimmy's still a homebody, and who's complaining? Nobody here. It's nice to have a Heath around the town. (p. 39)

I made another recording that year with Milt Jackson. We started in August and needed three dates to make it, August 30, October 31, and November 7. Since Milt was traveling with the MJQ, it was hard for him to find the time to make studio recordings. The 1962 record was titled *Invitation*, and Kenny Dorham wrote a number of the arrangements for this one. Also on the date were Ron Carter, bass, and Tommy Flanagan, piano. I was very pleased with the way this record turned out because Milt was a perfect soloist. On that album, Dorham's "None Shall Wander" became a favorite of mine, and I used it with my students when I later began to teach. Kenny is one of my all-time favorite composers, and that was the second time I was on a record with him.

In March 1963, I recorded *Swamp Seed: Jimmy Heath and Brass*, one of my last LPs for Riverside. I stretched out and used two French horns and a tuba. I wanted to add other orchestral sounds to the earlier instrumentation. The tuba had been used by Gil Evans, and Mingus had used it with bass. I liked the way the tuba and the bass sounded together. I later lent this recording to McCoy Tyner when he was putting together a larger ensemble. He was curious about what I had done with the tuba and wanted to check it out.

I also gigged with Donald Byrd that year. We had made a couple of recordings together for Blue Note, which hadn't been released at that time, so I asked him to be on the *Swamp Seed* date. The other cats were Julius Watkins and Jimmy Buffington, French horn; Don Butterfield, tuba; and Herbie Hancock and Harold Mabern, piano. Among the tunes we recorded were Thelonious Monk's "Nutty" and my "Six Steps," which used the six steps above the tonic of a major key, the relative minor, as the concept for the title. "Swamp Seed" was Percy's composition; it's a country expression for rice, "eatin' those swamp seeds." "D. Waltz" and "Wall to Wall" were my compositions, the latter named because we were all wearing beards from ear to ear. I thought of it as our having on a "wall-to-wall rug." Herbie Hancock played on "Wall to Wall."

JOE CHAMBERS

Around '63, I was in a group with Donald and Jimmy. Donald was back and forth between Europe because he was living in Paris at the time. I got a call from Jimmy after he heard me at a jam session. You know what happens when you come on the scene; when you're young and you have a little talent, word spreads around. It was different back in those days. Monday night was the off night for all the clubs, which it still is right now pretty much. All the major clubs had a jam session band, and they would have an open jam session, but it would be a little bit more organized, with a house band. The veteran people would come out and check out the new talent. Back in those days, you could get jobs from jam sessions. One Monday night Jimmy was playing with Lee Morgan at Birdland, and I sat in. The next thing I knew I got a call. We got together when Donald came to town. One time we went up to Syracuse, and we also went into Birdland. It was very strange because Jimmy and I didn't communicate too well in the beginning. I was a young player, and Jimmy was used to more veteran-type players. I thought I was doing something great, but I wasn't, so Jimmy used to come over to me on the side while we were playing and say, "Give me a little more fire. Give me a little more fire." I was trying to get in there, and we got through it. I really learned a whole lot at that time. I thought I was a hot shot, but it takes a little time for you to get things under your belt.

Since then, I've played on several occasions with Jimmy and with Byrd. Around 2000, we did a workshop and concert up at Cornell University. It's always a great musical experience. Jimmy writes beautiful tunes, and he's a great arranger. Any time we played with Byrd, the music would always include several of Jimmy's arrangements. Jimmy is one of the leaders of what I call the second wave out of the bebop era—the first wave being Parker, of course—but Jimmy's right there. I list him among the top composer-arrangers in jazz along with the late Thad Jones, Slide Hampton (who's still on the scene), Tom McIntosh, Benny Golson, and Frank Foster.

7

Maintaining the Groove

■

By late 1963 into 1964, things started to get rough. Riverside was in bad shape as a company. According to the liner notes, my last Riverside album, *On the Trail*, which was recorded in the spring of 1964, featured Paul Chambers, Tootie, Kenny Burrell, and Wynton Kelly. This was the first time I recorded "Gingerbread Boy" and two of my other originals, "Cloak and Dagger" and "Project S." Since the company was in trouble, it released this recording later. The title "Gingerbread Boy" comes from a chance meeting with Jimmy Oliver, the legendary tenor saxophonist. We were still in Philly when Mona was pregnant with our son Jeffrey. On one summer day, we were walking to the Showboat on Broad Street when we bumped into Jimmy. When he noticed that Mona was pregnant, he said, "A little gingerbread boy." This was a reference to Jeffrey's being the product of an interracial relationship. So I wrote a tune and called it "Gingerbread Boy." Jeffrey was born September 28, 1963.

For on *On the Trail* I also recorded a popular song by Bernard Bierman called "Vanity." Much later, in a 2004 e-mail I received from vocalist Michelle Pirret, I read Bierman's reaction to my recording of his composition:

> I was taken aback when I heard Jimmy Heath's recording of "Vanity" for the first time. Although I had written it in 1955, I didn't recall ever hearing an instrumentalist's rendition. Working as a staff writer for Shapiro/Bernstein, I was most familiar with the pop recordings

made by vocalists namely Sarah Vaughan and my favorite version sung by Hadda Brooks. Upon listening to Mr. Heath, I was pleasantly surprised. It is an amazing performance that demonstrates how a straight pop ballad can lend itself to a jazz conception. What is most impressive, aside from his tone and inventive improvisational lines, is that the rendition is kept within the framework of the original melody. I appreciated that the melody could still be completely understood. That was wonderful to behold. To this 95-year-old geriatrician, you are still a "kid" with all the opportunity to continue with your beautiful playing. I hope to have the pleasure of meeting [you] before this nonagenarian passes from this world.

The records I made with Donald Byrd for Blue Note in 1963 weren't released then because of problems between Donald and Al Lion. That year I had been working at Birdland with Donald, who had a sextet with Sonny Red, alto; Spanky DeBrest, bass; Tootie, drums; and me on tenor. On piano was a relatively new artist in town, Herbie Hancock. At that time, Herbie was being wooed by Miles. Donald and Herbie were schoolboys who were constantly searching and experimenting with harmony and sequences. Because I had been around during the bebop days, I could see that their experimentation was a continuation of that era. Donald had written "Fly Byrd Fly," and Herbie was reharmonizing tunes like "Secret Love." Sonny Red and I were also contributing music. Herbie had recorded "Watermelon Man" in 1962, which became a hit; Mongo Santamaria's version of that song made a lot of money for Herbie. A lot of jazz musicians like Miles and Freddie Hubbard were into sports cars at this time. Donald had a Jaguar XKE, a black fastback, and Herbie bought the newest thing out, a Ford AC Cobra. When I went with Herbie to the dealer, I asked the salesman if the Cobra was too fast for a first-car buyer. The salesman said, "If he has the money, I'm going to sell it to him." The Cobra had a big Ford Fairlane engine in a little AC Bristol sports car body. It was super fast. We frequently went to the racetracks, and we also kept up with racing car stats. The Corvette could go zero to sixty in thirteen seconds, but the Cobra could do it in ten or eleven seconds, and it had a loud exhaust system. Herbie eventually wrote a song called "King Cobra."

In the summer of 1963, Miles was working down at the Village Vanguard in New York, and Herbie, who was gigging with Donald Byrd and me at

Birdland at Fifty-second and Broadway, would get in his fast Cobra and drive down to the Vanguard while we were on break. Herbie got a speeding ticket practically every night on his way down Broadway to the Vanguard. I had a rich friend, a young white guy named Harvey Brown, a handsome, blue-eyed, blond-haired, wild, music-loving sports car enthusiast from the Shaker Heights district in Cleveland. Harvey's dad had left him a lot of money, and Harvey became a philanthropist. Wynton Kelly, Paul Chambers, Tootie, Cliff Jordan, and I were all helped by Harvey. He was a beautiful person. Harvey gave money to a lot of musicians to help them out if they were in need. On one occasion, he invited the Donald Byrd group to Cleveland. I drove with Tootie in his Porsche. Herbie got a speeding ticket on the Pennsylvania Turnpike.

I did other concerts here and there with Donald's sextet. "On the Trail" was one of the staple compositions in the repertoire, and it was on his 1966 recording *Mustang!* Donald arranged the tune by placing another song, "Pavanne," as a counter-melody behind it. Probably the reason it wasn't released was that Donald had argued with Al Lion during the session and stormed out of the studio. I was with Riverside then, so I recorded Donald's arrangement with Kenny Burrell, Wynton Kelly, Paul Chambers, and Tootie. I also recorded "Gingerbread Boy" on that date. My recording of "On the Trail" was released before Donald's, so I was given credit for the arrangement. The tune was originally Ferdinand Groffe's from the *Grand Canyon Suite*, an American classic.

The *On the Trail* LP was in the can when Riverside started to have trouble and was taken over by Orpheum Productions. The owner of Riverside, Bill Grauer, died mysteriously in December 1963. Bill was initially interested in recording race car sounds, and early Riverside records covered racing and sports cars revving up before the race. Ironically, a lot of us musicians were also into race cars.

I still kept going back to Philly for gigs, and between 1960 and 1964, in addition to the Sahara, the Showboat, the Uptown, and Pep's, another club I worked in Philly was the Underground, located at Broad and Pine streets. The Underground had a number of rooms and a few different bars. In one room were women dancers, and in another was a comedy act. I was playing in the Underground with Sam Dockery, Mickey Roker, and Buster Williams when I first met Bill Cosby, a native of Philly, who was bartending at the Underground and telling jokes at the same time. When we talk about those days, I tell him, "I was big-time and you were behind the bar."

When Mona and I got married in 1960, one of the guys who came to the wedding, Sam Reed, was a friend of Tootie's. Sam became one of my sax students and got a gig as the leader at the Uptown Theater, run by Georgie Woods. He was the DJ and used to say, "Georgie Woods delivers the goods." He was also the R&B producer at the Uptown, which was a big venue for the black community. Sam had the band there, so I worked with him in 1963 so I could save money to move to New York. Playing R&B arrangements, we worked behind Gladys Knight and the Pips, James Brown, The Impressions, Gary "U.S." Bonds, Sam Cooke, Chuck Jackson, Jerry Butler, The Supremes, and others. I didn't write for those groups; we just played those long, repeating vamps. The songs were short and the vamp would be for an hour while all the performers danced around. There were certain points in the arrangements when the guitarist would take a solo, and I soloed sometimes as well. It was basically a reading job, just playing the music. While working in the show band at the Uptown, I met Leo Morris, who later became Idris Muhammad and was then playing with Jerry Butler, the "Ice Man." Also in the group on guitar was Curtis Mayfield. Leo and I hit a groove right away, and I invited him to my house. At that time, I was driving my first sports car, a British racing green Triumph TR3. I was young and a lot of the beboppers had fast sports cars. Afterward, whenever I saw Idris, he always reminded me of that night. He said I was driving fast and wildly. I didn't think I was.

In 1963, near the end of my association with Riverside, Mona and I were planning to move to New York. After Bill Grauer died, the company got into financial difficulty, and that's why certain recordings went out of print and they stopped releasing for a while. The company was out of money, in bankruptcy, and involved in court actions. The estate was probably in receivership when the company was taken over by Orpheum. After some time, records started to come out, so sessions done earlier might have been released at a later point. Riverside's going under affected Mona and me economically because it was the main source of income. In addition to my own recordings, I had been arranging quite a bit for them and was getting royalties for my compositions.

After Riverside folded in 1964, I didn't have another record contract until the early seventies, when I recorded albums for Cobblestone and Muse—respectively, *The Gap Sealer* and *Love and Understanding*.

In 1964, I went to Boston to play as a soloist at a place called Connolly's.

The trio was headed by bandleader and pianist Sabby Lewis, who had a considerable name in the Boston area. The bassist was adequate, and the drummer was a postal worker by day. When I played more than three or four choruses, he got tired and would say, "Let's take it out." There was a jam session on Sunday, and a trumpet player and drummer sat in. The trumpet player was Dusko Goykovich, who was attending Berklee, and the drummer was a very young and talented guy named Tony Williams, who I recorded with much later. Tony played more in one set than the postal worker did all week. He was about seventeen and very confident, and he informed me that he could "take it out." I told him I would prefer to keep it "in," swinging. Not long after that, he joined Miles, and the rest is history. We played together later on several occasions and recorded in March 1979 in Havana, Cuba, with the CBS Jazz All-Stars, including Cedar Walton, Percy, Stan Getz, Dexter Gordon, Arthur Blythe, Hubert Laws, Woody Shaw, Bobby Hutcherson, and a couple of trumpets from the Fania All-Stars. Cedar and I did the arrangements. Tony Williams told me he didn't want my drum part; he just wanted a lead sheet. He bombed out my intro on "A Sound for Sore Ears," and when we mixed the recording, we had to make some serious adjustments in the studio. He was always a little cocky but very talented.

CEDAR WALTON

Tootie and I were band mates with J. J. Johnson, and we were both in the Jazztet after that. Jimmy and I were more personal friends and still remain musical colleagues. When Riverside Records was flourishing as much as a jazz label can, they signed Jimmy, and I was on three of his first dates. I had admired his style on records prior to meeting him. He had done some important things on records playing-wise and composition-wise with Miles Davis. I was acquainted with Jimmy's style. He's a prolific contributor to this musical genre.

The Riverside period was a very healthy time. It was in the sixties when Blue Note was the leading producer of jazz recordings. Then Riverside came in as sort of an alternate, signing artists on the level of Thelonious Monk. Thelonious had done at least one if not more with Blue Note, but then he did a series of recordings with Riverside, as did Cannonball. I did some work with Kenny Dorham during that time, so Riverside picked up the slack, recorded the artists that Blue Note hadn't covered. Blue Note seems to have covered some artists on a one-time-only basis, but Riverside enlarged that association by doing more than one or two projects with their artists.

Jimmy's a consummate musician and his playing is impeccable; he's quite prolific on soprano and tenor. He's very creative and innovative and still stands up strongly as a one of the pure, authentic styles of the modern jazz movement, bop and post-bop. He was into bop in the forties, and when he returned in the sixties, he joined the post-bop movement in the blink of an eye. He's not lacking on any end. "A Time and a Place" is one of my favorites of Jimmy's compositions, and so is "C.T.A.," which goes back to his days of recording with Miles Davis. Miles was wise enough to choose that among the Heath songbook. Later Miles heard me playing "Gingerbread Boy" at the Vanguard and asked whose tune it was. He then called Jimmy for the music.

The recording sessions were very businesslike, very straightforward, and there was total preparation on his part, which made it easy for me. He knew how to write for a jazz pianist of my stature at that time, which was not that much. I was just a friend of his little brother. Jimmy had heard some of the records I had made with Kenny Dorham, who was a very close associate of Jimmy's. Jimmy admired Kenny's work. Jimmy's and Kenny's styles, their concepts, are similar. We dove into his projects with quite a bit of enthusiasm. Technically, I found their penmanship, their sense of perfection harmonically, and their sense of melody to be similar. That was the period when Jimmy had the Triumph sports car and it seemed to be a happy time in his life.

All of the musicians who played in Philadelphia were invited to the Heath household on Federal Street for at least one meal. One time, Jimmy's father, mother, Jimmy, Tootie, and I were all watching [Igor] Stravinsky on TV. He was probably conducting The Firebird or Rite of Spring. Stravinsky was quite old, and we were wondering whether he was really conducting. It was humorous. There was always humor in the presence of any of the Heath brothers. When his older brother, Percy, returned from the Air Force, Jimmy gave him a crash course in music, and in two years he was playing with the likes of Charlie Parker. He jumped right into the thick of things without hesitation. Jimmy used to tease Percy by telling him that John Lewis of the MJQ taught him how to read.

We moved to New York on July 2, 1964, when the World's Fair was happening in Queens. By then, the twenty-four-hour leave restriction was over. Clark Terry was instrumental in our getting a place at the Dorie Miller Co-op in

Corona, Queens. One of the main reasons we moved to Queens was that I had two friends there, Cannonball and Clark, who had been on my Riverside recordings such as *Really Big!* Clark suggested that if I was going to move to New York, I should move to Dorie Miller, and Cannon sanctioned the idea. The co-op was very reasonable, with a low down payment. As tenants, we owned shares in the corporation, and we knew that we would always have a place. I got a U-Haul truck and moved the piano from my parents' house. We had little else at the time, so I asked a few of my friends in Philadelphia to help me move. After moving our belongings, I drove my Triumph TR3 with my son Jeffrey, then nine months old, in the back seat, which was a piece of foam rubber on top of the gas tank. We got a flat tire on the Brooklyn Queens Expressway, and that was a harrowing experience.

Tootie and Clifford Jordan were living in a loft at Thirty-first Street and Sixth Avenue, and they also helped us move in. The Dorie Miller was close to both airports, LaGuardia and Idlewild (now JFK), which was convenient. When I began to travel to Europe years later, I had easy access. I wanted to get back into the New York music scene I had already witnessed when I was there in the fifties. The Philly scene was much smaller by comparison. I was back on the scene, but with my family, which meant a big adjustment in my life. When we moved in, we had to make do with a lot of things. We didn't have any furniture so we had to build it. Since I had attended an industrial high school, I was able to work with my hands, and Mona and I built living room furniture. The sofa was made from a door, and we used iron pipes for the legs and foam rubber for the cushions, which Mona covered beautifully.

Milt Jackson gave us an old, boxy TV. It lasted a month or two before the picture kept getting smaller and smaller until it was just a line across the screen. By that time, I was beginning to work around New York. I remember buying my first black-and-white TV for $150 during my Riverside period, which ended that year. Between the work for Riverside and the gigs around town, I was keeping things going economically, and Mona started substitute teaching in 1970. We were keeping life's groove and surviving hard times.

MONA

When we first moved to Dorie Miller, we had medical assistance. Before that, we didn't have any medical coverage for the children. When you had children,

especially babies, and you had a certain income, you qualified for medical as-
sistance through a special city program that came in with Head Start.

Around 1964 and 1965, I was also working with the trumpeter Art Farmer, and my compositions were getting around to different bands, which were recording them. Farmer recorded "A Time and a Place," "Gemini," and "The Gap Sealer." I recorded with Art on his Columbia release *The Time and the Place* (1967), titled after my composition, and on *From Vienna with Art* (1970), which included "The Gap Sealer."

I was basically freelancing in the mid-sixties, and I started going to Europe more regularly in 1968, playing gigs with the radio orchestras. One of the most important new directions I took in the sixties involved Jazzmobile. Based in Harlem, Jazzmobile is basically a free music program for students who need training but can't necessarily afford it. The program was started by pianist and composer Billy Taylor and arts patron Daphne Arnstein, and I was at the first meeting establishing the program, which took place at a bank on 125th Street in Harlem in 1964. Taylor became president of Jazzmobile and appointed the bassist and composer Paul West as director. Billy had the idea, but Mrs. Arnstein had financial connections. They worked on getting private sources to fund street concerts, workshops, and lecture-demo concerts in the schools. Jazzmobile worked, and it's still going. There are a lot of people who are making a wonderful living from playing African American classical music the way they want to and are very happy doing that.

In 1964, I began teaching at Jazzmobile every Saturday at I.S. 201 on 127th Street and Madison Avenue. Jazzmobile was a lifesaver from two standpoints: It helped me to get a little bit of money every week, and it kept the music in the community. We were teaching people from the community the continuum of our music so that it wouldn't die. We wanted young people to have the option of making a living in different ways—writing, performing, recording, and teaching. We as teachers weren't making the biggest dollar, but we were surviving musically and doing something that we loved, that we thought was worthy of continuing. Some of the early teachers were "Dahoud" Freddie Waits, Tootie, Richard Davis, Billy Mitchell, Jimmy Owens, Lee Morgan, and Kenny Dorham. Later, others came in such as Frank Foster, Ted Dunbar, Lisle Atkinson, Sonny Red (Kyner), and Frank Wess. Jazz Interactions, another community-based program, started by trumpeter Joe Newman and his wife, Rigmor, was also happening at that time, and I was teaching there as well. In addition to freelancing around town and teaching, I also did a few school programs with Billy Taylor, lecture-demo concerts tracing the evolution of jazz through the different eras. Blue Mitchell and Sonny Red were on some of those gigs, which were sponsored by Jazzmobile and particular intermediate schools in the New York public school system. I had done some teaching privately—Ted Curson, Sam Reed, and Jimmy Garrison had been students of mine back in Philly—but Jazzmobile was my experience teaching in an institution. Those who taught at Jazzmobile always had a place where they could feel wanted and important. It was good for our egos. We had something valuable that music students would come to Harlem to get, and we could offer it to those who couldn't afford to go to music school. This was the beginning of my wanting to teach, a goal that I would later achieve at Queens College.

At Jazzmobile in the early days, Paul West and Billy Taylor had a problem, so Paul went to the Henry Street Settlement to teach jazz, and Dave Bailey was brought in to take his place. Dave had a varied background and was a very good director for Jazzmobile. He was a great drummer, who had played with Billy Strayhorn, Gerry Mulligan, and Art Farmer. He recorded extensively and was also a jet pilot. He had been the private pilot for another Bailey—the attorney F. Lee Bailey—before coming to Jazzmobile. Dave is a very astute man who knows how to run things.

BILLY TAYLOR

Jimmy Heath as an arranger-composer has really contributed some of the most important music in the jazz repertoire. At Jazzmobile, we commissioned him to write several important pieces. We played them in many venues around the world, actually. The kind of music that he writes embodies the process that jazz musicians go through when they play. You hear the vocabulary; you hear the perspective of a master player in all of his writing. Jimmy Heath has something that is unique. It's what one expects from a jazz musician. He gives a personal touch to everything he does. He influenced John Coltrane. He influenced Miles Davis. He influenced a whole lot of people, and Dexter Gordon made reference to some of the things that Jimmy did in his playing. You can hear that if you listen to what Jimmy does. (Inter-Media Arts Center, 1991)

During this period I also became associated with an organization in Baltimore called the Left Bank Jazz Society, which gave cabaret parties one or two Sundays a month. The organization would provide my transportation to Baltimore, where I would play with a local rhythm section. Since I knew so many musicians, I became their New York connection. Their logo was a little guy with a tenor saxophone, and I always said that it was an image of me—and nobody denied it, because I was the first one to bring in the musicians. They would call me and ask, "Jimmy, who can you get for the next concert?" I recommended Kenny Dorham, Pepper Adams, and other artists. The audiences were very jazz-oriented, middle-aged people who really liked the music. They would bring their own food and booze, and they had fun eating, drinking, and enjoying the music. They didn't make noise during the performance, but they partied all the same. The cabaret afternoon was held at the Alho Club at first; later, they moved to the Madison, and after that to the Famous Ballroom near the train station, where they were located for many years. I was associated with that organization for a long time. One of the club members, Dr. Charles Simmons, became the president of Sojourner-Douglass College in Baltimore, where I later received my first honorary doctorate.

The New York cats loved going to the Left Bank Jazz Society because of the audience. Most of us jazz artists were playing around the world, mostly for whites or other ethnic groups. When we went to the Left Bank Society Club or even back to Philly, the audiences would be mixed but predominantly black with maybe 25 percent white. The Left Bank was a different kind of groove; we were going to have some fun. Almost all the big-name jazz artists, East Coast and West, played at the Left Bank in those years—Coltrane, Duke Ellington, and many others. It was an integrated organization, but the leaders tended to be black. Simmons, Benny Kearse, Leon Manker, and Vernon Welsh, who was white, were the key figures in the organization. They decided collectively at their meetings who they wanted to invite to perform. Although I helped them to bring individual musicians, they also started to invite groups.

Although the Left Bank gigs, freelancing in and around New York, Jazzmobile, and Jazz Interactions kept me busy during this period, Mona and I were struggling economically. It was a struggle in those days because I had to re-establish myself in the New York area. I was still writing and recording, which provided funds. I wrote the title song for Blue Mitchell's album *The Thing to Do* on Blue Note in 1964 and rewrote "Mona's Mood," resulting in a shorter version for a quintet. Miles heard Cedar Walton playing "Gingerbread Boy" and called me for the lead sheet. He included the song on the 1966 jazz album of the year, *Miles Smiles.*

I was working at Slugs in the East Village with Art Farmer when Coltrane died on July 17, 1967. We played late sets, and I was very tired when I went to the funeral on July 21 at the old gothic-style Saint Peter's Lutheran church at Fifty-fourth Street and Lexington Avenue, with the Reverend John Gensel as pastor. That building predated the Citicorp Center site where the church is currently located. I sat next to Sonny Stitt during the funeral. I had been asked to be a pallbearer, but I couldn't handle it. I was in tears when I saw Trane in the coffin. His face didn't look anything like him. It resembled a puffed doll. I noticed his hands, which were just as they had been, and then it hit me that it was John. His whole life flashed back on me, and I was overwhelmed with sorrow. I had been so close to him during all those years with Dizzy and the many practicing sessions. I remembered when he was in Philly practicing all day and hanging out.

People were at the funeral from all over the country and the world. It was a big event, and I realized that the humble beginnings he had come from were similar to my own—more even than I realized at that time. For him to have risen to such a point and to then to have been snuffed out made me think of the old expression "life begins at forty." Lying in the casket, he was forty and gone. He was out of here. It was overwhelming, and I couldn't really handle it. Dizzy was sitting in back of me, and there were musicians in the balcony playing free jazz. Dizzy said, "If they play that stuff when I die, Lorraine [Dizzy's wife] will come in here and shoot all of them." I get calls all the time asking me to give interviews about Coltrane. When I did a lecture at New York University (NYU) in 1998, they wanted me to talk about my life as well as Coltrane's and Charlie Parker's.

My musical relationship with Coltrane was strong in the beginning, but when I went to prison it was severed. While I was away for four and a half years, he just kept doing what he had been doing, and when you do it all the time, you get better at it. When I came back, Trane had gotten big and was very busy, but we still had a chance to get together and talk. I didn't play with Trane after I came back home in 1959 because by then he had a different status. His musical direction also had changed, as did the musicians surrounding him. I have a postcard with Trane writing on my behalf, asking Miles to choose me to replace him. Later I wrote "Trane Connections" in tribute to John. (I had also written "One for Juan," which some people think is a tribute but really isn't.) His reputation and status surpassed everyone's.

He was definitely a pioneer in a new direction; he wanted to do things in a different fashion. He established a certain style that is undeniably "Coltrane." However, I didn't like *Ascensions* because it was too dense, too many layers, with everybody playing together. To me, it sounded chaotic. In the New Orleans style of playing, there are three or four people playing together; J. J. Johnson does this and calls it "clam bake." When three horns are playing, you can still hear the differences and the connections. When Trane used more than three horns in *Ascensions*, it left me cold. I think John peaked with recordings such as *Count Down, Giant Steps, A Love Supreme*, and especially on the compositions "Naima" and "Count Down." "Naima" was on a higher level. Later versions were freer and more dense. Coltrane had one of the most compelling sounds on the tenor saxophone, though I didn't like his soprano sound as much; it was strident. What he played on either instrument was undeniably wonderful, technically and creatively, but I'm referring to the sound on tenor. His tenor sound had a cry that was dignified. There are certain types of crying on the horn that resemble begging. Kenny G, David Sanborn, and some other musicians sound like crybabies, but Coltrane had a cry that had dignity and quality. It was heavenly and spiritual. Some of those crying sounds are imitations of the black soul saxophone players such as Hank Crawford. Grover Washington played in that vein, but he had a hell of a sound. This was way above begging for someone to go to bed with. It was as if he were saying, "I'm not begging you to like this, but you'll have to like it because it's a true expression." That sound is what made Trane so unique. Nobody else in the history of the tenor saxophone had it. There are musicians who have imitated Coltrane's style and his notes, but no one can get that sound, which is personal, coming from his spirituality, dedication, and constant practice. He knew the sound he wanted and he achieved that sound. The way Trane played "Naima" on the earlier versions shows that sound. He used a kind of straight tone, which could leave a cold feeling, but Trane got warmth out of a straight tone. There is a certain warmth in his vibrato, which came later, but it all comes down to something personal.

Ben Webster is another tenor player who had one of the greatest saxophone sounds ever. Webster, Lester Young, early Sonny Rollins, and Trane are the greatest sounding tenor players — and don't forget Don Byas and Paul

Gonsalves. Johnny Hodges had one of the greatest alto saxophone sounds, but I also like the sound of Cannonball Adderley on alto. On soprano, Branford Marsalis and Lucky Thompson both have a hell of a sound.

Between 1965 and 1968, I played various festivals. With Howard McGhee's big band, including Clifford Jordan, I played the Newport Jazz Festival in Rhode Island. We were also at the Randall's Island Jazz Festival, but I didn't play the Monterey Jazz Festival until after I did the *Afro-American Suite of Evolution* in 1976. In 1968, I went to Europe as a single to perform in a club in Paris, Le Chameleon. It had been twenty years since I had been in Paris. The booking was just for me because the French rhythm section was already there, local musicians. There were a lot of jazz musicians from the States in Europe at that time, such as Dizzy Reese, Arthur Taylor (A.T.), and Kenny Clarke, who had been there for years. I also saw Philly Joe, Hank Mobley, and Slide Hampton, who sat in with me at Le Chameleon. Hank's behavior was a little erratic. The next time I saw him was when he returned to New York and we did a couple of gigs together, one for Joe Fields at a short-lived club in the Village and the other at Slugs. We called the group the Two Tenors. On bass on one of the gigs was Sam Jones, and on the other was Stanley Clarke, the film-score writer, who was playing upright then. On that Paris gig, I played with a French pianist named Georges Arvanitas, with Jacky Samson on bass and Charles Saudrais on drums. They were the house rhythm section, the best of the French jazz musicians. One night a woman came in the club, and George told me that she was Sidney Bechet's widow. She called me over after the set and told me she really loved my soprano sound. That's a compliment I will never forget.

A.T., the great drummer, and I had been good friends in the early 1950s, when I was staying with Philly Joe in New York, way before A.T. moved to Paris. We had made one very fine recording in 1960 with Kenny Dorham—the music of Jerome Kern from the Broadway play *Showboat*. The other musicians on the date were Kenny Drew on piano and Jimmy Garrison on bass.

My Sugar Hill buddy, A.T. was collecting interviews from American jazz musicians. He said he was sick of the critics, who were mostly white, telling our story. He asked me for an interview, and at that time I refused. That was stupid on my part, since he eventually published a wonderful book called *Notes and Tones*. When Arthur came home for good in 1981, our friendship blossomed. We recorded *Mad about Tadd* in 1982. He also started his own group called Taylor's Wailers and recorded two of my songs, "C.T.A." and "Gingerbread Boy." A.T. loved "C.T.A." and used it for his theme song. He called me a dumb "mf" because I didn't play it often on my gigs. One day while he was hanging out at my pad, he pulled out his tape recorder and convinced me to let him do the interview. I did it, but I still regret not having done it the first time he asked in Paris. Arthur/author or author/Arthur, as he sometimes called himself, was a great musician and a wonderful human being.

All through the sixties, Mona took care of raising Roslyn and Jeffrey, allowing me space and time to create. In 1969, back in the States, I was on Tootie's recording called *Kawaida*, and that was the first time I played with my son Mtume, who gave me the Swahili name Tayari, which means "he who is always ready." Around that time, Mtume gave Swahili names to a lot of other musicians too. Mtume's whole family identified me as Tayari. None of the kids ever called me Jimmy or "grand"—and that's from Ife, the oldest one, to the great-grands.

Mtume had studied political science at Pasadena City College and was a cohort of Maulana (Ron) Karenga, the originator of Kwanzaa and founder of Organization US. When Mtume was attending Pasadena City College, he was also striving to be the first black Olympic swimmer. He didn't want to be a token, so he didn't continue with that pursuit. Mtume hooked up with the conga player Big Black in California, and that's when he started playing congas. His first album with me was *The Gap Sealer*. Mtume was (and is) the most involved in the Afrocentric movement, and it was partly through him that I got interested in Afrocentric issues and culture and wrote songs like "Heritage Hum," a 6/8 Afro-feeling piece, and "Faulu," named after one of my grandchildren, Mtume's second-born child.

MTUME

I gave Tayari the Swahili name in 1969, around the time we were doing the Kawaida album, Kuumba's session with Don Cherry, Herbie Hancock, Billy Bonner, Ed Blackwell, Buster Williams, and me. Kuumba told me to write the music for it. I was surrounded by these great composers like Herbie, but I was fortunate to have clarity about what I was shooting for. They opened their arms to me when I was just really starting out. I didn't expect to do most of the writing, but Kuumba said, "Here, you got it." Kuumba gets the credit for bringing Tayari and me together on the album because it was Kuumba's project.

I was with Organization US in L.A. then, and I gave Swahili names to some of the cats. They came down to the organization meetings and heard lectures by Karenga. I started with Herbie Hancock, who I named Mwandi-shi. Billy Hart took the name Jabali, and Buster Williams, Mchezaji. Don Cherry got a name too, and so did Joe Henderson, Keytu. Most importantly, the Swahili names had to do with the whole cultural identity changes that were happening.

Back then Tayari and I were starting to have musical discussions, and Tayari was starting to experiment with sound. I don't think he used an electric piano before that period.

When Tayari used the title The Gap Sealer *for one of his albums, it showed he was unlike a lot of the cats, who were closed. In the early seventies, I had been with Miles, and there were certain things I felt that musicians and composers of Tayari's stature could start to embrace that were in contemporary popular music.*

During this time, I took a position about the music scene, especially while I was with Miles. That was an intense period for the whole music industry. There's a great book by a guy named Henry Pleasants called The Agony of Modern Music. *He was a European classical music critic, but what he said also applied to jazz. He said that the European classical music arena had suffered from three things: aesthetic decay, social obsolescence, but more importantly, technical exhaustion, meaning there was nothing else to be played on those instruments that hadn't already been played over the last couple hundred years—unless you were one of the masters like Tayari or Sonny Rollins; that's different. The rest of us coming after them weren't going to play anything beyond that. We needed to make new music, to access new sounds. It was a hell of a schism that happened, acoustic music versus electronic.*

Gradually, I pretty much carved out my own realm in California, but then Mickey Roker, when I went to see him playing with Lee Morgan, told me, "Man, you cool out here but you still ain't tested if you don't come to New York." I never forgot that. When I joined Freddie, that's when word was kind of getting around about who my father was. I didn't use the Heath name or let people know that Tayari was my father. I was James Mtume. People didn't make the association with Tayari, and I initially didn't want that association publicly. In the contemporary popular world, which I was moving towards,

*unless someone told somebody, there was no way of making that connection.
I've always been hard on the "sons and daughters of" thing. "You're so-and-so's
son," or "You're so-and-so's daughter." I didn't want any extra consideration.
I wanted everything I did to be on my own. I was running from "the son of"
thing because I wasn't looking to fill nobody's shoes. I was looking for my own
sandals, but after playing with Freddie for a while, he started introducing me
on the stage as "the son of Jimmy Heath." I was like "okay."*

When I signed my band with Epic Records and did my bio, I told them
I didn't want any references to Jimmy Heath being my father. A lot of people
would think that's a little weird, especially record company people, because
his name was something they could use to make a bigger story. I said, "No,"
because I hadn't yet accomplished what I wanted to accomplish. I had issues
with the concept. I used to say, "I hate that son of Sam." That's what I called
it. The way the general public got to know that Tayari was my father was
through Casey Kasem's TV show American Top 40. When "Juicy Fruit"
[1983] was number one for eight weeks, that's when the Heath connection was
made because they would identify Tayari as my father. They'd show pictures
of Percy, Tayari, and Kuumba. The cat was out the bag then, but by that point
I was fine with it because I had accomplished what I wanted on my own.

I had established my position in the jazz world too, in that arena, especially after my five-year stint with Miles at "MD University." Tayari knew by
then that I was really into the music business. However, I hadn't seen Percy
since I was thirteen or fourteen, and he hadn't heard me play. One time with
Miles, we were playing Paul's Mall in Boston, and the Modern Jazz Quartet
was playing a concert somewhere that night. I didn't know that Percy was in
the audience. When we got off stage for a break, Percy evidently had gone
backstage to see Miles in his dressing room, and I went in the other dressing
room without even knowing he was with Miles. One of the road managers
came over to the dressing room where I was and said, "Man, Miles wants to
holler at you." When I saw Percy, I said, "Hey," but Miles gave me a gesture
not to say nothing else. Miles looked at Percy and said, "You were just asking
me who the fuck was that conga player. This is him and he's also your moth-
erfucking nephew." That was a crack-up moment. It was like "Oh, shit," which
is exactly what Percy said. It seems that after the set Percy had commented on
how well he thought I played but had no inkling who I was. That was the first
time Percy had any knowledge that I was in it like that.

When I was back East, Tayari and I did a lot of Jazzmobile gigs in New

York. We also played together when I had a band called the Umoja Ensemble, which means unity, and we were hitting this gig in Boston. It was after the Alkebu-Lan *album* was released in 1971. As ususal, whenever I played with the Umoja Ensemble, the cats were gracious enough to be there. There were more of us on the stage than in the audience. That night on the gig at the New England Conservatory, the lights went out. I said to the audience, "It ain't nothing but blackness," and I could tell that some of them started to get upset. It was a mostly white audience, and the political temperature at that time caused a reaction.

Tayari and I also did a TV show in Trenton, New Jersey. We got to the set and saw that they had it arranged like it was a tavern. I mentioned to them that I thought it was very disrespectful in terms of the presentation. Why are we in a tavern? They could have designed a concert setting. They had corny plaid red-and-white tablecloths. It was a certain mentality they were projecting with that tavern set.

Once I was playing a gig at SUNY [State University of New York] New Paltz with Tayari, who was the leader, and Billy Higgins was on drums. It was the first time I had a chance to play with Billy. The gig went great. When we were all in the car coming back, Billy said to me, "I don't like conga players." And I said, "Neither do I," because my model, my inspiration, was Elvin Jones. For me that was confirmation from Billy. I wasn't into the Latin thing. I was into polyrhythms, playing in different time signatures, which conga players don't usually do, like 7/4 or 5/4. Tayari looked over and said, "Wow. You're really there now."

PART THREE

■

Third Chorus

(1969–1986)

8

Stretching Out

■

Jazz Transitions

Mona and I took the family to Europe on some of the gigs I had as a soloist. Children could travel for free if they were under a certain age. I took the family to Europe in 1969 and 1972. In 1969, we went to Vienna, where I had a performance at the America House with the Austrian Radio Sextet, including Art Farmer. Farmer, who is one of the nicest men I ever met, was responsible for my getting gigs in Europe. He would give me addresses of promoters on the Continent, and all I had to do was write to them. My brother Tootie helped me get gigs in Copenhagen, where he was living at the time, and Clark Terry always recommended me for dates in Europe. In Austria, my daughter, Roslyn, who was nine at the time, was attracting attention because she had a big Afro, and people would run up to her and try to touch her hair, which she didn't like. They couldn't believe her hairstyle. When I performed in Austria on that date, it was the first time that my children realized I was important to other people. I was someone other than just "Daddy." At the end of the concert, through the crowd of admirers came Jeffrey, who was six years old, shouting, "Daddy, Daddy." He wanted me to recognize him. That was the first time he realized that I was a performing musician who had the attention of the public. We also went to Sweden and Denmark in the seventies. We traveled around Amsterdam in 1972, when Roslyn was eleven. We were really stretching out as a family.

ROSLYN HEATH

[The house at] 1927 Federal Street was where I spent the first four years of my life. My grandparents opened their hearts and their house to my mom and dad and I arrived shortly thereafter.

An interracial couple in 1960 was not a cool thing to be, at least not in the eyes of many. But this was the fresh start that my dad needed, and the foundation of his success stems from his family. That home was a wonderful place to be. I received a lot of attention from Grandpop, who taught me the alphabet forwards and backwards (almost) and read to me and sang to me. I was his angel, as he would say. My grandmother took me to church on Sundays and then came home and cooked wonderful soul food meals for my dad and his musician friends. She taught my mom how to cook soul food. The basement, though dark and damp, was the spot for Dad and his friends to listen to recordings and have jam sessions. Music was always a big part of our world; my grandmother would blast her Mahalia Jackson albums and recordings of Dr. Martin Luther King, Jr., on the record player. These are the sounds I remember growing up in that house on Federal Street.

I can remember moving to New York because it was traumatic because we were leaving my grandmother and grandfather, my home. I can remember my father trying to get the piano out into the moving truck, and it got stuck in the hallway. At Dorie Miller, we had an electric piano in the back room and the same piano from Philadelphia in the living room. My dad spent most of his time in that back room with that electric piano, and that's where he kept his horns and where he practiced. For at least six hours a day, he was back there practicing and writing. My mom, my brother, and I would be out in the front playing or doing housework and my dad would be in the back working and creating. He would start at about eleven o'clock when he felt the neighbors were up and would just keep practicing until dinnertime. That was his world. Sometimes I'd knock on the door and interrupt him, and when he came out, he would hang out with us.

If he worked a nine-to-five job, he wouldn't have been home till six and we wouldn't have been able to hang out with him as much. The discipline and work ethic that he displayed was something that I admired. The fact that he was home a lot made me feel secure, but sometimes he would go away for up to a month at a time. He would go to Europe for a month and we would miss him so much, but he always called.

In 1969, when I was nine, and then in 1972, he took us to Europe with him on a tour. That was fun. The first time, we stayed three weeks. It was hard to jump from one city to another, and I got a glimpse of how really difficult it was to be on the road. We went to Brussels, Vienna, Austria, and Copenhagen. We had great adventures together in Europe, and I realized how many fans my dad had outside of the U.S.

When we went to Europe in 1972, one night, when we came back to the hotel room after dinner, the woman who was running the place said she had a message for my dad from out of town. She told my dad that his mom had passed. We were thousands of miles away. That was the only time that I saw my dad cry. When I saw him, I just broke out crying. Dad was cool for a while and then he just said something to me about how she was better off because she had been very sick. It was just such a strange feeling because we were so far away from home, and I know he felt he should have gone back, but he was in the middle of a tour. He didn't go back for the funeral, and I know it hurt him.

When I was seven or eight, I would listen to the Jackson Five for a while, and then I would put on Wes Montgomery's record or Jobim music because my mom was into Brazilian music. I used to play those old records a hundred times. My mom liked to listen to Count Basie too.

I used to listen to my dad on records, but I was into The Beatles in the sixties. We had a lot of other albums in the house. I used to like listening to my father's music, and one of my favorite records was Wes Montgomery's old album. I used to play that thing over and over, and also some of my dad's Riverside records.

Dad would use me as a sounding board because he knew I was listening to a lot of R&B; he wanted to know what I thought of his music, and he would ask me. He used to say, "Listen to this, Roz. How do you like it?" I always thought it was good.

Our stereo was in the living room, and in the process of walking to the back to do his work or going out, Dad would walk through the house. My music would be blasting, Motown from the early seventies, soul music. Dad would say, "What's that junk?" He would really put it down and say, "Why don't you turn that down. It's too loud. I don't know why you have to listen to it so loud and they're not doing nothing. They're saying the same thing over and over again." He always had something to say about my music. He's such a musician with an uncompromising ear, but his music isn't the only kind that's *good. I would try and convince him. I said to myself, "Why doesn't he ever listen to my music?" Then one time I was playing "Spirit" by Earth, Wind & Fire. I played it over and over again. My dad was walking by and he said, "What's that, Roz?"*

I said, "That's Earth, Wind & Fire."

He said, "I like those changes right there, and I like what they're doing with that synthesizer. That's pretty good."

And I said, "Listen to this one." I played the albums for him and we got into it together, just the two of us. I would come home from school and we would play those albums. We would play those albums to death, and we bought second copies of those albums because we wore them out. He loved them, and when they came to town in 1977 for a concert, we got tickets. I said, "Come on, Dad. Let's go." It was sold out at Madison Square Garden and we were way up in the back in the last row. The group had their costumes; they had a whole presentation. I was jumping up and down on my chair and screaming and my dad was standing next to me and just going crazy. He was on his seat going just about as crazy as I was. The next time they came through, my mom came with us. Dad said, "Mona, you got to hear this. You got to see these guys. They have such a presentation and they are really together. They have the dancing and the lighting all going together and they get the audience participation and everything." We went back again and we really enjoyed it. They were doing something more technical and more musical than just the beat and saying the same thing over and over again. They had lyrics and arrangements.

Uncle Tootie, who knew the arranger for Earth, Wind & Fire, told my dad to talk to Tom Washington (Tom Tom 84). My dad hooked up with him somehow. Tom told Dad that he really admired him and had liked his Riverside records and really had been influenced by him, which made my dad feel good. One time when they were in town, Tom came by the house and they talked and talked about my dad's records, and my dad talked about how he had made arrangements with the big bands. Tom knew about that, and it really made my dad feel good. Tom said, "We're going to be flying out but if you come by the airport, you can meet the group."

I said, "Dad, we got to go." My father wanted to go too, and this is the only time I really saw my dad nervous about meeting somebody. We met Earth, Wind & Fire in the airport. Dad was talking to Verdine [White], the bass player. Dad loved the bass licks and the way he played the bass. Dad was trying to talk to him but was so nervous that he was stuttering. I wanted to tell him what to say. You wouldn't think that of him, as many famous people as he knows. He wasn't nervous around Dizzy and Miles. These were all his friends, but when he met Earth, Wind & Fire at the airport, he was nervous.

My dad has always been uncompromising as far as his music goes. It has to be of a certain quality, to a certain level. He won't stoop down just to sell records, and he was always like that. I used to hear Grover Washington's records. I would say, "Dad, man, you could do that. He's not playing anything, and he's got a little beat behind him, and you could sell millions of records like that." My father would say, "That's not me. I'm not going to do that." He just kept integrity in his music. Even though he's had synthesizers and used the computer to compose, it's still his music and he's going to bring it to his level. He won't compromise. He's growing and always has.

In 1970, Mtume moved back East from California with his wife, Kamili, and my first grandchild, Ife, who was about a year old. That same year, when Percy was in Sweden with the MJQ, our father passed away. I went to the funeral in Philadelphia, which was a really sad occasion. It was written up in the Philadelphia papers, the *Independent* and the *Daily News*, about Pop and his three famous musician sons. Before his death, Pop had been taking care of Mom, who had hardening of the arteries and diabetes. Mom never really got over Pop's death, and she just lost her will to live. When she was near the end, she wouldn't eat. In 1972, the family had to put her in a mental institution because she had lost her mind. She couldn't recognize me and would call me Percy or Tootie. I had a gig in Europe, and although my mother wasn't doing well, I went along with Mona and the children. Before we left, the doctor told me that she wouldn't last another week because she had given up on eating. When I saw her before the trip, she would slip in an out of consciousness. When she was conscious, she would say, referring to my father, "Percy slipped off and left me." They had been married so long that she never rested without him. We got the word of her death when we were in Brussels at the Pension Alpha. Percy was in the States, so he made all of the arrangements along with our sister, Elizabeth. Mom was sixty-nine when she died. Percy had been absent for Pop's funeral, and I missed Mom's.

Tootie was living in Copenhagen around that time and was the house drummer at the Montmartre Club, with Kenny Drew on piano and Niels-

Henning Ørsted Pedersen on bass. It might have been on that tour in 1968 that I performed with the Danish Radio Orchestra in Copenhagen for the first time. I used about five or six big band arrangements of my songs or others for our performance, which was broadcast for a half hour or so. Those gigs were funded by the Danish government.

In the club, Niels played everything I called or had music for. He was brilliant, and at the radio recording, I asked him if he had written my compositions and arrangements because he played them so well. Whenever I went to "Cope," he was there. After many years, in 1986, we played together along with Monty Alexander, Slide Hampton, and Kenny Washington on a Philip Morris tour to Europe, Japan, Australia, and the Philippines. There were two groups. The other had James Moody, Jon Faddis, Jimmy Smith, Kenny Burrell, Grady Tate, and vocalist Barbara Morrison. The music and the accommodations were first-class, thanks to Dave Bailey and Johnnie Garry. I saw Niels later with Oscar Peterson. Niels was always a giant of a musician.

In years to follow, I did similar performances with Swedish Radio in Stockholm, Austrian Radio in Vienna, Norwegian Radio in Oslo, Belgian Radio in Brussels, and German Radio in Hamburg. I used compositions I had written up to that point, but I had to write new arrangements especially for those gigs because I didn't have a lot of big band arrangements at that time. For those European radio gigs, I composed en route and in the hotel rooms. Sometimes I would finish copies on the plane. I wrote sketch arrangements on the plane as ideas came to me. The complete arrangement would be finished by the time I arrived in Europe to perform. I rewrote compositions from my Riverside recordings, which those audiences might have heard, such as "Gemini" and "Big P." I expanded those songs from the ten-piece arrangement to a big band score. In Austria and Denmark, I arranged all the tunes I had written up to that date, about twelve to fifteen tunes. On succeeding trips, I would add a new arrangement.

The European trips gave me the opportunity to keep my hand in with big band writing, because those radio orchestras welcomed American jazz people and their music. I mostly used my own compositions, although I did use a couple of standards I had arranged for a previous recording, such as "When Sonny Gets Blue," which I enlarged for the big band. I also arranged my composition "The Gap Sealer" and a song I wrote for Yusef Lateef, "Angel Man," which I recorded with the Austrian Radio Orchestra.

The Austrian Radio Orchestra often featured Art Farmer because he was living there at that time.

ART FARMER

The first time I saw Jimmy was when he came out to California with Dizzy. Dizzy had at that time a small group of six pieces with Jimmy, Milt Jackson, Percy Heath, the drummer Specs Wright, and John Coltrane. They were play-ing at a place called the Club Oasis on Western Avenue in Los Angeles, and at the same time Miles had just come out with a group that was led by Billy Eckstine, which was also a small group including Art Blakey on drums. One day I had to go over to see Miles. (I had known Miles since '46, when he first came out to California with Benny Carter's band.) Jimmy, Miles, and the others were all staying at someone's house. When I went by, they were just getting up out of bed, and they immediately started talking about music and playing stuff. That's what it was all about. That was the first time that I met Jimmy and the first time I ever heard of him. Jimmy was a very good player, and everybody there was very interested in music. This was around 1950 or the very late forties. Later on, around 1952, I came back to the East Coast for a second time with Mat Mathews's band. I left Lionel Hampton in '53.

I didn't work with Jimmy until the mid-sixties, around '65 or '66. Monty Kay was my manager at the time, and he was also the manager of the Modern Jazz Quartet. I had been working with a quintet featuring Jim Hall on guitar for about a year, but then Jim Hall didn't want to travel anymore, and I was sort of trying to decide what I wanted to do. Monty told me that Jimmy Heath was available, and I think Jimmy had just moved to New York. He was staying in Philly at one time and coming over to New York and doing what he had to do and then going back to Philly. I gave him a call, and he said yes.

We did recordings and gigs with my group around New York, Chicago, Boston, Baltimore, and Philadelphia. We never got out to the West Coast. In Philadelphia, we worked in a club called the Aqua Lounge. In New York, we worked at Slugs, the Five Spot, and the Dome in the East Village. In Boston, we played Connolly's, Lennie's on the Turnpike, and the Jazz Workshop; we worked for the Left Bank Jazz Society in Baltimore. We recorded together on The Time and the Place *and* Art Farmer Quintet Plays the Great Jazz Hits *[both 1967], featuring hit songs that were made by other people.*

Jimmy recorded with me in Europe also after that. At that time I was spending more and more time in Europe, and then Jimmy started coming over. Sometimes we would wind up playing on the same gig. A German record producer contacted me about making an album, and I knew that Jimmy was going to be over at that time, so I got him on the album also. Jimmy and I worked together in Germany and some one-nighters in Scandinavia, and we did some things in Holland, Oslo, and Berlin.

Jimmy is an extremely well-rounded musician as a writer and as a player. I have never seen him in any situation where he was incapable of bringing something of real value to it. His presence would certainly be missed if he wasn't there, again as a writer and as a player. Either way, he could be just a writer or be just a player, and if you cut out one part, what would be left would still be fantastic. Some players are not as good players as they are writers and vice versa, but Jimmy is rare because he's excellent on both sides of it. He has the combination of intelligence, feeling, and maturity. That makes him so great because he's not weak in any part; he's got it all covered, and he still has conviction and fire. He's not just going along for the ride. He still has his enthusiasm. Some people who have been playing not even as long as he has leave their enthusiasm somewhere in the past and they stop growing, and they just sort of go along for the ride and make their appearance and get the money and then go ahead and do what really interests them. In Jimmy's case, he has always been completely interested in the music, and that was the first thing that impressed me about him when I first met him in California.

To this day he is the same, so he hasn't lost that. He's very intelligent and that comes out in his music. He has intelligence and he has taste. You never hear him doing a thing that sounds silly or stupid. He has integrity and he stays with the music. He stays with his values, what's a part of him. He doesn't change that because of what somebody else is doing. It doesn't matter if somebody else says, "You ought to do this or you ought to do that; if you want to do this, then you got to do that." Jimmy is not the kind of guy that's going to be swayed by other people's suggestions. What feels good to him and what's valid to him is what he's going to do.

We're compatible because we have certain things in common and certain tastes. It's hard for me to imagine that Jimmy would do something that I wouldn't be able to like. That's good grounds to work together. I've played a number of Jimmy's compositions, "The Time and the Place," which I remember very well, "Gingerbread Boy," and "One for Juan." When we decided to work together, we called a rehearsal and he brought some tunes with him. We ran them over and played what seemed to go the best.

Jimmy is a thorough musician in every regard. He's a creative musician and he's also a complete craftsman. He can do whatever you want as long as it's in good taste, as long as it's real music. His contribution has been one of consistency, sticking to the art form, and being a fantastic example for the ones who came after him. Everybody has the highest respect for Jimmy.

I worked with the Danish Radio Orchestra two or three times. Later, the orchestra hired Thad Jones, who had moved to Copenhagen in 1978 and took over the ensemble. Ray Pitts, who was living in Europe, was also writing for the Danish Radio Orchestra. I considered moving to Europe because at that time things were slow in the States and jazz was being put on the back burner. In Europe, we were welcomed as artists. A number of jazz musicians left the States and went to Europe—mostly those who were either single or married to European women. Such was the case with Art Farmer, who was married to an Austrian woman, and my brother Tootie, who married a woman named Anita from Sweden. It would have been a different story for me, Mona, and the children to uproot and relocate in Europe. That wasn't an option we could seriously consider, but because of the employment opportunities and the respect jazz received in Europe, I did think about moving there.

Jimmy Woode, who always called me "namesake," was living in Austria when I went there in the 1970s. He was playing bass and writing in Vienna. He was occasionally with the Rundfunk Orchestra (Oesterreich) run by Erich Kleinschuster. Woode's experience with Duke, who he called the "maestro," left him with a lot of inside info and wonderful stories. I played with Jimmy on many gigs through Europe, since he moved from country to country—Holland, Sweden, Belgium, Germany, and Switzerland. My last gig with him was with the very fine Dutch Radio Orchestra, doing a tribute to Benny Carter. The soloists included Roberta Gambarini, Johnny Griffin, Toots Thielemans, and me. The arranger was Henk Meutgeert.

In the 1970s, I had the distinct pleasure of playing with Jo (Jonathan) Jones on two occasions, once in Staten Island with George Wein at a college, and once in Boston at LuLu White's, a kind of New Orleans–themed club. On both gigs, the feeling was uplifting and inspirational. I felt honored to be playing with such royalty.

During this period, I was also going back and forth to Philly, where I performed with groups at the Showboat, owned by Herb Keller. Herb regularly asked me to get the trumpeter Lee Morgan because he liked the way we sounded together. I would pick Lee up in my car, and we would drive down to Philly for the gig at the Showboat.

After I went to Europe a few times as a soloist, I was asked to bring a group in the early seventies, and that's when I organized a group with Curtis Fuller, Stanley Cowell—who I met in Stockholm—Sam Jones, and Billy Higgins. Curtis had been on my first album in 1959. In the late sixties, jazz was at a low point. It had never been America's number one music, but at this time it was at a lower point than usual. The music wasn't being publicized and marketed in the same way as R&B and so-called rock 'n' roll, which took over the American entertainment industry. The media tells people what to wear, what to listen to, what to eat, and what to see. Critics tell people to see certain groups, claiming a certain thing is what's happening, and most people just go for it. There was a point when even Sarah Vaughan didn't have a recording contract, someone of that level who had a strong recording track record. Some jazz musicians started working day jobs. Kenny Dorham had to work a day job. J. J. Johnson and Curtis Fuller at one point in their careers were working in an auto factory. Musicians had to survive and maintain their families. Clubs were closing and so were record companies. Some musicians, such as Miles, who was still with Columbia, were able to survive that period as recording artists. The Collective Black Artists, founded by Jimmy Owens, Reggie Workman, Stanley Cowell, and Kiane Zawadi, was one organization that helped jazz musicians to survive during the difficult sixties.

JIMMY OWENS

Along with Reggie Workman, Stanley Cowell, and Kiane Zawadi, I helped to found the Collective Black Artists (CBA), which was in existence from 1969 to about 1978. One of the things that we initiated was a big band. For the CBA, Jimmy arranged such compositions as "If You Could See Me Now," a wonderful ballad that was sung by Dee Dee Bridgewater, and the CBA Ensemble performed his "Heritage Hum." Jimmy also performed in CBA concerts.

The CBA was made up primarily of younger musicians who were activists and wanted to change things. A lot of the musicians who had come up the generation before us were not activists. Tootie Heath was at the first meeting, so Jimmy Heath could appreciate this group of musicians because they were *dealing with the legacy that he was a part of building. We started by taking up a collection of $18 at that first meeting, held in New York at the studio of Warren Smith, and we went from $18 to building an organization that had something like $175,000 a year coming in through contributions, concerts, grants from the New York State Council on the Arts and the National Endowment for the Arts. Behind the CBA was a business philosophy, and it just happened that the musicians involved were primarily black. There were also white people who took advantage of the workshops. It wasn't restricted to only black people.*

Jimmy is by far one of the great jazz composers. Besides "Gingerbread Boy," he wrote compositions that other musicians have played for quite some time, "The Gap Sealer," "Nice People," "Cloak and Dagger," "Big P," "A Time and a Place," which Jimmy and Art Farmer used to play when they worked together. I place Jimmy with Tadd Dameron, Benny Golson, Horace Silver, and Thelonious Monk as jazz composers. Jimmy hasn't written a lot of songs with lyrics, but he's still one of the great jazz composers like Duke Ellington.

I studied Jimmy's scores when I copied some of the music for the CBA Ensemble. I saw how Jimmy arranged for saxophones, trumpets, and the other instruments, so I learned a lot from his arrangements. You can tell a Jimmy Heath arrangement just as you can tell an Oliver Nelson arrangement, by the way he voices for the brass or the saxophones, and just by the sound he gets. That's akin to telling the difference between Coleman Hawkins and Lester Young. Jimmy's saxophone playing showed individuality all along, even when he was known as "Little Bird" and was supposedly copying Charlie Parker. At some point, he moved away from the whole concept of Charlie Parker to expressing more of how he felt. . . .

In 1986, at a big tribute to Miles Davis at Radio City Music Hall, I was on the program with Jimmy Heath and J. J. Johnson. In the dressing room, J.J. and Jimmy started talking about Miles. It was just fantastic to hear them. Jimmy Heath is walking history.

There was a time when Jimmy wasn't working a whole lot because musicians of his generation didn't have the backing of the record companies or the managers. A lot of musicians were affected by "Jazz in the Middle Ages" when they were under sixty years of age. After Jimmy turned sixty, he found himself working more than he had in his whole life; he landed the job teaching and directing the program at Queens College. Jimmy became a legend, but to the musicians, he had been a legend all along.

Jimmy as a saxophonist cannot be overlooked in the history of jazz performance; as a composer, the same situation. He took the knowledge from Gil Fuller and Tadd Dameron and re-molded it into what he wanted to express. In the years that he was incarcerated, Jimmy practiced and learned how to write music more expertly. He never gave up wanting to improve himself, and that's what is important for any artist. Jimmy has that drive to improve and to search for the unknown. He pushed a lot of boundaries, and he excelled in everything he did. For years, he took lessons with [Rudolf] Schramm, although at that time Jimmy knew how to write music. He knew how to arrange, but he was improving himself by studying with Schramm. It's a never-ending process, but many musicians forget that. Some musicians get to a point where they think, "Well, okay, I know it." Jimmy seems to be a person who says, "Hey, I know it but there's more for me to know."

Free jazz was happening during the sixties, in the hands of people like Ornette Coleman and Don Cherry—the ones who really came up with the idea—but what they did was to influence a lot of "sad" musicians who couldn't really play but tried to do what Ornette and Don were doing. That development turned off audiences. On the other hand, Horace Silver always appealed to audiences because he had earthiness that grabbed blacks as well as some whites. Free jazz leaned toward avant-garde Western classical music and the advocates of European classical composers such as Arnold Schönberg and Alban Berg who promoted atonalism and abstract kinds of music. That type of music turned off black people. In the sixties, free jazz contributed to our losing black audiences, who preferred music they could understand more readily, such as R&B. Jazz fusion had its place, and there were audiences who liked that style because it fused jazz and R&B. It was a time of transition in the jazz world. I was part of a kind of fusion too, since I was trying to evolve and create music that was acceptable to the generation of the sixties and seventies. In fact, I've been told by certain people that they started listening to jazz as a result of what the Heath Brothers were recording in the seventies and eighties.

Mostly, I stayed pretty much with the traditional straight-ahead jazz form, with the exception of my later recordings, when I tried to appeal more to younger audiences. That was the purpose of *The Gap Sealer* in 1972. I was trying to seal the gap between the younger people's music and the bebop generation, where I came from, because I thought there had to be a connection. You always have to make a connection with the youth, and that's what we emphasized. I added an element of R&B, and the title tune had a kind of funky beat. It was the first time I ever used electric piano on any of my recordings.

As a writer, I employed other musical ideas in *The Gap Sealer*. I used my son Mtume, who played percussion; Kenny Barron, piano; Bob Cranshaw, electric bass; and Tootie, percussion. Tootie had always tried to move with the trends. After not having been recorded for a while as a leader, I recorded *The Gap Sealer* as a result of my contact with producer Don Schlitten. I had recorded with Red Garland and Art Farmer, but not as a leader. Also on the album was "Alkebu-lan," which means the "land of the blacks." It was written by Mtume and was influenced by Coltrane, who had written melodies with a drone sound in the background. "Alkebu-lan" uses a pattern similar to that one. I had also been making gigs with my son Mtume, who had a group that was playing free jazz with an Afrocentric influence. Later on, in the Columbia days, we used Mtume's encouragement and knowledge of what the world of music was accepting. We started to use the Moog synthesizer and the funk beat. *The Gap Sealer* also included "Heritage Hum," a composition relating to my blackness. At that time, we wore dashikis and were really embracing being Africans.

I was interested in using different instruments at this time. *Love and Understanding*, recorded on June 11, 1973, included cello and French horns. (I had also used French horns on *Swamp Seed*, released by Riverside in 1963). Jazz critic Gary Giddins, who wrote the liner notes for *Love and Understanding*, talked about my use of the cello:

One manner in which Jimmy chose to express love in this album is in the use of a cello. "I use the cello for the tenderness it represents. Some music is turning violent and I don't want to be considered in that bag because I'm not." He first heard Bernard Fennell when they were working in the orchestra of the 1972 play, *Lady Day*, with music by Archie Shepp. Fennell is classically oriented, Heath points out, but he would like to learn to improvise. The cello parts are all written. This isn't the first occasion Heath has employed an instrument associated with the European tradition to vary his palette. In 1961, he was using French Horn to broaden the colors of the usual trumpet, tenor and rhythm quintet.

I also used keyboards on that recording, and that's where Stanley Cowell came in. I always wanted a change in sound. I wanted different colors and textures. From an educational standpoint, we know that people get tired of the same thing over and over. You have to come up with something different. That's what Dizzy, Bird, and the others did when they came up with bebop. They were put down. Every time somebody comes up with something new, the old guys are going to say, "Oh, that ain't nothing."

I was influenced by what was happening in the world too. I didn't have blinders on. I could see the changes, and some of the compositions had contemporary inflections throughout. That was the first time we did "Invitation" in 6/8. Mtume's playing the congas inspired me to get the African 6/8 beat in there. Dizzy also emphasized the African beat. The only person who objected to it on our recordings was Percy, who was too European-minded in his concept of music—but I didn't want to forget my heritage. When Mtume distinguished himself on the congas, I had to get him on one of my recordings.

While I was teaching at Jazzmobile one Saturday afternoon, February 19, 1972, Lee Morgan dropped by my classroom with a very nice-looking young woman who had a big Afro. She looked similar to Angela Davis from the sixties. Lee interrupted my class and said, "Shorts, how do you like my girl?" I knew that Lee was going with an older woman named Helen, who had helped him to get away from drugs and back on his feet. He was working again, traveling, and doing fine. I knew he was playing at Slugs on the Lower East Side that Saturday night. So I said, "Lee, I'm teaching my class. She's all right. Good for you." He split with the young woman. Later that day he was driving her Volkswagen and was stopped by the police for driving without a license. They let him go with a reprimand. That night, Lee went to work at Slugs with Harold Mabern and Billy Harper. Paul West called me at 4:00 A.M. the next morning and said, "Jimmy, we lost Lee."

I said, "Man, why are you calling me this time of night? What are you talking about?"

He said, "Lee came to the club with this young girl, and Helen came down on pay night with his gun in her pocketbook." According to Paul, Lee pushed Helen outside into the cold without her coat, but she was still holding the pocketbook. Lee went back inside to hang with the younger woman. Helen came back inside the club and said, "Mogie. He don't know that I'll kill him and that bitch." Lee turned around and Helen shot him right in the center of his chest. It looked as if someone had used a tube of lipstick to make a red dot in the center of his chest. It was all internal bleeding. Helen fainted after she shot him.

JOE McLAREN

Around 1972 or '73, when I went down to Jazzmobile to try out for the flute class, I had to play for Jimmy, who was doing the screening of prospective flute students. It was an awakening moment for me because I realized that I had a lot to learn if I was going to attempt to play jazz as an amateur. I had heard about Jimmy from a former Jazzmobile student and high school classmate, Ron Maxwell, who had studied with him earlier, and from the late Enos Payne, a music major and piano student at Queens College (City University of New York), my alma mater. Enos later taught at the Brooklyn Academy of Music and was active in the Queens and Brooklyn jazz scene. Another of the first-time students back then was vibraphonist Bill Jacobs, who would also try out for the "Mobile," as we called it. That Saturday, before participating in an orientation session with then Jazzmobile head Billy Taylor in the auditorium of I.S. 201, I first heard Jimmy play live. When I walked into the auditorium before the orientation, the hall was empty, but from the floor above I heard a cascade of beautiful flute sounds, complex scale patterns that echoed through the open hall. When I looked up, I saw Jimmy, who was wearing a knit skull cap. He had been practicing.

Later, when I tried out, he gave me material to read and asked me to play something. I bombed out completely on both. I had picked up the flute maybe a year before and had tried to teach myself. I thought I could play something, but I was mostly rambling. Jimmy was serious and let me know in a real way that I didn't make the cut for the intermediate level, which was the only flute class at that time, and I needed to go home, woodshed, and get it together. It was a disappointing moment, and one of self-realization. A week or so later, I received a letter announcing that Jazzmobile had opened a beginner flute class and the teacher was the legendary alto saxophonist and flutist Sonny Red Kyner. That was a moment of true elation. Sonny taught us about the discipline and practice necessary to play jazz and how to develop a sound by playing long tones.

After moving through Jazzmobile workshops, four years later I got into Jimmy's advanced flute class, and there I found out why Mtume gave him the Swahili name Tayari, meaning "he who is always ready." Among other things,

Jimmy taught us the 2-5-1 progression, and when he played changes for us on piano, he insisted on accuracy and attention to the melody and the changes. One time, I thought I knew the melody to the break in Dizzy's "A Night in Tunisia," but when I kept playing the same opening phrase over the changes, Jimmy said, "You're playing it wrong. What if Dizzy walked in here and heard you doing that?"

Jimmy and the other Jazzmobile instructors, like Lisle Atkinson, Frank Foster, Buddy Terry, Jimmy Owens, Sharon Freeman, and Norman Simmons, opened up the world of jazz professionalism for those of us older students who aspired to play the music. They were "no-nonsense" type teachers. I was fortunate to be in the flute ensemble that played at Town Hall when Jimmy premiered his Afro-American Suite of Evolution, *less than a week after my daughter Anikah was born. (Jimmy met my older daughter, Natasha, along with Anikah at the Schomburg Center for Research in Black Culture in Harlem, when he played there for the "Father's Day Gift" concert in June 1999.) Years after my first Jazzmobile workshops—I went back for piano lessons too—and after finishing graduate school, I contacted Jimmy about working with him on his autobiography. Our collaboration continued my learning experience. Through numerous interviews with Jimmy's fellow musicians and in conversations with him, I learned the history of a jazz life as told by one of the absolute geniuses of the art form.*

Teaching at Jazzmobile was very rewarding, and in addition to the Saturday workshop, sometimes I would give private lessons at home. In June 1973, I was approached by a student named Ed Levine, who wanted to take saxophone lessons. From his musical appetite and our meetings, a friendship developed, as well as a support system. Ed would later become a prominent food critic. We struck a beautiful and resounding chord that's still reverberating.

ED LEVINE

I first met Jimmy Heath in 1973. I had just graduated from Grinnell College with a degree in American Music. I was working for the New York City Parks Department's Department of Cultural Affairs, producing concerts in parks and museums. I booked Jimmy for a series we were doing at the Studio Museum in Harlem. I was blown away by Jimmy's playing and his compositions. I stayed in touch with Jimmy, and a few months later, I found myself listening to him at Boomer's, a jazz club on Bleecker Street in Greenwich Village. I'm not much of a drinker, but I managed to gulp down two cocktails to screw up my courage to ask Jimmy to give me saxophone lessons. To my utter shock and amazement, he agreed to teach me. I had never, ever played the saxophone (or any other musical instrument, for that matter) seriously. In fact, the first thing that Jimmy and I did together was buy a saxophone for me to play. We found a used Selmer Mark VI, which I still own to this day. I started going out to Jimmy and Mona's apartment in Queens once a week. I will never forget the education that Jimmy supplied. I ended up getting saxophone lessons, jazz history lessons, and life lessons, all for one ridiculously low price.

Around this time, I had started to find gigs for a couple of other musicians I had met (Howard Johnson and Gil Evans), so I started booking gigs for the Heath Brothers. Jimmy officially made me their manager. I remember feeling so proud that I was the manager of the Heath Brothers, a newly minted college graduate with an unabated passion for jazz that continues to this day. We designed a brochure for the band that I thought was the slickest thing I had ever seen. We played the Vanguard, the Left Bank Jazz Society, Blues Alley, the Jazz Showcase in Chicago, and the Lighthouse in Hermosa Beach. I thought that I had died and gone to heaven. Here I was, taking saxophone lessons from Jimmy Heath, managing the Heath Brothers, and going on the road with them. The road was the greatest jazz and life classroom any music lover ever had. Eventually I went to work for Ted Kurland, a booking agent in Boston, who also booked Keith Jarrett and Pat Metheny, and I brought the Heath Brothers with me.

In 1984, after twelve fantastic years, I left the jazz business, but I have stayed in touch with Jimmy and Mona to this day. Quite a few years ago, I went to a concert at New York's Lincoln Center honoring Jimmy upon his retirement from Queens College. I went backstage and saw Jimmy, Tootie, and Percy. Percy came up to me and asked me if I regretted all the time I spent with Jimmy, Tootie, and him. "Regret it! Are you kidding me?" I said to Percy. "My only regret," I told him, "is that I didn't get to spend more time with all of you, to truly complete my jazz education. You see, Percy, I only got my B.A. in Heathology. I still need my Ph.D."

9

Marchin' On

■

The Heath Brothers

y musical direction changed when my brothers and I organized the Heath Brothers ensemble. The Modern Jazz Quartet had been on a hiatus from 1974, and that created the opportunity for Percy, Tootie, and me to get together and form a family group. The nucleus of the group took form in Europe, where in 1974 I had been on a three-week tour with the Clark Terry Big Bad Band, featuring Ernie Wilkins, reeds; Chris Woods and Arnie Lawrence, alto sax; Grady Tate, drums; Bobby Timmons, piano; Sonny Costanzo, trombone; and Richard Williams, trumpet.

The first gig was in Malmo, Sweden. On the plane, Bobby Timmons was sick with phlebitis, and he had been drinking too. He wasn't wearing any socks and was out of it. When the band set up in Malmo and was ready to hit, Bobby went to the bar. He was weak on his feet when he started drinking, and he fell straight backwards. We crowded around and tried to help him when a woman, a doctor, pushed her way through. She asked about his medication and condition. We told her what we knew and that he was subject to blood clots. Bobby was flown back to New York, and Clark Terry replaced him with Horace Parlan, who was living in Europe at the time. Other than that incident, the three-week tour went very well. Richard Boone, the trombone player who had been with the Basie band, was living in Europe, and he joined us too. Boone was going with Jenny Armstrong, who had booked the tour and who later married the great composer-arranger Ernie Wilkins. After Ernie passed away, Jenny returned to booking in Europe.

Ernie, who had written for Basie, Dizzy, Sarah Vaughan, and others, also wrote some things for Clark's band. One night at the Monmartre in Copenhagen, Ben Webster came in. I had been featured on Ernie's arrangement of Duke's "All Too Soon." Ernie asked Ben if he wanted to play on the song, which he had played so beautifully when he was with Duke, and he said yes. I'll never forget that night. Ben started to play, as only he could, with that breathy, luscious tone. While he was playing, I noticed a photo on the wall of Coleman Hawkins. The moment was like a music history lesson.

Arnie Lawrence and I played together many times with Clark Terry, and he was on the three-week tour in Europe, booked by the great lady Jenny Armstrong-Wilkins. Arnie and I roomed together without any problems. However, when we went to Germany, Arnie (who was Jewish) was really uptight. I told him to just be cool. This is the kind of pressure I feel all the time in America. He survived it. Another time on our trip to Freeport in the Bahamas with Clark, we played a show with a comedian, Irwin C. Watson, and singers Dee Dee Bridgewater and Al Hibbler. Clark took us to Count Basie's house in Freeport, and Basie came to the gig at the Holiday Inn to check us out. This trip had some bizarre moments. At the airport, I introduced Hibbler, who was blind, to Dee Dee, and he reached for her breasts to "Braille" her while saying, "You're so fine." Of course, she pulled away and Dee Dee and I fell out laughing. The second crazy incident was when Arnie took Hib to the casino. At the crap table, Hibbler began rolling the dice. He made a few passes and began winning. A crowd gathered to see the blind man gamble. Sensing the moment, Hib then wound up like a pitcher and threw the dice in the corner of the room, at which time the maitre d' told Arnie to take his pal out there as he went to retrieve the dice. Arnie was a person who tried his best to bring people together. When I went to Israel, I played as a soloist in Tel Aviv and Jerusalem. Arnie was there trying to bring Jews and Arabs together socially through music.

Prior to forming the Heath Brothers, Percy and Tootie had played on my recordings, and Tootie and I had played together on live sets. The three of us initially toured as the Heath Brothers in Italy in 1974 on another trip to Europe after the Clark Terry tour. We played twelve concerts in such places as Bergamo, Pescara, Parma, and Firenze. In Bergamo, we opened a festival that also featured Elvin Jones and his group, which followed us. Elvin had Steve Grossman on saxophone, and Elvin and Steve got into an argument on stage. It even got to the point where Elvin threatened to punch Steve in the mouth after the performance. The argument had gotten to that point, and we could hear it offstage. Another volatile personality, Charles Mingus, followed Elvin and his group. On tenor Mingus had George Adams, who wasn't afraid of Mingus, although a lot of people were. Backstage, George, who knew Mingus better than any of us, showed us a knife, implying that if Mingus did anything to him, George would use it. It was a tense atmosphere. Mingus had an ongoing reputation for being erratic. Once Tootie was working with Bobby Timmons opposite Mingus, and one day Mingus just broke up his bass, destroyed it. Mingus never really asked me to play in his band. I never wanted to work with him because he often hollered at his musicians on the bandstand and wouldn't hesitate to stop a performance. I loved his music, but I didn't want to play with him because I was intimidated by him.

In Italy, Mingus was huge physically. When we were having lunch, they brought out a big bowl of salad and Mingus told the waiter, "Bring out another one for the other guys." The cooks and the waiters came out to stare because the bowl of salad was so big. I couldn't believe that anybody could eat that much.

When the Italian tour came up, it was more financially feasible for just Percy, Tootie, and me to do it. Overall then, we didn't work together that much as just a trio—though we did on certain recordings. We recorded "For Minors Only," "C.T.A.," or "Gingerbread Boy" as a trio. We also played standard tunes and Broadway tunes.

The following year, Stanley Cowell joined us on piano, and we toured Europe that year as the Heath Brothers and Stanley Cowell, traveling to Germany and Denmark. We made our first recording as the Heath Brothers, *Marchin' On*, on October 22, 1975, in Oslo, Norway. The album was dedicated to our mother and father, who had passed away. On the album cover, we used a picture of our parents in their Elks uniforms. My father had played the clarinet for the Elks Band, and my mother was in the ladies' marching club, which accompanied the band in uniform. We were following in the footsteps of our parents, who had "marched on," passed away. Stanley had especially urged us to do the recording because he and Charles Tolliver had a record company, Strata-East. Stanley said, "While we have this thing going, let's record it." It was a unique recording, with Stanley on piano and kalimba, African thumb piano; Tootie on drums and flute; me on flute, soprano, and tenor; and Percy on the baby bass, a jazz cello, and the big bass. When we rode on trains in Europe, we practiced in the compartment with our flutes and smaller instruments as if we were a chamber music group. People crowded around and listened to what was a unique sound. When we performed on stage, we used the smaller sound and opened it up to the big sound.

I wrote a four-part composition that year, dedicated to Billy Higgins, called the *Smilin' Billy Suite*. The first part featured Tootie and me on flutes, Percy on cello, and Stanley on kalimba. In the suite, we had a 3/4 part and a funk part on the ending where Percy switched to the big bass and I played tenor. There was also a part where we played flutes in front, and I played soprano in the waltz part. I dedicated that suite to Billy because he is a natural musician who has incredibly impeccable time. Regardless of what's being played around him, his time is constant. He has a meter and time feel that make the audience move and shake their heads or tap their feet. Even though he came on the scene with Ornette Coleman, who was playing avant-garde music (free jazz), Billy didn't play the bash-and-crash style like other drummers, but he's made an impact on the music world because he was able to make the audience feel that style of music. As dissonant as the free jazz sounded, Billy could really make you feel it.

Billy had worked with me on the recordings *Love and Understanding* and *Picture of Heath*, and we also worked together on out-of-town Jazzmobile gigs in Washington, D.C., and Buffalo. That was when Tootie had moved to Europe and Billy was around town in New York. He was the drummer of choice for Art Farmer and others because he could swing. Billy smiles all the time when he's playing. He's happy back there rocking and smiling, and so I called the suite "Smilin' Billy."

The suite was released as side two of *Marchin' On*; side one had Ellington's "Warm Valley," which we did with the small combo, Tootie's "Tafadhali," Percy's "The Watergate Blues," and Stanley's "Maimoun." We had a cooperative concept because, in addition to Ellington's composition, the album had a song by each person in the group. Tootie played drums and lead flute on "Warm Valley," "Tafadhali," and "Maimoun" and an African double reed instrument in part three of the suite. We were all striving for an Afrocentric sound, and we wore dashikis and other African clothing.

The gig and recording in Oslo were the result of my having been there before and meeting up with Stanley and journalist Randi Hultin. She was such a jazz enthusiast that she called the lake in her back yard the Eubie Blake Lake. Friends with Trane and Sonny Rollins, she had been a jazz woman all her life, and all the jazz musicians who went to Oslo knew her. She had been instrumental in getting musicians to travel to Norway. Phil Woods wrote a song for her called "Randi." I stayed at her house when I was doing a tour as a single. In her scrapbook, she had clippings and photos of the Basie Band and other greats. There's a video about her released in Europe, and she wrote a book titled *Born under the Sign of Jazz*. I met another jazz enthusiast that year, Ole Hall, in Aarhus, Denmark, when we were gigging at a club called Tagskëgget. Ole became an avid collector of my recordings. Over the years, I've kept in touch with him and his wife, Lissi.

The popularity of jazz in Europe contrasted with its decline in the States at this time because of the onslaught of pop and rock music. Oddly enough, black musicians created the R&B thing, but Elvis Presley and The Beatles were freezing us out even in R&B to a degree. Of course, there were always James Brown and others who were holding the fort in R&B. In the States, if you weren't playing in a certain style, you weren't about to get a recording contract. Miles Davis had a contract, but he had been off the scene for six or seven years, gave it up. He had a freer sounding band in the 1960s, and after that he went into retirement for a while. When Miles came back, his music related more to R&B. His recording *You're under Arrest* (1985) featured a Cyndi Lauper tune. He also recorded songs by Michael Jackson, Prince, and other R&B artists, which showed Miles's move to more popular forms of music. When an artist is with a record company, the pressure is on to sell more records, and if the company can convince you to compromise the music and play more popular forms, you might bend to it.

In Europe—and later on in Japan—you could play your music the way you wanted it to be. Europeans were still looking at jazz as the greatest thing that America had created artistically. Western classical music came from Europe, and America had African American classical music, "jazz." However, America objected to its black jazz musicians claiming their rightful position socially and musically. This is not to say that Europeans hadn't been slave traders or racists, but art was respected in Europe, and it was freer socially in Europe in terms of race relations. The Scandinavian countries and France were more liberal in thinking of a human being as a human being, whereas other countries weren't. There was enough interest in Europe so that you could perform your music the way you wanted it to be played without compromising.

The cats were going to Europe to play in the sixties and seventies. There was a whole movement of musicians who went to Paris. The free jazz guys stayed in Paris; Roscoe Mitchell, Frank Wright, and Anthony Braxton were living there, a whole colony of experimental guys who had come along after Ornette had set the pace. The Germans also liked free jazz. Europeans in general still liked traditional jazz, but free jazz was something new coming out of America, and it was very important to European enthusiasts.

In 1973, I had submitted a grant proposal, along with Dave Bailey of Jazzmobile, to New York State's Creative Artists Public Service (CAPS) program, for funding to write an extended work, the *Afro-American Suite of Evolution*. I received a grant of $2,900 for what I thought was an ambitious proposal. I knew it was going to take a lot of study on my part to write the suite, and it was fortunate that I was studying at the same time with Professor Rudolf Schramm at Carnegie Hall studios, Fifty-sixth Street and Seventh Avenue in New York. I continued my studies with Professor Schramm for two years to learn more about composing extended works, string writing, and choral writing. I also had to research the history of ragtime. Schramm, who was originally from Leipzig, Germany, had come to America with his wife, a ballet dancer. Eventually he became the musical director for the Eleanor Roosevelt Radio Broadcast. He taught the Schillinger System for some twenty years at NYU. Eubie Blake, Mercer Ellington, Eddie Barefield, and Gil Fuller (who wrote for the Dizzy Gillespie big band) had studied the Schillinger system under Schramm. Schramm lived in Queens, on Eighty-fifth Street in Jackson Heights. I took lessons at his office on the tenth floor of Carnegie Hall; he taught me about counterpoint, harmonization, chromatic harmony, and other devices related to the Schillinger System. He gave me assignments and corrected them.

The Schillinger System is a number system for writing music. George Gershwin and other composers studied the system. The Berklee College of Music in Boston was originally called Schillinger House. However, after all of his years of teaching this system at NYU, Schramm said that Schillinger's idea that all art could be attributed to numbers wasn't true. Schramm realized that there are human, emotional factors that go into writing music. So he changed from being an all-Schillinger teacher to his own system, the Schramm System, which was a combination of Schillinger and traditional harmony. He was a wonderful teacher, and I had a great relationship with him. He used to say in his broken English, "Heath, you're a worker." He liked people who worked hard, and I had always been curious and intense in terms of learning and writing. However, he respected the knowledge that I had prior to studying with him. He knew that I had been composing for recordings and that I had been a staff arranger for Riverside Records, writing for Cannonball, Blue Mitchell, Sam Jones, and other Riverside artists. He knew where I was musically, and he didn't take me back to things that I could already do. He took me from where I was to where I wanted to be. Those were two of the most important years in my musical life because he opened me up to being a better teacher, writer, and performer. Being his pupil made me a better musician. I still apply some of what he taught me, the Schillinger System and chromatic harmony.

When Wynton Marsalis, who has become a wonderful composer, came to me for a lesson, I told him about one of the things I had learned from Schramm, and Wynton didn't come back for another lesson. Then on one occasion, when I was at the University of North Florida in Jacksonville for a ten-day residency, Wynton was in town for a concert, and I sat in with him. Earlier on, he came to the university when I was teaching and told the students, "I took a lesson from Mr. Heath and he showed me something that was very important." I said, "But you never came back." He said, "There was so much in what you told me that I didn't have to come back." He said he was still working on it.

Schramm taught me to recognize how any one note can go through the whole chromatic scale. That's what I had shown Wynton. I'd never thought about that concept before I studied with Schramm. A lot of musicians knew that concept—that one note can fit the whole chromatic scale, according to how tense or how mild you want the chord to sound—but they never really concentrated on it or exploited it. A typical weekly session with Schramm was an hour lesson for $25 or $30. I used up the $2,900 grant taking lessons with him. CAPS got their money's worth. I don't know if Schramm learned anything from me, but he wrote examples of jazz licks by Charlie Parker and others for his students to analyze. Schramm was into musical shapes from a scientific standpoint. He used the example of jumping up on a table and how one would use target points to jump up.

For Schramm, music had shape and design. When he wrote his group of jazz licks, he included one of mine. I'm fully aware that he had analyzed some of my music to see how I was going about things before I started studying with him.

The *Afro-American Suite of Evolution* was my second suite, after *Smilin' Billy Suite*, which we recorded as the Heath Brothers. Duke Ellington, Billy Strayhorn, Oliver Nelson, Quincy Jones, and others had written extended works, and I wanted to do the same thing. The *Afro-American Suite of Evolution* was more involved than the *Smilin' Billy Suite* because it included a choir, African percussion, and a big band. The big band contains all kinds of possibilities.

The Town Hall premiere of the *Afro-American Suite of Evolution* on May 1, 1976, was a milestone in my career. It was performed in the second half of the concert. The first half included a performance by the flute ensemble, made up of my students from Jazzmobile, playing a composition that I'd arranged for the occasion and that was well accepted. In the ensemble were Joe McLaren; Galen Robinson; Jimmy Cruz, who organized a group called the Spirit Ensemble; Tony Hinson, who later played with Mongo Santamaria, Gail Freeman, and others. Karen Atkinson, who married Jazzmobile teacher and bassist Lisle Atkinson, was also a flute student. She would later play bass with Lisle in his Neo-Bass Ensemble. Also performing was the Jazzmobile student big band—with students like Chip Shelton, the dentist-turned-flute-specialist, who played saxophone that night, and Eugene Rhynie, the saxophonist now known as T. K. Blue—along with such faculty as Frank Foster, Charli Persip, Sonny Red Kyner, Kenny Rogers, and Ernie Wilkins. Percy Heath, Quentin Jackson, Stanley Cowell, and Buddy Pearson were active professionals.

The *Afro-American Suite of Evolution* was the feature presentation of the concert. It was an ambitious work, which encompassed elements I hadn't used in the past, such as strings. The violin section included Noel Pointer, John Blake, and others. The movements started with the idea of being in Africa. I used a tape of ethnic drum sounds and animal sounds from Africa, fusing them in with the live drums. I also had a tape of field hollers from the African American experience, followed by gospel, ragtime, blues, swing, bebop, bossa, and R&B, ending with the avant-garde. I did some of the text, and my niece, Beth Jackson, who is a poet, did the bulk of it. Her way with words is incredible. She is blessed with the Heath wit also. Each section of the suite was dedicated to a musician who epitomized a particular era of the music. The first part was dedicated to the elders in the African community; the gospel section was dedicated to James Weldon Johnson—and to my mother and grandmother, who sang in a Baptist choir; the ragtime to Eubie Blake; the boogie woogie to Meade "Lux" Lewis; the swing to Basie; and the bebop to Dizzy. John S. Wilson, who reviewed it in the May 3, 1976, *New York Times* piece "Musical Tribute for Jimmy Heath," thought that I had "caught the spirit of the various periods" (p. 41).

DAVE BAILEY

Jimmy was always on top of the game. He is a natural teacher, and Jazzmobile added greatly to his skills at teaching—a teacher, composer, and arranger. He took those skills and transferred them over to his students. He has the knack of being a communicator, and he's a wordsmith. He can take words and turn them into anything he wants—to tragedy, to humor, to love, to hate. He just loves words, and he does that with many people at many times. He takes people's names and transposes them just like he would do with music. He uses one of my phrases I mentioned at a lecture he did at the Schomburg Center for Research in Black Culture in Harlem, on the confluence of rap and so-called modernists with the more traditional players like himself. Somebody in the audience challenged Jimmy about the age of his music, and I got up and said, "What was good is good." He uses that phrase quite often. Jimmy was one of the finest teachers we had at Jazzmobile, along with Frank Wess, Frank Foster, Ernie Wilkins, and others. Many of his students have gone on to greater heights. He is very jocular in his own personal way, but he's never jocular about his music.

He's a prolific composer. Some of his compositions have stood the test of time. "Gingerbread Boy"—they still play "Gingerbread Boy." They're still playing "Big P." Jimmy's trying to communicate with people, and he says musically some of the things that maybe he can't express verbally. He's as close to genius as you come if not already there. With the Afro-American Suite of Evolution, Jimmy really musicalized the whole black tradition from Africa to modern jazz. I was responsible for the work being performed, first at Town Hall in New York. We did it again in Winnipeg, Canada, in 1977 with the members of the Winnipeg Symphony Orchestra, and Jimmy did it in California at the Monterey Jazz Festival. In the suite you can see the respect for the drum, which is the basis of it all.

Jimmy and I were both raised around the corner from the American Legion Post in Philadelphia. It was Lincoln Post Number 89. This marching band affected so many of us, and what we liked about it was the drums, and maybe that's why Jimmy is very picky about drummers. He loves drummers who play the drum as an instrument and who don't beat on it as if it's some bastard instrument.

Jimmy has also been a great mentor. Many of his students from Jazzmobile turned out to be fine musicians. He did the same thing teaching at Queens College, where Jeb Patton, the piano player, was one of his students. Jimmy recognizes a quality student when he sees one. He encourages them and he'll hire them. Without exaggerating, Jimmy is appreciated and worshiped, not in an ecclesiastical sense.

Jimmy loved to play Jazzmobile because he knew that the people who came to Jazzmobile concerts were the real jazz lovers. Jimmy always played Grant's Tomb, one of the best Jazzmobile venues for summer concerts in New York. It was always packed. Jimmy, Art Blakey, and Dizzy always packed Grant's Tomb.

FRANK FOSTER

In the sixties, Jimmy and I were instructors at the Jazzmobile Workshop in Harlem. We taught saxophone, harmony and theory, and arranging. We were really brothers under the skin at that time. He was such a funny guy, and he was quite entertaining to be around. Some of the things he said might not have actually been funny, but it was the way he said them that made you laugh. He had an inimitable style of speaking.

One time we were playing a jazz festival in Upstate New York or somewhere, and I was grossly overweight, weighing about 210 pounds. I was really unhappy with being that overweight. The first time Jimmy saw me that evening, he said, "Hey, wide body." Just that one phrase both cracked me up and made me sad, made me realize that I really had to lose that weight.

Another time, we were rehearsing the Lake Placid Suite, which I was commissioned to write by Jazzmobile, for the Lake Placid Winter Olympics in 1980, and Jimmy was a part of the Jazzmobile All-Stars, which performed that work. During the rehearsals at Lake Placid, he had so much of value to contribute musically, and wit-wise he just cracked everybody up.

His music is a reflection of him as a witty, funny individual, and some of his titles show that too. I heard him perform with his band at the Blue Note

for his eightieth birthday celebration, and he made a commentary on the tab-
loids concerning famous people under the microscope. One of his song titles
was "Sources Say," as in "sources say" that Angelina and Brad are heading
for a break-up, for example. His song musically nails down the phrase. He
has an excellent command of orchestrational facilities, and he is able to put
into the music practically whatever he feels. He uses the big band as a vehicle
for expression. His playing style is what I call a "no-nonsense-straight-ahead
modern bebop approach," which is full of correctness, validity, and humor as
well. But the most important thing about it is "no-nonsense-straight-ahead."

Jimmy's expression on his instrument is totally characteristic of the bebop
or the post-bebop genre, and it's punctuated with his knowledge of the music,
his knowledge of the principles that make up the genre, physical principles
which all of us hold dear, such as the ability to relate the music horizontally to
the music vertically, which means to play melodies which are perfectly in line
with the chords or to improvise melodic solos that correspond with the existing
vertical harmonies.

His overall contribution is as valid as anyone's in the music industry. My
idols were Tadd Dameron, Oliver Nelson, George Russell, Benny Carter,
Gerald Wilson, Sy Oliver, Quincy Jones, Ernie Wilkins, and a couple of
others. Jimmy ranks right up there with all of them in musical knowledge and
capacity for self-expression. Jimmy is at the top of his game. He doesn't have
many peers in modern jazz, and he is well deserving of much more recognition
than he probably has received, but it seems as though he has been content to
remain in relative obscurity while certain others have received wide acclaim.
He deserves just as much acclaim as anybody.

He is high on musicality, a combination of the three elements of music:
harmony, melody, and rhythm. His validity can never be denied.

In 1976 Dizzy took me, along with Ben Brown, Mickey Roker, Al Gaffa,
and Mike Longo, to South Carolina on a five-day tour, playing a different
city each day. When we played Walterboro, I called Percy and said, "Guess
where I am?" He had no idea and was surprised when I told him. Walterboro was where he was stationed after leaving Tuskegee as a pilot with the
rank of second lieutenant. It's also the place where I slept in the bunk of
one of his fellow officers while he went into town to see his girlfriend. In-
cidentally, if the sergeant checking beds had seen how short my legs were,
the absent officer and I would have been in trouble. I had been there at the

time with Calvin Todd's band out of Philadelphia. When I arrived in the afternoon, I asked where I could find Lieutenant Heath. They told me his squadron was the one that was flying over.

I met Ben Brown, who I called "Big Ben," on the South Carolina tour with Dizzy. Ben was a talented, bright young man, and we hit a groove right away. Throughout the eighties, he worked in my quartet along with Tony Purrone and Akira Tana. Besides being a fine musician, Ben knew a lot about the Mac computer, and he mentored me when I got my first Apple computer and notation program, Finale. I have been using it ever since. In 1989, I took the quartet to Europe, which was one of the highlights of my career, going to Vienna, Nice, Stockholm, Kongsberg in Norway, London, and other festivals. Later we did the Black College Network tour in the States. Being a curious person, Ben was always finding electronic gadgets. He made the recording *You've Changed* with me in 1991 and the Grammy-nominated *Little Man Big Band* CD in 1992. I liked the fact that he played the upright and "uptight" bass (bass guitar). I now call him "Thin Brown" since he's lost a lot of weight.

In South Carolina in 1976, we went to Dizzy's hometown, Cheraw, and my mom's hometown of Sumter. In Columbia, we played at the South Carolina Legislature. This was significant because they were honoring Dizzy for his cultural achievements and celebrity. We played a couple songs, and after the presentation of an award, Birks had to give a speech. Dizzy pulled out a written speech. He both praised and trashed the state and the country, leaving some of the legislators squirming. After what seemed to be about five minutes, Mickey whispered to me, "And that's just the first page." We laughed. That night we were invited to the governor's house for dinner. When we sat down at the table, the governor spoke. He stated that he had heard Dizzy and Charlie Parker on the jukebox when he was attending college in Philadelphia. He said that never in his wildest imagination had he dreamed he would be the governor and be honoring Dizzy Gillespie in his home. Birks accepted the accolades. Then he told this story about Louis Armstrong.

Dizzy said "Pops" had told him, early in his career, before the civil rights movement, that he was playing a gig in a white hotel. He was living in the hotel secretly. They would sneak him up to his room on the freight elevator to keep the guests from knowing. One night after his performance, he went to his room, where he had left the window open. When he got there, he found a raccoon in the room. Pops called down to the desk and shouted, "Come get this coon out my room." The receptionist answered, "We know there is a nigger up there." Pops said, "I'm the nigger; come get this coon out my room." We all fell out laughing, including the governor.

When we left South Carolina to go home, Dizzy told us he was going to stop in Durham, North Carolina, to visit his friend Mary Lou Williams, who was sick at the time. He would always visit his friends when they were down.

As a family, Mona, the children, and I continued to survive economically through the seventies. In 1970, Mona started teaching at I.S. 229 in Maspeth, Queens, which helped us to make ends meet. After we recorded *Marchin' On* for Strata-East as the Heath Brothers in October 1975, the group had some gigs over a period of a few years—possibly while Percy was still working back and forth with the MJQ because of Milt Jackson's leaving from time to time. In 1978, I met Bruce Lundvall, who had heard me play when I was in Lewisburg and he was attending Bucknell University. Lundvall had become president of CBS Records' jazz and popular music division, and he approached Percy and me about making a recording. Later that year, he agreed to sign the Heath Brothers.

In 1977, while doing a single in Connecticut, I had met a very talented guitarist, Tony Purrone. I recognized that he had enormous potential. After I signed with Columbia, I told Tony that we wanted him to be in the group. Of course, he agreed because he hadn't gotten that kind of exposure. The group still needed a permanent drummer. Tootie had moved to California and remarried. He was interested in getting into the movies as an actor and wasn't really concerned with playing with the Heath Brothers. Percy and I were shocked. How could he quit being a brother? Tootie agreed to make the first record with Columbia, *Passing Thru* (1978), but only as a guest. He didn't want to sign the contract with Columbia. After that recording, Tootie returned to L.A., where he lived with his wife, Beverly.

ALBERT "TOOTIE" HEATH

When the Heath Brothers had a recording contract with CBS in 1978, there were a lot of good things happening, although I was never really a part of planning things. I was just the drummer and a brother, but Percy and Jimmy made all the decisions about the contractual stuff, and we basically played Jimmy's music. I was fine with that. The Heath Brothers started up when the MJQ had gone into retirement and Percy was available, but we had this conflict about the music. My living in California made it a little difficult for them. I don't know if it bothered Percy as much as it bothered Jimmy, who just couldn't get with that. A manager is really what we needed. I think we would have stayed together longer if we had someone to handle our business. At that time, it was a lot of responsibility for Jimmy. Percy would always equate everything with the MJQ, which wasn't a reality for us. He would always say, "Man, why are you doing this? Why don't you call so-and-so? Let them do that." That means paying people, but we didn't have that kind of money. Then there was a conflict with George Butler and CBS. That got stupid because Butler wanted us to do more mainstream pop jazz and Percy didn't want to do that.

Jimmy is a very sensitive, caring, and loving human being. Jimmy was very serious about helping his students, but he didn't have a lot of black students when he taught college. He's passing on the legacy to white students who want it, but the black people want it too. A lot of young people don't have the notion that it's even there. It's not a part of their everyday thing. If you ask a young person who John Coltrane is, he probably wouldn't know, and Coltrane was popular. Someone of their generation might not even know about Wynton Marsalis. Jimmy had some prize students like Antonio Hart. Those are the guys he feels closest to.

Jimmy loves me, man. He's my brother and I love him too. I love playing with him and I love his music. Percy's my favorite bass player and Jimmy is my favorite saxophone player of anybody in the world. Charlie Parker, Coltrane, I don't care who it is. Jimmy is one of my favorite writers too.

When we start playing, all of our little differences are gone. There's an appreciation for each other as family members that you don't feel with others. I had the opportunity to travel and play with the MJQ. I would always say to Percy right before a concert, when we would walk out on the stage and the people would give us a thunderous applause, "Percy, man, I wish Mom and Pop could see us now." And he would say, "Don't worry. They see us." Jimmy wasn't there, but I'm sure he has experienced it too, that our parents are watching.

On that first recording for Columbia, we had Tony on guitar, Stanley on keyboards, Mtume on percussion as a guest for a couple of tracks, and, of course, Percy on bass. On *Passing Thru,* I used overdubbing for the first time on a recording. All of the tunes were originally played in a quintet setting, but on a few of the tracks—"Mellowdrama," "A New Blue," and a ballad contributed by Tootie, "Light of Love"—horns were added, which provided another color, another texture to the sound. In my earlier recordings on Riverside, such as *Really Big! The Quota,* or *Triple Threat,* I had used French horn. I liked the idea of the French horn and the type of musical quality it added to an ensemble. On "Mellowdrama," which was used as a theme song for a jazz radio program in Los Angeles, I used tuba and French horns. *Passing Thru* sold eighteen thousand copies, which at that time was considered good. For our second recording for Columbia, we wanted the same kind of theme. *Passing Thru* was similar to *Marchin' On,* and the next one was titled *In Motion,* which also had to do with continuing to progress in our musical lives. The choice of the theme title was a collective decision, especially between Percy and me. After *Passing Thru,* we continued to use Tony and Stanley, but we had a new drummer, Keith Copeland, son of trumpeter Ray Copeland, who had played with Monk and others and who had also been a teacher at Jazzmobile. As a group, the Heath Brothers played in California just before the second album was released, and that's where the album cover picture was shot. Columbia, with its jacked-up budget, sent us to Long Beach by way of limousine to take the photo.

For *In Motion,* I suggested to Columbia that we should have an album cover that showed us "moving." We had played the night before and had to get up early and go for the long drive to Long Beach for the photo shoot. Columbia spent a lot of money for that. The cost was deducted from our budget, a "nonrecoupable." When the cover came out, it really didn't look as if we were in motion. There were only two or three impressions, but there should have been multiple ones to show more motion. We also had to go to California to do the mixing. CBS Records did a lot of good things, but there were also a lot of things that were excessive. They helped us with tour support, and they bought uniforms for us so that we were real clean-looking on stage, Cardin outfits from Barney's clothing store. Our image was positive, but all of those costs were charged against the budget. Our record had to sell in large numbers to pay for all of the frills and extras. This was the start of the height of our popularity as a result of the exposure we were getting at that time.

CBS Records, which is now Sony, was one of the biggest recording companies in the world. Their distribution was worldwide, and that resulted in greater exposure. With the Columbia tours, we began to travel all over America, to places like Iowa or Minnesota where the average jazz group wouldn't have had access. I had played those areas earlier in my career with the Nat Towles Orchestra. With promotion and distribution, one of Columbia's oversights was that some of their distributors in Europe didn't have enough historical background to know that we had all been to Europe before, so some records didn't get released there. It was a drag for us because some of the recordings we made with Columbia went as imports rather than as part of the usual distribution. This happened in England.

In spite of this, we became popular in England and toured there, particularly after our third record with Columbia, *Live at the Public Theater*, recorded in 1979. That recording was nominated for a Grammy in 1980. One of the tracks, "For the Public," was one of my compositions produced by Mtume and using the Moog synthesizer. The funk beat was played by one of Tootie's students from Jazzmobile, Howard King. By this time, the drummer with the Heath Brothers group was Akira Tana, who replaced Keith Copeland, who hadn't gotten along that well with Percy. Since I had played with Keith, I suggested him, but it came to the point where Percy couldn't take Keith's playing, and once it almost came to a confrontation. Keith blew up and quit after Percy criticized him on the bandstand. Keith said, "Tell me that after we get off the set. Don't give me that stuff on the bandstand when I'm playing and make me look bad. James, I'm going to have to resign. You and I are fine, but Percy and I can't get together on the stage."

When we recorded *Live at the Public Theater*, Akira was on most of the tracks, but on "For the Public" Mtume wanted to use Howard King, who had played with Roberta Flack. King's nickname was "the Locksmith" because of his even groove. Knowing that Akira didn't play that particular style, Mtume produced "For the Public" with Howard as the drummer. Other than that, most of the tracks were recorded live. "For the Public" was successful as a single and received a lot of air play. Ted Ross, the guy who played the lion in the musical *The Wiz* on Broadway, did the announcing on the recording.

On "For the Public," we used a funk concept. With our first two recordings for Columbia, the use of funk style was my idea; Percy didn't completely agree with that choice of style, but we were trying to sell more records, the expectation of most artists who sign with a big company. If you're not selling more product with each recording, you're considered dispensable. On

In Motion, I had written "Feelin' Dealin'," which was more commercial, but for *Live at the Public Theater*, George Butler, who was a vice-president at Columbia and our producer, suggested that Mtume, who was with Epic Records, should be involved. The result was a Grammy nomination and more recognition.

When we toured in London, we didn't perform at Ronnie Scott's, the popular London jazz club. Instead, we played in a dance hall setup for young kids, and the place was packed. We played the tunes from the album that had a more contemporary beat. The Columbia Records guy in London who didn't distribute our record, Hugh Atwald, came to the gig and saw the response of the huge crowd, and he said that he was sorry he didn't have the insight to distribute the record. He had chosen one by another Columbia artist—Arthur Blythe. Percy said, "You dumb motherfucker. You don't know that the Heath brothers have been in and out of Europe since the 1940s, and you preferred somebody new like Arthur Blythe." Even as an import, *Live at the Public Theater* received so much attention that we had gotten that London gig.

In early March 1979, the Heath Brothers made musical and cultural history as part of a project called Havana Jam. Many of the other artists on the CBS roster participated, including the Jazz All-Stars: Dexter Gordon, Stan Getz, Hubert Laws, Arthur Blythe, Woody Shaw, Cedar Walton, Tony Williams, and Willie Bobo. We stayed in Cuba three or four days. Besides enjoying the beautiful weather, we were taken on an interesting sightseeing tour of the Ernest Hemingway house. At the concert, we recorded Cedar's arrangement of "Tin Tin Deo" and my composition and arrangement of "A Sound for Sore Ears." When the record was released, they gave Dexter credit for the solo I took on my song. It was great being there with all the name musicians and meeting Paquito D'Rivera.

PAQUITO D'RIVERA

Three decades ago, wearing worn-out yellow/black dotted swimming trunks and accompanied by my four-year-old son, Franco, I was strolling the forbidden sands around one of those "foreigners only" hotels of the eastern beaches of Havana. Suddenly, I was surprised by the improbable image of a happy group of people: Jaco Pastorius, Hubert Laws, Harvey Mason, John McLaughlin, and the brothers Percy and Jimmy Heath. The explanation for such an unusual gathering of jazz luminaries ninety miles away from the U.S. coast was that they were part of the impressive musical troop organized by CBS and Bruce Lundvall—its president at the time—to produce the gigantic show "Havana Jam," held March 3–5, 1979, at Miramar's Karl Marx Theater.

For the occasion, the gringos brought together a few planes of gear and technicians, as well as a constellation of jazz and pop artists, such as Stan Getz, Dexter Gordon, Weather Report, Tony Williams, Willie Bobo, Billy Joel, Kris Kristofferson, Rita Coolidge, Woody Shaw, Bobby Hutcherson, Stephen Stills, and the Fania All-Stars. The latter group featured prominent U.S. Latin musicians and singers such as Héctor Lavoe, Johnny Pacheco, Roberto Roena, and Rubén Blades. Representing the Cuban musicians, there were percussionists extraordinaire Tata Güines and Guillermo Barreto, Orquesta Aragón, Irakere, and the political singer Sara González, sort of an overweight Spanish-speaking Joan Baez. That is how the musical extravaganza was inaugurated by the chronic drunkard Armando Hart, Minister of Culture, who was (for a change!) out of tune from the start. After his final words, the huge curtain of the theater slowly opened and out of a cloud of white smoke came the unmistakable sound of the great Jaco Pastorius, as the group Weather Report presented its credentials. Behind them, an enormous screen simulated a dark-blue and infinite universe with millions of shining stars—the perfect backdrop for music that sounded, to many of those in the audience, as if it were coming from another planet.

At the end of the show, we were informed that the revolution had assigned us the mission of representing Cuba at the Montreux Festival in Switzerland, as part of the CBS delegation to the annual celebration, along with Alvin Batiste, McLaughlin, Stan Getz, and the Heath Brothers with Tony Purrone on guitar, Akira Tana on drums, pianist Stanley Cowell, and the fantastic Slide Hampton on trombone. It was like a dream come true, since those men were among our heroes for a great part of our lives.

A couple of years later, already established in the City of Skyscrapers, I found myself at Avery Fisher Hall in Lincoln Center, seated in Dizzy Gillespie's Dream Band saxophone section, along with Frank Wess, Frank Foster, and Pepper Adams. As soon as I took my position on third alto, a voice coming from my left said, "Hey, amigo, did you bring those swimming trunks with you?" The voice on the other side of lead alto Frank Wess belonged to none other than Jimmy Heath. That was his funny way of welcoming me to the "Jungle." Ever since, we have cultivated a professional as well as personal relationship, from which I've learned so much, musically and humanly. Luck-

ily, many years ago, the tenor man found a caring, lovely lady on his path. Besides his music, Mona was the best that could happen to him, and he deserved it.

My mother always said, "Quality perfume comes in small bottles," so I would say that Jimmy Heath is a good example of that concept, isn't he!

During our tenure on the CBS roster, there was also a group on the label called John Lee and Gerry Brown. John was the bass player and Gerry was the drummer. Percy and I became friendly with John, who was about to get married. He said he would be honored if the Brothers would consider playing at the event. On December 30, 1979, in a loft in Lower Manhattan, they had an interdenominational ceremony with a gazebo and all the trimmings. This was unusual for Percy and me, since both of us married interracially and were ignored by our wives' parents.

When the summer of 1980 came around, I had the chance to visit Senegal in West Africa. I had related to Africa through my music, as in the *Afro-American Suite of Evolution*, but this was my first trip to the continent. The event was the celebration of the twentieth anniversary of the independence of Senegal, whose president was the poet Léopold Senghor. I was on a set with drummer Darryl Washington, Dizzy, saxophonists Clifford Jordan and Sonny Fortune, trumpeter Jimmy Owens, Percy, and Kenny Clarke. It was overwhelming to see the massive crowd and to hear their response to our music. We were really playing "for the public."

MTUME

In 1976, when I played with Tayari at Town Hall on his Afro-American Suite of Evolution, *I was proud. It was a hell of a piece. Not only that, it was the completion of a circle for him. It covered so much stuff, and it was a joy to play on and a deeper joy to listen to. It was one of those things when you're playing, you got to watch what you're doing because you're listening to all this shit. It was just great.*

Tayari was always open. One day he came to see me work in the studio when I was doing maybe the Stephanie Mills album. He saw how serious I was about recording technology. It had an influence on him. After Tayari saw me working in the studio, he said, "Why don't we do something together on Live at the Public Theater?*" It was his suggestion.*

Things really got deep when we were . . . recording Live at the Public

Theater *in 1979, when the Heath Brothers were really getting notoriety. Percy would really get pissed off, but I was patient with it because I understood. It was that resistance to change. I don't think he had ever really heard what a Moog synthesizer could do, a bass Moog, and on one of those tracks, I had his bass line doubled with a Moog. I told him, "The bass you play only goes here. We can take that shit down to here and double it and put you on top with that bottom." He hated it, but that sound was a motherfucker. For most of the cats from Percy's generation, that was out. It was Tayari and people like Miles who just kept it going. Percy was very resistant to the new sounds. We had to fight hard for him to agree to that because he was saying, "No, no. It's not pure." Stanley was also resistant. We finally got around it, and the recording was a success, one of their biggest records. It wasn't hard-core funk, but it was just a way to bridge that gap.*

We didn't want to do anything that sacrificed the authenticity of a true artist. It wasn't going to be "We want the funk." I thought about a texture that would get them some airplay but in no way take away from the integrity of the Heath Brothers. I brought in my drummer Howard King on "For the Public." On the next recording in 1981, Expressions of Life, I produced the cuts "Dreamin'" and "Use It (Don't Abuse It)." On this session, I added Edward "Tree" Moore, guitar, with Howard and Edward Walsh on synthesizer. Also, as on "For the Public," Tawatha Agee and I were backup singers. Tayari and I co-wrote "Dreamin'." It was almost like a soft R&B, but it was still the Heath Brothers.

10

"For the Public"

■

The Heath Brothers

The albums with the Heath Brothers marked the peak of my recording success. *Passing Thru* sold eighteen thousand copies, *In Motion*, twenty-five thousand, and *Live at the Public Theater*, thirty thousand. We were working regularly as the Heath Brothers and establishing a reputation. Even now, people approach me and mention that they first knew about the Heath Brothers from those Columbia recordings. Sometimes they want to know whether those records are now available on CD. One compilation of *Expressions of Life* and *In Motion* was released on Collectables Records. Columbia is probably waiting for us to die, and then they'll put out those recordings on CD and clean up the catalogue. It's narrow-minded on their part, but they deal in big numbers.

Our numbers never came up to what CBS Records expected. However, after we recorded *Live at the Public Theater* and began to get more recognition and sell more pieces, we did a fourth album for Columbia in 1981, *Expressions of Life*. Mtume was involved on two tracks: "Use It (Don't Abuse It)," which was my composition, and "Dreamin'," which Mtume and I wrote together. The fourth record sold over forty thousand albums, which by any standard for a jazz record is a big number. At that time, we still had in the group Akira Tana, Tony Purrone, Stanley Cowell, Mtume, the Locksmith (Howard King), and a guitarist named Tree, who Mtume used on "Use It" and "Dreamin'." As a group, we were definitely on an upward plane with record sales, but at the same time, a move was taking place at CBS Records to cut all the jazz guys. Jazz artists were known at CBS as Bruce's pets because we weren't selling in the neighborhood of pop artists like Michael Jackson, whose *Thriller* sold over thirty million back then. We were being thrown in the same bag with the pop artists, and our sales appeared minuscule in comparison, but with any other jazz label or small label that produces jazz, forty thousand records could guarantee a contract.

In early 1981, CBS cleaned house and dropped the Heath Brothers, Cedar Walton, Bobby Hutcherson, Dexter Gordon, Woody Shaw, and most other jazz guys. They even dropped Freddie Hubbard, who had sold around eighty thousand records, an astronomical number for jazz, though his sales were diminishing. Bruce Lundvall, who had originally signed the Heath Brothers to the label, was also dumped and ended up at Warner Brothers. Wynton Marsalis was brought in as the new jazz artist for CBS's catalogue, and they kept Weather Report and Miles Davis. Percy and I were shocked. We didn't know that we had been dropped until Mtume told us. Mtume had sold a lot of records for Epic, a division of CBS, and was on the inside, and he told us that George Butler could have saved us but didn't. All he had to say was that we were on the way up, that we would perhaps sell fifty, sixty, or seventy thousand records the next time out. I don't know if we even received a letter from CBS. We were really hurt by that. We had compromised a little musically for CBS, but we still kept our integrity, playing things we liked also. We had tried to meet the younger audiences halfway. People have often said to me, "I didn't listen to jazz until I heard the Heath Brothers." On three of our recordings for CBS, we included compositions aimed at younger audiences, and the other tracks were compositions we really wanted to record. We never gave in totally and made an all-crossover or all-funk recording. We were still going to do our thing. Ninety percent of the recording was going to be what we wanted. On *Live at the Public Theater*, we not only had "For the Public" but also "Warm Valley" and "A Sassy Samba," which shows the kinds of selections we wanted to play.

Despite our compromising, Percy had been opposed to a lot of things that were happening when we were with CBS Records. He thought it was condescending. On most of the compositions contributed by Mtume, the bass played figured bass, a certain figure over and over. Percy never liked that kind of thing. He liked the freedom to walk and play four-four in the swing and bebop traditions, but he was swept up by our success and just went along with it. He would say, "James, you got the music anyway." This was similar to his situation in the MJQ. John Lewis "had the music," which means he was primarily responsible for the tunes they played and recorded. With the Heath Brothers, it was my responsibility, but I didn't mind that because I naturally fit in the middle, since I was born between Percy and Tootie. I, a Scorpio, was in the middle of the road and could go any way. Percy was the oldest brother, Taurus the bull. His mind was set on where things were supposed to be, and he didn't usually change. Tootie, the last brother, was Gemini, and he was very flexible and wanted to go with what would be successful. I was trying to find a way to make the music better but always realizing that we had to sell records for the label. How could we do that? We had to do a balancing act, or we had to give up all of our integrity. I wasn't going to do that. I wasn't going to do a whole record that was in a direction that I didn't feel I should go.

Percy and I used to always argue about the music. I said, "Well, man, you cross over to Western classical with the MJQ. It's okay to cross over to white people's music, but you don't want to cross back to your black roots." He fumed at that. He used to say, "But John Lewis can swing." I said, "Yeah, he also acts like Bach was the greatest composer in the world, not bop." John didn't like congas either. That's too black. He didn't like Dizzy because Dizzy kept the conga drums in there. John wanted to sound like the European style. The MJQ crossed over into the European classical but not into African American classical. On the other hand, when we were with Columbia, Percy didn't hate it when we sold forty thousand records.

After we got dumped by Columbia, we hooked up with Antilles Records, a subsidiary of Island Records. Percy and I recorded *Brotherly Love* (1981) with Tony, Stanley, and Akira. Tootie returned for our second Antilles record, *Brothers and Others* (1983). We also had Slide Hampton on trombone and Joe Kennedy on violin. What a beautiful thing it was to have Tootie back with us again as part of the Heath Brothers. It had been hard for Percy and me when we went to California to play a gig, knowing that he was in the audience. Tootie had joined the Actors Guild and had hoped to get into the movies. He was on a couple of television shows, one with Dizzy in 1987, *Frank's Place*, a black show based in New Orleans. He had also played some gigs with us before his comeback recording.

Akira left in a fashion similar to what happened with Keith Copeland. Percy, who was very particular about the drummer in any situation, hadn't been that satisfied with Akira either. From back in the forties, he had gotten spoiled by Kenny Clarke, also known as Klook. Percy had played with Klook with the Symphony Sid All-Stars, the MJQ, and others. Percy loved Klook all his life. Connie Kay of the MJQ had also been cool with Percy. Connie could fit, but there was nobody like Klook. For Percy, there would never be another Kenny, but Percy was always looking for a drummer like him. He was concerned with the drummer's overall groove. Kenny and Percy worked well together because Kenny could swing and was also sensitive. Percy thought Keith Copeland's foot was a little heavy, but in the music of that time, the drummer's foot was usually heavy. Percy liked the way Kenny played four-one, and Akira never played four-one like that. He would play four and one. It's a settling thing to feel the fourth beat. Akira was more "modern" in that he did things that a drummer like Elvin Jones would do that were more polyrhythmic.

While we were still on the CBS merry-go-round in the late seventies, we had a gig in Atlanta where we met one of the up-an-coming drummers of his generation, Winard Harper. Along with the performance, we conducted a workshop at Clark College, where the saxophone player James Patterson is a professor. At the end of our presentation, we listened to a tune played by the Harper Brothers, Danny on piano, Philip on trumpet, and Winard on drums. Winard was the one who took charge, doing all the talking. Percy and I were impressed. This was when Winard was still in high school. A number of years later, we played in Connecticut at the Hartt School, University of Hartford, where our friend and master saxophonist Jackie Mc (McLean) had established one of the most productive and creative jazz programs ever. Winard was there, having received a scholarship. He sat in and I knew then he had it. In every generation, there are a few outstanding performers. He is one of them. When he left Hartford and entered the New York scene, his energy level and smile captivated everyone who saw or played with him. He has the drive of Art Blakey and the persona of Papa Jo Jones. I call him "Happy Harper" or "the energizer," like the "Energizer Bunny" from the TV commercial. He just keeps going and going and going.

During that Heath Brothers period, there were some tensions between Percy and me, but we never really had a blowup over personnel or the music. I had liked both Keith and Akira and had been instrumental in getting both of them, since I was the music director. There were other differences between Percy and me as far as where we were with our careers when we started the Heath Brothers. Percy had been with the MJQ for over twenty years, and he was disappointed when Milt Jackson left and the group had to disband for a while. Percy had been in a safe and secure position, but I was freelancing and was aware of a lot of changes that were happening musically. I had to make the musical contacts for myself, and I did okay.

In 1982, while we were still with Columbia, we also made a trip to Japan, a brand new experience for me. Percy, of course, had been there with the MJQ; Tootie wasn't with us. We went to Beppu in Kyushu, the southern island. Beppu has hot springs, and there were monkeys running around. I tried the hot springs along with Ira Gitler, who was there as a writer. It was very different for me—the environment, the people; the respect they had for the music was overwhelming. The Japanese audience was so quiet; they don't scream or say anything while you're performing. When you stop, they give you thunderous applause. Obviously, they're paying attention in a way that's different from African Americans, who get into the music with you while you're performing, with responses like "Yeah, man, yeah." Black people get all up in it with you when they hear something they like. They aren't going to wait until the end. If they feel something, they'll let you know it during the course of the performance.

After that first trip, I went back so many times on different occasions with the Heath Brothers. In 1983, we played the Live Inn in Tokyo, this time with Tootie. I've recorded with several Japanese artists since then. I was a soloist on vocalist Keiko Lee's *Day Dreaming* (1999), and I also played on trumpeter Tomonao Hara's release *Hot Red* (1996). While teaching at Queens College, I had Japanese students like the singer Nabuko Kiryu. Her singing on my arrangements of Ellington's "In a Mellow Tone" and Bobby Troup's "Route 66" can be seen on YouTube. I also wrote arrangements for the Filipino singer Marlene de la Pena, who was very popular in Japan in the seventies and eighties. Of course, one of my main connections with an artist of Japanese ancestry was with Akira Tana, who was in the Heath Brothers for a good period of time and is a lifelong friend. We always hang when I go to California or when he comes back East. I sometimes stop by his house to see him and his wife, Margie. They're great people. He's a fine performer and just an all-around nice guy.

Despite setbacks, we continued as the Heath Brothers in the early eighties. We recorded two albums for Antilles, but their distribution wasn't as good as CBS's. We were still getting some response from fans as a result of having been with CBS. And then, when Tootie returned, Percy was ready to go back with the MJQ. The price was right, and Milt Jackson wanted to return. When Percy left to rejoin the MJQ in 1981, that was just about the end of the Heath Brothers as a CBS recording group. Stanley Cowell's family life situation also changed at that time, and he left to take a job teaching at Herbert Lehman College. For a while Tootie and I continued to work in a quartet with Tony. I couldn't afford to carry a quintet, so I figured that the guitar would be a better instrument to complement the saxophone. I had become accustomed to playing the melodies with the guitar from the CBS days, but Tony had a different role when we had Stanley on piano. Sometimes Tony would play the chords, and other times Stanley would have that role. Tony and Stanley had it worked out. I found that the guitar was a more flexible instrument, one that could blend with the saxophone while playing unison melodies as well as chords. That's when I preferred to use Tony in the quartet situation.

With Percy's departure, I was out there struggling. It was difficult for Tootie to remain in the quartet, since he was in Los Angeles, but occasionally, when the price was right, I could get him to play. Otherwise it was the Jimmy Heath Quartet.

STANLEY COWELL

I met Jimmy around 1969 at the Collective Black Artists big band rehearsal at Westbeth Artists House on West Street, where I was living. I was rather surprised to see him there, but evidently Reggie Workman had convinced him to come and play with us. He became a regular member of that group. I had known of him before, of course, because of his having been with Miles Davis. I was somewhat in awe because he was a recording artist, probably the most notable person in that band at the time.

In 1972, I toured with a group that consisted of Billy Higgins, drums; Sam Jones, bass; and Curtis Fuller, trombone, and the following year, I recorded with Jimmy on Love and Understanding *on the Muse label. Jimmy was always very humorous and kept things light. He shared many stories with us about his life, good and bad things, and there was continuous wordplay. He could turn a word around very quickly into something that would make you laugh, and he also could do the same thing with music. He could find melodies in whatever you played. After you played something, he would quote something else. You thought you had played something original. Once the*

Heath Brothers started in late '73 or '74, the wordplay just tripled with the Brothers because they all had the similar quality of putting things in a humorous perspective.

On tour in Europe, we used to play music on the train, Tootie and Jimmy on flutes, Percy on his baby bass, and I had my African kalimba tuned chromatically so I could play Western scales. I call it "couchet" music because we played in the sleeper cars. We developed a repertoire of tunes with the two flutes that included "Tafadhali," a piece by Albert, and Jimmy's Smilin' Billy Suite came out of that. We got to Norway, and I convinced them that they should record all this stuff in the studio, so we went into a studio in Norway and recorded. My company with Charles Tolliver, Strata-East Records, released it ultimately on that label. When I came back, it was sold to another producer, and Jimmy bought the master back in 2004.

I was influential in introducing certain Afrocentric elements like the kalimba. Strata-East and the Collective Black Artists were examples of how black artists could take control over their own musical destiny. There was in a way an eschewing of European elements and more of a focus on African or non-Western elements. There was a heavy influence from my generation even though musicians like Art Blakey and Max Roach used Afrocentric elements. Musicians of my generation were the benefactors; we ran with it. I was with the Heath Brothers from '74 to '83.

Jimmy is an expressive classicist with the older tunes, forward-looking, but always desirous of creating lyricism amid sophisticated harmony. He and Percy shared that classicist approach, and from my standpoint as a younger musician, I was trying to create things that didn't necessarily agree with them. Sometimes Percy would remark, "Who wants to hear something like that?" referring to a composition I created. The youngest brother, Albert, was trying to mingle and mix contemporary rhythms into that kind of classical approach of the two older brothers, which was always a point of contention because he wanted the older brothers to modernize and accept some other music styles, like rock and funk. I was even younger than Tootie and had a closer connection with the more contemporary pop music of the seventies. After a while, Jimmy began to change.

With the CBS contract, Jimmy's response was to write some excellent tunes, and Jimmy purposely bent over backwards to write music that George Butler thought would sell, crossover music, with contemporary funk, rhythm and blues, and pop-ish beats. Percy probably bit his tongue quite a bit in the studio with what George Butler wanted. We might play a beautiful ballad and then George would say, "I think we need to sweeten that up a little bit. Stanley, can you overdub Fender Rhodes on that?" His mentality was that the sound of the contemporary music could hook people and they would come over and listen to the older approaches that we were employing, playing a ballad in the typical style. I'm sure that George would have liked to have seen an electric bass on some of those things. However, the money was very good. The tunes were quality songs. They weren't just something Jimmy just threw together. There was a lot of craftsmanship and all of the elements of his style came out, the lyricism and the harmonic movement, but they were a little boring at times for the background parts because the rhythm had to be locked down in that style of music. It was boring I think for Percy to play those repetitive patterns. . . . Because those kinds of tunes only accounted for 10 percent of the music that we played, Percy lived with it. There was a balance.

However, sometimes there were loud arguments, and I found myself getting caught up in the middle of stuff. Eventually I said, "Let me get out of this. I'm not one of the brothers." That's when I began to not be available and gradually departed the group. It was my decision to leave. I wanted to do something else, and I had also started teaching in '81 at Lehman College, City University of New York. My leaving coincided with the Modern Jazz Quartet getting back together again, so it kind of worked out well for everybody.

When Akira Tana was in the band, he was just as crazy as Tootie and just as much fun. We were roommates a lot on the road. One night in Belgium in the eighties, it just got so ridiculous that we started singing opera on the stage. It was just a heady state; we were probably tired, had been traveling and playing the repertoire as usual. Something happened and it triggered some sort of spontaneous response and I started singing and then Akira started singing. It may have come out of a tune with an ending that had a sort of classical or operatic sound. Jimmy and Percy weren't actually singing, but I think that they were contributing to it. Percy may even have gotten his bow out and started bowing.

Jimmy is a very flexible musician. He's been on my recording of world music, on an album called Regeneration. The idea was to feature all these Afro-Asian instruments, mostly African instruments. Jimmy also performed with my piano choir in Washington, D.C., along with the Eastern High School Choir, a very well-known black school. He was the featured soloist. He also performed with my trio in Port Washington in the early nineties, and I *brought him back for his seventieth birthday with his big band. My wife and I presented him at Prince George's Community College in Maryland.*

Jimmy's compositions for big band and orchestra, as well as his many songs and tunes, are going to be the big legacy that people will continue to tap for inspiration. Jimmy's playing is masterful and that will always be remembered, but I don't think Jimmy's legacy when compared to a Sonny Rollins, Coltrane, or Ornette Coleman will be in terms of innovation.

PERCY HEATH

After the MJQ broke up in 1974, I was figuring out what I was going to do after twenty-two years of that. Now it was a chance to play with my brothers. We hadn't really done that since the MJQ got together. James was doing his own thing. I said, "We'll get the Heath Brothers together. How about that?"

The first recording had our mother and father on the cover, Marchin' On (Strata-East). Lois Gilbert, a host on WRVR radio, liked us, and we had a lot of play on that station. In 1978, we got an offer from Columbia, but we made a mistake in getting a black lawyer to negotiate the contract in the first place. Columbia's lawyers looked at his demands and laughed. It was a mistake because those lawyers at Columbia did not show any respect or regard for our contractual stuff, what we thought we were going to get. It wasn't there. They had no respect for a black lawyer. Our lawyer didn't know the ins and outs. I think he was connected with a number of people in the music business, but in dealing with these high-powered Columbia lawyers, he was just out of his league.

We were so glad to get a contract with Columbia. We thought that was going to be it for the Brothers. George Butler gave us his sweet talk. "Oh yes. You're going to be jazz on our label." Dr. Butler was a middleman between these people. They weren't thinking about art. All they think about is money and record sales. They didn't give a shit about the art form of jazz. The classical music series that Columbia records calls the Master Works Division had been carrying on for years and years. It's practically subsidized. We met some of those classical musicians in the airport, and they told us they never sold over three thousand records in all the years that they had been recording, and they record every year. It's a separate category in their catalog. One of the guys said, "You guys sold twenty or thirty thousand?" We said, "Yeah." They said, "We never sold five thousand." "No kidding," we said. They just keep recording and paying them. They were white classical musicians. They put us under the category of "Black Music." I knew that was a mistake when I realized there was such a category in the company. When I was recording with the MJQ for Atlantic, we never had a quota, and we never had a budget to fill out so that we owed for limos and flying to California for mixing. With Columbia, it was in the budget for each record. The corporation said, "We'll give you a $75,000 budget for this record, and if you don't use it, you're stupid." The seventy-five grand we had to pay back out of royalties, which we could never pay back. We did four albums, and we sold as many as forty thousand on the last one. We still owed them $150,000 or something. We never recouped $150,000 or more for limos and other bullshit like flying so-and-so's buddy to California to do the mixing—studio time here, mixing there.

With the MJQ and Atlantic, we were getting royalties on our records for years and years. We never spent that kind of money to make a record in the first place. Some of those albums for Atlantic were done in three or four hours of studio time or at least two double sessions. We would play the music for a month, two months, six months before. Then it was time to make a record. We would go to the studio. It was just like being on the gig. "Okay, start the tape, doom, doom, doom, we ran it down. Okay. That's it." The difference between what happened with the Heath Brothers is this jive big company approach to making records. All this studio time, thousands of dollars of studio time. They didn't have anything to do with booking us. We had a booking agent, Ted Kurland.

The whole rub in the Columbia association was that they pulled James off to the side, and because he was the arranger and composer, they would tell him, "Look. One of the songs will have to be geared toward the bullshit." They had the audacity to say to James, "Your son Mtume will produce a funk tune in this record just to sell it." I told James, "You can't get anybody to like apples by feeding them oranges. You won't sell jazz music if you use hyphenated jazz, funk jazz, punk jazz, skunk jazz, crossover bullshit. If you got to do that, then you're not going to reach the audience because the audience that is interested in jazz won't go for it, and those kids that you're trying to reach don't know enough to go for the real music." The musical difference between me and James started right there. On top of that, all of a sudden drums were the main thing in the band with that "dup dit di papi diti," that half-time music, which is not "ting tiki ting tiki ting," which is jazz. That's the difference between jazz and any other music in the world, that feeling. Once you compromise that feeling, you've left it.

That "ting tiki ting" is the basic cymbal rhythm. I remember when drummers were just playing snare drums. "Boop dap booba dap boop dap," and it was from the church, the Baptist church. That hand clapping, that after beat, but what they did to make the so-called pop jazz, I can't stand it because they are clapping on the wrong beat. They're clapping on three according to the subdivision they're making. "Data datadata boom." Tootie being a drummer was going right along with it. He would put funk on everything, but there was no funk beat for "Confirmation." Trying to please the record company, James included that stuff in the repertoire.

I told him it wouldn't matter if you didn't sell no more than forty thousand records, which was a bitch for a jazz sale. They give away that much for those punk records to get it played on the radio. They sell half a million. As far as I'm concerned, it didn't sell any more records. They never sent a letter saying, "No. We're not going to pick up your option." Nobody ever told us we were no longer recording for Columbia. Never. We found out when they didn't set up a next recording date. We had four albums and they were sitting on the shelf. A lot of good music was there, James's compositions and all, and those four or five things that were written to please. "For the Public" was one of them. The public never dug it anyhow. When we went to the recording studio, some dude was in there telling James, "You're playing too many notes. They'll never understand it." James wants to be a well-known composer. I guess James wanted to sell a million. He told me he wanted his music to reach the kids. I said, "Well, James. For twenty-two years I never had to worry about who listens to what we do."

With the Brothers, the rest of the repertoire was all right, but when it came down to those songs that were supposed to be new, for the kids, it wasn't really what it was supposed to be.

Overall, we had a good time. It was nice to play with James. We flew Tootie in from California to make the first album, but I could never get Tony to turn the volume down. He always played too loud. That would make the drums play too loud, and that would make me have to turn up the amplifier on the bass. I hate an amplifier on the bass. I never had to use an amplifier on the bass before. Horn players need more drums. That's okay too, but it just made everything too loud to enjoy the music. I enjoyed the gigs, but we were still playing kind of small venues.

My involvement with the Brothers eventually took a turn. Mr. Jackson (Milt) reconsidered his financial situation, I suppose, and found out it was *rough being a bandleader. In order to carry his own group with the caliber of musicians that he wanted, it was much more expensive and demanding. Every place we went with the Heath Brothers, somebody would always say, "When are you going to get together with the MJQ?" The quartet (MJQ) sort of got back together in '80 or '81. We actually started working so much that it was difficult for me to tell James when I'd be available and when I wouldn't be available. Also, Stanley got a teaching job.*

The Brothers never rose above a certain financial venue. Kurland was doing the best he could, but there was just not enough money. We played the festivals. The money they were getting for the Brothers and the money the quartet could command for the same amount of time was quite different. With the Brothers, James and I were just getting a little bit more than the other guys in the group. If the gig paid over two grand, we'd give them three hundred or four hundred apiece. Me and James would take five hundred and give them three hundred and use the other two hundred for transportation. We didn't take out the money for ourselves, but there was never enough really. We couldn't expect Stanley to go on the road for nothing, so eventually he needed more money so he got this job as a professor at Lehman College. He wasn't as available as he used to be. Then the MJQ resumed, and they started offering ten or fifteen thousand dollars a concert. It wasn't the money. John Lewis said, "Well, you owe it to us after all the twenty-two years of hard work. You owe us something too." It put me in a bind there for some loyalty that was due. I told him, "Well, listen. In 1974, when Jackson walked away from it, we were making six hundred dollars a week every week of the year, work or not. That ain't it."

James and I were both really disappointed because the Heath Brothers had progressed along quite a bit in five years, and we had the potential of moving up into another category financially. Everybody seemed to want to go for the kids who were buying the records. It was a selfish attitude on my part because I never had to do that.

James is the complete musician in the family. My favorite of his compositions is "A Time and a Place." It had broken rhythm; there was a swing part in it. That was quite a composition. "A Time and a Place" wasn't straight-ahead swing all the way, and it had a contrast in it with a sort of a Latin-type influence. Then it came to the swing part in the middle. The public liked it, and we liked to play it too, because it was really effective and built up into a good feeling on the bandstand. James had some other nice ones too.

James still enjoyed being in Dizzy's band occasionally, when every now and then Dizzy got a big band together. Dizzy hadn't changed too much in all the years. James is an excellent saxophone player. He is quite a musician. I'd really like to hear him go back to his alto sometime. Charlie Parker was the one who chased them all off the alto—Trane too. I've been trying to needle James up on that, but I think he's doing what he really should be doing, which is teaching, because James is an excellent teacher. He knows a lot about the music, and he knows how to teach people. I've had kids ask me, "Are you taking any students?" What students? I'm a self-taught bass player. What am I going to teach them? James is a teacher, and he's wide open as far as electronic instruments, which he uses to compose. I don't think he intends to be a synthesizer player, but he's using that to compose. He's becoming more of a composer than a player, actually, and a professor, a teacher. He's got off the road a bit because of that little heart shake up that scared us all pretty much. He changed his diet and everything since then.

He goes out and performs occasionally when he feels that he wants to; that's all good. He had jobs with radio stations in Europe that gave him a chance to play his orchestrations. I think James is doing very well.

AKIRA TANA

My given name is Japanese, so many listeners around the world who see me and also see my name on recordings assume I'm Japanese-born and are quite impressed at my fluency in English for a Japanese and are quite surprised to learn that I'm American-born. Japanese promoters have treated differently Japanese musicians who have lived and worked in New York. Because the music is American, most promoters have historically not encouraged American bandleaders to bring Japanese musicians to Japan to tour.

Performing with the Heath Brothers in Beppu, Japan, in 1982 was my first experience performing music in Japan. The Beppu event was a big affair, at the height of the economic "bubble" in Japan, so there were a number of U.S. groups and musicians and also many well-known Japanese players invited to participate. Dizzy, Paquito, Toshiko [Akiyoshi] and Lew Tabackin, Bernard Purdie, Freddie Hubbard, Kenny Barron, and Donald Bailey were all there. In addition, Motohiko Hino, Terumasa Hino, and other well-known Japanese musicians were part of the festival. Beppu, which is on the southern island of Kyushu, is famous for its hot springs. I went to the hot springs bath with Dizzy, Bernard Purdie, Jimmy, Ira Gitler and his young son at the time. There were a few others as well, and the looks of all the Japanese bathers when a group of non-Japanese entered the bathing area was something. Because Japan is such a homogeneous country whose people are relatively small in comparison, foreigners really stand out.

I can't imagine working with siblings, but Jimmy and Percy have been partners in music way before the formation of the band (that includes Albert as well), so it was natural with their compatible but different personalities that they formed a band, unlike Elvin, Hank, and Thad Jones. I can't imagine how their strong egos would have meshed into a working band later in their careers. By far Jimmy was the musical leader of the band, the composer, the arranger, and the producer, though Percy definitely had strong input in all areas, and he might have been more influential in organizing the band from his experiences with the MJQ.

The band, when I was a member, had a guitarist, and Jimmy, being the composer and arranger, always had an "open" ear to contemporary pop music. This was also partly because of the CBS contract the group had at the time, which allowed Jimmy to explore more melodies and sounds in a pop vein. All three Heath brothers are understandably hard-core boppers, and even with Percy's experience with the MJQ—an original fusion group if I've ever heard one—I sensed that Percy was the most stubborn in resisting Columbia's pressure to sell more product by commercializing their sound and approach. All in all, Jimmy was and still is true to his musical convictions, which are vast and infinite. It is definitely evidenced by his illustrious career as a composer and arranger. I can't imagine what the dynamic would be if I had to do it with my three brothers, but for the Heaths, because of their shared experiences in the spirit of music, together and separately, it worked and still works. Nevertheless, siblings have differences, and boy did they get into disagreements. It seemed like sound checks were a great time to vent frustrations and the effects of fatigue from travel. With an electric guitar in the band, volume was also an issue, especially with Percy, coming from the more "sedate," controlled sound environment of the MJQ. I recall seeing the Brothers at the Vanguard way before I joined the band, and seeing Albert wearing a jumpsuit playing funk beats on "All the Things You Are." He had a crash cymbal behind him—reverse slam dunks on every crash! Albert, the youngest and free-spirited; Percy, the eldest and most proper; and Jimmy, in the middle, relating to both in a very diplomatic fashion. Jimmy has written so many wonderful compositions, but a favorite of mine to play on is "A Sound for Sore Ears," which has transitional sections that allow the drums to be creative, bridging the sections.

After the CBS contract ended, the HB's signed with Antilles. At the recording session for Brotherly Love, which was released in 1981, Percy was trying to read a bass part and complained about the notes being too high above the staff. Jimmy went in and promptly turned the page around. Percy had the music upside down!

I was also part of a State Department tour we did of South America in 1981. We had to go to the airport early to catch a plane in Brazil. I was sitting in the backseat between Jimmy and Percy; early morning travel can be stressful, and this morning was no exception. They were "wolfing" at each other. I happened to be caught in the crossfire. I can still hear it now. Also on the same tour, I learned about how a traveling, working band is really a family on the road, and despite the personality differences, helping each other out is tantamount to a successful band. The State Department tour in 1981 also coincided with the Malvinas (Falkland Islands) controversy between England and Argentina.

Our concert was canceled in Buenos Aires, and we were trying to get to Lima, Peru. The U.S. Consulate was supposed to host us and help us with the travel arrangements. We were stuck without any assistance at the airport—the U.S. Embassy had been evacuated—and we needed to get Percy's bass case on the plane and had plenty of luggage to check. The overweight and oversize costs were usually waived, but without the assistance of U.S. officials, we were on our own. We had to scrape together all of our cash to add to Percy's credit card charge to pay for the extra costs to get out of the country. We barely made the flight, had to fly through Santiago, Chile, and finally arrived in Lima in the early morning hours. To add insult to injury, Percy's luggage was vandalized and his wife's jewelry was stolen. Even after arriving at that late hour, the group was met with hostility of the racial kind by a redneck Texan at the hotel in Lima, who made derogatory comments about the band. Stanley Cowell and I had to be restrained from going after this person. This experience is certainly mild compared to what African American traveling musicians experienced in the South decades ago, but, nevertheless, after a harrowing day of travel, this run in was no walk in park.

In 1983, I was back to freelancing. There was less money coming in after CBS, but I had established a pretty good reputation as a writer, which helped to supplement my income. A few small commissions, royalties, the CBS monies, and gigging kept me in manageable financial shape, so Mona and I weren't really hurting. We had survived harder times in the sixties without really serious consequences. Despite the setbacks, I was on a pretty good roll in the eighties because my nature wasn't to be extravagant with money. I was a saver, so I had a nest egg that would take the family through the harder times. I learned to save when I was a youngster. If you get something, you better hold onto it. My parents had some difficult times over the forty years that they were together, and I learned from them how to survive.

I continued working with Tootie on and off, but I felt strange about calling our group the Heath Brothers. I hadn't felt the same way when it was just Percy and I because we had originally signed the contract as the Heath Brothers. After Percy left, I called the group the Jimmy Heath Quartet featuring Albert Tootie Heath, as opposed to calling it the Heath Brothers. I'm sure that Tootie had a reaction to that. When Tootie and I played together without Percy, people in the audience would ask, "Where's Percy?" because Percy and I were more identified by the public as the Heath Brothers. Since Tootie had been on *Passing Thru* only as a guest, people didn't necessarily consider him as a key part of the Heath Brothers, as we did.

In reality, Percy and I are much older than Tootie, and from the beginning, when I was with Howard McGhee, we were the two professional musicians in the family. Tootie is nine years younger than I am. Percy and I had been professionals before Tootie started playing. It made for a strange situation, and I felt guilty sometimes. Once, we were supposed to play a gig in Vail, Colorado, and Percy didn't want to go because the money wasn't right, so Tootie and I made the gig and used the name Heath Brothers. At a certain point, Percy wasn't that anxious to work a lot of gigs because he had gone into retirement, and unless the money was really right, he wouldn't travel. On those occasions, I had used the name Heath Brothers even if Percy wasn't there. Tootie and I were the Heath Brothers too. It's an honest identification, even if it wasn't the same two or three Heath Brothers that some audiences might expect.

We went back to Wilmington for "Heath Brothers Day," February 24, 1983. The mayor pro tem, Luther H. Jordan, Jr., came to the airport to meet us. A reporter asked me what was different about that day and when I was in Wilmington before. I said, "You coming here to meet us as a reporter and a white man to document this occasion. Back when I graduated from high school, if I walked down the street in the wrong neighborhood, I was just a nigger to everybody." It was nice to perform in Kenan Auditorium on the campus of the University of North Carolina, Wilmington. We performed in Wilmington again in 1985, at Thalian Hall. The city had declared May 25 "Jimmy Heath Day," and when we performed, a lot of my schoolmates from Williston High School attended. Many others had passed away. The concert was produced by Larry Thomas, the son of one of my classmates at Williston. Larry is a proud African American man—a historian, author of two books, producer, promoter, jazz supporter, and DJ. One of his books is titled *The True Story behind the Wilmington Ten,* about the group of civil rights activists, including the Reverend Benjamin Chavis, Jr., who were imprisoned in 1971 on arson and conspiracy charges and spent nearly ten years in jail before their sentences were overturned. Larry has done a lot of research on the Barn, the Wilmington club where Ellington and Lionel Hampton played. For many years, he has presented me, the Heath Brothers, and many other performers in concert throughout the state of North Carolina. I consider him the North Carolina jazz connection. Larry and his wife, Candace, an artist, are champions for black folks' causes. When I want to know what's happening in North Carolina, I contact them. I kid Larry by calling him "Sleepy time," from the song "Sleepy Time Down South," but he is completely aware of what's going on, not sleeping.

That fall, on October 18, 1985, I had a chance to hear some of my compositions played at Rutgers University, the home of the Rutgers Institute of Jazz Studies, directed by Dan Morgenstern and Ed Berger. The Institute is in Newark, but the event was held at the New Brunswick Campus. I was the guest artist at the concert, which the Rutgers Jazz Ensemble, headed by saxophonist Sahib Shihab, a legend in his own right, finished off by playing "C.T.A.," "A Sassy Samba," "The Voice of the Saxophone," "Gingerbread Boy," and my arrangement of Kenny Dorham's "Una Mas." Years ago, I had heard Shihab with Tadd Dameron and Babs Gonzalez, and after that we had played together on a couple occasions, including a gig with Art Blakey's Messengers big band and a recording for Discovery with Gil Fuller's band in 1949. In the late sixties, I witnessed his wedding in Copenhagen. The last time we played together was with Jay McShann in Paris for the Charlie Parker celebration.

In the eighties, I continued to record occasionally with other musicians, like Slide Hampton. My basic survival kit for gigging was the Jimmy Heath Quartet, although I made a number of other gigs. When I got back from a tour in Europe, I was asked by Sonny Costanzo to teach saxophone for one day a week at Housatonic Community College in Bridgeport, Connecticut. I taught there in 1984 and 1985, during which time I was still teaching on Saturdays at Jazzmobile. In 1984, my daughter's first son, Michael, was born, and because Roslyn was working at Memorial Sloan-Kettering Cancer Center in Manhattan, Mona took over as babysitter. She was proud to do it. My teaching helped out economically because this was a slow period for jazz recordings, and I didn't have many record dates during those years. After teaching at Housatonic, in 1985 I started teaching at the City College of New York as a replacement for Gil Evans when at the last minute he didn't show. John Lewis was at City College during his hiatus from the MJQ, as was bassist Ron Carter. I was there for one semester, but I left because the Ted Kurland Agency, which had been booking me for years, arranged a European tour for the winter of 1985. Although City College asked me to stay, I told them that I was going back on the road, thinking that the tour with my new band to Europe was going to happen. Then I got another call that the tour had fallen through because of a tragic car accident in Europe involving the group Oregon. The promoter was so shaken up that he canceled my tour. I had been traveling to Europe over the years as a soloist performing with European radio orchestras, but I had been depending on that tour to get over there with my own band. I was disappointed, of course, but by the summer of 1986, I was part of a group called the New York Jazz Sextet, which was booked on a three-week tour of Europe starting out at the North Sea Jazz Festival in The Hague.

A couple of days before going to Europe, Mona had gone into Manhattan, and while she was gone, in a down moment, I smoked a "Thai stick," really potent grass. I felt like I was going to die. When Mona called me, I told her I felt terrible. I had congestion in my chest and could hardly breathe. The next day I went to the doctor and told him I needed an exam because I was going to Europe. I realized then that it wasn't what I had smoked that had made me feel so out of it. The doctor detected something strange on the electrocardiogram but said I would be all right and could go on the tour. He told me that when I got back, I should have more tests taken. The next day I called the guy I got the Thai stick from and asked him what was in it because I still thought that it was the cause. Later that day, a very hot day, Mona and I drove over to the supermarket, and when I walked into the air-conditioned store, I could hardly breathe. I started to feel weak and dizzy. While Mona was shopping, I went out to car, put the seat back, and rested. The sun was hot but I felt pretty good.

The next day I flew to Europe for three weeks with the New York Jazz Sextet. We had Hilton Ruiz on piano, Jimmy Cobb on drums, Percy on bass, Slide Hampton on trombone, and Jimmy Owens on trumpet. The North Sea Jazz Festival was like a reunion, a big jazz party, and a lot of cats were there who I hadn't seen in a while. I saw Miles and spoke to him in his room. His son, who I had never met, was there. He was just a very young child at that time. I spent the whole first day talking to a lot of the musicians I knew: John Lewis, Clark Terry, David "Fathead" Newman, and others.

That night, Miles was playing in the tent, an outdoor venue that held some three or four thousand. The New York Jazz Sextet was in a big building that was like a jazz supermarket, not a pleasant place to play. Groups were playing in different areas of the building. It was good in that you could meet all of your fellow musicians. When we started to play "Invitation," with me on soprano sax, I began to feel congested. I told Jimmy Owens that I wasn't feeling well, and he said that there was a medical person available in case someone had a problem. I left the stage while someone else in the group was taking a solo, and had my blood pressure taken. They brought the wheelchair for me. My horn was still on the stage. John Lewis was in the audience, and he reminded me later how well he thought I had played. I was taken to another room for more tests. My blood pressure and heart rate were strange, and they took me to the hospital in an ambulance. I told Percy to pack up my stuff. Since the day I had smoked the Thai stick, this was the third occurrence of that strange feeling. I was taken to a very comfortable hospital, Bronovo in The Hague. They took blood tests and an EKG, and the result was that I had an irregular heartbeat. The next day they were going to let me know what they thought I should do. When the doctor came the next day, he said, "Mr. Heath, I don't know what your tour schedule is, but I think that if you go on tour, within a year's time you will have a major heart attack." He recommended an angioplasty, a medical procedure in which a catheter is inserted in an artery. Before that, they put a catheter in my groin and ran it into my heart. On the monitor, I could see the wire passing up into my heart. That procedure wasn't painful, but when they shot the dye up inside of me in order to take photographs of my heart, I felt a burning sensation for a few seconds, as if I were on fire. They took me back to my room so that I could get some rest.

The next time I saw the doctor, he told me that I had a blockage in my major arteries. He recommended an angioplasty, where they would go back in through the catheter they left in place and open up my artery with a balloon. That would stretch the artery and remove the plaque. After that I would have to change my diet and I probably wouldn't have the problem again. But he said that if they put the balloon in and something went wrong, if the artery collapsed, I would have to have a bypass. I was given time to think about it. My illness brought on a blue interlude of doubt and despair.

The tour was supposed to go from The Hague to San Sebastian, Spain, and on to Italy, where Mona, who hadn't been to Italy, was going to join me, but she came over early after the hospital called her. When she arrived, the doctor discussed the procedure with us, and he told me not to worry because 90 percent of angioplasties are successful. I was worried about possibly needing a bypass, where they would have to cut into my chest. What I found comforting was that the doctor at Leiden asked me if I had known Charlie Parker, and I said yes. The surgeon was a jazz lover. I was comfortable with him after I found out that he liked jazz and Bird. I had the procedure on July 17, 1986. (Ironically, Coltrane passed away on July 17 back in 1967.) They put me to sleep and ran the balloon up into the catheter in my groin, and it worked. Fortunately, I didn't have to have the bypass—I took the "underpass."

Afterwards, during the rehab, the staff was very surprised that I had so much energy. The nurse took me on walks, and the test for my lungs showed that they were super strong. The procedure and the hospital stay cost about five thousand dollars. In the States, it would have cost twenty thousand, and they weren't doing that procedure as often there. Nat Adderley had a bypass at the Howard University Hospital in Washington, D.C.

After I had the angioplasty and was recovering, I would get a call from Bill Cosby almost every day. The staff at the hospital would ask me, "Is that the real Bill Cosby?" Bill would always say to me, "In person." They really thought of me as a celebrity, especially after the calls from Bill. Also, one of the nurses, knowing that I was a jazz musician, asked me, "Do you know 'Groover' Washington," slightly mispronouncing his name. Later, when I would see Grover, I would call him "Groover." Her naming him was appropriate because he really did groove. Grover and I played together on many occasions, in Philly and D.C. James Moody planned a three-tenor gig with Grover and me for Moody's seventy-fifth birthday, but Grover passed away before that.

I kept the list of people who called me, people I never knew cared about me. I was overwhelmed by the calls from the States. A lot of the musicians came by to see me before I was taken to Leiden. Clark Terry came by and gave me five hundred dollars; David "Fathead" Newman and others came by. Of course, Percy was there immediately after he got off the stage that first night. Lionel Hampton, Dave Brubeck, and other celebrities called from the States. I stayed in the hospital for ten days, and Mona stayed at the house of my dear friends, Hilde and Cees Slinger, a Dutch pianist who recorded with Don Byas, Zoot Sims, Ben Webster, and Philly Joe. Cees is one of the most renowned pianists in Holland. I had played gigs with Cees but never recorded with him. Cees and Hilde took Mona in and treated her like family. When I got out of the hospital, I spent a couple of days with them as well.

PART FOUR

■

Fourth Chorus

(1986–)

11

■

Reharmonization

■

Queens College

When Mona and I got on the plane for the States after my operation that summer in 1986, I was still feeling a little weak. Just before we were about to take off, something went wrong with the engine; smoke was coming out of it. We just sat there for about an hour and a half until they fixed it. All I could think of was the seven-hour flight back. This rough experience was enough for me to give up smoking weed forever, as I had done with heroin. That's that, from here to eternity!

MONA

Jimmy was in the hospital that Friday in July 1986 for observation and he called me. He said, "Don't worry. They're just checking me out." Saturday morning, in a serious thunderstorm, Johnnie Garry of Jazzmobile took me to the airport. When I arrived in Amsterdam, Cees Slinger and his wife, Hilde, picked me up and took me to the hospital to see Jimmy. The hospital was very small, quiet, and resembled a Swiss Hotel. I expected to see Jimmy looking like a basket case, but they had taken such good care of him that he looked like a baby, very calm. The nurse, who looked like Brooke Shields, was very excited by the many calls he got, including more than one from Bill Cosby. Some of the musicians who were at the festival came by to visit. After the diagnosis, a blocked artery to the heart, Jimmy was sent to the University Hospital in Leiden for the angioplasty.

When we were riding in the ambulance, the attendant told us not to worry because if anything happened, they would just take him upstairs, saw open his chest, and do a bypass. Why did he say that! Jimmy thought he might never play another note on the saxophone. At the hospital in Leiden, the doctor who performed the angioplasty, and who had been trained in the States, said that's where the procedure was developed. He did three or four cases per day and wondered why more angioplasties were not done in the States. If Jimmy had just come home, who knows what the result would have been. In about twelve days total, we were ready to return home. Cees and Hilde took care of us the whole time. They were part of our family.

SLIDE HAMPTON

In the early eighties, at a club that's no longer in existence, called Seventh Avenue South, Jimmy and I worked together in a quintet with Ron Carter, Kenny Barron, and Art Taylor. Jimmy is one of the more important saxophone players. He's one of the guys who really make a lot of music. His whole attitude is to have the greatest musical result possible. We did a recording, Mad about Tadd, on May 4, 1982, and played some great music of Tadd Dameron. Jimmy, as always, played great solos, very wonderful lines, never trying to overdo things, but just trying to make it as musical as possible. Some musicians try to impress people with their technique or their range, but Jimmy's the kind of guy who just tries to make as much music as he can, and his solos are really fantastic.

Once in Europe, we were playing at the North Sea Festival in 1986, and for some reason Jimmy played longer than usual. It was a great solo, but as soon as he finished playing, he had a heart attack. At the time, maybe he thought that he was tired or had indigestion. He wanted to go on playing. We told him he couldn't do that. Jimmy Owens told him to check with the paramedic on the side of the stage, and luckily he was taken to the hospital. He was there for a couple of weeks. I don't think it was that long solo that caused him to have the heart attack. Now he always jokes about it, saying that I had played so much before he played that it gave him a heart attack.

Jimmy's very humorous, and like Curtis Fuller, there's a lot of intelligence in the humor. Jimmy's humor is usually about something that really happened in life, and when you think about it, it either makes you laugh or cry. Jimmy says that Dizzy had commissioned him to write an arrangement for one of his bands, so he wrote the tune for Dizzy, "Without You, No Me," but, as Jimmy says, "Did you know he never paid me?"

Jimmy's a fantastic arranger-composer. Composers are born. It's not just an inspirational thing. You can't just make yourself a great composer, but you can study and become a great orchestrator. Jimmy's one of the few guys who has both of these. His natural talent for composing is something that most musicians are in awe of because the rest of us don't have that kind of ability to compose. His arrangements are like his playing, very musical, very inspiring. Jimmy uses a lot of lines in the trumpet, trombone, and saxophone section that are like the lines he plays in his solos. His arrangement on "Gingerbread Boy" is an example.

Most saxophone players favor the saxophone section, but for a real orchestration you have to be very partial to brass. They're usually the first voices, the leading instrument. He writes beautifully for the saxophones, and some of his voicings for the trumpets, where they are playing things not quite in the ensemble, are wonderful voicings too, as are his trombone parts. Jimmy doesn't get the credit that he deserves, and that's usually the case with people who are really dedicated to what they do. Lots of guys who are big names never include him on one of their dates or one of their concerts. If there was a great trombone player around, even the younger guy, and he played really good, even better than I played, I would include him on my concert or date. You don't see Jimmy on these guys' concerts. You don't see him on the concerts of Sonny Rollins, or on Joe Henderson's when he was alive. How can these guys avoid making an effort to show their respect for each other by hiring a guy for a recording or something? There used to be a time, when these guys were coming up, that somebody would hire them. Dizzy would hire Sonny Rollins, Sonny Stitt, and Stan Getz. It's sad. It's gotten to a place where guys who play the same instrument avoid giving the others any kind of recognition.

It's something a little bit different from being competitive. All the guys are great players, so they don't have to compete with anyone. If you're going to have a restaurant, you're going to get the best cooks in there that you can. If you're going to have a classical orchestra, you're going to get maybe sixty or seventy of the best violinists you can get. You're not going to get one guy and say, "I'll make sure you don't get anybody else who plays as good as I do." It's a mistake. I have a group with five trombones. They're the best trombone players I could find, and they're so good that they make me practice. Whenever I'm able to hire a guy like Jimmy or Roy Hargrove, I hire him.

When I got back to New York, I stayed home for a week, and after that I went to Boston for a gig. I was so nervous, thinking that I might fall out or worse. I got over the nervousness, and the gig was all right. The next week, I went to Australia with the Philip Morris Superband tour. Dave Bailey, director of Jazzmobile and my good Philly friend, was the tour organizer and manager. Two bands were involved; I was in the number two band, which included Slide Hampton, trombone; Monty Alexander, piano; Kenny Washington, drums; and Niels-Henning Ørsted Pedersen, the Danish bassist. The number one band had Jon Faddis, trumpet; James Moody, saxophones; Kenny Burrell, guitar; Jimmy Smith, organ; Grady Tate, drums; and Barbara Morrison, a vocalist from California. That was my first trip to Australia, a long seventeen-hour flight. We landed in Sydney and then took another flight to one of the farthest west cities, Perth. We also went to Adelaide, Brisbane, Coolangatta, and Surfers Paradise.

MONTY ALEXANDER

Around 1966 or '67, I saw Jimmy when he was playing with Milt Jackson, and I also worked with Jimmy on a Jazzmobile concert. I think it was in a group including Milt Jackson. I knew of Jimmy before that because I used to listen to a Milt recording on which Jimmy was playing. It was a big band featuring Ray Brown and Milt Jackson, and some of the arrangements and one composition—"Dew and Mud"—were by Jimmy. That name came from the fact that Miles's middle name was Dewey and Miles played this Muddy Waters lick. They were playing in a soulful style of music that had grits in it, but it was also streamlined and at the same time connected to the roots. It was down-to-earth, and I loved it when I heard it. I realized that Jimmy was this awesome arranger, and that he was Percy Heath's brother, but Jimmy was completely apart from Percy, who I saw as more formal, from the image you associate with the Modern Jazz Quartet. They struck you as so reserved. I said, "Those guys couldn't be brothers."

Jimmy is a unique master of his music. You can't help but tap your foot to his music. It was connected to black America and soul just like the music of Jamaica, where I come from.

After you hear just a few notes of his horn, the way he phrases and his tone, you immediately know that's Jimmy Heath. This is something that seems to have gotten away from us, where individuals have an extremely unique quality; you can see the person in front of you after six notes. Maybe we've lost some of this because of saturation.

Jimmy's compositions always bring a smile to your face. The way he constructs a song reflects his own personality. Each has its own story, and there's an underlying quality, soul. It's harmony of a certain kind. His statements are so strong that they're cast in stone. They leave an indelible impression on you. Milt Jackson used to play that way too. It comes from a certain approach that was happening around the fifties and into the sixties, and then it kept developing. You could hear church music in their playing, in their beautiful ballads and harmonies, but all of it was roots music.

Jimmy always had this vision or nuance and could say the funniest thing. He has a way of taking the language and turning it into a Jimmy Heath comment that's memorable. He is a master of coming up with names for people. After he said something, word got around and someone might say, "You know what Jimmy Heath said?" I remember the joke about his turning fifty-nine. He would say, "Yeah, I'm coming into Central Park South now," referring to the street numbers in New York. A musician who would get all the jobs was Grady Tate . . . the busiest musician around. Jimmy called him Gravy Taker because Grady would "take" all the jobs. Jimmy would see you with a big Samsonite suitcase and would say that it was so heavy that it took Samson to lift it up.

There's no one like him. He's nonpareil. His unique sound and his experience are all there, wrapped up into that man of slight stature, but he's a giant. Musicians absolutely admire and respect him for his ageless approach. Here's a man now in his eighties who has eternal youthfulness, and he certainly puts his fingerprint on his music. His music always has a smile on it, a good feeling. When I saw him performing at the Vanguard in October 2007 for his eighty-first birthday, it was like being in his living room. He brings that family concept and great entertainment, a great uplifting experience. You can't forget it.

In Australia, Johnnie Garry of Jazzmobile and I would take long walks on the very flat, white beach of Coolangatta, one of the most beautiful beaches I had ever seen. The distance between the water and the houses was almost a block long. The audiences were wonderful at all the performances in Australia. Red Rodney, the trumpeter who I knew from Philly, and who had played with Bird, was there. Red was in residency at one of the schools in Sydney, and we got to talk quite a bit. We also went to Manila in the Philippines and Japan during the three-week tour.

DAVE BAILEY

I put together several Philip Morris tours for the purpose of trying to give exposure to some younger musicians by having them play with some of the stalwarts. We had veterans like Jimmy, Slide Hampton, Donald Byrd, Phil Woods, Kenny Washington, Kenny Barron, Monty Alexander, and Bob Cranshaw. The concept was to give exposure to some younger musicians who didn't have a lot of recognition in Europe. We took Joshua Redmond, saxophone; Lewis Nash, drums; Christian McBride, bass; Mike LeDonne, piano; Ryan Kisor, Mike Leonhart, and Jesse Davis, trumpets; and singer Nnenna Freelon. We had the older guys play a set and the younger guys play a set, and then we had a finale where they all performed together. It was incredible. The young guys gave the old guys a run for their money from time to time and vice versa. It was a beautifully competitive thing in terms of the quality of what was happening. Each made the other play stronger. Jimmy kind of co-led with Slide Hampton.

JOHNNIE GARRY

I met Jimmy when I worked with Sarah Vaughan, a long time before I was the manager at Birdland on Fifty-second Street, from 1960 to 1965. Jimmy's a little giant in the music. For thirty years he's been doing the Jazzmobile concerts, and we did the Philip Morris tour together. Before that, when he had that heart attack in Europe, I took his wife to the airport. When he got out of the hospital, he was part of the Philip Morris tour to Australia, and I was the stage manager. I didn't think he was going to make the tour, but he did. His doctor said he had to walk a couple of miles every morning, but Jimmy hated to walk alone, so I said, "Well, man, call me. I'll get up and I'll walk with you." That's what I did at six o'clock in the morning in Australia. When we talked and walked on the beach, Jimmy would be cracking jokes all the time. I had to keep up with him. Jimmy's very strong.

I was stage manager for the Jazzmobile concert he did for Dave Bailey when Dave retired. Jimmy put a big band together for the occasion. Dave was fond of that tune "Una Mas," and Jimmy played that tune with a group of all-stars at Marcus Garvey Park in Harlem. That was a tremendous deal on the big stage, and the audience was overflowing with about eighteen hundred people. Jimmy was also in the band when we did Ernie Wilkins's Four Black Immortals at Avery Fisher Hall in 1994 to celebrate Jazzmobile's thirtieth anniversary. The piece was also performed at Town Hall. The immortals were Paul Robeson, Jackie Robinson, Malcolm X, and Martin Luther King, Jr. When it comes to African American subjects, money is no object for Jimmy. He just does it. He's just a unique person.

He gets the quality musicians and does quality jobs, and Jimmy is never uptight like a lot of musicians. He just sails along, cracking jokes, especially on the road. He keeps you in stitches. Backstage he's always got something funny to say.

When I came back from the Philip Morris tour, I had made enough money to pay off the balance on my new car, a Volvo. It was one of the better-paying tours. The rest of that year, I gigged around town and continued to compose. In 1986, I was offered a teaching position at Queens College, one of the branches of the City University of New York (CUNY). I thought that my health would be jeopardized if I traveled too much, so I decided to take the offer. I told my wife that after years of being on the road, this would be a good opportunity to give up part of the traveling lifestyle.

I was brought on board at the request of Dr. Howard Brofsky (Dr. Bebop), a jazz trumpeter who was on the faculty, and Maurice Peress, the symphony conductor at Queens, who was a friend of Duke and Strayhorn. Peress had conducted the Cleveland Symphony when it featured the MJQ. In September 1987, I started teaching undergraduates improvisation, jazz harmony, and theory. This was a period of recapping my musical experiences and passing them on to students in a harmonic relationship.

HOWARD BROFSKY

I met Jimmy in the late seventies at a jam session at a mutual friend's house. I had just gotten back into playing jazz trumpet. At Queens College, I started the M.A. in Jazz Performance, and I recommended Jimmy as our first appointment in 1987. I had liked him as a person, and I had tremendous respect for him as a musician. I knew of his many abilities. A number of people applied because it was an open search, but I pushed for Jimmy and the committee hired him. He was a triple threat. I was impressed by his many abilities as a performing musician, as a composer, as an arranger, and by his personality. He fit into the academic environment even though it wasn't his background. I knew that he had been teaching at Jazzmobile and that he would be wonderful with students. That was my sense, and it was borne out by his work there for ten years.

Around the year that Jimmy's appointment was pending, the New Grove Dictionary of Jazz came out, and it was mentioned in Jimmy's entry about his drug arrest and his incarceration. Concerned that this would affect his application, Jimmy called me up and said, "Oh, man. That's it. They're not going to hire me. Forget it. They'll see that." Even though the department committee had approved him, it was up to the president to hire him. I reassured Jimmy that it wouldn't affect him. Even if they did see it, which was unlikely, it was in the past, and that would not cause him to lose the appointment. That's the way it turned out.

I observed him directing the big band at Queens when I sat in. I was very impressed with how he made up riffs right on the spot to be played under a soloist. He would suggest a riff figure to the saxophone section and then right on the spot suggest a complementary trumpet figure against that saxophone riff. When he directed the band, he never scolded anybody or was overly critical but got the best results from them in a very constructive way.

I've had the good fortune to play several concerts with Jimmy at Queens. We tried to use themes; for example, we did a Monk concert and a Tadd Dameron concert. They were fifty-minute programs, and we generally hired an outside rhythm section. One of the pianists might have been an adjunct faculty member. Sometimes we did Jimmy's originals or a couple of mine, and those concerts were recorded by the college. At one of those concerts with Jimmy, we played a jazz arrangement of mine on the old Russian folk song "Dark Eyes." I used this piece on a CD that I put out in 2000 called 73 Down: Dr. Bebop.

In '92 I retired from Queens and moved to Vermont to run the Vermont Jazz Center. Jimmy very kindly came up there several times and did a birthday concert with me. He was very well received. He's a crowd pleaser, and when he performs, he has such joie de vivre. He communicates this joy of music and engages the audience, and with this spirit, he engages the other musicians on the stand as well.

Donald Byrd was hired on Jimmy's recommendation. For a couple of years, Donald and I had adjoining offices. I knew of Donald and his early work, but I didn't know what he'd been doing at that time. He was having problems with his chops. Musically, he was sort of a shadow of his former self.

Jimmy was instrumental in making the program one of the top jazz educational programs in the country. When I went back fifteen years later to teach jazz history, I was impressed with the level and the diversity of the students from all over the world—a trumpet player from New Zealand, a pianist from

Switzerland, and so forth. The reputation of the program worldwide is really attributable to Jimmy's work.

The first important thing that happened after I was appointed at Queens College involved the Louis Armstrong House. Located in Corona, Queens, at 107th Street, not far from my co-op, the Louis Armstrong House, where he and his wife, Lucille, lived from 1943 until his death in 1971, had been designated a National Historic Landmark, and Queens College had been given the responsibility of running the house and overseeing its upkeep. Then president of Queens College, Shirley Strum Kenny, asked me if I would arrange for a gathering of musicians to play for a major press conference to announce the gift from the city of the Armstrong House and archives. In the fall of 1987, I was able to get Jabbo Smith, Roy Eldridge, Jonah Jones, Dizzy Gillespie, Clark Terry, Doc Cheatham, Art Farmer, Red Rodney, Jon Faddis, Jimmy Owens, Ted Curson, Leonard Goines, and Wynton Marsalis.

The emphasis for the October 19 affair was the trumpets, which played a fanfare and some of Louis's music. Aside from that, the Louis Armstrong Alumni, Arvell Shaw, Marty Napoleon, and other musicians from Queens, Wild Bill Davis, Frank Wess, and Arthur Prysock, were asked to attend the press conference. I also contacted Illinois Jacquet and Dexter Gordon, who had played with Armstrong. One of my students from Queens played on the occasion. CNN, NBC, ABC, CBS, all the major television networks and other media were there. Soul food was served in the large garden and in the house itself. People were all over the place, and the press conference was a complete success. I became an advisor for the Louis Armstrong House.

Shirley Strum Kenny and the other head administrators at Queens hadn't realized that I had those kinds of connections in the jazz world. They probably hadn't thought that I could have pulled off something like that. I think my involvement with that event was instrumental in my getting early tenure at Queens in 1992.

In 1987, I was commissioned by Queens to write a piece for the school's fiftieth anniversary, to be performed by the Queens College Symphony Orchestra and a five-piece jazz group. I was given very little money, three thousand dollars, to do it, but that didn't matter so much because I had never written for symphonic instrumentation. It was something I wanted to do but never had the opportunity. The copying of the music probably cost more than what I received as commission. *Three Ears* took me quite a bit of time to compose—six or seven months to a year. I used a lot of what Professor Schramm had taught me from the years I studied with him when I was writing the *Afro-American Suite of Evolution*. I also consulted Maurice Peress, who helped me a lot with *Three Ears*—especially with the bow marking for the strings.

It was an important day in my life when *Three Ears* was performed on April 17, 1988. The performance went off well except for one thing. We had rehearsed the piece with the students playing the string parts, and to me they sounded beautiful. It almost brought tears to my eyes, and I was really pleased with the way my string writing sounded in rehearsal. However, the day of the performance, *Peter and the Wolf* was on the program, with Tony Randall, the actor from *The Odd Couple*, doing the narration. They had brought in alumni string players to supplement the students, and the alumni were very snobbish in their reaction to my piece, which included the jazz quintet. The alumni didn't really think much of the music, or they were just Western classical music snobs. Maurice Peress, however, wasn't one of them. Most of their rehearsal time was spent with *Peter and the Wolf*, a piece they had probably played numerous times, and when they got to *Three Ears*, they cut the rehearsal short and took it very lightly. Consequently, when they performed it, everybody played quite well, except for one passage of strings, which really fell apart. I felt disappointed, and Maurice, who conducted the orchestra, was courageous in holding it together because they really screwed up that part. Classically trained people in the audience probably noticed the mistakes, but the average person most likely didn't. It seemed as if the audience enjoyed it and it was well received.

The concept behind *Three Ears* was that music is heard in three different parts of the body: the mind's ear, the heart's ear, and the body's ear. Music enters through the ears, and some people hear it with their minds. They are very scientific and analytical. Other people hear music with their hearts, especially when the music has a soulful feeling. Then others hear it through their bodies; they move physically with the music. I dedicated the piece to my mother, Arlethia. The jazz combo was integrated into the piece—Stafford James, bass; Akira Tana, drums; Tony Purrone, guitar; and Lou Soloff, a fine trumpeter. I had wanted Jon Faddis to play trumpet, but he was busy and unable to make it. A number of my friends and colleagues were in the audience, Stanley Cowell and Gil Fuller, who liked the piece, even though Gil told me what he would have done with the string section. He criticized it, which was okay because he had been one of my orchestration teachers. That was one of the last times I saw Gil, who passed away in 1994.

MAURICE PERESS

I took Howard Brofsky's advice that Jimmy would be the right person to lead the new jazz program at Queens College, and it proved to be true. He and Sir Roland Hanna got us off to an extraordinary start, and theirs was a very hard act to follow. They came with a century of personal one-on-one knowledge of the jazz world and produced some wonderful players. I'm a symphony con-ductor, but with a good, strong jazz background, and I feel attached to that community. Jimmy has been kind of my connection. Also, Jimmy and I are both still working full out in our seventies and eighties. We have wisdom, and we know that time is running out. We kind of say to each other, "Keep doing it. If not us, who?"

I worked with Jimmy on his tone poem Three Ears, *performed by the Queens College Orchestra in 1987 and 2006, the latter for his eightieth birth-day year. A lot of jazz musicians are in awe of the symphonic tradition and they shouldn't be. They see a guy look at a score with thirty lines on it and say, "Oh, my god," but you don't grasp a full symphonic score in one gulp. It takes time to study it, to go through it and learn it. I now stand in front of a symphonic score, and it doesn't scare me at all. I think Jimmy has lost some of that fear. It's doable. You can have a score with eighteen or twenty lines. It's not just trumpets, trombones, saxes, and rhythm, but now you have a whole bunch of colors and a whole bunch of instruments to work with, and each one has its own limitations and challenges—horns in F, various instruments in various keys—and you have to learn the comfortable and uncomfortable ranges of these instruments. All that stuff, Jimmy's got. Maybe in the process of putting his pieces together, I've helped him.*

Jimmy is a great composer. I don't know if he sees himself as that, but I think he is one of the finest composers of American music, African American music—it's all African American music. Jimmy's tunes are better and more interesting than Dizzy's. The notion of having your music played by a sym-phonic ensemble has been around since Gershwin wrote Rhapsody in Blue *and before that. Stepping out and working with symphonic musicians has been a very important thing for a lot of "jazz" composers. I used to score for Ellington with the symphony orchestra. Jimmy knew about all of this, and* he wanted to do some pieces that required symphonic scoring. He wanted to somehow marry his music with that, which I thought was a healthy and a wonderful thing. I've been a great proponent of that marriage. There are a lot of people who say it can't be done, that it's always a disappointment. I don't believe that's true, and I think I've proven that it's not true.

We did Three Ears twice. The first time it was like curry in a hurry, and it didn't have the kind of maturing process we would have liked. Then came his eightieth birthday, and I asked him for the materials, the parts and score; I did a little tweaking, not a lot, and I got to understand what he was after. I got to study the piece in greater depth, and I understood some of the ideas that weren't as clear to me the first time. I gained respect for the work, and I was able to teach it to the orchestra, to guide them through it in a way that gave it an artistic and successful hearing. It was very exciting, the idea of having a symphonic orchestra perform with a true jazz ensemble with real improvisers like Mike Mossman, Antonio Hart, and a rhythm section. The orchestra had a lot of licks of its own, and they rose to the occasion. I think it was fun for the kids to be playing those bebop licks.

Jimmy does things that come out of the Ellington "extended works" tradition. In 1999 at Avery Fisher Hall, I heard Jimmy's Sweet Jazzmobile, a profound piece for chorus, orchestra, and jazz band. I said to him, "I hope this has a future," because the text was kind of one-dimensional, but what he was able to do musically and spiritually was a masterful thing. I don't think the man who runs Lincoln Center Orchestra could write as well or as interestingly. For Jimmy, it seemed to be very natural and very easy, although he might have worked extremely hard on it. In another life, he might have developed more of these pieces. You've got to be commissioned to do that, as he was by Jazz at Lincoln Center. You can't just do it in the abstract and say, "Hey, here's my new piece; play it." This opportunity came to Jimmy because of his reputation, and he showed that he's a true composer. He's the real thing.

When I sit down and play jazz piano, it's like the clock stopped for me in 1954. My changes are fairly traditional, my substitutions are kind of obvious but nice. Jimmy sits and plays the same tune, but he finds within a bar transitional chords, substitute chords, that are so much more detailed and so much richer. He opened my ears to possibilities I didn't realize, and to the intricacies and the artistic skills of a musician of his stature. I've learned that from Jimmy.

■ Heath Brothers concert, Umea Jazz Festival, Umea, Sweden, 1975. *Left to right*: Jimmy Heath, Percy Heath, and Albert "Tootie" Heath. (Photo by Gunnar Holmberg)

■ *Afro-American Suite of Evolution*, Jazzmobile concert, Town Hall, New York, May 1, 1976. *Top row, left to right*: unknown (percussion), Percy Heath (bass), Stanley Cowell (piano; kalimba), Charli Persip (drums), unknown (percussion), unknown (tuba), Barry Domfort (trumpet), unknown (trumpet), and unknown (hidden; trumpet). *Middle row, left to right*: Sharon Freeman (hidden; flugelhorn), Ted Dunbar (guitar), Victor Gaskin (bass), Quentin Jackson (trombone), and unknown (trombone). *Bottom row, left to right*: unknown (hidden; violin), unknown (violin), John Blake, Jr. (violin), Carl Ector (violin), Noel Pointer (violin), Dave Bailey (Jazzmobile director), Jimmy Heath (conductor), Ernie Wilkins (tenor sax), Frank Foster (tenor sax), Buddy Pearson (alto sax), and Sonny Red (alto sax; flute; clarinet). (Photo by Morty Yoss, Jimmy Heath Collection)

■ All-Star Band, Twentieth Anniversary of Independence Concert, Dakar, Senegal, summer 1980. *Left to right:* Darryl Washington (drums), Dizzy Gillespie (trumpet), Clifford Jordan (tenor sax), unknown (drums), Jimmy Owens (trumpet; flugelhorn), Jimmy Heath (tenor sax), unknown, Sonny Fortune (alto sax), Percy Heath (bass), and Kenny Clarke (drums). (Photo by Jérôme Schwab)

■ Backstage, Live Inn, Tokyo, Japan, November 24, 1983. *Left to right:* Albert "Tootie" Heath, Percy Heath, and Jimmy Heath. (Copyright © K. Abé/ctsimages.com)

■ Louis Armstrong's house, Corona, Queens, October 19, 1987. *Standing, left to right:* Leonard Goines, Howard Brofsky (hidden), Ted Curson, unknown student, Red Rodney, Cecil Bridgewater, Lou Soloff, Art Farmer, Jimmy Heath, Jimmy Owens, Clark Terry, Jon Faddis, Wynton Marsalis, Marty Napoleon. *Seated, left to right:* Jonah Jones, Dexter Gordon, Illinois Jacquet, Dizzy Gillespie, Roy Eldridge, Jabbo Smith, and Doc Cheatham. (Courtesy of Queens College)

■ "Hearts for Ella" rehearsal, Avery Fisher Hall, Lincoln Center, New York, February 12, 1990. *Left to right:* Slide Hampton, James Williams, Hank Jones, Dizzy Gillespie (at piano), Teddi Jones, and Jimmy Heath. (Jimmy Heath Collection, photographer unknown)

■ *Little Man Big Band* session, BMG Recording Studios, New York, 1992. *Left to right:* Ted Nash (tenor sax), Jerome Richardson (hidden; alto sax), John Mosca (with his back turned; trombone), Loren Schoenberg (tenor sax), Danny Bank (baritone sax), Eddie Bert (with his back turned; trombone), Jimmy Heath (conductor; tenor sax; soprano sax), and Bill Cosby (producer). (Courtesy of Luigi Cazzaniga)

■ Jazz at the White House, White House lawn, Washington, D.C., June 18, 1993. *Left to right:* unknown photographer, Eric Reid (piano), Joe Williams (vocalist), Dick Hyman (hidden; piano), unknown (hidden), Jimmy Heath (tenor sax), Dorothy Donegan (piano), unknown (hidden), Grover Washington (soprano sax), Jon Faddis (trumpet), Illinois Jacquet (tenor sax), Bill Clinton, unknown (hidden), Bobby McFerrin (vocalist), and unknown photographer. (Jimmy Heath Collection, photographer unknown)

■ Queens College graduation, Flushing, New York, 1993. *Left to right:* Antonio Hart, Jimmy Heath, and Darren Barrett. (Courtesy of Queens College)

■ Jimmy directing his big band, Grand Hyatt Hotel, Grand Central Station, WBGO Radio New Year's Eve gala, National Public Radio live broadcast, New York, December 31, 1997. *Left to right:* Danny Bank (baritone sax), Jimmy Heath (conductor), and Bobby LaVell (tenor sax). (Copyright © Alan Nahigian)

■ Jimmy with friends, eightieth birthday celebration, Blue Note, New York, October 2006. *Standing, left to right:* Roy Haynes, Jimmy Heath, Benny Powell, Slide Hampton, and James Moody. *Seated, left to right:* Frank Foster and Hank Jones. (Photo by Carol Friedman)

■ Jimmy Heath, Birdland, New York, 2008. (Photo by Richard Conde)

The same year that *Three Ears* premiered, I had the good fortune to record with one of my idols, the "King," Benny Carter, on his date for *Over the Rainbow*. I later wrote a piece called "Jimmy Heath: 1989 Artist in Residence," for the March–April 1989 issue of *Saxophone Journal*, where I talked about his influence on me:

> In 1940 I heard *Cocktails For Two* by Benny Carter, and his playing knocked me out. I was only fourteen, and I dreamed of someday being able to play like him.
>
> Benny's tone is like velvet, his execution is flawless, and his ideas unique. He was my first influence and I continued to practice and listen to him on records. Then, in 1944 I went to see him at the Earle Theatre in Philadelphia. He had a big band that included Max Roach and J. J. Johnson. This was when I heard him play trumpet too. His band was great and he did most of the composing and arranging. Shortly thereafter he released a record playing "Malibu" on alto on one side, and "I Surrender Dear" on trumpet on the other side. After that, I knew I would be a Benny Carter fan for life. (p. 6)

BENNY CARTER

I've known Jimmy for a number of years. I've admired and respected him as a musician, composer, and a wonderful gentleman. I recorded an album in 1988, and Jimmy was part of that recording. That was a very interesting project. It was a saxophone session, five saxophones and rhythm, and Jimmy was one of the tenors and Frank Wess was the other. . . . For a while we weren't sure whether he was going to be available, but once he told us of his availability and confirmed that he would be there, we were all very, very happy. Jimmy had been one of my favorite musicians for many, many years; he's done some very interesting things. He's following a wonderful career, where he's doing a number of projects in education; everyone who has worked with him and witnessed what he does has commended him and spoken so very highly of what he does. Of course, his writing just speaks for itself. For one thing, Jimmy's got to be intricate in dividing himself into two or three different pieces. It's all part of the one career, but they involve different functions. Jimmy has this great ability to write like he does and create this wonderful music and then to pick up the horn and play anything he wants to.

Soundwise, he brought a beautiful tone that he gets from the instrument to blend with the other four saxophones, and he contributed advice about phrasing. There was so much that he and everyone else brought to it. Although it was my session, it was a collective effort; we all probably soloed equally. In that recording session, everyone was offering suggestions. Sometimes I would dare to offer one. Much of the music was written, and what was not written was improvised, and you certainly can't tell anybody how to improvise. They play what they feel, what they hear, and they create accordingly.

Jimmy has a sound that I like. There are so many different sounds that people get from instruments these days, and one musician pursues the sound that he has heard from somebody else and he wants to emulate. . . . Musicians emulate their peers or their contemporaries. It's just the influence they want to be under and what they hear that they like. I can't say that someone should emulate an eighty-year-old man like me—not necessarily, because I find myself at my age being influenced by younger musicians. . . .

Jimmy's skill as a reader is highly expert, no question, and his improvisatory skills are fantastic. He is acknowledged among his peers as an innovator, as a contributor, and as a great performer.

While teaching at Queens, I got involved in local activities in the New York area. When the movie *Bird*, by Clint Eastwood, was released in 1988, Gil Noble, who has had the long-running program *Like It Is* on WABC TV, New York, wanted to have some musicians connected with Charlie Parker on the show. Gil was raised in Sugar Hill in Harlem along with Jackie McLean, Sonny Rollins, Arthur Taylor (A.T.), and others, and in fact had played piano as a young man. On the program that fall were Dizzy, Jackie, A.T., Max Roach, and Roy Haynes. We all spoke about the movie and how it emphasized Bird's womanizing, not his musical genius. It was an honor for me to be on Gil's show, since I've watched it religiously on Sundays when at home. I never understood why it didn't have a national syndication. It's invaluable to African Americans and should be to all Americans. Gil has documented our history and culture in all its phases—politics, education, music, and art—through interviews with giants.

That fall I was also on the move again internationally. With my quartet, I went to the Malaga Jazz Festival in November 1988. It wasn't my first time in Spain; I had gone there in 1974 with Clark Terry's Big Bad Band. J. J. Johnson's quintet was on the schedule, as were Celebración Latina with

Paquito D'Rivera, Tete Montoliu, the Michel Camilo Trio, and Sammy Figueroa. The Festival Internacional de Jazz, as it was called officially, was held at the Teatro Miguel de Cervantes.

Malaga was a beautiful place, especially the landscape. We were near the beach, and it was like stepping off into heaven or someplace of rare beauty. The people, who were of all different persuasions, were very kind and in tune with the music. It was just a wonderful occasion. The Spanish hold the American musicians in high esteem, like we're something special. In general, Europeans don't think of jazz musicians as being black. We're Americans. Although we look at it as African American music, they just know that it comes from America, and America is exotic to them. All throughout Europe they treat us as artists, not just as ordinary people who are musicians. That's the difference. They're definitely aware of the racial situation in the States, and I guess that was an added bonus, that we came from not such pleasant circumstances to present this glorious music.

Back during the Heath Brothers' CBS period, we opened in Madrid for B. B. King in a sports stadium, and there were ten thousand people there. I had never played for that many people, but maybe Percy had with the MJQ. Years later I played in a main club in Barcelona, the city where the pianist Tete Montoliu was born. Tete was on one of my gigs somewhere in Germany, when I went over as a single, as I used to do in the sixties, seventies, and into the eighties. He was a super talent. I was fascinated by how he was able to play with such dexterity and competence although he was blind. He would never miss anything. He was very precise, very accurate. If he swung his hand way up high, he would hit the right note when he brought it down. He was exceptional. When Tootie lived in Copenhagen, he had played with Tete a lot. Tete spoke English pretty well, so we were able to communicate. For some reason, when I played with him, there's one song that I called that he wouldn't play. I said, "Tete, let's play 'Just in Time.'" He said, "I don't play that tune." He just turned his head away and no explanation was given. I don't know what his reason was, because he could play any song I asked, and I'm sure he could have played that one. It meant something to him, but he never explained it to me.

Not long after the premiere of *Three Ears*, we decided to launch a Master of Arts program in jazz at Queens. We started recruiting students from all over the world who had undergraduate degrees. At that time, the new program at Queens was probably one of the only master's programs in jazz performance in the city. We had to change the curriculum and the course descriptions to suit the program. I worked on that part of it. With the master's program, we needed another faculty member besides me, so we began a search. At one of the faculty meetings, one of the professors in the classical division said to me, "Can you get Winston?"

I said, "I think you mean Wynton." Wynton Marsalis had been getting a lot of recognition at this time at Lincoln Center.

The professor said, "Oh, Wynton."

I said, "I don't think Wynton is ready to start teaching at this point. He's still a performing artist, and he's still doing a lot of other things. But I can get Dr. Donald Byrd, who is highly qualified and has taught at other institutions in the country."

When Donald and I went before President Kenny, Donald, who was a pilot, got into a conversation with another of the faculty members who was a pilot as well. Donald really made a strong impression as a teacher of music with his background and his degrees from Wayne State University, Manhattan School of Music, and Howard University, where he got a law degree. The committee thought very highly of him, and he came on board. Donald helped design the master's curriculum, but he stayed only a couple of years because he had a big problem with Charles Burkhart, the professor who was head of the graduate music division.

Donald really wanted a free hand; he wanted to take over the jazz program, but they weren't ready to give him that control. Donald was still under the head of the graduate music division, which included the classical and jazz programs. Donald had a run-in with Burkhart. It was brought to a head when we were trying to get another jazz professor for the program, pianist Sir Roland Hanna. Donald went over the head of the Personnel and Budget Committee (P&B) and the powers in the classical division. He went directly to President Kenny, and she advised us to get Sir Roland Hanna. In doing so, Donald didn't follow the proper procedure. He was supposed to have consulted the professors in the Music Department, who would have had to approve it before it was sent to the president. Donald's move rubbed the Music Department heads the wrong way, and Donald was reprimanded. One night, Donald cleared everything out of his office and left the program. It caused me a lot of embarrassment because I had been instrumental in getting him there. He should at least have come to me beforehand to tell me he couldn't handle it any longer. Donald wanted autonomy; he wanted to be head of the jazz program. I didn't have the power to give him that authority.

I wasn't the only person who was pissed at Donald; he had done that kind of thing before. When he came to Queens, his lady friend in Jersey said, "I hope he stays." He sets up programs and then doesn't always follow through. At Queens, he really wanted to control the jazz curriculum and get it all together. He had the expertise to do it. We had several run-ins with Burkhart about various things. Once it was about musical terms used in exams. We told Burkhart that we jazz musicians have our own musical language. We don't use all of the Italian terms used in Western classical music—only basic terms such as pianissimo and fortissimo. Burkhart had a problem accepting that.

Donald didn't like the letter of reprimand he received from the department for announcing we were going to get Sir Roland Hanna before the routine search and the P&B process. We had been told by President Kenny to get him. I have to give Donald credit because he worked very hard on the program. Though we worked together on it, Donald had more experience with curriculum because he had organized jazz programs before, like the one at Howard University. I basically let him have that part, and I concentrated on teaching. He often stayed at the college until nine o'clock at night, working on the project with his clerk assistant. Donald tried to shape a jazz curriculum with all the necessary exams, but since our program was under the larger graduate division, there were certain requirements we had to meet that Donald couldn't accept. I was disappointed because Donald just left and didn't even come back to give his students grades. He later taught at Delaware State University.

The music school at Queens had been in existence for fifty years, and I was the first full-time appointee in the jazz program. There had been adjunct jazz professors prior to me, Frank Foster and Bud Johnson, and later we had as an adjunct the well-known trumpeter-arranger Cecil Bridgewater, who had played with the Thad Jones–Mel Lewis Orchestra and Max Roach. The lack of full-time jazz musicians on the faculty prior to my period showed where the program at Queens was in terms of jazz as music. It took them such a long to time to recognize jazz, and when I got in, it was a hard row to hoe. Queens has a major Western classical program, comparable to that of any city university system in the country, and a lot of private institutions as well. Those in the Western classical program didn't want to be pushed out, and they still aren't ready for the movement that is happening in this country.

Some of the professors were kind and respectful to me, but Donald did get sort of a raw deal because the president had encouraged him to go after Roland. As a new head, President Kenny, who specialized in early European classical music, also had a problem with some of the administrators at Queens because she had to deal with those who had been entrenched and who had power.

During my years with the program and since, most of the people I recommended stayed on. Following Donald's departure, we went through the procedures and hired Sir Roland in 1993. I was also instrumental in getting Michael Mossman into the program. Todd Williams was the last hire I recommended, and he came on after I left in 1998. When he left, I urged them to get my number one student, Antonio Hart, and they did. When Queens was looking for someone to run the Louis Armstrong House, I recommended a friend of mine, Julian Euell, who had been a director at the Oakland Museum in California and who had also worked for the Smithsonian before Martin Williams. Julian had also headed the Har-You program in Harlem. Julian didn't stay long, though, because he couldn't get along with one of President Kenny's assistants.

One day, during a semester at Queens in the 1990s, I discovered that I needed emergency dental surgery, and I was lucky to have as my dentist Phil Terman, the "Miracle Worker." Phil is the brilliant dentist who helped many of us in the music profession, including Duke Ellington, Harry Carney, Stan Getz, Phil Woods, Sonny Rollins, Donald Byrd, Dizzy Gillespie, Betty Carter, Terence Blanchard, Jerry Dodgion, Joe Temperley, Toshiko Akiyoshi, and others. I met Maceo Parker, James Brown's saxophonist, in Phil's office one day. What made Dr. Terman so special was that he was also a great clarinetist who could have continued as a professional musician if he had chosen to. We all used to talk about how he saved our careers when we were in doubt. Without his skill and compassion, I wouldn't have made it as long as I have. Hats off to the "Dental Giant," Phil.

When I started at Queens, I made the bold statement to my wife, Mona, that I was going off the road but that I wasn't going to lock myself up in my music room and constantly write. That was a big lie. At Queens it was my responsibility to conduct the jazz ensemble, which was a big band. I started writing for performances that took place every semester, and that led me to writing more and more big band music. In the ten years that I was at Queens, I wrote more big band music than I had ever written before, at least forty or fifty compositions and arrangements. I didn't write many arrangements of jazz standards. I continued writing extended compositions, such as *Upper Neighbors Suite*, a commissioned work that premiered at the Concordia University Concert Hall in Montreal on October 6, 1990. Four years later, on August 4, 1994, *In Praise (from J. to J.)*, another longer work I had written, premiered at Alice Tully Hall, Lincoln Center, New York, with Joe Henderson, the Heath Brothers, and Wynton Marsalis and the Lincoln Center Jazz Orchestra as part of the performance. By 1995, my second SteepleChase recording had been released, *You or Me*.

12

Up-Tempo Mode

■

I had some really good students at Queens. Some of them haven't gotten the recognition they deserve. One of my saxophone students was Donald Hanson, an exceptional player, who was teaching in the school system. Other students of mine were Alan Mandel and Antonio Hart, who was nominated for a Grammy in 1998, "Best Jazz Instrumental Solo," for a performance on his CD *Here I Stand*. Antonio is now a professor at Queens in the jazz program. He came to Queens from Berklee in Boston to get his master's degree. At Berklee, Antonio had studied with Andy McGhee, my partner from Wilmington, North Carolina, and he had also played with Roy Hargrove. Antonio reminds me very much of my buddy John Coltrane in his dedication to the music. He's always practicing, always trying to learn something new, always picking up different instruments. When he wanted to learn the flute, he took lessons. Now he's writing big band music fluently because he wants to do some of those college-type performances. He's a wonderfully talented saxophonist. He's always improving, and the reason he improves is that he's one of the hardest-working musicians in the mold of John Coltrane. For the album notes for Antonio's 2004 album *All We Need*, I wrote, "It is rare when a musician is able to sing, swing, create and communicate on his instrument. On this recording, Antonio does all of the above, on alto, soprano and flute. His compositions and arrangements are 'Hart-warming.' I am honored to be a part of this project." He's performed my compositions, and we've played together in the Dizzy Gillespie All-Star

Big Band. When Antonio came to Queens, he brought with him another young player, trumpeter Darren Barrett. Darren took first place in the 1997 Thelonious Monk International Competition in Washington, D.C.; another of my students, the Argentinian Diego Urcola, took second place that year.

Many of my students at Queens became teachers or performers. Some were from out of the country or different parts of the States. We had a saxophonist originally from New Mexico, Cynthia Mullis, who played with Diva (No Man's Band) and has a band of her own, New York Confidential. A lot of the students who came to the program had been at the New School in Manhattan, which had an undergraduate jazz program and steered people our way. Eventually we started to get more students who had been at Berklee because Andy McGhee recommended the program at Queens. Also, Paul Jeffries, the saxophonist who played with Monk, would send us students from Duke. Our program was developed through a lot of recruiting and eventually through some ads in *JazzTimes*. Another one of our students, Jeb Patton, ended up working with me in the Heath Brothers after graduating. He got his master's under the tutelage of Sir Roland Hannah and graduated summa cum laude in 1997. I grabbed him up real quick. Percy loved him; he didn't want another piano player after we got Jeb in the group. Jeb is a very talented young man in both genres—Western classical music and African American classical music. He's done all his homework. He's transcribed and performed Tatum compositions. Jeb is wonderful.

My teaching schedule was three days a week, from 2:00 to 7:00 P.M. At 2:00 P.M., I would start with my saxophone students. I might have two a day, one hour each. Then my classes would go from 4:00 P.M. until 6:30 P.M. I taught composition and improvisation, conducted the big band, and, of course, had to prepare my lesson plans. When I was on tour, I would go over my class work while on the plane. I used very high-caliber substitute teachers, such as Tom McIntosh, Benny Golson, Frank Foster, and Cecil Bridgewater, who would teach my composition class and direct the big band; they all had experience in those areas. With teaching and touring, I was really in an up-tempo mode.

ANTONIO HART

At Berklee College of Music, I had some really great teachers, but at Queens College, my intention, more than getting a master's, was to be around someone who actually contributed to the legacy of jazz and someone who was important—not just a saxophone player, but a composer and arranger like Professor Heath.

If you just look at the recordings—the Heath Brothers recordings and all the things that he's done as a leader, and the things that he was a part of— he's just part of the legacy. I had some great, great teachers at the college at Berklee, but none of them had that connection to the history like Mr. Heath. That's what I was looking for. I had an academic education, and it was a great education, but I wanted to be with somebody who had been in the trenches with all the masters.

Mr. Heath was a wonderful teacher. I wanted to be a protégé or an apprentice, not just a student. I made it a point to ask a lot of questions. I would ask him a lot of life-type questions, a lot of historical questions about what it was like when he came up with John Coltrane. He told me that sometimes they would go to the library and listen to Stravinsky. He told me about John Coltrane's work ethic and what it was like playing with Miles and leading his big band, the kind of things he did when he practiced, before he even started playing tenor, about being influenced by Charlie Parker. Mr. Heath has a reverence for everybody. He's just a very humble, unassuming man, and to me he's like an Apple computer on the highest level. He's just real fast, real bright, and funny. All of the positive qualities I would look for in a man, especially an African American man, Mr. Heath seems to embody all of that. He seems to be a great father, an amazing musician at his craft, an amazing teacher, and he seems to be a really good friend. When I visit his house, I might hear him giving Sonny Rollins a call, or back in the day Milt Jackson would call, or Benny Carter. He always talks about Dizzy Gillespie being the teacher, and he's always the teacher too. He'll sit at the piano and talk about what Dizzy did or show you different harmonic structures and how he came up with melodies. When I think of Dizzy Gillespie and that picture of people around him at the piano, I think that Mr. Heath is actually doing the same thing.

"Like a Son" is a composition he dedicated to me. It was touching. One day I went over his house and he was in his computer room. He said, "Antonio, check this out. I've been working on this." He played this composition for me and asked me what I thought of it. I said to myself, what am I supposed to say? It's great. Everything you touch is gold as far as I'm concerned. He said, "Look at the title." When I read "Like a Son," he just looked at me and I looked at him. I thought, wow, he actually wrote something for me, and he thinks of me like that. I think of him the same way, with the same kind of fondness. That's

probably one of the greatest honors anybody could have in life—if someone would create something with you in mind. To have my mentor, somebody who I totally respect, actually write a composition for me, there are no words to really describe that.

He'll come up with names for everybody, and they're really fast and very witty, and they're pretty appropriate to the character of the person—like he'll call Gary Smulyan "Scary," and Roy Hargrove, "Roy Hardgroove."

I recorded with Mr. Heath on Turn Up the Heath. He chooses the players according to what they can do, almost like a Duke Ellington thing. Mr. Heath knows exactly what you're capable of doing, and he hires you for that particular reason. That big band was like a family situation. We loved Mr. Heath so much that we wanted to make sure that his dream, his vision, came across exactly the way he wanted it. That was a very enlightening musical experience, where everybody's on the same page and everybody is trying to take it to the highest level. Nobody's really out for self. In the studio, it was just like a love fest. He has a way of presenting material and getting the best out of it in a way that's serious but also light at the same time. You hear that wittiness and that humor. It's humorous; it's sensitive; it's visionary; it's imaginative. It's who he is. Every time we would play a composition, we would say how great it was and then look at Mr. Heath. He's just this little, unassuming man, but he's like a hundred feet tall. It's a real lesson for me to know somebody who's so powerful in a lot of ways but still expresses a very, very high level of humility. He's definitely earned the right to throw attitude if he wanted to, but he embodies what I think Christ talks about in the Bible, how you're supposed to let your life shine, how you're supposed to treat people the way you want them to treat you. It's not fake. It's real.

The composition that has moved me the most for quite a number of years is the one he wrote for Dizzy Gillespie, "Without You, No Me." That's a powerful composition, and the spirit comes through it. Every time I play it, I just get chills. When I sit next to James Moody in the Dizzy Gillespie All-Star Big Band, Mr. Moody knows when it's coming up and he just looks at me. He'll gesture because I've been playing it for so long.

Mr. Heath is a really sensitive human being, and that sensitivity really comes through when he plays ballads. He surrenders right away, and that allows the music to really flow. When you hear him, you don't hear the mind getting in the way of the creativity. You just feel the flow, and when he plays the soprano, what a voice. He has one of the most gorgeous soprano sounds of anybody.

As a result of writing music for the big band at Queens, I accumulated a lot of arrangements. In 1991, I was given an opportunity by the American Jazz Orchestra—Loren Schoenberg and John Lewis, music directors, and Gary Giddins, artistic director—to give a concert on October 18 at Cooper Union in New York. The concert, which was critically acclaimed, featured my big band music. This was a huge moment for me because I had been working for years on big band arrangements, but it was also another time when I was looked at as being "discovered," which is what the title of Peter Watrous's review in the October 18, 1991, *New York Times* was trying to say: "Jimmy Heath Comes into His Own." Watrous wrote:

> Jimmy Heath is like a man who has just inherited a fortune. After years of being overlooked, Mr. Heath, who is 64 years old and one of jazz's finest saxophonists, is working more than he ever has. And a concert tonight by the American Jazz Orchestra at Cooper Union, featuring a rare program of Mr. Heath's orchestrations, should make clear to the uninitiated that the musician is one of the great arrangers of his generation. (p. C16)

Bill Cosby heard about the performance. In fact, while I was at Queens, I had recorded a couple of CDs produced by Bill; one was called *My Appreciation*, which came out in 1991, the same year I signed with SteepleChase Records. Bill got us on the *Joan Rivers Show*, and we had a piece on *Arts and Entertainment* to push his record. At the time of the Cooper Union concert, Bill had one more record to do under his contract with Verve, and since he didn't want to do another Verve record in his own name, he suggested that I record a big band CD. Bill produced *Little Man Big Band* in 1992, and he was there when we rehearsed and recorded it, January 30–March 3 of that year. Also, one of my favorite bassists, Ben Brown, who played with my small group, was on the date.

Without any promotion, the CD was nominated for a Grammy in 1993, the same year the Heath Brothers were elected to the Walk of Fame in Philadelphia. I was up against Miles Davis and Quincy Jones, which is a tough combination to beat. I went to the Grammy ceremony in New York, but *Little Man Big Band* was beat out by *Miles and Quincy Live at Montreux*, which was a throwback to the Gil Evans materials. Wallace Roney played some of the solos that Miles would have played because Miles, who passed away in 1991, was ill when the CD was being recorded.

It seems that the world likes to honor those who have passed away, rather than the living. When *Live at the Public Theater* was nominated for a Grammy in 1980, the award for a small group was given to Bill Evans, who also had died. (Percy told me that when the MJQ had been nominated for a Grammy earlier, Evans won that year too, though he was alive then.) After you die, you become larger than life. I was also nominated for a Grammy in 1995, the thirty-eighth Grammy Awards, for the liner notes for a Coltrane compilation, *The Heavyweight Champion* (1995).

MTUME

I went to a rehearsal for Tayari's big band album Little Man Big Band *in 1992. Tayari and I were also together once for the* New York Undercover *TV series, when I was doing the scoring in the 1990s. Tayari did some cues, some horn things, on one of the episodes. But the funniest thing involving Tayari happened when they were shooting the pilot just after I got the* New York Undercover *gig. Bill Duke was directing the pilot, and you know they didn't want no brothers in there anyway, so it was a struggle, but finally Dick Wolf said, "Okay." It was on location on the East Side. As I was walking up the street, all of a sudden I heard Dick Wolf say, "Who the fuck is that? What the fuck?" Everybody was losing it. "Who is that guy?" Then as I turned around, I saw it was Tayari. The scene involved a woman who was lying in front of a parking lot. She had just gotten mugged. Coming out of the parking lot, Tayari said, "Hey, somebody help this lady," and he didn't understand why nobody was helping her. It was a scene. He inadvertently had just walked on the set. I said, "Man, that's my father." That was a roar.*

The up-tempo pace continued in the spring of 1992. Being from Philadelphia and having heard about the Kelly family for years, I was thrilled to go to Monaco in June to perform at the Johnnie and Jazz Masters in Monaco event, sponsored by the Scottish distillery John Walker and Sons. The famous actress Grace Kelly, whose father had a big name in construction, was married to Prince Rainier III of Monaco. In Philadelphia, her brother had run the Vesper Boat Club, where Mtume trained to be an Olympic swimmer. The Jazz Masters event centered around the faculty of the Department of Jazz, headed by David Baker, at the Indiana University School of Music. The jazz professionals gave master classes and performed with their own groups and with students. Some of the artists were guest faculty at the school. The event headliners were Dave Brubeck, the Woody Herman Band, Michel Petrucciani, Betty Carter, Jerry Coker, Nathan Davis, Ted Dunbar (who I knew from Jazzmobile), Dominic Spera, Joe Henderson, Freddie Hubbard, Louie Bellson, Frank Tiberi, and David Baker and the Indiana University Jazz Big Band. Tootie and I were supported by Tony Purrone on guitar and Stafford James on bass. One of the venues was the Princess Grace Theater, where we all got a chance to perform at least once. Brubeck, who would in 2000 have an institute established in his name at the University of the Pacific in Stockton, California, gave a great show. I love his compositions like "In Your Own Sweet Way" and "The Duke." Brubeck and I had a chance to hang out in Monaco. Monaco was great except for one incident where Tootie, who was wearing African clothing, was refused entrance into the casino.

DAVE BRUBECK

Jimmy Heath, renowned saxophonist, composer, and arranger, the middle one of the three talented Heath brothers, was a Jazz Master and legend long before officially designated as such by the National Endowment for the Arts. Jimmy is one of the all-time jazz greats of the last half century. His life story parallels the story of jazz, beginning in smoke-filled dives and ending with performances in the finest concert halls, lecturing in universities (including my own Brubeck Institute at the University of the Pacific), and receiving lifetime achievement awards and honorary degrees from prestigious institutions that once frowned upon the music he loved and pioneered. Jimmy's story is compelling because, like his music, it is honest and from the heart.

The Philip Morris tours kept me out of the classroom for the longest period of time. I had an understanding with the Music Department at Queens. They knew that I was a performing artist and would be going out on the road. In the fall of 1992, I took an extended trip of about three weeks with the Philip Morris Generations Tour, which paired a younger group and an older one. The older group consisted of Donald Byrd, trumpet, who was at Queens at the time; Slide Hampton, trombone; Phil Woods, alto; Kenny Barron, piano; Bob Cranshaw, bass; and Kenny Washington, who was quite young at that time, on drums. The guy who ran the Philip Morris organization, Buzzi, really liked Kenny, so he put him with the older guys. The young group had Christian McBride, bass; Mike LeDonne, piano; Joshua Redman, tenor; Jesse Davis, alto; Lewis Nash, drums; and Ryan Kisor and Michael Leonhart, trumpets. On the tour were also Nneena Freelon, vocals, and Norman Simmons, piano, accompanying her along with Bob Cranshaw and Kenny Washington. David Sanchez on tenor was a special guest with that small group.

Touring, teaching, and other projects kept me busy. Another of the young lions, Winard Harper, whom I had met back in the late seventies, asked me to do arranging for his 1991 Harper Brothers recording *You Can Hide Inside the Music*. He has that ability to light up a room like old man Jo Jones. Winard smiles, he loves what he's doing, he's enthusiastic, he swings hard, and he gives you everything he has every time he's on the stage. I love to play with Winard. When I'm not performing with Tootie, Winard's my first choice. The other thing is that he has respect, complete respect. He's always been that way, and he was raised that way. During my tenure at Queens, Winard worked on some of my gigs, and at the college I got him to do the faculty concerts. He always touched people. On the *You Can Hide Inside the Music* date, he had Ernie Andrews as vocalist. I co-wrote a composition with my niece Beth Jackson, a poet and lyricist, called "You Can Hide Inside the Music." Ernie objected to the lyric and title because of the way one of his children shut everybody out while listening to "his music." Ernie halfheartedly recorded that song. Many years later, he apologized to me for not understanding the lyric, which made reference to all kinds of music.

WINARD HARPER

When I was sixteen, I was into jazz, and I had some of Jimmy's recordings in my collection, like Live at the Public Theater. *After I met him, I really started checking out some of his recordings before that period. I first met Jimmy around 1978 or '79, when he had the Heath Brothers band with Percy, Stanley Cowell, and Akira Tana. They came to Atlanta for a workshop involving the Harper Brothers and the Heath Brothers. Afterwards, Jimmy and Percy gave us tickets to the gig in Atlanta that night.*

At their workshop, Jimmy sounded knowledgeable about the history of the music, certain licks the guys played and where they came from. I was im-

pressed by his knowledge of the history, and I already knew about his dedication to the music. I had a chance to play with him when I was in school at the University of Hartford with Jackie McLean. Jimmy came into town, and Jackie used me as part of the rhythm section at a club. It was cool. Jimmy was gracious. I was about nineteen or twenty years old then. The gig was a lot of fun. We were students and still working on the music. Later, my brother and I had a track record. I was working with Dexter Gordon and Betty Carter, and Philip was working with Art Blakey. Between 1988 and '89, the Harper Brothers took off, and every now and then Jimmy would call me for gigs. I called Jimmy to do arrangements for one of the Harper Brothers records, You Can Hide Inside the Music, *named after one of Jimmy's compositions.*

I always wanted to tie up the generations, to show how they go hand in hand. I wanted to borrow from the artists who came before me, like Cannonball Adderley and Ernie Andrews. Not many people had really heard of Ernie Andrews, so I wanted to do a project with him. We also had Harry "Sweets" Edison and Jimmy McGriff. Here was this band of young guys, the youngest being eighteen or nineteen years old, up to me, twenty-five or twenty-six at the time. I knew Jimmy had the understanding and the knowledge. He knew the sound of my group, and that I had expanded the Harper Brothers to a sextet. There weren't too many guys around like Jimmy, who had the expertise to arrange for three horns.

Jimmy's been like a big brother or father figure to a lot of us, like me, Antonio Hart, and Jeb Patton. Jimmy and Mona are one of a couple of jazz families that have been very good to us. Working with Jimmy is always a pleasure, and I like the spirit that he brings to the music and to the bandstand, even though it's serious business. He's one of the few guys who still understand that there should be some joy and fun in it, and you can make it pleasurable and entertaining to an audience.

When you get the Heath brothers together, it's always hilarious. Hearing Jimmy talk about some of his experiences has been very memorable and touching, from his speaking about playing in some of the big bands, when they had to play twice, once for the white audience and once for the black audience, or being on those road tours and being pulled over by the police and having to say, "Yes, sir."

When we went to Canada once with the group called Faddis, Hampton & Heath, Jimmy still had to go to the police station to get an authorized letter saying that he has been a model citizen because of his involvement with drugs years ago. It was a kind of a warning sign for us. Things you do in life can stay with you for a long time, whether it's fair or not.

I know it can be difficult having a "brothers" group, and I remember that period when a couple of the Heath brothers didn't get along well. I can understand it because I got to a point where I had difficulty with my brother, but later on, seeing the Heath Brothers hook back up together was inspiring. Time and the Creator have a way of healing wounds and bringing things together.

For my generation, Jimmy is the connection between the Charlie Parker and the Dizzy Gillespie way of living. Jimmy is one of the few guys who were able to pass on that knowledge and information by going into the educational system. With the diminishing of the club scene and working bands, that kind of education was replaced by going to school to get the music. Jimmy is part of the system that helped to kick that off.

In the mid-1990s, I continued to compose and gig around town as a solo and with the Heath Brothers small group. I always liked to play close to home, and I had an opportunity to work with the Queens-based pianist Bross Townsend on February 15, 1995, for an event at the Queens Theatre in the Park. It was sponsored by the Black American Heritage Foundation, headed by Clarence Irving, who had been working in the trenches and promoting Queens artists for a long time. Clarence invited me to play as guest artist.

From about 1996, my group included guitarist Mark Elf, who replaced Tony Purrone and who stayed with the group until around 1999. Mark was an extremely talented guitarist who also had his own record label, Jen Bay Records. I recorded with Mark on *The Eternal Triangle*, released on his label, with pianist Hank Jones, bassist Ray Drummond, and drummer Ben Riley. Mark was instrumental in helping to promote some of the Heath Brothers releases through his own pipeline.

In 1996 I finished a suite I had been working on for Howard University. *Leadership*, a three-movement composition for solo saxophone and jazz orchestra, was commissioned by the Inaugural Committee for H. Patrick Swygert, Howard's fifteenth president. It premiered at Cramton Auditorium on April 11, conducted by Fred Irby III, director of the Howard University Jazz Ensemble. The theme of the inaugural activities was "Leadership for America." In addition to writing for the jazz orchestra, I also contributed a lyric for their choir:

Your leadership in education
That leadership is what we need.
Don't forget from dedication
Flowers grow from tiny seeds.
Hearts and minds need elevation.
Your leadership is what we need.
Takes leadership to build a nation.
Good leadership should be our creed.

When my youngest granddaughter, Benin, entered Howard University in August 1999, she took a course titled "Blacks in the Arts." One day the professor played some of *Leadership* from the CD they made of the 1996 concert. The professor explained that it was written by Jimmy Heath, "legendary saxophonist and composer." Benin shouted out spontaneously, "That's my grandfather!"

I was really active during the nineties while teaching at Queens. In actuality, I had three jobs—teaching, writing, and performing. After Roland came on, things went very well at Queens. Before I left the program in 1998, I suggested that they hire Mike Mossman. Cecil Bridgewater, a great arranger, applied for that position as head of the jazz program, but Michael Mossman got the job. Cecil's personality is a little subdued, but Mike, who could do the same things Cecil could, and may have had more degrees as well, was more outgoing. It was like my going up against Wynton Marsalis for a gig. You know who would get the gig in that situation. Cecil left after that for the New School. Through my urging, Todd Williams, who was an adjunct professor at Queens in the Music Department, was later hired as a full-time professor. I wanted Todd to take my place as the saxophone teacher, and I recommended him highly.

While at Queens, I had other interactions with jazz students. In April 1997, I was invited by Wynton Marsalis to be a judge at the Second Annual Essentially Ellington High School Jazz Band Competition and Festival. Horace Silver, one of the most prolific composers and bandleaders ever, was also one of the judges. (In 1959, I had asked him to send me some of his songs, and he sent me one hundred lead sheets.) The other judges were Ronald Carter, a professor at the University of Northern Illinois and one of our dedicated young men with a serious spiritual commitment to the music; Wynton, the jazz warrior, who is constantly leading the fight for the respect and dignity of our musical creation; and the late Michael Brecker, the hard-working, super-talented saxophonist from my hometown. We judged twelve bands from around the country, and during one of our breaks, Mike told me that his brother, Randy, had a picture of me in the house when he was growing up. After the concert, I had the panel members sign a poster for me. Michael signed, "To Jimmy, My Hero."

My connection with the Thelonious Monk Institute of Jazz in the nineties led to my receiving more recognition. I was on the board of advisors and later became a trustee. Max Roach had been one of the trustees, but he backed out. Since I had been an advisor from the beginning of the institute, I was chosen to take his place. Max Roach, Clark Terry, and Herbie Hancock, who had become very active in the institute, were also on the board. Back in 1985, the institute was first discussed by percussionist T. S. Monk, Thelonious's son, and Maria Fisher, head of the Beethoven Society, in conjunction with Tom Carter and Art Monk, a second cousin of Thelonious's who played for the Washington Redskins and is now an NFL Hall-of-Famer. I was also one of the founders of the institute. In 1986, I attended a meeting at the Tavern on the Green in New York City with T. S. Monk, Tom Carter, Clark Terry, Max Roach, drummer Willie Jones, and bassist Leonard Gaskin. I was also present at a series of meetings to decide where the institute would be located. In 1994, I received a Founder's Award. Others who were eventually involved on the board were Illinois Jacquet and Grover Washington; Ron Carter and Wayne Shorter also really got involved. As a board member, I was privy to the funding sources, and I also made suggestions for the annual international competition guidelines.

Working with the Thelonious Monk Institute was very rewarding. When it was located at the New England Conservatory, I often conducted workshops. Two groups of students were selected to participate in the program there, and each group was there for two years. In September 1999, the institute moved to the University of Southern California (USC). I was involved in selecting the instructors and administrators for the new location. At our board meeting, we selected Patrice Rushen to run the institute at USC. Clark Terry did the first residency, and I followed in October 1999 for a week of instructing the new appointees. The six or seven students selected for the two-year appointments had all their costs covered, all by funds from private sources. After USC, the institute moved to Loyola in New Orleans.

When the institute first started, Thelonious, Jr., brought in Tom Carter as the overall director. Tom and his wife were well connected in Washington and knew the Clintons and the Gores. This led to my being invited along with other musicians to attend various receptions where President Clinton and Vice President Al Gore were present. I went to receptions at the Gore residence two or three times, and I also visited the White House in connection with the Kennedy Center Honors in 1996. The Kennedy Center Honors that year were given to dancer Maria Tallchief, playwright Edward Albee, country singer Johnny Cash, actor Jack Lemmon, and Benny Carter, my idol. Benny asked me to play for that event, and afterward I attended the White House reception for the honorees.

Before that I had visited the White House for a gathering of the Newport Jazz Festival participants in June 1993. It was held outdoors, and was the first time that jazz had been played on the lawn of the White House since the Carter administration. Bill Clinton, who played saxophone, liked jazz. Bassist Milt Hinton (the "Judge"), T. S. Monk, trombonist Al Grey, Jacquet, Clark Terry, and I had played for a rally at the Sheraton in New York when Clinton ran for president the first time in 1992. I met Caroline Kennedy, Arthur Ashe, and Governor Mario Cuomo that night. Clinton said, "If I get in, we are going to have jazz in the White House." He kept his word, and in 1993, George Wein was honored for his contribution to jazz through the Newport Jazz Festival. The artists at that affair included Illinois Jacquet, Clark Terry, Red Rodney, Jon Faddis, Grover Washington, Bobby McFerrin, Herbie Hancock, Dick Hyman, Michel Camilo, John Lewis, Elvin Jones, Dorothy Donegan, Joe Williams, Rosemary Clooney, Joe Henderson, Charlie Haden, and Joshua Redman, who played on Jacquet's set. I was in the bebop set, which included Henderson, Red, Faddis, and Christian McBride. Joe played "Lush Life" from a recent release of his. The Wynton Marsalis Septet also performed. The big performance on the lawn was taped for a PBS special called *In Performance at the White House*, which the Monk Institute produced as *A White House Jazz Festival*. Kareem Abdul-Jabbar, who is also connected with the institute, was in the audience.

When we closed, we played "All Blues" with Joe Williams, who started off the tune. President Clinton came up to jam with us. Since he didn't have his horn, he asked Jacquet to borrow his. I had heard President Clinton on TV playing in the key of F. However, "All Blues" is in G. I warned him by saying, "We're in G, Pres." He stumbled, but he landed on his feet.

I know he knew what I meant when I called him Pres, the title given Lester Young, the great jazz tenor saxophonist.

Since its beginnings, the Monk Institute has stretched out. It sponsors young students who play at sports events, and aside from the annual competition, which receives the most attention, there are various programs in California and Aspen, Colorado. However, there's a lot of work done by the institute in the background involving student instruction. The main thrust is to produce future great jazz artists. While the competitions are going on, the institute has on occasion been involved in television spots. I participated in two of the ABC television events called A *Celebration of America's Music* (1996 and 1998), the first network special program in decades focusing on jazz.

If it hadn't been for my connection with the Thelonious Monk Institute, I wouldn't have met Bill Clinton. In my conversations with President Clinton on two or three occasions, I came away with the impression that he was a very special kind of person, especially for someone who held such a high office. He listens and pays attention when a person talks to him, regardless of where that person comes from. He listens and responds to what you're saying. Richard Nixon, George Bush, and other presidents seemed to be nervous and always conscious of their security. They didn't seem to really listen to what people had to say, unless it was a remark by a head of state or someone they were supposed to listen to. Clinton had an interest in the music; when he was running for office, he played saxophone on the *Tonight Show*. Stanley Turrentine, David Sanborn, Phil Woods, and I were asked by an interviewer to critique his playing. Our comments, reported by Ron Givens, were posted on the *Entertainment Weekly* Web site in June 1992. I thought that for a person in his position, Clinton was pretty good. After all, he didn't really practice all the time like a professional musician would. I said, "His tone was a little harsh, but at least he has a concept of the way music should sound. I admire his courage for exposing himself. When you're standing up and playing before an audience, you're being scrutinized at every moment."

I also attended receptions at Vice President and Tipper Gore's house before certain Thelonious Monk Institute competitions. Tipper, who was actually a drummer, became a supporter of the Thelonious Monk Institute high school program. On my first visit to the Gores, I saw a red set of drums in the living room. When I asked who played them, she said that she did. The second time I went there with some others from the Monk Institute, the drums weren't there. Tipper said that her son was also playing drums, and they had to put the set in the garage. One time, Tipper visited New York City to speak at the High School of Music and Art; Percy, Clark Terry, and I went to the affair. When one of the students at the school asked her how she became interested in jazz, she told him that she had played the drums in her high school band. Al Gore was also a very nice person. In the summer of 1999, there was an event celebrating the music of Ellington and Gershwin held at the Gore residence under a tent.

Two summers earlier, in 1997, I worked with trumpeter Jon Faddis's group, which he called Faddis, Hampton & Heath, with Slide Hampton on trombone. Faddis, Hampton & Heath sounded like a law firm to me, but in fact it was a beautiful sextet à la Miles's sextet, when it included J.J. and me. Faddis's group also reminded me of J.J.'s sextet, when I played with Brownie. The difference was the focus on our mentor, Dizzy. Jon's brilliance, consistency, and sense of humor were obvious, and we had big fun. In June, we played a gig at Scullers in Boston with a rhythm section that included Mulgrew Miller, piano; Ray Drummond, bass; and Lewis Nash, drums. We also played the North Sea Jazz Festival in July and toured Canada and Japan.

JON FADDIS

Mr. Jimmy Heath is a "musician's musician." I first met him over thirty-five years ago at the Village Vanguard in the early 1970s, when I was playing first trumpet with the Thad Jones and Mel Lewis Jazz Orchestra (now the Vanguard Jazz Orchestra). Soon after, Jimmy and I found ourselves playing together in a big band that Dizzy Gillespie put together for an appearance at Buddy Rich's club (Buddy's Place) in New York. Since then, I've played in Jimmy's big bands, and Jimmy has played in groups that I have led, most notably Faddis, Hampton & Heath, as well as both the big band and small group configurations of the Dizzy Gillespie Alumni All-Stars. Mr. Heath has also arranged for my Carnegie Hall Jazz Band (now the Jon Faddis Jazz Orchestra of New York), and he's played as a featured guest artist with the Chicago Jazz Ensemble, for which I'm artistic director.

Over the years, as our friendship has blossomed, what has impressed me most about Jimmy is his honesty, his wit, his passion for and depth of knowledge about music, and his willingness to share by teaching. Hearing Mr. Heath not only play music but also recount stories about Dizzy Gillespie, Charlie Parker, John Coltrane, and others is, for me, an inspiration. Jimmy makes me want to do better and to work harder, on music and on my life.

Mr. Heath has a very subtle wit with both his words and his music. Once, commenting on a musician's weight, Jimmy slyly jested, "Here comes Menachem Big-Un!" Everybody cracked up. Laughing is easy with Jimmy; he is self-deprecating and humble in so many regards, and his jokes, if they involve others, always show an underlying affection for their targets too.

I believe that this same wit, intelligence, and humor is reflected in Jimmy's music, whether he's quoting a popular song during one of his improvisations, playing with puns in his song titles (such as "Ellington's Stray-Horn" or "Without You, No Me"), delivering one of his home-spun "raps" like "Bebop, the Cream of the Crop," or answering a question about the differences between bop and hard bop by pronouncing simply, "All bop is hard." I can tell you that's true.

Jimmy also keeps jazz history more honest. One such example I recall is Jimmy remarking on Miles Davis's autobiography, "Miles says that he didn't learn anything from other trumpet players. Shit, I remember Fats Navarro kickin' Miles's ass every night on the bandstand and there wasn't anything that Miles could do except to sit there and take those ass whippin's!" Jimmy knows; he was there, and yes, he walked with giants and he witnessed the paths they really took too. He's a "giant" himself in the best of ways—huge heart, great mind, enormous curiosity about the world, a tremendous capacity to share, and his music will endure for ages.

Sharing the stage with Mr. Heath is a lesson in comportment and professionalism. As with many leaders, a look or a word from Jimmy goes a long way. On stage with ten saxophonists at the first James Moody Scholarship Concert at Purchase College, April 9, 2005, a "young lion" came to play, looking a bit unshaven and unkempt, a little like what used to be referred to as a ragamuffin. Jimmy took one look at this youngster (whose music I think he respects quite a bit) and said of his attire, "Come on, man! That's disrespectful!" Jimmy gives respect, yet he also commands it himself and on behalf of others. He wants to show people to advantage, and he wants them to be the best they can be in all regards.

"One never knows (do one?)" what someone else's relationship is like when the door is closed, but the loving and lasting marriage between Jimmy and Mona is a joy to behold. I know that being in an interracial relationship is still not fully accepted by too many in our society, yet when I see Mona's eyes as she listens to Jimmy soloing, or when I listen to Jimmy's voice as he speaks about his wife, it shows me that there is something very special going on there.

Jimmy and Mona embody the principle that there is really only one race, human. My wife, Laurelyn, and I are blessed to have Jimmy and Mona as friends; they've enriched our lives in more ways than they'll likely ever really know.

Jimmy is fond of saying that when you become fifty-nine years of age, you enter the park. This is a reference to the start of Central Park in New York City at 59th Street. As you age past fifty-nine, you begin your journey through the park. Central Park ends at 110th Street, and Jimmy says that he hasn't met anyone that has made it out of the park yet.

Thank you, Mr. Jimmy Heath. I'm proud to know you. Here's to you making it out of the park!

In October 1997, the Thelonious Monk Institute competition focused on trumpets. It happened on my birthday, and that day we also went to the State Department, where I met Secretary of State Madeleine Albright, who wished me a happy birthday. Being with people of that ilk was one of the highlights of my life. Also on that occasion, two of my students from Queens, Darren Barrett, born in England, and Diego Urcola, from Argentina, had come in first and second, respectively, in the competition. I was very proud that they had been my students. Avishai Cohen from Israel was third.

My academic life had gone well, and graduate students at other institutions were getting interested in my work. Leon Latimer Dunkley, Jr., wrote his doctoral dissertation on topics relating to my *Afro-American Suite of Evolution*. He called it "The Icarus Endeavor: Jazz, Narrative History, and the Idea of Race. The Case of James Edward Heath and *The Afro-American Suite of Evolution* (1976)." He finished it in 1997 at the University of Pittsburgh, where he worked with Nathan Davis, and the things he said were true about what I was trying to do: "Heath's composition is a racial statement. It is, even in its title, sharply qualified by race." He also said that he wanted to "explore the intersection between music and the idea of race as these two forces function in the American academic and intellectual environment" (pp. 18–19). It was good to read how academic people were interpreting my composing.

In the late nineties, I continued to record with my brothers Percy and Tootie, sometimes just as a threesome. Our first record on Concord, *As We Were Saying* (1997), has just the three of us on the track called "South Filthy," and another recording, *Jazz Family* (1998), is also a threesome.

The concept of bass, saxophone, and drums has been used by a lot of musicians such as Sonny Rollins, Coltrane, Ornette Coleman, and Joe Henderson. Miles used to do it while he had a pianist. He would tell the pianist to lay out, stroll, and Trane did that as well. That format frees up the soloist to experiment in different ways because you have to match only one line, one note, when you're playing. It's a free-expression type of form if you can maintain the groove and the interest. It's a wonderful thing because it gives you possibilities that you don't have with the piano, which locks you into the harmony. When you play without the piano, you don't have to worry about being locked in because there are only twelve tones and all are relevant to whatever tone the bass is playing at the time. We wanted to be just the Heath Brothers because we thought that it would be something unique.

I always enjoyed the successes of the Heath Brothers, but when I was honored personally on January 9, 1998, at Alice Tully Hall, Lincoln Center, I felt that my teaching and learning had all paid off. Bill Cosby and Wynton Marsalis were part of the event, which was sponsored by Queens College president Allen Lee Sessoms and the Trustees of the Queens College Foundation. It would lead to the establishment of a chair in Jazz Studies in my name at Queens College. Later that year, in July, when I was asked to be a panelist at the Washington, D.C., Jewish Community Center along with Artie Shaw, David Baker, Joe Wilder, and Loren Schoenberg, I immediately said yes. The topic to be discussed was "The Relationship between Blacks and Jews in Jazz." My instant decision was based on my interest in the subject and wanting to meet Artie. He had been a hero of mine from the time I was in high school, when I had heard the Gramercy Five and his wonderful big band stuff.

When he was told that I would be on the panel, he said that he knew who I was and he liked my music. However, according to the person who handled the contract for the panel, he said that he liked Coltrane better. The moderator for the panel was Congressman John Conyers, who I had met many years before when he and other members of the Black Congressional Caucus initiated the resolution to make jazz a National Treasure. At one time, Conyers had a jazz show on the radio in Washington, D.C.

The morning of the panel, Artie, John, my wife, and I had breakfast together, and we listened that day to Artie's life history. In the afternoon, the Smithsonian Jazz Orchestra directed by David Baker played some of Artie's music. During the performance, Mona and I sat with Artie, who didn't make any comments about the performance of his music. When the concert was over, people in the audience moved in on Artie for autographs. He told them that he didn't give autographs, had stopped doing that years ago. He said to them, vehemently, "What are you going to do with them anyway?"

Following the concert and after a few speeches, one by noted jazz writer A. B. Spellman, the panel began, or, I should say, Artie took over. The first thing he said was "This is a great country, but there are a lot of idiots in it. That's why I went to Spain for a while." The most fascinating of his stories was the one about his relationship with Billie Holiday. He had met Billie when they were around seventeen or eighteen. When his band became popular, he hired Lady Day for a tour down South. Artie knew that he would have a problem because of the racism down there, so he had a contingency plan that if any problem with rednecks occurred, the valet would hustle Billie out to the band bus, take her to the next town, and return for the band.

On the first night of the gig, it happened. In those days, the band was the attraction, not the singer. They played several numbers and then it was Lady's time. She sang one song, and as she began to leave the stage, a cracker down front screamed, "Let the nigger wench sing another one." At that point, Billie, who was known as a person who took no shit, called the heckler "a cracker motherfucker." Then the commotion started, so the valet bus driver took Billie out to the bus and executed the plan. This happened only on the first gig and not after that.

Artie also told a story about Michael "Dodo" Marmarosa, who he said never pulled out his music because, being a very competent musician, he had memorized it. Artie had many requests for his own hits. On one gig, he said he played "Begin the Beguine," and soon after, another fan came up and asked for it again, so he played it once more. Dodo told him that if he played it again, he would leave. Later on, someone asked for it again and Artie obliged. He said Dodo got up from the piano, and Artie never saw him again.

Later that summer, in August 1998, I had a chance to hear Sonny Rollins, who is one of the most creative forces in the world of music, an excellent saxophonist and composer. Besides that, he has been a dear friend for fifty or more years. I first heard him on "Wail" with Bud and Fats when he was seventeen. I'm still always listening in anticipation. They don't get any better. Newk, as I call him, phones me all the time when he's home. He likes to write cards from all over the world. I always say, "If I had a dollar for every card that Sonny wrote me, I'd be rich." He might not say anything but "What's new?" or "Hey" or whatever, but it's a greeting card, a postcard. I would say I got near a hundred. I've received cards from Cedar Rapids, Iowa; Monterey Bay, California; Ft. Lauderdale, Florida; St. Thomas, Virgin Islands; and Kyoto, Japan, to mention a few.

Sonny just keeps creating. He's a monster of a musician. When I heard him live at Lincoln Center's Damrosch Park in 1998, he was supposed to play two sets. I was sitting over on the side with his wife, Lucille, and I asked her, "What time is Sonny going to take a break?" She said, "He's already past the break." He played straight through for two and a half hours. There were about eight or ten thousand people out there. He just kept playing. When he gives a performance, he gives all every time.

Sonny's a highly creative artist, and some say he might have even influenced the painter Bob Thompson. It so happened that just a couple of months after I saw Sonny, Wynton Marsalis and Lincoln Center thought that it would be very apropos for me to perform at the presentation of Bob Thompson's art work at the Whitney Museum in October 1998, because I was around when Bob was hanging in the Five Spot and painting people like Trane and Jackie McLean, who was a friend of his. Jackie couldn't be there, so I was chosen because I knew him, his wife, and his sister-in-law. They came to the event on October 6 and I performed solo. In my solo, I was trying to connect to Bob Thompson's visual concept. It was only the second time that a jazz musician had performed live at the Whitney. The first was Duke Ellington, who recorded at that time.

SONNY ROLLINS

Jimmy's a great player with great integrity. This is the word that always sums up Jimmy to me, integrity. It's a big word when it comes to music. Jimmy has it. Thelonious Monk had it. There were other musicians who we were associated with who had it. When you hear Jimmy as a saxophone player, you're going to hear a big sound, you're going to hear that straight-ahead forwardness, directness, and you're going to hear the love. You're going to hear the history of the music. You're going to hear that whole period when Coltrane and all those guys were hanging out together in Philly. That's what I hear when I hear Jimmy play. That's a remarkable contribution because a lot of people

will be playing like that. A lot is due to Jimmy's being on the scene and to his
playing the way that he does. (Inter-Media Arts Center, 1991)

Sonny is one of the giants, and so is Frank Wess, "Magic," who I had the
pleasure of working with again in the summer of 1999 in Japan. Things
started to get busy for me that fall, and playing the Monterey Jazz Festival in September was another chance to hook up with musician friends
and giants. At that festival, the big performance was Saturday and featured
"Eastwood at Monterey," with songs from his movies. Eastwood's son, Kyle,
is also a jazz musician, a bassist, and he was on an earlier set. Clint, who is
himself a jazz lover, as you can tell from the music in his films, plays piano
and admires people like Kenny Barron and Barry Harris. They were on
the live recording *Eastwood after Hours: Live at Carnegie Hall* along with
James Moody. At the festival, I played with Clark Terry on "'Round Midnight," and Chris Potter, Joshua Redman, Lew Tabackin and I, all tenors,
got to blow on "Lester Leaps In."

It seemed in this period that events honoring jazz giants were taking
place in all areas—even South Orange, New Jersey, where my son Mtume
lives. "Giants of Jazz III," their third annual concert, was held in October
1999. I played my piece "The Voice of the Saxophone," and Mtume presented me with a plaque. It was really a special honor to get that award from
my son—to have his recognition too. Also that fall, on October 29, I was
part of Jazzmobile's Thirty-fifth Anniversary Gala at Avery Fisher Hall, at
which my friend Bill Cosby was the emcee. It was a tribute to yet another
of the giants I had walked with, Milt Jackson, recognizing his sixty years
in the jazz world. Percy, Frank Foster, John Lewis, Bob Cranshaw, and
Kenny Washington performed, and in the second half, Coleridge-Taylor
Perkinson, the black "classical" composer, directed a performance of my
commissioned work *Sweet Jazzmobile*. We had a chorus of twenty singers
along with my big band. *Sweet Jazzmobile* was my way of praising the organization that continued to be so important in the community. Earlier,
when I was working on the project, Joe McLaren wrote a cover story about
it ("Jimmy Heath: Jazz Legend") for the January–February 1992 issue of
Beth Turner's magazine *Black Masks*:

> *Sweet Jazzmobile* expresses Jimmy Heath's sense of history and the
> legacy of African American musical giants who have furthered the

developments of jazz and have contributed to its international recognition. In the lyrics to the choral section, Heath describes in poetic and historical terms the importance of past artists and the value of an organization such as Jazzmobile. (p. 15)

I wanted to express in the lyrics for the choral section my feelings about the legacy of Jazzmobile:

> We won't let our History
> Become a Mystery.
> Just remember those who died.
> In them we must take pride.
> Jazzmobile, keep it real.

FRANK WESS

Jimmy's always been a beautiful writer, player, musician, man, and teacher. I was with Jimmy on a nice tour in Japan with "Ellington Forever" from August 21 through 29, 1999. It was in the summer and it was hot. We had a good time. I took my grandson with me. That was his first trip out of the country. We had a good band. Being with Jimmy on the road was always pleasant, never any downs. It was always up. He and his brothers always had plenty of jokes, and they were nice to be around. They never had any down side.

Jimmy and I were also teachers at Jazzmobile. Jazzmobile presented the opportunity for those who didn't have the chance to get proper instruction. And then, too, it brought music to the people. We did long tours up in New York State and in the five boroughs. It was a very unique organization formed by Billy Taylor. It's been around a long time, and they still have their regular classes and good teachers. It's been very beneficial for a whole lot of young people and older people too. We didn't discriminate. Whoever could come was welcome.

But I had heard of Jimmy even before Jazzmobile. We knew of each other. I was with Basie on the road, and he was moving around in other circles. Over the years, we had a number of gigs together. They were all nice experiences. We were both with the Dizzy Gillespie Dream Band. That Dream Band was a nice thing. I contracted that band for Diz. We had a whole band full of beautiful players and Jimmy was one of them. We taped a TV show from Lincoln Center on February 16, 1981. I also played with the Dizzy Gillespie

All-Star Big Band for a while. I played lead alto and Jimmy was one of the tenor players in the section. We also did a nice little session for Benny Carter with Jimmy, Herb Geller, Joe Temperley, and me in the reed section, Over the Rainbow.

When Jimmy plays, he's Jimmy. He plays good and he's consistent. He's got the background for whatever. He's very musical all the time and his writing is really superb. He's got a good big band now too.

As a composer, Jimmy's top class. Any of his compositions—"Gemini," "Gingerbread Boy," "Without You, No Me," which he wrote for Diz—are all beautiful compositions and well written.

He's contributed immensely to jazz and he's done it all. He's written, he's played, and he's taught. He's given a lot to the kids. I admire him for that. He deserves all the praise that you could give. He's a great musician and a beautiful person.

13

Aroma of the Roses

■

When the new millennium rolled around, I thought about how long I had been a professional musician and all the giants I had known. It really hit me when Jimmy Cobb, who was with Miles in 1959, and I were asked to attend the book signing for *Kind of Blue: The Making of the Miles Davis Masterpiece*, by Ashley Kahn. Cobb was the only surviving member of Miles's group who had recorded on the album. When Kahn called me earlier asking me for a statement about being in Miles's band just after the recording, I was surprised. I asked him why he was writing a book about one recording. He said, "You don't know?" I said, "No." He told me that *Kind of Blue* (1959) was the biggest-selling jazz recording of all time. I was shocked. In the book, Ashley used my comment about how Miles told me to play modal tunes, using the white keys and the black keys. The signing was held at Barnes and Noble across from Lincoln Center in New York, with radio host Phil Schaap as the moderator. Cobb was asked if he knew that the recording would be so large, and he said, "No. I've made a lot of recordings in my life."

PHIL SCHAAP

The Heath and Schaap families have known each other since I was a young child. During my adolescence, Jimmy Heath became one of the primary musicians who nurtured my need for jazz information. Over the forty years that I have played Jimmy's music on WKCR Radio in New York, he has become

more and more tolerant of my limited musicianship and more and more will-
ing to field questions from a discographical perspective. That Jimmy has so
adapted and that we continue to feed each other jazz information allows me
to think that I may actually be doing something for him. Jimmy Heath has
done oh so much for me.

I started to really smell the roses when I continued to receive recognition
for things I had done, some of them involving my longer compositions. I
was honored on May 21, 2000, by the Presbyterian Jazz Society of Mount
Vernon, New York—that small city above the Bronx where they've had a
number of black mayors, where actor Denzel Washington was born and
grew up, and where the actress Phylicia Rashad lives. They called the event
"A Tribute to a Legend Concert." Delores Bell, the wife of the late Aaron
Bell, who played bass with Ellington, was a big part of that organization.
Another type of recognition was having the opportunity to hear my longer
works performed. On April 21, 2001, *Birmingham* premiered at the Carver
Theatre in Birmingham, Alabama, a historic site where black groups played
in the past. Then in October at Lincoln Center, there was a two-night celebration concert for my seventy-fifth birthday. I played with small groups
and led Wynton's Lincoln Center Jazz Orchestra. That night Wynton told
me that he was close to raising all the funds needed to build the Jazz at
Lincoln Center complex.

The aroma of the roses became intoxicating when I was given an honorary doctorate in music at Juilliard, the first one presented in the field of
jazz. At the commencement on May 24, 2002, at Alice Tully Hall, Lincoln Center, Bill Cosby gave the address, and he also received an honorary
degree, along with soprano Shirley Verrett, playwright Edward Albee, and
dancer-choreographer Helgi Tomasson. President Joseph Polisi made the
presentations. Cosby said in his address to inspire the graduates, "The day
that you go for an audition and you decide not to show up, that's the job you
lose." He was talking about being sure of yourself and being who you are.

I went back to Wilmington, North Carolina, for another "Jimmy Heath
Day," October 19, 2002, with the quartet, including Paul West, bass; Tootie;
and Jeb Patton, piano. We played on the "wrong side" of town, and it was
very sparsely attended. The mayor, Harper Peterson, who happened to be
a white man from Queens, New York, came to the concert. I don't know
how he got to be the mayor of Wilmington. Other than my family and a few

friends, not many folks were there. It was at Town Hall, on the side of town where Williston High School used to be. When we played at the University of North Carolina, however, people of all races attended. It made me think that nothing has changed. We just go through changes; things look better and then it goes back to the same old thing. Look at the Supreme Court decision in June 2007 that reversed some of the gains of the *Brown v. Board of Education* decision of 1954. This touched me deeply because of what Thurgood Marshall and his allies did to get us into better schools in other neighborhoods. The new Chief Justice John G. Roberts is the chief drag because he threw us back. If we don't get into other schools, it throws us back because our schools aren't going to be at the same level financially, and the teachers will be different. We move to move ahead.

In January 2003, at the International Association for Jazz Education (IAJE) Conference in Toronto, I received the National Endowment for the Arts (NEA) Jazz Masters Award. I had been going to Toronto over the years, and also to Montreal, which was always good for jazz. The people up there like the music, and they have some great players. That year, the NEA also gave awards to Abbey Lincoln and Elvin Jones. Since then, they've given the award to four or five other jazz artists, which is nice. Joe McLaren was in Toronto at that time, and he came to the ceremony with Amrita Persaud. There was a session where some young musicians played, and Abbey was taken aback because there were no black youth playing, mostly white players, but it's like that. If she'd been teaching in an institution, she would have known it's like that. We need more of our people to accept jazz as something special. She said to me and Elvin, "This is not real." She didn't stay to get her award. She went back to her hotel room, and I didn't see Abbey later that night. Elvin and I stayed and we each got our twenty grand. We thanked the people. I wasn't that gracious because my award was signed by George W. Bush. I made a face when I heard the words "Signed by George W. Bush." Everybody recognized that I didn't like that.

The roses kept coming after I received the Duke Ellington Fellowship at Yale in September. October 17, 2003, was one of the most exciting and rewarding days of my life. I was being honored at a conference in Washington, D.C., by the National Visionary Leadership Project (NVLP), created and administered by Dr. Camille Cosby and Renee Poussaint, wife of Dr. Alvin Poussaint. The purpose of the organization was to document, through video interviews recorded in their homes, the life histories of African Americans over seventy years of age who could be considered vision-aries. The organizers planned to publish a book each year with the goal of passing on the information to black students in secondary and higher education.

My day to be honored started out at LaGuardia Airport, where Mona and I met the Honorable David Dinkins, former mayor of New York—still my mayor—and his wife, Joyce, for the flight to D.C. When we arrived, we shared a limo to the Watergate Hotel and later attended the Intergenera-tional Summit on the State of Black America at the Library of Congress. At the event were activist and former president of the National Council of Negro Women, Dorothy Height, who I knew from other occasions, Con-gresswoman Cardiss Collins, Senator Edward Brooke, Mayor Dinkins, and historian John Hope Franklin. There were also two college students there as interns. The moderator was CNN correspondent Bernard Shaw. Honorees Dorothy Height, Senator Brooke, Mayor Dinkins, and John Hope Franklin were presented with their NVLP sculptures. Renee Poussaint and Dr. Ca-mille Cosby read a brief bio for each and declared them "visionaries." Just hearing their accomplishments, I was on cloud nine. The panel was very informative, and there were questions from many young black people in the audience and responses from the panelists.

A black-tie gala was held at the Kennedy Center that night, and that's where I received my honor. On the bus going to the center, I had big fun talking to Buck O'Neil, the former Negro League baseball player, who I had met before in Kansas City when I was a panelist at the American Jazz Museum. That panel was about Charlie Parker. It was incredible how well-informed Buck was about jazz history. That night at the Kennedy Center, Mos Def played a song he had written, and he played the piano, not skill-fully but in a heartfelt way. He talked about musicians he heard and knew. After a reception with all the elders, the program presenting the Visionary Leadership Awards started and the excitement began. First they showed a video with short clips of each elder. The video, introduced by Phylicia Rashad, was put together very artistically. The recipients at the evening cer-emony included Ruby Dee and Ossie Davis, Ray Charles, Geoffrey Holder, Dick Gregory, Odetta, and me. I knew that I was in the company of kings and queens, heroes and heroines—giants.

For each visionary, a young person or persons who had been inspired by that person performed. For health reasons, Ray Charles couldn't be there.

His manager accepted the award for him, and then a young sightless man, whose last name was Hall, sang and accompanied himself beautifully on piano. His performance was soul-shaking. Ms. Rashad was visibly moved, as we all were. She then called Dick Gregory to receive his award. His acceptance monologue was funny and enlightening. He was brilliant. Then they showed some excerpts of my video, as they had done for Ray and Dick, and I was next. I was so full of pride as I accepted my award and gave my speech, giving thanks to Arlethia and Percy, my mom and pop. I thanked the NVLP for coming up with such an important idea, for pulling it off, and for choosing me. I then announced my two favorite young masters and former students, Antonio Hart, saxophone, and Jeb Patton, piano. They began to play as I stood in the wings. As they played a medley of my compositions in a clever suite form, I was flushed and had to hold back the tears. They started with "Gingerbread Boy," then segued into "Mona's Mood," "New Picture," "Gemini," and ended with "C.T.A." They spoke about me in a way that touched me deeply. Next was Geoffrey Holder. When he spoke, his voice shook the whole building. He cited his mom, dad, and brothers. When he finished, there was a thunderous applause as he gestured and moved gracefully on the stage. He then introduced a magnificent young protégé, who danced as if he were floating through the air. The audience was spellbound.

Next came Ossie and Ruby. After their video and eloquent acceptance speech, they introduced a young actor who was performing in a play called *Emergen-see!* Daniel Beaty began his monologue about the direction of today's video-culture youth and how they are being deliberately exploited along with the so-called artist. He was so strong and convincing that we all jumped to our feet with approval. The last visionary was Odetta, saluted by Tracy Chapman, who had been inspired by her mentor. She gave a stirring performance and the audience responded in kind. To top off the evening, Stephanie Mills was her usual strong and positive self. What a night, one I will cherish forever.

Receiving awards, accolades, and blessings is like an endless chorus. They just kept coming. Another memorable night occurred on February 9, 2004, at the Schomburg Center for Research in Black Culture in Harlem. It was a "Salute to 'Giants of Black History,'" and I was privileged to be among giants once again. Tennis great Althea Gibson was honored posthumously, and the other awards were given to Dr. Ivory T. Nelson, president of Lincoln University; Dr. H. Patrick Swygert, president of Howard; and the Reverend Calvin Butts of the Abyssinian Baptist Church in Harlem, who had become president of SUNY College of Old Westbury. On the music side, Arlene Smith of the Chantels, Dr. Billy Taylor, and my son Mtume were recipients too. They also recognized my favorite jazz station, WBGO, Newark, New Jersey, where Rhonda Hamilton, Michael Bourne, Gary Walker, and Dorthaan Kirk are on the staff. If that wasn't enough, the thirtieth anniversary of Harlem Week was commemorated. It was an evening filled with performances by the cast of *Hairspray*, the Billy Taylor Trio, and the Marie Brooks Pan Caribbean Dance Theater.

In June, I saw a lot of my old friends when I went back to Queens College to receive an honorary doctorate in music, not just in "humane letters." That honor "knocked me to my knees," as Lester Young might say. That summer in July, I performed with Percy and Tootie in Kensington, California, at Coventry Grove, Danny Scher's three-hundred-seat amphitheater at his home. It was a fund-raiser for Berkeley's "Jazzschool," a well-known program serving students of all ages. The setting for the concert was spectacular, with a giant redwood tree on the grounds. Danny, who's a music producer, filmed the concert, along with interviews. The resulting film, *Brotherly Jazz*, premiered at the Monterey Jazz Festival in 2005 and was released on DVD the following year. Percy and I were also on another DVD, *Jazz Master Class Series from NYU: Jimmy and Percy Heath*, filmed in 2005 and produced by John Snyder, for Artists House Foundation, and Dr. David Schroeder of the NYU Steinhardt Jazz Studies Program. Gary Giddins did the interview segments. My extended works were also getting more exposure. On August 21 and 22, 2004, *Bird Is the Word*, an extended work I had written, premiered at the Charlie Parker Jazz Festival in New York. On October 29 of that year, I was in the audience for the grand opening festival of the Frederick P. Rose Hall at Lincoln Center, for which Jazz at Lincoln Center had commissioned me to write a composition. The theme of the concert was "Let Freedom Swing: A Celebration of Human Rights and Social Justice," and my composition *Fashion or Passion* dramatized Lyndon B. Johnson's 1965 speech on civil rights. Along with my composition were several others by notable composers, framing texts by people who stood for freedom: Vaclav Havel, Lyndon B. Johnson, Robert F. Kennedy, Eleanor Roosevelt, Martin Luther King, Jr., Desmond Tutu, and Nelson Mandela. The composers were Toshiko Akiyoshi, Billy

Childs, Darius Brubeck and Zim Ngqawana, Emil Viklicky, and Darin Atwater.

Coming back off of a cruise that Saturday morning, Mona and I, along with my guest Maurice Peress, went to Lincoln Center for the last performance of the three days. Glenn Close read from President Johnson's 1965 "American Promise" speech for *Fashion or Passion*. She was wonderful, and the ovation was thunderous. I was completely overwhelmed. Some of the other narrators were Morgan Freeman, Keith David, the Reverend Calvin O. Butts, Mario Van Peebles, Alfre Woodard, and Patricia Clarkson. In the audience were then Secretary General of the United Nations Kofi Annan and other dignitaries.

Wearing hard hats, Percy, George Benson, and I had visited the site of Jazz at Lincoln Center when it was under construction. To recall that and to be part of the opening ceremony was incredible. This whole experience is etched in my memory forever, thanks to Wynton, a super jazz giant.

The next year, we lost Percy, who died on April 28, 2005, two days before his eighty-second birthday. Percy had been hospitalized about six months before his death. He was visited by ABC anchor Peter Jennings at South Hampton Hospital, near where Peter lived. Peter's visit impressed the staff so much that they placed a sign in the hallway with an arrow pointing to Percy's room. I don't think Peter had been diagnosed at that time with cancer. When Mona and I went to see Percy, he was sedated. We woke him up and tried to get him to eat some of the food that we had brought him, but he ate very little. Percy was resigned to the fact that it wouldn't be long.

This was one of the lowest points of my life, but things were continuing to happen musically. Early the next month, on May 7, another of my extended works, *For the Love Of*, was performed at Richardson Auditorium, Princeton University, where the jazz orchestra was headed by Anthony D. J. Branker. Etched in my memory of that spring were not my achievements but Percy's memorial, which was held at the Abyssinian Baptist Church on June 10, his son Percy III's birthday. It was attended by a lot of people, some of whom performed, like Randy Weston and Keter Betts, who came up from Washington. The church was quite full. Ironically, Keter passed a couple weeks after that. Buster Williams, Cedar Walton, and Antonio Hart played, and so did Tony Purrone and Mark Elf, two of the guitarists who had been with the Heath Brothers.

Other musicians were there, like Roy Haynes, who was up in the balcony, and Roberta Gamberini. Stanley Cowell played a duet with his daughter on viola. They played one of Percy's compositions, "Suite for Pop," which he had written for my father. Jeb and I played a piece for Percy, which I later arranged for big band. My niece Beth from California had written a poem called "A Lonely Bass," and I took the idea from that and wrote a piece called "From a Lonely Bass." I played it on soprano. It was hard to get through that without crying. The most touching performance at the memorial was by trumpeter Joe Wilder, Percy's childhood buddy. He played "It's Easy to Remember (But So Hard to Forget)" with Michael Weiss on piano. It's so hard for me to forget that moment.

The speakers were Maestro Maurice Peress from Queens College, Stanley Crouch, and Percy III, who spoke very eloquently about his dad. Jazz critic Gary Giddins, who writes for the *Village Voice*, spoke, and so did another writer, Ira Gitler. Peter Jennings sent someone from his staff in his place because he was very sick at the time. The woman read Peter's words, which were very touching. I also spoke about Percy. All in all, it was a very difficult experience for me to get through.

On Peter Jennings's birthday, July 29, 2005, his wife Kaycee asked a few of us musicians to surprise him at his house. Peter had always been a friend and a big supporter of the music. He gave benefits for unfortunate people on Long Island or emceed at events like the Friends of Charlie Parker Annual Benefit. Jon Faddis, Gene Bertoncini, Jay Leonhart, and I went out to South Hampton. When we arrived, Peter was lying out by the pool, and when I looked up I saw a helicopter circling his home with a sign that read "Happy Birthday—WNT" (World News Tonight). We played a couple of songs, and at one point, he began to tap his feet to the music, but he was very weak. After we stopped playing, I went over and told Peter that after he visited Percy, Percy became more famous than Peter was. Peter smiled.

The aroma of the roses was getting stronger. On October 21, 2005, I played a beautiful concert at Yale, where Willie Ruff sat in on French horn with the Heath Brothers. That day was also significant because it would have been Dizzy's eighty-eighth birthday. Early the next morning, I was taken to the Franklin D. Roosevelt Presidential Library and Museum for the presentation of the Four Freedoms Award. These awards have been given every year since 1982 to individuals who have advanced the "Four

Freedoms" outlined by President Roosevelt in his speech to Congress in 1941. The affair was held in a large tent set up in a banquet style. The first recipient was Tom Brokaw, who received the Freedom of Speech Award. The second, the Freedom of Worship Award, was given to Dr. Cornel West. The Freedom from Want Award went to Marsha Evans. Thomas Kean and Lee Hamilton received the Freedom from Fear Award.

The last Four Freedoms Award, the Freedom Medal, was presented to President Bill Clinton, and I played a solo piece when he was announced. Before the medal was given, the presenter said to President Clinton, "We have a surprise for you." At that moment, playing "There Will Never Be Another You," I walked over to the steps and onto the stage. President Clinton was genuinely surprised and smiled throughout my performance, after which, to thunderous applause, he hugged and thanked me. Before I left the stage, I was also hugged by Cornel, who's a good friend and admirer of the Heath Brothers. The feeling is mutual. When President Clinton started his acceptance speech, he first commented that he was grateful to me as one of the great saxophonists of the world, and that's what he possibly could have been if he hadn't chosen public service. Of course, he was joking. After his speech, two soul sisters, Gretchen Reed, contralto, and Marva Dark, piano, performed "The Battle Hymn of the Republic." As the whole audience began to sing, Gretchen beckoned me to join in, and I did.

When we sat down for lunch, I sat with the Clintons, and Bill immediately said that "Another You" was a favorite of his, and of Hillary's too, and they started reciting the words. Next to me at the table was a familiar face, and when I looked at the name card I saw that it was Joe Louis Barrow, Jr., who is the son of the great boxer Joe Louis and is on the Board of Directors of the Roosevelt Library and Museum. In the brief moment that the Clintons weren't swamped by people, Bill and I talked about saxophones. He told me about the one he owned that was made by Adolphe Sax himself in the 1860s. He said that he would bring it to his Harlem Office one day and let me try it and that he couldn't find B-flat on it but maybe I could.

The year 2005 was really up and down for me. On the upside, I found out that a saxophone teacher, James Farrell Vernon, had completed his doctoral dissertation at the University of Northern Colorado on my saxophone playing: "Jimmy Heath: An Analysis and Study of His Tenor Saxophone Improvisational Style between 1959 and 1998 through Selected Transcriptions." What he did was different from what Leon Dunkley had done. Vernon's was more of a musical analysis, and he was right on. Something he said in the beginning made me think about smelling the roses and how I had been passed by during my career:

> Given his impressive list of awards, accolades, and achievements—a list which certainly is not comprehensive—the reader may ask how Heath could be described as "perennially overlooked," as in the quote at the beginning of this chapter. The answer, which is complex, is the impetus of this paper. (p. 3)

He was quoting what the jazz critic Peter Watrous had said about me in 1991.

The following year was very eventful and especially meaningful because it was my eightieth. Wynton's new piece *Congo Square* premiered in New Orleans in April. I had gone to a rehearsal of the Lincoln Center Jazz Orchestra when they were preparing it. Wynton had a number of Ghanaian drummers, including Yacub Addy. Wynton's reflections on Congo Square reminded me of my *Afro-American Suite of Evolution* because I had African drummers open up the piece, bringing us over from Africa on the slave ships. Wynton's drummers were playing authentic music from Ghana, and a Ghanaian singer performed in one section. Later, Wynton gave me a copy of the two-CD performance. It's a very elaborate piece that has all kinds of instrument variations with E-flat sopranos and clarinets, B-flat bass clarinets, woodwinds in different sections, and chanting by the band, trying to match the chants of the African performers. In this piece Wynton is honoring black classical music. The authenticity is prevalent. His composition took me to a home I've never known. It touched me not in my home in Philadelphia where I was born, but my home in Africa as an African American. I've never experienced my ancestors' home of Africa in the way I did in that piece. My suite touched Africa in the beginning. Being born and raised in the United States, I mostly touched the African American input: field hollers, gospel, ragtime, boogie woogie, swing, and bebop—all the different styles that people of African descent have created in this country since coming over. To a master composer, Wynton, thanks for your loyalty and respect.

Another of my longer works, *The Endless Search*, was first presented November 4 and 5, 2006, in Seattle. The first performance, on Saturday night, was at Benaroya Hall–Nordstrom Recital Hall, with another performance on Sunday at the Kirkland Performance Center. Earlier that year, on June 24, I went to Harpers Ferry, West Virginia, to perform and receive the Don Redman Heritage Award along with the great Hank Jones. It was an honor to get this award, since Don Redman and Fletcher Henderson were responsible for creating the big band sound. Being with Hank has always been a pleasure, and playing with him is like walking through a colorful harmonic garden. The ceremony was held at the Harpers Ferry Historical Park. The next day we were driven by a National Park ranger to D.C. During the drive to National Airport, I pulled out my iPod to get my morning spiritual and musical medication from the a capella gospel group Take Six. I told Hank that I also listen to Take Six at night. When I played "Feels Good" for him, tears began to flow from his eyes. He was overwhelmed and amazed by their religious dedication and harmonic depth, as most musicians are. He told Mona and me that he was raised in the church, his father having been a deacon. Even though I had played with Hank and his brothers, Thad and Elvin, I didn't know about their father. It made me realize how much more the Heaths and the Joneses were alike. A couple days later, I sent Hank three Take Six CDs.

HANK JONES

I have known and admired Jimmy Heath and his boundless talents for over fifty years. Since the 1960s, Jimmy has been a major force in the evolution of jazz culture. His influence has been felt in his superb playing on tenor, alto, and soprano saxes, and on flute. Having excelled on all these instruments, he would have added baritone and bass saxophones if not for their enormous size. As if all the above accomplishments were not enough, Jimmy is one of the best (if not the best!) arrangers in the business. And, yes, he is an outstanding instructor. I am privileged to call him my good friend.

Later that summer, in August, we finished the mixing for my second big band recording, *Turn Up the Heath*. Mtume, who has "big studio ears," really helped with that part too. Nat Hentoff reviewed it the following year in "A Complete Jazzman" in the March 2007 issue of *JazzTimes:*

Jimmy knows the value of space. He lets the music breathe; and accordingly, the ensemble players and the soloists always sound like their natural selves—a multitude of individual voices cohering into a wholly distinctive conversation. Jazz, at its most enduring is, after all, constitutional democracy in action, with all of its individual stories becoming a mosaic of interdependence. And in Jimmy Heath's writing, as intensely swinging as it often gets, there is an implicit obbligato of singing lyricism. Anyone who can write like this knows what he was born to do in this world. (p. 82)

BENNY POWELL

When Jimmy asks you how you're doing, he really wants to know. I'm a big Jimmy Heath fan. That's one of his attributes, one of his strong points. He cares about truth, and he has a nice way of telling you the truth so that it doesn't hurt. He's one of the wittiest people I've known, and he talks sort of in puns. He could rhyme the Constitution. Emceeing one time, he was like Dizzy Gillespie, announcing people like Rufus Reid as Roughus Reid, and Jon Faddis as Jon Fat Ass. It was all a playful joke, but he had it right on. He greeted one person as Belly Dee Williams for Billy Dee Williams. Jimmy's a wit and a punster. He'll say things that are so witty that it takes a minute to get it. He has a funny outlook on life, period. Other times on a break, he'd relate some of the tragedies in his life in such a comical way that you would think he's doing stand-up comedy. He had a job at one time selling shoes, and he said he used to put shoes on the side until he got off in the evening. He said he would take them up to the barbershop and ask, "Who needs 11D or whatever?" He entertained on his own recording dates when we'd take a break. His life involved comedy and tragedy because the stuff gets so tragic that it's really comical, and he can see the comical side of it.

I was on both of his big band recordings, and he always relates musical phrases to verbal ones. When he wanted to explain the opening for his tune "Gemini," which goes, "de de dee, de de dee," he said, "Get a job, get a job." He'll add little words to make it simpler for musicians to grasp. When I was on the date for Turn Up the Heath, *he explained very complex phrases by just singing them. On paper it's very complex, but when he sings it to you, it becomes very simple and you get it right away. When I taught at Jazzmobile with him, I wished that I could have been a student in his class because he uncomplicates things. Jimmy writes like Frank Lloyd Wright, the architect. Every note is placed in the right place on the score. Everybody who's playing it can hear the part they're playing and the parts all around them, how they all fit, because it's all so correct. I like the way Jimmy explained how he learned to write music by looking at scores and figuring out what the writer was doing. He later studied formally, but earlier on he would look at the part he was playing and at everybody else's part and figure out how they all went together. His writing for the trombone is perfect. It's never high, never too low, and it's always meaningful. It's never subservient to the trumpet part. It's some of the most balanced music I have ever played. He writes challenging music, but it's not anything that's unplayable, and once you play it and hear how great it sounds, it makes you feel good to play it every time afterwards. You feel like you're contributing and not just furnishing background for somebody else's solo.*

I was fortunate to play that same role with J. J. Johnson and Thad Jones, two other giants. The fact that they chose me made me feel very good about myself. That's what Jimmy Heath does. He can make you feel good about yourself, and he's not an aggressive figure. He doesn't hit you over the head with anything. It's all done very subtly with a lot of wit and humor. Anytime I've been on any gig with him, it's always been a lot of fun, not really jump up and down fun, but just intelligent fun. The way he couches things, the way he tells you how to do things, it's unique unto him, but he gets a lot of results from it, from his own unique way of putting things to musicians. He's a great manager of musicians. I don't think he ever has any problems with musicians being rebels because his stuff is so right. He's the last person I would ask if a note is correct. A lot of times when composers ask you to play it down, to read your part, they ask that if you hear anything wrong, mention it to them so they can check it out. I don't think I've ever found anything wrong or even questionable about Jimmy's music.

I am very good friends with Mona as well. I've known her for a very long time, even before I met Jimmy. They're one of the most balanced couples I've ever met. She's a very supportive person. Jimmy wrote a song for Dizzy, "Without You, No Me." I feel that Mona is like that to him as well. She balances him just perfectly.

Also in August, Nancy Wilson's *Turned to Blue* was released. John Levy and Nancy asked me to be on the recording. They had most of the stuff already recorded, but they were finishing up in New York. It was around the time that the International Association for Jazz Education (IAJE) convention was in town. They gave me the song called "Knitting Class," a 3/4 composition with a very interesting harmonic structure, a couple of days before the session. It was a brief recording session because they had already gotten it together. All I had to do was put the solo on it. I never even dreamed it would be on a Grammy-winning recording, and I think I did a pretty good job on it. They thought so too.

In 2006, I was literally among giants at the Romare Bearden Jazz Jubilee Tribute Gala held at the Lighthouse on Twenty-third Street, near the Hudson River, on September 18. Kareem Abdul-Jabbar and Randy Weston were there. I have a picture with the two "twin towers"—Randy is six-foot-six, and Jabbar made Randy look small. At the affair, I played with pianist Jason Moran as a duo on a composition called "Sea Breeze," written by Romare Bearden. Besides being a great artist—a painter and a sculptor—Bearden also wrote music. "Sea Breeze" had been recorded earlier by Billy Eckstine and Dizzy and more recently by Branford Marsalis. The basketball star Grant Hill was there with his parents. They had taught their son to appreciate paintings by African Americans, and Grant has a collection of Bearden's work. I'm a big basketball fan and know Grant's career, but I didn't get a chance to meet him; he had to babysit because his wife, the Grammy-nominated R&B vocalist Tamia, had a gig. I did get a chance to speak with his mother, a lawyer, and his father, Calvin Hill, who went to Yale and was the running back for the Dallas Cowboys when they were champions. It was obvious that Grant came from a very fine family.

After celebrating my section buddy James Moody's eightieth birthday six or seven times in 2005, it was my time in 2006. Moody, the most giving person I have ever met, started my celebrations in March at SUNY Purchase along with bassist Todd Coolman and Jon Faddis, who are professors there. The second eightieth-birthday event for me was at the Bethany Baptist Church in Newark, pastored by Moses William Howard, Jr., where in attendance was my long-time friend and WBGO jazz radio special events coordinator Dorthaan Kirk, widow of multi-reed player Rahsaan Roland Kirk. It was a glorious, spiritually uplifting Sunday that touched me deeply. The third celebration, which was small but appreciated, was in Memphis, and the fourth was a huge five-day party held at the Blue Note in New York, the same time the club was celebrating its twenty-fifth year of existence. On October 11 and 12 at the Blue Note, in addition to having my big band and introducing the new recording *Turn Up the Heath*, my homeboy Bill

Cosby was emcee. We had a ball, and "North Philly Billy," as I call him, was gracious, funny, and generous, as he always is. He calls me "South Philly Shorty." The next two days, October 13 and 14, were incredible, with Clark Terry as guest. Clark, who has helped me throughout my career, insisted I do "Mumbles" with him. It made everybody happy, although I was surprised by it. On Sunday, October 15, James Moody was the guest. He played the flute and his tenor as only he can. Moody always knocks the audience out with his songs "Benny's from Heaven" and "Moody's Mood for Love." It was a love-in with my friends and the friends of all my friends being there.

Talking about smelling the roses, just being in front of a great group of musicians and having them play your music is heavenly: the rhythm section: Lewis Nash (drums), Peter Washington (bass), Jeb Patton (piano); trumpets: Frank Greene, Terell Stafford, Diego Urcola, and Tanya Darby; trombones: John Mosca, Steve Davis, Jason Jackson, Doug Purviance; saxophones: Mark Gross (alto), Antonio Hart (alto), Bobby LaVell (tenor), Andres Boiarsky (tenor), Gary Smulyan (baritone). Peter Washington has made a reputation around New York as almost the number one call other than Ron Carter. I heard him extensively with Tommy Flanagan's trio, and he reminds me of Paul Chambers in his solo work. Peter's a great support person as well as a great soloist. The week was like a "who's who of jazz." Some of my friends sat in; Paquito D'Rivera, Monty Alexander, and Steve Turre were killing. Hank Jones, Barry Harris, Roy Haynes, T. K. Blue, Slide Hampton, Jimmy Owens, Dennis Mackrel, John Lee, Frank Wess, Frank Foster, Benny Powell, Eric Alexander, René McLean, Jerry Dodgion, and my son Mtume, the producer of the big band CD, were there. Tom Bellino showed, and so did two brilliant photographers, Carol Friedman and Roy DeCarava. Carol was there every night taking historic shots.

In addition to all the jazz lovers, there were celebs like actor/director Laurence Fishburne, who brought me a cheesecake; even though I couldn't eat it because of my diet, the band grooved on it. I had met Laurence at the Iridium when he was checking out one of Slide's groups. We talked about his love of music and my love and appreciation of his film *The Tuskegee Airmen*. He knew Percy as a musician, but he didn't know Percy had been a Tuskegee Airman also. Tavis Smiley, the TV talk show host, and Dr. Cornel West came together. Cornel is a fan of the music and comes occasionally to hear the Heath Brothers perform at the Blue Note or wherever. He's also a friend of my son Mtume, who invited him to celebrate Tootie in New Jersey in 2002. Mtume had organized an affair celebrating my younger brother's musical life, and Cornel spoke about Tootie. I also hung out with Cornel at the FDR museum when he received the Freedom of Religion Award. At the Blue Note, Cornel, Tavis, and I talked in the dressing room. Cornel was aware that I knew something about contemporary music, rap, but Tavis didn't know it. I talked to them about that. Clark Terry, who was the guest that night with the big band, was in the room as well. Tavis and Cornel were amused by my imitation of Ludacris, when he says, "When I move, you move."

Jean Bach, the producer of the jazz documentary *A Great Day in Harlem*, and Phoebe Jacobs of the Louis Armstrong Foundation came twice to the celebration. On opening night, President James Muyskens of Queens College came, along with Edward Smaldone, chairperson of the Music Department, and my good friend the Borough of Queens president, Helen Marshall. It was also wonderful that my daughter, Roslyn, my son-in-law, Dwayne, and my grandson Joey, came up from Atlanta to celebrate with us. They came to the club a couple of nights, along with Mike, another grandson who lives in Jersey. Joe McLaren also attended.

On Tuesday, October 17, I went back to Philly to be honored for the sixth time. A reception and performance was held at the Kimmel Center, where I received a proclamation from Mayor John Street and the Jazz Masters Hall of Fame Award from Temple University. Under the direction of Terell Stafford, the Temple Jazz Orchestra played some of my compositions and I soloed. Stafford, who played trumpet on *Turn Up the Heath*, is also the director of Jazz Studies at Temple. I saw some of my old friends there. What made it even better is that Temple announced that my friend Julian King's massive collection of jazz recordings, photos, and memorabilia would be housed in their institution. They also started the Julian King Scholarship. Julian's widow, Shirley, their daughter, Andria, and Julian's sister Jean were also there. The concert was very successful, with many of my friends and Julian's in attendance. The Clef Club event honoring me around that time was very nice too, because the club is located in my old neighborhood in South Philly. What a night of nostalgia. Harrison Ridley, Jr., another of Philly's jazz collectors and a radio host, created a great archive of documents and interviews at the Clef Club, including one with me.

Wednesday, October 18, was the seventh glorious day for me because the event was held back at Queens College, where I'm Professor Emeritus. My friend Maurice Peress, the conductor of the Queens College Orchestra, performed my composition *Three Ears* for full orchestra and a five-piece jazz group. The performance was superb, with professors Antonio Hart and Michael Mossman as soloists. I had been commissioned to write *Three Ears* in 1987—the same year I was appointed—for the fiftieth anniversary of the College's Aaron Copland School of Music. Both times, the house was full, and on the program this time were compositions by Will Marion Cook and Duke Ellington. There I was again, walking with giants or in "Fast Company," which was the title of one of my earlier albums.

The eighth celebration was on my actual birthday, October 25, when I played at the Herbst Theatre as part of the San Francisco Jazz Fest. I was joined by my brother Tootie; Tony Purrone, guitar; Jeremy Pelt, trumpet; Jeb Patton, piano; and young Joe Sanders, bass. It was a party, and the creativity was happening. My nieces, Gwen and Beth, came up from L.A. to hang with me. I was in seventh heaven out there in San Francisco.

For over thirty-six years in San Francisco, the Mecca for young aspiring jazz artists has been the Stanford Jazz Workshop, started by Jim Nadel, who I consider the number one advocate for our music out West. His tenacity is evident and his love lasting. During my several visits over the years, I've been privileged to be with the pros from the world of jazz as well as the young wide-eyed students of all races and ages. This is truly democracy at its best. Jim Nadel is an "Educational Giant," along with his great staff of dedicated workers and volunteers. He's one of the keepers of the flame.

The ninth celebration of my eightieth birthday happened in Seattle. The Seattle Jazz Repertory Orchestra received a grant from Meet the Composer to have an extended composition written for them. I was honored when Michael Brockman and Clarence Acox, the co-directors of the orchestra, asked me to do the piece. The performance dates were November 4 in Seattle, at Benaroya Hall, and November 5 in Kirkland, ten miles east of Seattle. I wrote a piece titled *The Endless Search*, in three movements, and it was about twenty or twenty-five minutes long. Seattle is one of the hippest jazz towns in the country. Even though it rained for four days, it never touched me. I was in a garden of roses. The orchestra played exceptionally on both concerts, and the audiences were enthusiastic, giving us standing ovations and asking for more. The people, the accommodations, the food, and the respect were tremendous. It was also a pleasure to play with tenor saxophonist Hadley Caliman, who I met in L.A. in 1950 when Trane and I were with Dizzy. The orchestra also played an afternoon concert at Seattle's Langston Hughes Performing Arts Center. The NEA and Arts West representatives were there for each performance. My longtime friend Willard Jenkins checked everything out for the Jazz Masters on Tour Program. That weekend really touched me where I live.

The tenth and final eightieth-year celebration was huge. It took place on the Norwegian Sun cruise ship, the Sixth Annual Jazz Party at Sea. Joe Segal, the producer from Chicago who has supported the jazz community for over fifty years, also turned eighty in 2006, as did saxophonist, composer, and arranger Bud Shank. Originally the Jazz Party was billed as 320 years of jazz and was to include Lou Donaldson, but he didn't show. Jazz cruises are social happenings. Besides having music played practically all afternoon and evening, there's lots of nostalgia. People on the cruises are from all over—the States, Canada, and Europe.

We boarded the ship in New Orleans on Sunday, December 3, 2006, and played that night. Monday was an off day, so I went to the casino to play the slots. My eightieth year continued with good luck when I hit the jackpot. Vibraphonist Bobby Hutcherson played with us twice, and Phil Woods replaced Lou Donaldson. Tootie, Jeb, and bassist Joe Sanders were at the top of their game. Joe, who was studying at the Monk Institute and was just twenty-two, was charming all the ladies. He had worked with us once, in the Healdsburg and San Francisco festivals in California. The hang was wonderful with David and Karen Newman, Benny and Bobbi Golson, Curtis Fuller, Phil and Jill Woods, Buster and Ronnie Williams, Benny Green, Russell Malone, Danilo Pérez and his whole family, "Senior" Mance (my nickname for Junior Mance), Donald Harrison, Joey DeFrancesco, Bud Shank and his wife, Willie Pickens, Eric Alexander, Jim Rotundi (Not so Rotund), David Hazeltine, and vocalist Jackie Cain. This was truly a jazz party. It was the best.

PHIL WOODS

I have known Jimmy Heath since before Vaseline. We were on the road with the Clark Terry big band around 1973 or '74 when the bus was left running for two weeks (as were we)—called her the "Idle Queen." Whenever I am doing some research on this music that we all love and can't quite put my finger on the answer, I ask "Little Bird." Nobody has the depth of knowledge that Jimmy has. He can spot a wrong 64th note at the speed of light. Ears? Can hear 'round the corner. In a section, lead, second, third, split fifth—don't matter. He plays the part, does not stick out, doesn't over-blow, shades and phrases with the lead wherever it goes. Sound easy? It is not easy. Whether writing a chart, rehearsing a band, giving a master improv class, or just doing the gig, no one does it better than my dear friend and Jazz Master, Mr. James "Lil Bird" Heath. And when I need to have a good laugh, Jimmy never lets me down! He embodies the true spirit of jazz music.

In December, I got a call from Tom Carter, who directs the Monk Institute, asking if Mona and I could meet with Gail, T. S. Monk, and him at Birdland in New York on December 13 to celebrate the birthday of Vaclav Havel, first elected president of the Czech Republic. He was a playwright and friend of my mentor, Dizzy; "Madam Secretary" Albright was also there. I asked Tom if Maurice Peress, who had just produced a musical tribute to Anton Dvořák at the Bohemian National Hall, could join us, and he did. Jeb Patton and I had performed on that tribute. At Birdland, I showed Secretary Albright a picture from the 1997 Monk Institute competition, where my students Darren Barrett and Diego Urcola won first and second, and she remembered. The Roy Haynes youth quartet was dynamic, and everyone had a ball at Birdland. I was in the company of more giants.

The final surprising event of the year occurred on December 21, when I attended an oral history interview with Kareem Abdul-Jabbar at the Museum of the City of New York as part of a program called "Harlem Speaks," sponsored by the Jazz Museum in Harlem. Kareem was interviewed by museum co-director Christian McBride and jazz writer Larry Blumenfeld. I went backstage to speak with Kareem before the panel began. Ferdinand Lewis Alcindor, Kareem's father, had been a jazz trombonist who played at Minton's Playhouse in Harlem. Since I was a sports nut and Kareem a jazz lover, we had a lot to talk about. Christian McBride was also a sports lover, so that made the whole thing complete. I had met Kareem many times at the Monk competitions, at the White House when President Clinton had jazz on the lawn, and at a Romare Bearden benefit earlier in the year, but this was our first hang. We exchanged stories and had many laughs. During the panel, I learned more about this extraordinary athlete and scholar. I admired him as an athlete, but now I respected him as an African American with knowledge and integrity. He was on a continuous search for black history. I spoke to Kareem about his life, about moving back to Manhattan, and about his father, who had been a jazz musician. We also talked about how drummer Ben Riley used to take Kareem to see Monk and about Kareem's connections to the music and sports worlds. Saxophonist Frank Wess knew his father from the Sixteenth Battalion Band back in 1941. Kareem is also a very great writer with a number of books, including *Brothers in Arms* and *On the Shoulders of Giants: My Journey through the Harlem Renaissance.*

14

Endless Stroll

■

The year 2007 was also a good one. On March 3, I was part of a ceremony in Washington, D.C., honoring all the living Jazz Masters. Billy Taylor was involved in organizing the event, where we received the Living Jazz Legend Award. Thirty-three of us showed up; the rest were either working or ill. It was quite a celebration, with James Earl Jones as the emcee. John Clayton's big band performed, and a few of the masters, like Phil Woods, Frank Wess, and me, joined them. We played together on "Eternal Triangle," arranged for the big band, and we soloed too. Nancy Wilson sang and Wynton played a duet with Dave Brubeck. Wynton wasn't a Jazz Master yet, as far as having received the National Endowment for the Arts award, but he just came to honor us. The NEA Jazz Masters honor is the highest government recognition given jazz musicians in this country.

When Dana Gioia was in charge of the National Endowment for the Arts, he really heightened the visibility of the Jazz Masters Award; before, we'd just get the award and that was it. He was trying to make it so that we got more media exposure. One such opportunity was *Legends of Jazz*, a TV program hosted by Ramsey Lewis that presented some of the Jazz Masters. In 2007, Jazz Masters received a fellowship of $25,000. When I got mine back in 2003 in Toronto, it was $20,000. Percy had gotten it in 2002. At one of the meetings afterward, I told the panel, "People in the other countries are giving hundreds of thousands of dollars. The Danish Jazzpar Prize is $30,000. Also, the MacArthur Genius grants, like Ornette Coleman, Cecil

Taylor, and Max Roach have gotten, can be over $300,000. Ornette got one from the Japanese government, the Praemium Imperiale award, for $150,000. You all have got to come up with this." So they went up $5,000. I said, "Is that retroactive? Can I get that?" They said, "Oh, no, Mr. Heath. We can't do it that way." Since I received the award in 2003, some of the others who got it were Freddie Hubbard, Frank Wess, Toshiko Akiyoshi, Nat Hentoff, Jimmy Scott, Curtis Fuller, and Ramsey Lewis.

Almost a week later, I was back in Washington, D.C. On March 9, 2007, Ahmad Jamal asked Donald Byrd and me to play with his trio at the Kennedy Center, and that was a pleasure and a challenge. Later that year, on September 2, I played with his group at Tanglewood in Massachusetts, and it was like coming full circle. It was mutual admiration, beauty beyond compare—picture-perfect. I courted Mona to his music, and listening to Ahmad has been an ongoing pleasure in our lives. We never miss going to hear him when he plays in our area. He had an influence on Miles and Gil Evans. For a long time, on Milt Jackson's gigs we always played "Ahmad's Blues," a beautiful song. On Ahmad's album *Pittsburgh*, he recorded one of my compositions titled "Mellowdrama," which he still plays. I always tell him that he owns it now.

A few months later, in May, I saw my old friend the Reverend Herbert Daughtry, my roommate from Lewisburg, when I played at the Five "A" Café in Brooklyn. The turnaround in both of our lives makes me realize that God is still in the miracle business.

THE REVEREND HERBERT DAUGHTRY

On Sunday, May 20, 2007, Jimmy Heath, the preeminent jazz musician, his wife, Mona, and Jeb Patton, a.k.a. the General—a superb pianist and former student of Jimmy's—came to the House of the Lord Church. It was the opening of the Five "A" Café, founded by the House of the Lord Church (THOTL) and the Downtown Brooklyn Neighborhood Alliance (DBNA). The purpose of the Café is to create a positive place where artists, athletes, academicians, activists, and the anointed (spiritual ones) gather to share their talents, knowledge, and experience, thus setting the stage for the emergence of another Afrocentric renaissance. Jimmy and the General played three songs—"'Round Midnight," "On Green Dolphin Street," and I requested "A Night in Tunisia." It is a song with a beautiful lingering melody. It was one of my favorites back then. Both musicians gave brilliant performances. The large audience's emotional expressions went from deep silent enthrallment to hand clapping, foot stomping, and verbal shouts of appreciation. After each song, there was a standing ovation. Also on the program was the House of the Lord Church Choir and the Youth Praise Dancers. My daughter, Sharon, the National Director of Music, Art and Dance, directed both. The Five "A" Café is coordinated by Sister Zakiya Russ. Between the music, Jimmy and I reminisced about our years together in the federal penitentiary at Lewisburg, Pennsylvania, over fifty years ago.

I first met Jimmy during the early fifties at Birdland, a nightclub named after Charlie Parker and located on Broadway near Fifty-second Street in those days. It was the jazz Mecca of New York, perhaps of the world; all the great musicians played there.

At the opening, I asked Jimmy, "What made bebop different?" He said, "It concertized and intellectualized music. You had to listen and think to appreciate it. Similar to a concert or a symphony, you went to those occasions to listen, not dance. Swing, which was prevalent at the time, was for dancing. There was also the New Orleans or Dixieland sounds and the Lindy Hop and the jitterbug dances, but Dizzy, Parker, and Monk speeded up the sound. You had to pay attention. It was creative, high energy."

Across the years, I think our positive qualities have deepened. After all, we have been to hell and back. Very little we have not experienced. We've been hurt to the depth of our beings. Scars are still with us. And we have hurt others too, and that is a part of our pain. But here we were, over fifty years later, laughing, kidding, joking as we had done a half century earlier. Now we were in a historic church that I, by the grace of God, had built from a storefront with a few parishioners. We had achieved our goals. We had gained the highest admiration and appreciation from people across the globe. We had been awarded many prestigious awards by religious, civic, corporate, and governmental institutions. I am eternally grateful to the almighty God through Jesus Christ who saved me and called me to minister.

The African beat was what they wanted in Puerto Rico when I went there in June 2007 for the Heineken Jazz Festival with the Dizzy Gillespie All-Star Big Band. The first time I went to San Juan to perform was in August 1980. On that trip, I met Ana Velez, the mother of Ivonne Soto, a friend of Dexter Gordon's. "Mom Soto" ran the record shop in the Old Town section of San Juan. Ivonne, her brother Ramon, and her mother were all connected with the music. The Heath Brothers performed on a television program in Puerto Rico, and the Sotos were involved in that. Ana Velez wrote a book about jazz called *En Torno al Jazz, Vol. 2* (1980) and was connected with Don Pedro Productions. Ramon came to the 2007 concert, and I found out that somebody else had the record shop but that Mom was still around and in her eighties. His sister, Ivonne, had been suffering with cancer. Before we went on stage, I was privileged to meet Bernie Williams, the former Yankee baseball star, who was standing in the wings when we were going on stage. I said, "Bernie, you still playing guitar?" He said, "Yeah. I'm still playing the guitar." I said, "You should also be playing baseball with the Yankees because that outfield sucks." He laughed. He was in great shape, and he loved the music also. At the concert that night, the audience wouldn't let us go until we played "Manteca," and we weren't about to get off the stage until we did. When we played it, they went nuts.

Summer in New York means Jazzmobile outdoor concerts, and that's where I get to see lots of friends who stop by after the set, like Dave Bailey, who used to direct Jazzmobile and who was there when I played the Grant's Tomb outdoor venue in August. Robin Bell-Stevens, the daughter of bassist Aaron Bell, became the president and CEO of Jazzmobile. Since Grant's Tomb is uptown, a lot of people from the Harlem community usually show up.

DAVE BAILEY

At Grant's Tomb, Jimmy showed that he's a communicator. He had the people in the palm of his hand. And that solo he took on "The Voice of the Saxophone" was orgasmic. A lot of the young players don't know how to play a ballad. Jimmy, Frank Wess, and Frank Foster are masters of playing ballads. You can't play love if you've never been in love. Jimmy has my highest respect. I love him passionately as a man, as a musician, as a composer, as a writer, and as a human being. He is one of a few of us left.

In September, I attended Sonny Rollins's Fiftieth-Anniversary Concert at Carnegie Hall.

After the wonderful performance, I told him, "Newk, you've played there almost as many years as they've been playing Bach and Beethoven's music," and we got a good laugh about that. Knowing that no one has a monopoly in music, I was overwhelmed that October by all of the talented musicians who came to hang with the "Brothers," me and Tootie, at the Vanguard in the "Apple" during the week of October 16–21. Tootie was living up to his Swahili name Kuumba, which means creativity. Jeb Patton, the "General," was brilliant as ever on piano, and David Wong, who had joined my group that year on bass, was unbelievable. We were inspired to a higher level when Roy Hargrove (Hardgroove) sat in. A number of musicians who I admire showed up—Cedar Walton, Kenny Barron, Monty Alexander, and Rob Schneiderman—and that's just the piano players. Others who came by were trumpeters Joe Wilder, Ted Curson, Marcus Printup, and James Zollar; bassists Ron Carter, Kiyoshi Kitagawa, and Cameron Brown; drummers Louis Hayes, Billy Hart, and Joe Chambers; saxophonists Frank Wess, Charles Davis, and Antonio Hart; and the outstanding guitarist Russell Malone. It doesn't get any better than that.

JAMES MOODY

I met Jimmy in Philadelphia in 1946 when I was twenty-one and Jimmy was twenty. I was with the Dizzy big band. They called Jimmy "Little Bird" because he played alto then. His family would have musicians over to the house, and they were gung-ho musicians. Jimmy was always writing, but I didn't know how to do anything like that.

Years later, I recorded two of Jimmy's compositions, "Heritage Hum" and "A Sound for Sore Ears," and the album was titled Heritage Hum. *Earlier on, I didn't know what chords were. I thought I would be doing vamps all the time. Tom McIntosh taught me my chords, and once when I was trying to play chords, Jimmy said, "No more vamps." That cracked me up, but it was right on the money too. I'm still trying to get these changes.*

Can you imagine the work that he does, arranging, composing, and playing? He's a phenomenal musician. His chords are right. They just sound right. With the Dizzy Gillespie All-Star Big Band, we play one of his compositions that he was commissioned to do by Dizzy years ago, "Without You, No Me." It's grandiose, and it sounds right now, what the reeds play, what the trombones play, what the trumpets play. When you're playing, you hear all of that and you say to yourself, "Wow."

We played together in the alumni band at the Blue Note on November 25 and 26, 2007. The first couple of nights, Clark Terry was the guest, and then they had other guests. Jimmy played on Sunday, and it was a good lesson-getter because Jimmy Heath blew his butt off as usual. The group was like the Dizzy Gillespie small group: John Lee, bass; Lewis Nash, drums; Slide Hampton, trombone and leader; Greg Gisbert, trumpet; and Roy Assaf, piano. They also had Cyrus Chestnut and Mulgrew Miller. The way Jimmy played "'Round Midnight" on soprano was like a warm meal that you enjoy, a Thanksgiving meal, like a Christmas dinner, like making love. All the emotions were in there and it was so beautiful. He'll go off somewhere and you'll say, "Oh, man," and then he'll come back. When he plays, you say, "Yeah!" and a musician says "Yeah!" because that's the way it hits you. He says, "Oh, yeah! Um um." When somebody plays and it sounds good, you say, "Yeah, okay. It's good." But when Jimmy plays, you say, "Yeah, oh!" because it's not just one thing that he's playing. It's the different things that he's connecting during the whole phase of the solo. Jimmy's got some shit, and he's passed it on to Antonio Hart.

Every time I see Jimmy, I say, "Section, I want to take some lessons, man." We call each other Section because we're in the saxophone section. Of course, I get the lessons when I'm playing with him anyway, but it's not the same. I can't give him enough praise. He's humble, funny, and very spiritual too. His sense of humor is acute. When he talks about the saxophonist Justin Robinson, he would say, "Just in time" or "Justification."

Jimmy is a master master. On the jazz cruise in 2007, he wrote an exercise for me, a tri-tone thing, and it's beautiful. He said he got it from Kenny Dorham. I'm trying to dissect it so I'll know what it is. It was so nice of him. I heard him play it and he said, "I'll write it for you." And when he says something, he does it. In 2005, he wrote a composition for me called "Moody's Groove," with lyrics too. Bum bah dee, dah dah dah, James Moo-dy, James Moo-dy, dah dah dah, bo bo bo. He wrote that in Savannah, Georgia, for my eightieth birthday. And for him, I always sing, "Who's the wife of Jimmy Heath . . . Mona," like the song "Moanin'" by Bobby Timmons. With all the stuff that he's doing, Mona is right there with him. She helps him to go along like my wife, Linda, who is everything to me. Mona is fantastic and Jimmy's fantastic. When you sit down with them somewhere and watch them talking, they're wonderful. You see them jesting with each other and laughing and going on after all these years. That's a wonderful thing, two incredible people doing that.

Jimmy Heath is a giant, giant, giant, giant. He's a hell of an arranger-composer and just a hell of a nice guy, and I love him dearly.

In 2007, I also started to work with my son Mtume on a hip-hop collaboration with Ohene, a classically trained pianist from Ghana, who is now a rap artist based in Philadelphia. His third CD was titled *Nina Simone by . . .* We're trying to connect to the hip-hop generation because the disconnect is a drag. That's what *The Gap Sealer* was about in '72, and so we're still trying to seal that gap. I played with Mtume once in Washington, D.C., in a park where white people didn't allow black people. One white guy got down wrong with some black people and they started rumbling. I think someone said, "We never could get in this park and you ain't got no business coming in here and telling us what to do." It was one of those things. I also played for Mtume behind Gladys Knight on "Good Morning Heartache" for *New York Undercover*, the TV series he did the music for, and once I wrote some of the horn parts for the O'Jays, when they were on the show.

MTUME

In 2006, Tayari and I addressed the entire Music Department at NYU. I had spoken at NYU before, and Dr. Lawrence Ferrara, Chair of Steinhardt Music and Performing Arts Professions, said, "I'd like you to come back and address the entire music school." I said, "Let me bring my pops and we can do it together. Then you'll have the whole history." On September 13, we did it and the students were blown away. It was just an incredible response. In the interview, one of the things I said was "You can't have access to new music without having access to new sounds." About two or three months later, Tayari called me and showed me an interview where he had made the same statement forty years earlier with Lee Morgan. In 2006, I co-produced with Doug Purviance Tayari's big band recording Turn Up the Heath. *The rehearsal for* Little Man Big Band *back in '92 had sounded great, and I just kept thinking about a big band album of Tayari's arrangements on hip hop. We would keep the authenticity of his arrangements, all that complex stuff, but on a "now" beat. It was about that "exhaustion idea." Great big band albums all sound the same conceptually, but I always wanted to find the difference in the familiar. I guess that's what allowed me to weave through those worlds, because I tried to figure out a way to blend things. In 2007, we finally got to work on it after* Turn Up the Heath. *After that, Tayari said, "You know what. I've done it. That's the last one. I want to do another concept now. Let's get on that."*

We started by gathering up some hip-hop cats, including this brother named Ohene, who's from Philly. We're thinking of having guests on it like Mos Def, Common, or Snoop Dog. I'm trying to get Jill Scott to sing a ballad. If it comes off right the way I hear it, this would be historical, the ultimate bridge. Both forms are authentic. We would have real cats who do these beats and one of the greatest jazz big band arrangers in the world coming together. It would be the first cross-generational big band album ever.

We've been laying down some tracks, and we got a bunch of people doing some beats. We're weeding out the ones that will work. Some of it might be too hard, so we have to find the balance. That's my gig, to find that balance. Tayari loves it. He's totally open, which is amazing. You're talking about a cat who's in his eighties. That's the beauty of the masters, as I call them. They were always open, as Miles was open and Trane was open. If you stay open, you can always go to another level. There's no such thing as being stuck because there's too much sound available. You're only stuck if you refuse to walk out of the house.

In February 2008, Black History Month, I received the Carter G. Woodson Award of Mercy College at the Manhattan campus, thanks to the efforts of history professor Roger Gocking. I was joined by Mona; longtime friends like Sandra, wife of Milt Jackson; saxophonist Charles Davis; and Dot Hampton, my Dorie Miller neighbor. The emcee was Dr. Stella Maars, who wrote that "believing in miracles is the foundation of Love." I also saw Grace Metivier of the Wynton Kelly Foundation and one of my Jazzmobile saxophone students from many years back, Donald Morales, who teaches at Mercy. Mtume's daughters, Ife and Benin, and son, Faulu, were there too—my grandchildren. There was an African feeling in the room when they brought out drummers and dancers. With her direction, the leader even encouraged me to dance a few steps in front of the crowd. In my acceptance speech, I talked about attending high school in Wilmington, North Carolina, when segregation was in full swing. That wasn't my first time at a Mercy College event. I had given a lecture-demonstration at the main campus in Dobbs Ferry back in the late 1980s when Joe McLaren taught there.

During Black History Month, I also taught for a week at the Monk Institute at Loyola University. At the airport on our way to New Orleans, Mona and I ran into a giant of black literature, Amiri Baraka, who was going to Tulane University to give a lecture. Coincidentally, we were on the same flight. We had big fun just "reminiscing out of tempo." (Ellington titled one of his compositions "Reminiscing in Tempo.") We talked about family, careers, technology, and especially about the jazz greats we knew. Over a month later, I was honored again when I received a Hall of Fame award from North Carolina Central University in April. Not only was it satisfying that it was from an institution in North Carolina; bassist Larry Ridley was an influential member of the sponsoring organization, the African American Jazz Caucus and its research institute (NAJRI).

LARRY RIDLEY

Jimmy Heath not only has "walked with giants," but he is unequivocally one of the giants. We became friends in 1960, and our special friendship, mutual respect, and musical relationship have been eternally enduring. Jimmy's brother Percy was one of my idols, who continually encouraged and supported me. Tootie and I became friends and worked together many times. Tootie and Jimmy could have dual careers as fantastic musicians and comedians! The Heath family members—Pop, Mom, Jimmy's wife, Mona, and their children— all have a special place in my heart. "A Love Supreme!"

Now, in the days that seem like an endless stroll, I've been able to return to my passion for big band writing and directing. The Queens Jazz Orchestra made its debut in 2008. It all started back in 1998, when I was a part of a committee with the late Jo-Ann Jones and Marc H. Miller, when the Queens Jazz Trail was created and the map was drawn. Years later, after being on the Advisory Board at Flushing Town Hall and having played many gigs there, I was called by the newly appointed executive and artistic director Ellen Kodadek to discuss a project she had in mind. Clyde Bullard, producer and artist relations person, had spoken to me previously about Flushing Town Hall having a big band. At a meeting sometime in 2007, the idea was put on the table and a few names were suggested. I said, "Why don't we call the group the Queens Jazz Orchestra? You already have the Queens Jazz Trail with a trolley taking people by jazz greats' homes." All agreed with the title QJO. We talked about funding, fees, programming, commissions, and so forth. I left the meeting a bit skeptical as always, especially with the economy being what it was, but when they asked me if I would be the music director/conductor, I said yes.

Later, when I got one of their advance programs in the mail, I noticed they had scheduled the premier QJO concert for May 16, 2008. Still leery,

I put it in the back of my mind and continued with my gigs and commitments at hand. A few months before the proposed and advertised concert, Clyde called me and said they had gotten the funds and that it was a go. We then had another meeting that included the marketing folks, Betsy Enright and Cathy Hung. I also talked about personnel, rehearsals, and fees. The ball had started rolling, and I discussed which artists' music we should play on our first concert. Then I realized I had to go to work on the commission. We then called heirs, relatives, widows, and related musicians to get the music of the masters being honored. After a lot of preparation and hard work, the date came around and we were ready. Other than the weather causing some last-minute anxiety, the show went on with much more fanfare than I expected. We had citations from Mayor Bloomberg, Queens Borough President Helen M. Marshall, and the Honorable Ellen Young of the New York State Assembly.

That night, to a sold-out audience, we started the music with my commissioned, extended work *Cultural Crossroads*, named for Flushing Town Hall's location and significance. The orchestra sang the song I composed:

> A home for all the arts
> Is here where the mu-sic starts.
> The Queens Jazz Orchestra is here.
> The songs are old and new.
> We hope they will touch you too.
> The Queens Jazz Orchestra is here.
> We still love mel-o-dy.
> And folks live in har-mo-ny.
> The Queens Jazz Orchestra is here.
> This bor-ough of his-to-ry,
> No longer a mys-ter-y,
> The Queens Jazz Orchestra is here.

We followed with a set of compositions: "Struttin' with Some Barbeque," by Louis Armstrong; "Shiny Stockings," by Frank Foster, and my composition "Basie Section," both for Count Basie; "God Bless the Child," by Billie Holiday and Arthur Herzog; "Robbins' Nest," by Sir Charles Thompson and Illinois Jacquet; my compositions "Without You, No Me," for Dizzy Gillespie, and "Trane Connections," for John Coltrane; "What a Little

Moonlight Can Do," by Billie Holiday; "Bags Groove," by Milt Jackson, arranged by John Clayton; and "A Night in Tunisia," by Dizzy Gillespie.

The orchestra, which was mixed by both race and gender, was killin'— trumpets: Frank Greene, Tanya Darby, Terell Stafford, Michael Philip Mossman; saxophones: Antonio Hart, Sharel Cassity, Bobby LaVell, Charles Davis, Frank Basile; trombones: John Mosca, Michael Dease, Jason Jackson, Douglas Purviance; piano: Jeb Patton; drums: Dennis Mackrel; bass: David Wong; vocals: Antoinette Montague. The audience was of all ages, and they gave us a serious standing ovation. It was a spectacular event, and one that all will remember. The Queens Jazz Orchestra is here.

So much was happening in the fall as my birthday approached. Tootie and I recorded another Heath Brothers CD, *Endurance,* for the Jazz Legacy Productions label founded by bassist John Lee and Lisa Broderick. Barack Obama was in a heated campaign, and it seemed like things were going to change in this country. Around my birthday, I got a call from Sonny Rollins and we talked about Obama's chances of becoming president. Sonny didn't think he would be elected, but I was optimistic. On October 25, 2008, my eighty-second birthday, the groove of this endless stroll got deeper when I went to L.A. to judge the Thelonious Monk International Saxophone Competition. There were twelve talented semifinalists from Australia, France, Israel, and the United States. The five judges were saxophonists Jane Ira Bloom, Greg Osby, David Sanchez, Wayne Shorter, and I. This was my third time as a judge. Jon Irabagon, an alto player based in Astoria, Queens, won the award; second prize went to Quamon Fowler from Fort Worth, Texas, and third to Tim Green from Baltimore. After six hours of listening and choosing three finalists, Mona and I were invited to a reception where T. S. Monk, Billy Dee Williams, and Herbie Hancock spoke. Herbie announced that it was my eighty-second birthday, and they surprised me with a huge cake. My brother Tootie was there too. This was the night before the "Blues and Jazz: Two American Classics" Gala Concert at the Kodak Center in Hollywood.

The show the next night was spectacular and included high school students, Monk Institute students, judges, and many giants of the blues and jazz idioms; actor Don Cheadle and Quincy Jones were presenters. I played "Straight, No Chaser" with T. S. Monk, drums; George Duke, piano; Lee Ritenour, guitar; and John Patitucci, bass. On the finale, B. B. King, Wayne Shorter, Terence Blanchard, Greg Osby, Herbie Hancock, and I were joined by the horn section. Since B.B. was being honored, Bono, The Edge, Robert Cray, and Keb' Mo' joined in while Terri Lyne Carrington laid down a big beat on drums. I felt seven feet tall.

Now in my eighties, and having become one of the elders, I have been "rediscovered," since Jimmy Owens said you were discovered in your middle ages. My musical palette is full with composing, performing, recording, teaching, and participating in panel discussions. I have to pinch myself to make sure I'm not dreaming. It's truly amazing that I've been honored with numerous awards, citations, plaques, certificates, sculptures, and even financial awards. I appreciate all of them and thank everyone who presented them, but what I treasure more than anything is that I was fortunate to have met some of the most creative geniuses in music. I have been truly blessed. I walked with giants.

Appendixes

∎

he played sax to the max/////////// the people loved the way he blew
with little knowledge of all he'd been through/////////////////////////////

long after we're gone
it's the songs that live on/////////////////////////////

a man with giants is where he stood /////////////////////////////
but he dropped more music on the world than most giants ever
could/////////////////////////////

MTUME, July 22, 2009

Appendix A

■

Unique Names

Musicians who improvise live their lives creating, even in the way they talk. Louis Armstrong ("Pops"), Lester Young ("Pres"), Cabell "Cab" Calloway, and others started colloquialisms or hip expressions that have become part of the American language. This is a collection of names that I and others (Albert, Percy, Curtis Fuller, and Cedar Walton) created over time for our colleagues. Each shows the unique personality we see in our jazz friends. These names came to mind spontaneously over many years and include the old tigers as well as the young lions.

ARRANGER/COMPOSER

Carter, Benny: Carter's Crossings
Childs, Billy: Childs' Style
Clayton, John: Clayton's Crayon
Dameron, Tadd: Tadd's Tenderness
Ellington, Duke: Endless Ellington
Evans, Gil: Glorious Gil
Foster, Frank: Foster's Frostings
Fuller, Gil: Fuller's Fire
Golson, Benny: Golden Golson

Hampton, Slide: Slide's Slickness
Jones, Quincy: Quincy's Quickness
Jones, Thad: Thad's Thickness
Mackrel, Dennis: D-Maculate Perception
McIntosh, Tom: Mack's Knack
Shorter, Wayne: Wayne's Terrain
Strayhorn, Billy: Strays Ways
Wilkins, Ernie: Ernie's Empathy

BASS

Blanton, Jimmy: Blanton's Breakthrough
Booker, Walter: Bookity Book
Brown, Ben: Big Ben or Thin Brown
Brown, Ray: Brown Power
Carter, Ron: Carter's Clock or Ron Cartier
Chambers, Paul: Paul's Pulse

Clayton, John: Clayton's Crowd Control
Cranshaw, Bob: Crankshaft
Drummond, Ray: Drumsticks
Gomez, Eddie: Speedy Gomez
Heath, Percy: Big P
Hinton, Milt: Hinton's History
Jones, Sam: Homes' Tone

Lee, John: John Lee Booker
May, Earl: Earl's Way
McBride, Christian: Muslim McBride
McKibbon, Al: MacEbon
Mingus, Charles: Emperor Ming
Mraz, George: The Bad Check
Patitucci, John: Hoochie Coochie
Pedersen, Niels-Henning Ørsted: The Great Dane

Reid, Rufus: Roughus Reid
Ridley, Larry: Riddler
Sanders, Joe: Colonel Sanders
Veal, Reginald: Veal Chops
Washington, Peter: From Paul to Peter
West, Paul: Tall Mess
Williams, Buster: Buster's Luster
Wong, David: Ding Dong
Workman, Reggie: Regular Workman

DRUMS

Allen, Carl: The Brady Bunch
Blade, Brian: Razor Blade
Blakey, Art: Bu's Beat
Clarke, Kenny "Klook": Klook's Kicks
Cobb, Jimmy: Cobweb
Copeland, Keith: Cope-Land
Foster, Al: The Hat
Francis, Panama: Panama Dances
Harper, Winard: Happy Harper
Hart, Billy: Frownin' Billy
Hayes, Louis: Hayes Ways
Haynes, Roy: Haynes Reigns
Heath, Albert "Tootie": Tootie's Touch
Higgins, Billy: Smilin' Billy
Israel, Yoron: You're On
Jones, Elvin: Elvin's Elasticity
Jones, Papa Jo: Papa's Personality
Jones, Philly Joe: Philly's Sillies

Lock, Eddie: The Lock
Mackrel, Dennis: D-Mac
Nash, Lewis: Lewis Bash
Persip, Charli: Tippin Sip
Queen, Alvin: A&Q
Riley, Ben: Big Ben
Riley, Herlin: Whirlin' Herlin
Roach, Max: Max's Meter
Roker, Mickey: Stroker
Strickland, E. J.: E. J. Stickman
Tana, Akira: A Can of Tuna
Tate, Grady: Gravy Taker
Taylor, Arthur: Author Arthur
Thigpen, Ed: Headman Thigpen
Washington, Kenny: Washboard
Williams, Tony: Tony's Tempo
Wilson, Shadow: Shadow's Swing

GUITAR

Benson, George: Gorgeous George
Burrell, Kenny: Kenny B
Dunbar, Ted: Texas Ted
Elf, Mark: Market Self
Hall, Jim: Jim Bald

Malone, Russell: One Alone or Muscle Malone
Matheny, Pat: Pat Betweeny
Montgomery, Wes: Mid Wes
Purrone, Tony: Tough Tony

PIANO

Alexander, Monty: Monty's Magnetism
Barron, Kenny: Boundless Barron
Basie, Count: Count Spacey
Bryant, Ray: Rayfield
Corea, Chick: Slick Corea
Cowell, Stanley: Stretching Stanley
Drew, Kenny: Drew's Brews
Ellington, Duke: Duke's Depth or Duke Elegant
Evans, Bill: Evans's Heavens

Flanagan, Tommy: Fluid Flanagan
Garland, Red: Garland's Gift
Garner, Erroll: Garner's Groove
Green, Benny: Benny Mean
Hancock, Herbie: Herbie Handscapes
Hanna, Sir Roland: Rolling Hanna
Harris, Barry: Barry's Beauty
Hicks, John: Hicks' Tricks
Hines, Earl "Father": Hines' Lines
Jamal, Ahmad: Ahmad's Artistry

Jones, Hank: Hank's Harmony or Jones' Tone
Keezer, Jeff: Jeff Pleaser
Kelly, Wynton: Kelly's Keys
Lewis, John: Lewis's Logic
Lightsey, Kirk: Nude-wig Beethoven
Mabern, Harold: Mabern's Mits
Mance, Junior: Senior Mance
McCann, Les: More McCann
Miller, Mulgrew: Miller Heavy
Mixon, Danny: Danny's Drama
Monk, Thelonious: The Onlyest or Monk's Mystery
Patton, Jeb: The General
Pérez, Danilo: Daring Danilo

Peterson, Oscar: Oscar Speedyson
Powell, Bud: Brilliant Bud
Reed, Eric: Eric the Cleric
Rubalcaba, Gonzalo: Blueberry Cobbler
Shearing, George: Shearing's Hearing
Silver, Horace: Sanctified Silver
Tatum, Art: Tatum's Technique
Taylor, Billy: Taylor's Tapestry
Tyner, McCoy: The Real McCoy
Waller, Fats: Waller's World
Walton, Cedar: Wailing Walton
Weston, Randy: Eastern Weston
Williams, James: Cutie Williams
Wilson, Teddy: Teddy's Tenths
Zawinul, Joe: Joe Fifth Avenue

SAXOPHONE

Ammons, Gene: Jug's Hugs
Anderson, Wessell: Lessell
Bartz, Gary: Gifted Gary
Basile, Frank: Baserious
Bechet, Sidney: Bashing Bechet
Blanding, Walter: Walter Spicey
Bridgewater, Ron: Little Bridge
Byas, Don: Don's Dives
Carter, Benny: Classy Carter
Coleman, George: Big Cole-man
Coleman, Ornette: Little Cole-man or Ornette Goldman
Coltrane, John: Trane's Triumph
Cook, Junior: Cookin' Junior
Davis, Eddie "Lockjaw": Jaws' Paws
Desmond, Paul: Dangerous Desmond
Donaldson, Lou: Country Lou
Foster, Frank: Foster's Finesse
Getz, Stan: Stan Gets
Goines, Victor: Vicktation
Golson, Benny: Golson's Gloss
Gonsalves, Paul: Passionate Paul
Gordon, Dexter: Big Red Machine or Dexter's Drive
Green, Jimmy: The Green Giant
Griffin, Johnny: Riffin' Griffin
Gross, Mark: Remarkable
Hart, Antonio: All Hart
Hawkins, Coleman: Hawk's Talks
Henderson, Joe: The Mighty Joe

Herring, Vincent: Invincible
Hodges, Johnny: Royal Rabbit
Johnson, Bud: Uncle Bud
Jordan, Clifford: Cliff's Riffs
Lovano, Joe: JoLo
McLean, Jackie: Jammin' Jackie
McPherson, Charles: McPersonal
Mobley, Hank: Hankenstein
Moody, James: Moody's Melody
Newman, David: New Man
Oliver, Jimmy: Satin Doll
Parker, Charlie: Bird's Breaks
Potter, Chris: E. F. Hutton or Pottery
Red, Sonny: Señor Rojo
Robinson, Justin: Justification
Rollins, Sonny: Sonny's Syncopation
Sanchez, David: Searching Sanchez
Shaw, Jaleel: For Real
Shorter, Wayne: Wayne's World
Simms, Zoot: Zoot's Toots
Smulyan, Gary: Scary Smulyan
Stitt, Sonny: String's Stretch
Tabackin, Lew: Chew Tobacco
Thompson, Lucky: Unlucky
Warfield, Tim: Tenacious Tim
Washington, Grover: Groover
Webster, Ben: Ben's Breath
Wess, Frank: Magic
Woods, Phil: Fill Up Woods
Young, Lester: Lester's Language

TROMBONE

Davis, Steve: Stevie D or Stevie Delicious
Eubanks, Kevin: Birthday
Fuller, Curtis: Curtis Fooler
Gardner, Vincent: Vincent's Variations
Gordon, Wycliffe: Cliff-craft, Why-not Cliff
Grey, Al: In the Gray Area
Hampton, Slide: Slide's Side

Hayward, Andre: Andre the Giant
Jackson, Jason: Jayjax
Johnson, J. J.: Gentleman Jay
Liston, Melba: Melba's Melisma
Powell, Benny: Powell to the People
Purviance, Douglas: Reliance
Turre, Steve: Turre's Tours or Shelly
Westray, Ron: Ace Duce Tray

TRUMPET

Adderley, Nat: Bullet
Armstrong, Louis: Pops' Chops or Louie's Licks
Blanchard, Terence: Terrorist Blanchard
Brecker, Randy: Reb
Bridgewater, Cecil: Big Bridge
Brown, Clifford: Brainy Brownie
Byrd, Donald: Disappearing Dr.
Coles, Johnny: Spots
Curson, Ted: Fed Person
Davis, Miles: Miles Styles
Dorham, Kenny: Dapper Dorham
Edison, Harry "Sweets": Sweets Pleats
Eldridge, Roy: Roy's Range
Faddis, Jon: Faddisphere or Busy Gillespie
Farmer, Art: Charmer Farmer
Gillespie, Dizzy: Dizzy's Dazzle or Dynamic Diz
Gisbert, Greg: G Wizbert

Greene, Frank: Mountain Greenery
Hargrove, Roy: Roy Hardgroove
Hubbard, Freddie: Ferocious Freddie or Ready
Marsalis, Wynton: Wynton's Wisdom
Mitchell, Blue: True Blue
Morgan, Lee: Morgan's Mirror
Owens, Jimmy: Owens Knowin's
Payton, Nicholas: Payton's Pace
Roditi, Claudio: Romantic Roditi
Rodney, Red: Bread Rodney
Roney, Wallace: Styles Davis
Rotundi, Jim: Not so Rotund
Shaw, Woody: Goody Shaw
Sickler, Don: Stickler
Soloff, Lou: Strolloff
Stafford, Terrell: Staff Inflections
Terry, Clark: Clark's Clarity
Wilder, Joe: Joe Milder

VIBES

Hampton, Lionel: Hamp's Hums
Harris, Stefon: Step On
Hutcherson, Bobby: The Hutch Touch

Jackson, Milt: The Reverend or Metal Melter
Montgomery, Buddy: Bells by Buddy

VOCALS

Carter, Betty: Betty's Breakaway
Eckstine, Billy: B's Bigness
Fitzgerald, Ella: Ella's Elegance or Elegant Girl
Holiday, Billie: Lady's Luck
Horne, Lena: Lena's Look

Lincoln, Abbey: Abbey's Attitude
McRae, Carmen: Carmen's Charisma
Smith, Bessie: Bessie's Blues
Vaughan, Sarah: Sassy's Savvy
Washington, Dinah: Dinah's Dues
Williams, Joe: Joe's Indigo

Appendix B

■

Honors and Awards

MISCELLANEOUS

Cover story, *Jazz Improv Magazine*, December 2008

North Carolina Central University/African American Jazz Caucus Jazz Research Institute Jazz Hall of Fame, April 17, 2008

Carter G. Woodson Award of Mercy College, February 25, 2008

Living Jazz Legend Award, Kennedy Center, Washington, D.C., March 3, 2007

Lifetime Achievement Award, *Jazz Improv Magazine*, 2007

Humanitarian Award from National Endowment for the Arts, January 11, 2006

Don Redman Heritage Award, 2006

Juilliard Medal, Centennial Commencement Celebration, May 20, 2005

Honored at Oberlin Conservatory, May 14, 2005

Beacons of Jazz Award, at The New School, New York, February 22, 2005

Mount Airy Cultural Center Award, Philadelphia, September 4, 2004

Honorary Doctorate in Music, Queens College, City University of New York, June 3, 2004

Giants of Black History Award, Greater Harlem Chamber of Commerce, New York, February 9, 2004

Duke Ellington Fellowship, Yale University, September 5, 2003

Mid-Atlantic Arts Foundation Legacy Award, February 7, 2003

Named a 2003 American Jazz Master by the National Endowment for the Arts, January 10, 2003

Honored by the National Visionary Leadership Project, 2003

Artist of the Year, Flushing Council on Culture and the Arts, December 14, 2002

Honored with the mayor's proclamation of "Jimmy Heath Day" at a concert in Wilmington, North Carolina, October 19, 2002

Heath Brothers received the Diamond Award for Excellence from International Association of African American Music and a citation from the Mayor of Philadelphia, June 8, 2002

First jazz artist to receive Honorary Doctorate in Music at Juilliard School of Music, May 24, 2002

Benny Golson Jazz Master Award, Howard University, Washington, D.C., March 14, 2002

75th Birthday Tribute concert at Lincoln Center, New York, with Lincoln Center Jazz Orchestra Plus Guests, October 10, 11, 2001

Heath Brothers honored at tribute concert at Artist Collective in Hartford, Connecticut, March 24, 2001

New York State Governor's Arts Award 2000, November 20, 2000

Jazz Masters Award, South Orange Department of Recreation and Cultural Affairs, South Orange, New Jersey, October 14, 2000

Tribute and Proclamation, "Jimmy Heath Day," Westchester Board of Legislators, Westchester, New York, May 21, 2000

Heath Brothers honored at *JazzTimes* Convention, "Give My Regards to Broad Street: Salute to the Heath Brothers," New York, November 2, 1998

Dorie Miller Award at Dorie Miller Co-op, Corona, New York, June 25, 1998

Elected to the South Carolina State University Hall of Fame, April 10, 1998

Heath Brothers honored with the Count Basie Award from Queens Symphony, New York, April 2, 1998

Honored at "A Tribute to Jimmy Heath" concert at Alice Tully Hall, Lincoln Center, New York, hosted by Bill Cosby, to establish The Jimmy Heath Chair at the Aaron Copland School of Music, Queens College. Also received the Queens College Presidential Award, January 9, 1998

Life Achievement Award, Jazz Foundation of America, March 7, 1997

Phineas Newborn, Jr., Award of Excellence received at Jimmy Heath Tribute Concert, Merkin Hall, New York, January 6, 1997

Carter Woodson Foundation Award, May 10, 1996

Living Legends Jazz Award, Afro-American Historical and Cultural Museum, Philadelphia, February 2, 1996

Afro-American Classical Music Award, Northern New Jersey Spelman College Alumni, New Jersey, April 18, 1995

Appointed to the Board of Trustees of the Thelonious Monk Institute of Jazz, 1995

New York *Newsday* Front Page Award, November 22, 1994

Founder's Award, Thelonious Monk Institute of Jazz, November 21, 1994

The Dizzy Gillespie Achievement Award, New York, September 11, 1994

Greater Jamaica Development Corporation Award, New York, September 1994

Heath Brothers elected to the Hall/Walk of Fame, Philadelphia Music Alliance, April 2, 1993

Celebration of North Carolina Artists Award, Greensboro Cultural Center, Greensboro, North Carolina, September 15, 1990

Jazz Pioneers Award received from BMI at Copacabana nightclub, New York, June 25, 1990

The Barry Award received from Barry Harris, 1989

Appointed to the Advisory Board of the Louis Armstrong House and Archives, New York, 1988

Honorary Doctorate, Sojourner-Douglass College, Baltimore, 1985

GRAMMY NOMINATIONS

Grammy nomination for box set liner notes of *The Heavyweight Champion: The Complete Atlantic Recordings of John Coltrane* (Rhino), 1995

Grammy nomination for *Little Man Big Band* (1992, Verve), produced by Bill Cosby, 1993

Grammy nomination for *Live at the Public Theater* (Columbia), with the Heath Brothers, 1980

Appendix C

■

Selected Discography

ABBREVIATIONS

arr = arranger
as = alto saxophone
bs = baritone saxophone
cdr = conductor
comp = composer
fl = flute
ss = soprano saxophone
ts = tenor saxophone

JIMMY HEATH AS LEADER

1959   *The Thumper*, September or November 27 and 30, Riverside (ts)
1960   *Really Big!* June 24 and 28, Riverside (ts)
1961   *The Quota*, April 14 and 20, Riverside (ts)
1962   *Triple Threat*, January 4 and 17, Riverside (ts)
1963   *Swamp Seed*, March 11 and May 28, Riverside (ts)
1964   *On the Trail*, March, Riverside (ts)
1972   *The Gap Sealer*, March 1, Cobblestone (ts, ss, fl); reissued as *Jimmy*, Muse (1979)
1973   *Love and Understanding*, June 11, Muse (ts, ss, fl)
1974   *The Time and the Place*, June 24, Landmark (ts, as, ss, fl)
1975   *Fast Company*, March 11, 1963–March 1964, Milestone (ts) (Riverside reissues)
1975   *Picture of Heath*, September 22, Xanadu (ts, ss)
1985   *New Picture*, June 18 and 20, Landmark (ts, ss, fl)

1987   *Peer Pleasure*, February 17 and 18, Landmark (ts)
1988   *Nice People*, November 27, 1959–Spring 1964, OJC (ts)
1991   *You've Changed*, August, SteepleChase (ts, ss)
1992   *Little Man Big Band*, January 30 and 31, March 3, Verve (ts, arr, cdr)
1995   *You or Me*, April, SteepleChase (ts, ss)
1998   *The Professor*, date unknown, 32 Jazz (ts, as, ss)
2006   *Turn Up the Heath*, January 13, 2004, April 10, 2006, Planet Arts (cdr, comp, arr, ts, ss)

HEATH BROTHERS

1975   *Marchin' On*, October 22, Strata East (ts, ss, fl)
1978   *Passing Thru*, October, Columbia (ts, ss, fl)
1979   *In Motion*, January, Columbia (ts, ss)
1979   *Live at the Public Theater*, December (liner notes), Columbia (ts, ss)
1980   *Expressions of Life*, December, Columbia (ts)
1981   *Brotherly Love*, December 29 and 30, Antilles (ts, ss)
1983   *Brothers and Others*, May 16 and 17, Antilles (ts, ss)
1997   *As We Were Saying*, February 23 and 24, Concord (ts, ss)
1998   *Jazz Family*, May 29–31, Concord (ts, ss)
2004   *Brotherly Jazz: The Heath Brothers*, July, Dansun (released 2006), DVD
2005   *Jazz Master Class Series from NYU: Jimmy and Percy Heath*, November 21, Artists House Foundation (released 2008), DVD
2008   *Endurance*, October 5 and 6, Jazz Legacy Productions (ts, ss)

JIMMY HEATH ON RECORDINGS BY OTHER ARTISTS

1948   Howard McGhee Sextet (2 tracks, 78 rpm), "Hot and Mellow" ("Yardbird Suite") and "Messin' with Fire"("Donna Lee") February, Old Swing-Master (as) (supposedly recorded December 1947, Vitacoustic, at Argyle Show Lounge, Chicago)
1948   Howard McGhee/Milt Jackson Sextet, *Howard McGhee/Milt Jackson*, February, Savoy (as, bs)
1948   Kenny Clarke, *Paris Bebop Sessions*, May 14, France, Prestige (as)
1948   Howard McGhee Boptet (Sextet) (6 tracks, 78 rpm), France, May 15, Vogue (as)
1948   Erroll Garner, "I Surrender Dear" (live jam session, Théâtre Marigny, Paris, May 16 (released on I Giganti del Jazz 24) (as)
1948   Howard McGhee Boptet (Sextet) (6 tracks, 78 rpm), France, May 18, Blue Star (as)
1949   Gil Fuller Orchestra (78 rpm), June 11 or July 11, Discovery (as); reissued on Savoy Jazz, various artists, 2-lp set, *The Bebop Boys*, 1978 (contains Heath's first recorded arrangement on "Mean to Me")
1949   Dinah Washington, *The Complete Dinah Washington on Mercury, Vol. 1 (1946–1949)*, September 27, Verve (as)
1950   Dizzy Gillespie Sextet, *In the Beginning*, September 16, Prestige (as)
1950   Dizzy Gillespie Orchestra, *Strictly Bebop Jazz Classics, Vol. 13*, November 21, 1949, and January 10, 1950, Capitol (as)
1953   Miles Davis, *Miles Davis, Vol. 2*, April 20, Blue Note (ts)

1953	J. J. Johnson Sextet, *The Eminent J. J. Johnson, Vols. 1 and 2*, June 22, Blue Note (ts, bs)
1953	Kenny Dorham Quintet, *Kenny Dorham Quintet*, December 15, Debut (ts, bs)
1959	Blue Mitchell, *Blue Soul*, September 28, Riverside (ts, arr)
1960	Julian Priester, *Keep Swingin'*, January 11, Riverside (ts)
1960	Sam Jones, *The Sam Jones Soul Society*, March 8, Riverside (ts, arr)
1960	Nat Adderley, *That's Right! Nat Adderley and the Big Sax Section*, August 9 and September 15, Riverside (ts)
1960	Kenny Dorham, *Show Boat*, December 9, Time (ts)
1961	Sam Jones, *The Chant: Sam Jones Plus 10*, January 13 and 26, Riverside (ts, arr)
1961	Don Sleet, *All Members*, March 16, Jazzland (ts)
1961	Freddie Hubbard, *Hub Cap*, April 9, Blue Note (ts)
1961	Elmo Hope, *Homecoming!* June 22 and 29, Riverside (ts)
1961	Riverside Jazz Stars, *A Jazz Version of Kean*, October 31 and November 1, Riverside (ts, arr)
1961	Curtis Fuller, *Soul Trombone*, November 15–17, Impulse (ts)
1962	Pony Poindexter, *Pony's Express*, February 16, Epic (ts)
1962	Blue Mitchell, *Sure Thing*, March 7, 8, and 28, Riverside (ts, arr)
1962	Milt Jackson Sextet, *Big Bags*, June and July, Riverside (ts, fl)
1962	Sam Jones, *Down Home*, June 25 and September 16, Riverside (ts)
1962	Milt Jackson, *Invitation*, August 30, Ocober 31, and November 7, Riverside (ts)
1962	Lee Morgan/Jimmy Heath Quintet, *Live at Birdland*, November 17, Ozone (ts)
1963	Milt Jackson Quintet, *Live at the Village Gate*, December, Riverside (ts)
1964	Milt Jackson Orchestra, *Jazz 'N' Samba*, June 7 and August 6, Impulse (ts)
1964	Ray Brown/Milt Jackson Orchestra, *Brown/Jackson*, September 24, Verve (ts, arr); reissued on *Much in Common* (1996)
1964	Donald Byrd, *Up with Donald Byrd*, November 4 and 6, Verve (ts)
1964	Cal Tjader, *Soul Sauce*, November 20, Verve (ts)
1964	Donald Byrd, *Mustang*, November 24, Blue Note (ts)
1964	Milt Jackson, *In a New Setting*, December 9, 14, and 28 Limelight/Verve (ts, fl, arr)
1965	Carmell Jones, *Jay Hawk Talk*, May 8, Prestige (ts)
1965	Herbie Mann, *Latin Mann*, date unknown, Columbia (released also as *Big Boss Mann* (ts)
1966	Art Farmer Quintet, *The Time and the Place/The Lost Concert*, August 18, Mosaic (released 2007) (ts)
1966	Milt Jackson, *Born Free*, December 15, Limelight (ts)
1967	Art Farmer Quintet, *The Time and the Place*, February 8, Columbia (ts)
1967	Art Farmer Quintet, *The Art Farmer Quintet Plays the Great Jazz Hits*, May 16, 23, and 25 and June 7, Columbia (ts)
1967	Donald Byrd, *Blackjack*, May 27, Blue Note (ts)
1969	Albert Heath, *Kawaida*, December 11, Trip (ts, ss)
1970	Charles Earland, *Black Drops*, June 1, Prestige (ts, ss)
1970	Art Farmer, *From Vienna with Art*, September 7, MPS/Pausa (ts, ss, fl)
1971	Red Garland Quartet, *The Quota*, May 3, MPS (ts, ss)
1971	Art Farmer, *Homecoming*, July 1, Mainstream (ts, ss)

1971   Music Inc., *Music Inc.*, November 11, Strata-East (reeds, fl)
1972   Art Farmer, *Here's That Rainy Day*, date unknown, Jazz Heritage (ts, ss, fl)
1972   Curtis Fuller, *Smokin'*, date unknown, Mainstream (ts, ss)
1973   Albert Heath, *Kwanza (the First)*, June 4, Muse (ts, ss, fl)
1973   Don Patterson, *These Are Soulful Days*, September 17, Muse, (ts)
1974   Milt Jackson, *Olinga*, January, CTI (ts, ss)
1974   Mtume, *Rebirth Cycle*, February, Third Street (released 1977) (reeds)
1974   Clark Terry, *Clark Terry's Big Bad Band: Live at the Wichita Jazz Festival*, April 21, Vanguard (ts, arr)
1975   Sonny Stitt, *Mellow*, February 14, Muse (ts, ss, fl)
1975   Stanley Cowell, *Regeneration*, April 27, Strata-East (ss, fl)
1979   CBS Jazz All Stars, *Havana Jam, Vols. 1 and 2*, March 2, Columbia (ts, ss, arr)
1981   Various Artists, *God Rest Ye Merry Jazzmen*, December, Columbia (ts)
1982   Continuum, *Mad about Tadd*, May 4, Palo Alto (ts, arr)
1983   Don Sickler, *Music of Kenny Dorham*, November 12, Uptown (ts)
1984   George Benson, *20/20*, date unknown, Warner Bros/Prime Cuts (ts)
1984   Mtume, *You, Me and He*, date unknown, Epic (ts)
1985   Milt Jackson and His Gold Medal Winners, *Brother Jim*, May 17, Pablo (ts, ss)
1988   Arnett Cobb, Jimmy Heath, and Joe Henderson, *Tenor Tribute, Vols. 1 and 2*, April 30, Soul Note (ts, ss)
1988   Maurice Peress, Conductor (American Composers Orchestra), *Four Symphonic Works by Duke Ellington*, June 27, MusicMasters (ts, ss)
1988   Benny Carter Jazz All Stars, *Over the Rainbow*, October 18 and 19, Music Masters (ts)
1988   Mark Elf, *The Eternal Triangle*, December 22, Jen Bay Jazz (ts)
1988   Milt Jackson Sextet, *Bebop*, date unknown, East-West/Atlantic (ts)
1988   Sam Jones, *Right Down Front: The Riverside Collection*, date unknown, OJC (ts)
1988   Blue Mitchell, *Blues on My Mind*, date unknown, OJC (ts)
1989   Jay McShann, *Paris All-Star Blues: A Tribute to Charlie Parker*, June 13, MusicMasters (ts)
1990   Bill Cosby, *My Appreciation*, May 28 and 29, Verve (ts)
1990   Clark Terry, *Live at the Village Gate*, November 19 and 20, Chesky (ts, ss)
1990   Milt Jackson, *The Harem*, December 10 and 11, MusicMasters (ts, ss)
1992   New York All Stars, *Jazz Summit*, April 25, Jimco (ts, ss)
1992   Densil Pinnock, *I Waited for You*, August, Uptown Jazz (ts)
1992   J. J. Johnson, *Let's Hang Out*, December 7, 8, and 9, Gitanes/Verve (ts)
1992   Sonny Costanzo Jazz Orchestra, *Sonny's on the Money*, date unknown, Stash (ts)
1992   Antonio Hart, *Don't You Know I Care*, date unknown, Novus (producer)
1992– 1993   The Modern Jazz Quartet and Friends, *A 40th Anniversary Celebration: MJQ and Friends*, June 1992–July 1993, Atlantic (ts)
1993   Slide Hampton and the Jazz Masters, *Dedicated to Diz*, February 6 and 7, Telarc (ts)
1993   Various Artists, *Jazz at Lincoln Center Presents: The Fire of the Fundamentals*, February 14, Columbia (ss)
1993   Dusko Goykovich, *Soul Connection*, June 28 and 29, Enja (ts)
1993   Sonny Rollins, *Old Flames*, July and August, Milestone (arr, cdr)
1993   Riverside Reunion Band, *Mostly Monk*, September 20, Milestone (ts)

1994   Riverside Reunion Band, *Hi-Fly*, July 25, Milestone (ts)
1994   Antonio Hart, *It's All Good*, date unknown, Novus (liner notes)
1994   Quartette Indigo, *Quartette Indigo*, date unknown, Landmark (arr)
1996   Frank Wess, *Surprise, Surprise*, November, Chiaroscuro (ts)
1997   T. S. Monk, *Monk on Monk*, February 6–27, N2K (ts)
1998   Calvin Owens, *Another Concept*, date unknown, Sawdust Alley (as, ts, ss)
1999   Shirley Witherspoon, *Magic and Love*, date unknown, Hot Springs (ts)
2000   Dizzy Gillespie Alumni All-Star Big Band, *Things to Come*, September, MCG Jazz (released 2002) (ts)
2001   Pat Metheny and the Heath Brothers, *Move to the Groove*, January 28, 1983–November 25, 1988, West Wind (ts)
2001   Freddie Hubbard and Jimmy Heath, *Jam Gems: "Live" at the Left Bank*, June 13, 1965, Music Force (released January 30) (ts)
2001   Nancy Wilson, *A Nancy Wilson Christmas*, date unknown, Telarc (ts)
2003   Gerald Wilson, *New York New Sound*, August 26 (released), Mack Avenue (ts)
2003   Antonio Hart, *All We Need*, Sepember 11 and 12, Downtown Sound (released 2004) (ts)
2003   Angela Hagenbach, *Poetry of Love*, date unknown, Amazon (ts)
2004   Whit Williams, *"Now's the Time" Big Band*, September 28–30, Mama (released March 11, 2008) (ts)
2005   Dizzy Gillespie All-Star Big Band, *Dizzy's Business*, September 29–October 2, MCG Jazz (released September 26, 2006) (ts)
2005   Diego Urcola, *Viva*, November 18, 19, and 20, CAM Jazz (ts)
2006   Nancy Wilson, *Turned to Blue*, January 15 and 16, MCG Jazz (ts)
2008   Dizzy Gillespie All-Star Big Band, *I'm BeBoppin' Too*, date unknown, Half Note (released 2009) (ts, arr)

Appendix D

■

Compositions

SHORTER COMPOSITIONS

"All Members"
"Angel Man"
"Artherdoc Blues" (with Percy Heath)
"Basic Berks"
"Big P"
"Blue on Blue"
"Bop Ag'in"
"Bring It Home (To Me)"
"Bro' Slim"
"Changes"
"Chordnation"
"C.J."
"Cloak and Dagger"
"C.T.A."
"Dew and Mud"
"Downshift"
"Dreamin'" (with Mtume)
"D. Waltz"
"Ellington's Strayhorn"
"Far Away Lands"
"Faulu"
"Feelin' Dealin'"
"Forever Sonny"
"For Miles and Miles"

"For Minors Only"
"For the Public"
"Funny Time"
"Gap Sealer, The"
"Gemini"
"Gingerbread Boy"
"God Is the One" (with Beth Jackson)
"Heads Up! Feet Down!"
"Heritage Hum"
"Homes"
"Ineffable"
"Keep Love Alive"
"Life in the City"
"Like a Son"
"Longravity"
"Losing Game, A"
"Lowland Lullaby"
"Mellowdrama"
"Melodic Strains"
"Metal Melter, The" (with Milt Jackson)
"Mona's Mood"
"Mongo's Groove"
"Moody's Groove"

"Nails"
"New Blue, A"
"Newest One, The"
"Newkeep"
"New Picture"
"Nice People"
"Old Fashion Fun"
"One for Juan"
"Our Little Town" (with Percy Heath)
"Picture of Heath, A"
"Project 'S'"
"Prospecting"
"Quota, The"
"Re-Rev" (with Milt Jackson)
"Resonant Emotions"
"Rio Dawn"
"Sassy Samba, A"
"Six Steps"
"Sleeves"
"Smilin' Billy"
"Sound for Sore Ears, A"
"Sources Say"
"South Filthy"

"Stand for Jazz"
"Studio Style"
"Summer Afternoon, A"
 (with Beth Jackson)
"Tender Touch"
"Then What"
"Thing to Do, The"
"Thirteenth House, The"
"Thumper, The

"Time and a Place, A"
 (also titled "The Time
 and the Place")
"Togetherness"
"Top Shelf"
"Trane Connections"
"24-Hour Leave"
"Two Tees"
"Use It (Don't Abuse It)"

"Voice of the Saxophone,
 The"
"Wall to Wall"
"Waverly Street"
"Without You, No Me"
"You Can Hide Inside the
 Music" (with Beth
 Jackson)
"You or Me"

EXTENDED COMPOSITIONS

Afro-American Suite of Evolution, The, premiered May 1, 1976, Town Hall, New York

Bird Is the Word, premiered August 21 and 22, 2004, Charlie Parker Jazz Festival, New York

Birmingham, premiered April 21, 2001, Carver Theatre, Birmingham, Alabama

Cultural Crossroads, premiered May 16, 2008, Flushing Town Hall, Queens, New York

Endless Search, The, premiered November 4–5, 2006, Benaroya Hall–Nordstrom Recital Hall and Kirkland Performance Center, Seattle

Fashion or Passion, premiered October 29, 2004, Frederick P. Rose Hall, Jazz at Lincoln Center, New York

For the Love Of, premiered May 7, 2005, Richardson Auditorium, Princeton University, Princeton, New Jersey

In Praise (from J. to J.), premiered August 4, 1994, Alice Tully Hall, Lincoln Center, New York

Leadership, premiered April 11, 1996, Cramton Auditorium, Howard University, Washington, D.C.

Smilin' Billy Suite, recorded Oslo, Norway, and released on Heath Brothers, *Marchin' On* (1975)

Sweet Jazzmobile, premiered October 29, 1999, Avery Fisher Hall, Lincoln Center, New York

Three Ears (symphonic work), premiered April 17, 1988, Colden Auditorium, Queens College, Flushing, New York

Upper Neighbors Suite, premiered October 6, 1990, Concordia University Concert Hall, Montreal, Quebec

Appendix E

■

Chronology

1926   Born to Percy and Arlethia Heath in Philadelphia on October 25

1931   Attends Smith Elementary School, South Philadelphia

1932   Sees Duke Ellington and other bands at Pearl Theatre in Philadelphia

1936   Spends the summer in Wilmington, North Carolina

1939   Attends Williston High School in Wilmington

1941   Receives saxophone as Christmas gift from father; joins Williston High
        School Marching Band, whose members include Andy McGhee

1942   Studies saxophone in Philadelphia during the summer with Paul Amati; plays
        in jazz band called the Melody Barons, in Wilmington, North Carolina

1943   Graduates high school in Wilmington and returns to Philadelphia; works with
        local bands headed by Arthur Woodson, Mel Melvin, and especially Calvin
        Todd through 1945 (Calvin Todd Band includes Gerald Porter and Bill Griffin)

1945   Goes South with Calvin Todd Band; in May, joins the Nat Towles Orchestra,
        which would include Billy Mitchell, Hy Lockhart, and Felix Leach; on June 5,
        hears Dizzy Gillespie live for the first time at Academy of Music, Philadelphia;
        on July 3, plays what was probably his first gig with Towles in Wayne, Nebraska;
        in the fall, plays Prom Ballroom in St. Paul, Minnesota; travels extensively
        throughout the Midwest

1946   In January, plays Royal Theatre, Baltimore, with Nat Towles; leaves Nat Towles
        Orchestra and returns to Philadelphia; forms Jimmy Heath Orchestra, includ-
        ing John Coltrane and later Benny Golson; hears Dizzy Gillespie Big Band at
        Club Elate, Philadelphia, including Milt Jackson; meets Bertha Preston

1947   In January, Jimmy's son James (later Mtume) is born; on December 7, Jimmy
        Heath Orchestra plays at benefit performance at Club Elate, and Charlie

Parker sits in; Parker plays Down Beat Club, Philadelphia, with group including Miles, Tommy Potter, Duke Jordan, and Max Roach; Parker borrows Heath's saxophone for the gig; Howard McGhee takes over Jimmy Heath Orchestra for a couple of gigs; Heath works with McGhee in Chicago at Argyle Show Lounge; plays Three Deuces on Fifty-second Street in New York with McGhee

1948   With Jimmy Heath Orchestra, plays what were likely its final engagements; takes first trip to Europe in May; travels to Paris with McGhee for gigs at Les Ambassadeurs; on May 15, records with McGhee on *Howard McGhee Boptet*; plays and records with Kenny Clarke and Erroll Garner; records "Maggie's Draw" with McGhee, Heath's first recorded composition; records with Milt Jackson and McGhee group; plays Paradise Theater, Detroit, with McGhee

1949   Works with Gil Fuller's orchestra and studies orchestration with Fuller; plays battle of the bands at the Audubon Ballroom, New York, with Dizzy Gillespie and Gil Fuller bands; on July 11, records with Fuller on *Bebop Boys*, containing Heath's first recorded big band arrangement on "Mean to Me"; in September, hired by Dizzy for big band; on October 4, plays Wilberforce University with Dizzy Gillespie Orchestra (DGO); on November 21, records *Dizzy Gillespie and His Orchestra* for Capitol Records, along with Coltrane; plays Christmas engagement with DGO at Apollo, New York

1950   Tours with Dizzy's band; in March, plays Howard Theatre in Washington, D.C., with DGO; in June, DGO disbands; in the summer, plays with Dizzy Gillespie small group in California; in September, plays Ciro's, San Francisco; in November, plays jam session at Bop City, San Francisco

1951   In the winter, is fired by Dizzy; begins to play tenor sax; plays gigs around Philadelphia, including Down Beat Club; with Heath group, plays with Clifford Brown; travels to New York

1952   In New York, joins Symphony Sid All-Stars, including Miles Davis, J. J. Johnson, Kenny Clarke, Percy Heath, and Milt Jackson; tours with Symphony Sid All-Stars and plays such cities as Cleveland (Ebony Show Lounge), Detroit (Graystone Ballroom), and New York (Downbeat)

1953   Miles Davis records Heath's composition "C.T.A."; Jimmy records with Clifford Brown, J. J. Johnson, and John Lewis; Percy Heath joins with Milt Jackson to form Modern Jazz Quartet (MJQ); Jimmy plays gigs with Art Blakey's Jazz Messengers big band in New York

1955–   Off the scene, at Lewisburg Penitentiary in Pennsylvania, serves a sentence for
1959   narcotics possession; organizes inmate band; undertakes self-study in music and continues to compose and arrange; writes charts for Chet Baker and Art Pepper; begins to play the flute

1959   Back on the scene, returns to Philadelphia; meets Mona Brown; plays gigs with Kenny Dorham at Diamond Horseshoe in Philadelphia; is signed by Orrin Keepnews to Riverside Records, for which he will record six albums as leader; records with various Riverside artists, such as Blue Mitchell; in June, works with Gil Evans Band at the Apollo, New York; in July, joins Miles Davis's group at

Jazz Seville, Los Angeles, replacing John Coltrane; is part of group that includes Cannonball Adderley, Paul Chambers, and Jimmy Cobb; adjusts to modal sound; plays Regal Theater, Chicago, and French Lick, Indiana, with Davis group; records first Riverside recording as leader (*The Thumper*)

1960   Marries Mona Brown; records *Really Big!*; records with Julian Priester; opens for Ray Charles in Philadelphia; daughter, Roslyn, is born; records with other Riverside artists such Nat Adderley, Blue Mitchell, and Sam Jones

1961   Records *The Quota*; plays gigs in Philadelphia; around this time, meets Bill Cosby at the Underground club, where Cosby makes his debut as a stand-up comic

1962   Records *Triple Threat*; plays on Milt Jackson's *Invitation* with Kenny Dorham

1963   Records *Swamp Seed*; plays gigs with Donald Byrd; son Jeffrey is born; returns to Philadelphia for occasional gig

1964   Records *On the Trail*; moves to Corona, Queens, New York; freelances, plays and records with various artists; continues to arrange for Riverside; plays Connolly's in Boston with Sabby Lewis; Riverside, in financial trouble, folds; Jimmy attends first meeting for the establishment of Jazzmobile; begins teaching at Jazzmobile in Harlem; World's Fair is held in Queens

1965   Works with Art Farmer

1966   Miles Davis's *Miles Smiles*, jazz album of the year, includes Heath composition "Gingerbread Boy"

1967   Records with Art Farmer on *The Time and the Place*; Coltrane dies

1968   Begins to take more frequent trips to Europe for gigs

1969   Is given Swahili name Tayari (ready) by Mtume; records on Albert "Tootie" Heath's *Kawaida* release; takes family to Europe while touring; becomes part of Collective Black Artists

1970   Jimmy's father, Percy, Sr., dies

1972   *The Gap Sealer* is recorded; Jimmy takes family to Europe while touring; Jimmy's mother, Arlethia, dies; Lee Morgan is killed in New York

1973   Records *Love and Understanding*, including Stanley Cowell; studies Schillinger System and orchestration with Rudolf Schramm at Carnegie Hall

1974   Records *The Time and the Place*; receives grant to compose *Afro-American Suite of Evolution*; MJQ goes on hiatus, and Jimmy forms Heath Brothers group with Percy, Albert, and Stanley Cowell

1975   Heath Brothers tour Europe; Jimmy records *Picture of Heath*; *Marchin' On* is recorded in Oslo, Norway; Jimmy writes *Smilin' Billy Suite*

1976   On May 1, *Afro-American Suite of Evolution* premieres at Town Hall, New York; Jimmy tours South Carolina with Dizzy

1977   *Afro-American Suite of Evolution* is performed in Winnipeg, Canada; Jimmy attends Earth, Wind & Fire concert with daughter, Roslyn, at Madison Square Garden; meets guitarist Tony Purrone, who will later join the Heath Brothers

1978   Meets Bruce Lundval of Columbia Records, and Heath Brothers sign with the label; Keith Copeland joins Heath Brothers on drums; *Passing Thru* is recorded

1979   *In Motion* is recorded; Akira Tana joins Heath Brothers on drums; *Live at the Public Theater* is recorded; takes first trip to Cuba with Heath Brothers, for Havana Jam concert; meets Paquito D'Rivera

1980   *Live at the Public Theater* receives Grammy nomination; on his first trip to Africa, Jimmy goes to Dakar, Senegal, for the country's twentieth anniversary of independence, where he performs with Dizzy, Kenny Clarke, Clifford Jordan, Jimmy Owens, Percy Heath, Sonny Fortune, and Darryl Washington; performs with Jazzmobile orchestra on Foster's *Lake Placid Suite,* for the 1980 Winter Olympics in Lake Placid, New York; performs in San Juan, Puerto Rico

1981   *Expressions of Life* is released; *Brotherly Love* is recorded; Heath Brothers participate in a U.S. State Department–sponsored tour of South America; around this time, Percy returns to MJQ; Columbia drops Heath Brothers

1982   Takes first trip to Japan, where Heath Brothers perform in Beppu; with Slide Hampton, records *Mad about Tadd*

1983   *Brothers and Others* is recorded on Antilles; Jimmy plays Live Inn, Tokyo

1984   Teaches at Housatonic Community College, Bridgeport, Connecticut

1985   Records *New Picture*; teaches at City College of New York; receives first honorary doctorate, from Sojourner-Douglass College, Baltimore

1986   Plays with New York Jazz Sextet at North Sea Jazz Festival, the Hague; has emergency angioplasty operation in the Hague; takes first trip to Australia, with Philip Morris Superband (organized by Dave Bailey)

1987   Records *Peer Pleasure*; joins faculty of Queens College (City University of New York) jazz program; organizes all-star event for Louis Armstrong House, Corona, New York; is commissioned by Queens College to write first symphonic work, *Three Ears*

1988   On April 17, *Three Ears* premieres at Queens College; Jimmy is appointed to board of the Louis Armstrong House; records with Benny Carter on *Over the Rainbow*

1989   Works with his quartet in Europe

1990   On October 6, *Upper Neighbors Suite* premieres in Montreal

1991   American Jazz Orchestra, Cooper Union, New York, performs Heath's big band arrangements; Jimmy arranges composition for Winard Harper; signs with SteepleChase and records *You've Changed*

1992   *Little Man Big Band,* produced by Bill Cosby, is recorded; Jimmy performs in Monaco; participates in Philip Morris Generations Tour, including veterans and "young lions," such as Joshua Redman, Christian McBride, and Mike LeDonne; plays at campaign rally for Bill Clinton

1993   Roland Hanna joins jazz program at Queens College; *Little Man Big Band* is nominated for Grammy; Jimmy takes part in Newport Jazz Festival in honor of George Wein, White House lawn, Washington, D.C.; meets President Bill Clinton again; is elected to the Hall/Walk of Fame with the Heath Brothers, Philadelphia Music Alliance

1994   On August 4, *In Praise (from J. to J.)*, extended composition, premieres at Lincoln Center, New York; Jimmy receives Founder's Award from Thelonious Monk Institute of Jazz and Dizzy Gillespie Achievement Award, New York

1995   Receives Grammy nomination for liner notes for Coltrane compilation *The Heavyweight Champion* (1995); is appointed to the Board of Trustees, Thelonious Monk Institute; *You or Me* is released

1996   Mark Elf replaces Tony Purrone on guitar in small group; on April 11, *Leadership*, extended composition, premieres at Howard University, Washington, D.C.; Jimmy plays in celebration of Benny Carter, Kennedy Center Honors, Washington, D.C., and attends White House reception, where again he meets President Bill Clinton and the Gores; participates in the ABC television event *A Celebration of America's Music* (1996/1998), involving Thelonious Monk Institute of Jazz

1997   Heath's Queens College trumpet students Darren Barrett and Diego Urcola win the Thelonious Monk International Competition; Heath Brothers record *As We Were Saying* for Concord; Jeb Patton joins quartet on piano

1998   Jimmy is honored at Alice Tully Hall, in an event hosted by Bill Cosby; Heath Brothers record *Jazz Family*; Jimmy retires from Queens College; receives Dorie Miller Award at Dorie Miller Co-op, Corona, New York

1999   Visits Vice President Al Gore's residence for event honoring Gershwin and Ellington; on October 29, *Sweet Jazzmobile*, extended composition, premieres at Lincoln Center, New York

2000   Jimmy is honored by Presbyterian Jazz Society, Mount Vernon, New York.

2001   On April 21, *Birmingham*, extended composition, premieres in Birmingham, Alabama; Seventy-fifth Birthday Tribute concert for Jimmy is held at Lincoln Center, New York

2002   Jimmy is awarded honorary doctorate from Juilliard, first in the field of jazz; "Jimmy Heath Day" is established in Wilmington, North Carolina

2003   Receives National Endowment for the Arts (NEA) Jazz Masters Award in Toronto; receives National Visionary Leadership Project Award, administered by Dr. Camille Cosby and Renee Poussaint, in Washington, D.C.; is awarded Duke Ellington Fellowship at Yale University, New Haven, Connecticut

2004   Receives honorary doctorate in music from Queens College (City University of New York); on August 21 and 22, *Bird Is the Word*, extended composition, premieres at Charlie Parker Jazz Festival, New York; on October 29, *Fashion or Passion*, extended composition, premieres at Lincoln Center, New York, for opening reception of Jazz at Lincoln Center's Rose Hall

2005   Percy Heath dies; on May 7, *For the Love Of*, extended composition, premieres at Princeton University; Percy Heath Memorial is held at Abyssinian Baptist Church, Harlem; Jimmy attends Four Freedoms Awards honoring Tom Brokaw, Bill Clinton, Cornel West, and others

2006   Attends rehearsals for Wynton Marsalis's *Congo Square*, Lincoln Center, New York; on November 4–5, *Endless Search*, extended composition, premieres in Seattle; Jimmy records *Turn Up the Heath*, second big band recording; attends Romare Bearden Jazz Jubilee Tribute Gala, along with Kareem Abdul-Jabbar, Grant Hill, and Randy Weston; attends multiple eightieth-birthday celebrations; David Wong joins Heath's quartet

2007   Jimmy receives Living Jazz Legend Award, Kennedy Center, Washington, D.C.; plays with Donald Byrd and Ahmad Jamal at Kennedy Center, Washington, D.C.; performs for opening event at the Reverend Herbert Daughtry's House of the Lord Church, Brooklyn; plays with Dizzy Gillespie All-Star Big Band in San Juan, Puerto Rico

2008   Receives Carter G. Woodson Award from Mercy College, New York; launches, under his leadership, the Queens Jazz Orchestra (QJO), Flushing, New York; records *Endurance* (Heath Brothers) for Jazz Legacy Productions

Index

■

■

JIMMY HEATH, an NEA Jazz Master, is widely recognized as one of the greats in jazz. A saxophonist, composer, arranger, and educator, Heath grew up in Philadelphia with his renowned brothers, Percy, the longtime bassist with the Modern Jazz Quartet, and Albert ("Tootie"), a highly respected drummer. The three formed the Heath Brothers band in the 1970s. Jimmy Heath directed the Jazz Studies master's degree program in performance at Queens College (CUNY).

JOSEPH McLAREN is Professor of English at Hofstra University, author of *Langston Hughes: Folk Dramatist in the Protest Tradition, 1921–1943*, and editor of several additional titles.

BILL COSBY has been one of the most influential performers of the second half of the twentieth century. A best-selling comedian and author, he starred in two of the most groundbreaking television series—*I Spy* in the 1960s and *The Cosby Show* in the 1980s. His generous support of numerous charities, particularly in the field of education, has endowed many Americans with the gift of hope and learning.

WYNTON MARSALIS, the Artistic Director of Jazz at Lincoln Center, musician, educator, and composer, was born in New Orleans, Louisiana, and received his first trumpet from renowned musician Al Hirt at the age of six. Marsalis has released over sixty jazz and classical albums and has won nine Grammy Awards, in both jazz and classical categories. He is the only artist to have won Grammy Awards in five consecutive years. In 1997, Marsalis's oratorio on slavery and freedom, *Blood on the Fields*, became the first jazz composition to win the Pulitzer Prize in music.